Communications Policy and the Public Interest

Communications Policy and the Public Interest

THE TELECOMMUNICATIONS ACT OF 1996

Patricia Aufderheide

THE GUILFORD PRESS
New York   London

© 1999 Patricia Aufderheide
Published by The Guilford Press
A Division of Guilford Publications, Inc.
72 Spring Street, New York, NY 10012
http://www.guilford.com

Printed in the United States of America

This book is printed on acid-free paper.

Last digit is print number: 9   8   7   6   5   4   3   2   1

Library of Congress Cataloging-in-Publication Data

Aufderheide, Patricia.
    Communications policy and the public interest / Patricia
Aufderheide.
        p.   cm. — (The Guilford communication series)
    Includes bibliographical references and index.
    ISBN 1-57230-418-9 (hc.). — ISBN 1-57230-425-1 (pbk.)
    1. Telecommunication policy—United States. 2. Public
interest—United States. 3. United States. Telecommunications
Act of 1996.   I. Title. II. Series.
HE7781.A94   1999
384′.0973—dc21   98-54130
                                                              CIP

Acknowledgments

This book draws on my experience as a reporter on communications issues for a variety of newspapers and magazines, but especially *In These Times*, over the last two decades; on my advocacy work for the United Church of Christ in the mid-1980s; and the analytical work I have done as an academic at American University's School of Communication since 1989. In my effort to produce this work in a timely fashion, I had help from many people. While in Brazil on a Fulbright Regional Researcher grant, I benefited from the help of the Fulbright office, the University of Brasília, and the U.S. Embassy in investigating the newly passed Act. In the United States, people at most of the institutions listed in the Resources for Active Citizens shared time and resources. Trade association representatives, including people at America's Public Television Stations, National Cable TV Association, and U.S. Telephone Association were helpful. I owe thanks especially to Barbara Abrash of New York University; Andrew Blau, Larry Kirkman, and Kevin Taglang at the Benton Foundation; Lynne Bradley of the American Library Association; Angela Campbell and Lori Dolquiest of the Institute for Public Representation; William Drake of Georgetown University; the staff of the Federal Communications Commission; Jeffrey Chester and Kathryn Montgomery of the Center for Media Education, with their staffers; Ted Glasser at Stanford, in whose series this book is included; Robert Horwitz of the University of California, San Diego; Debbie Goldman of the Communications Workers of America; Douglas Gomery of the University of Maryland; Thomas Krattenmaker, Dean of William and Mary University Law School; David Lieberman of *USA Today;* Mark Lloyd of the Civil Rights Project, Inc.; Brian Moir of Moir and Hardiman; Andrew Jay Schwartzman, Gigi B. Sohn, and Joe Paykel of the Media Access Project; Mike Mills of *The Washington Post*; Stephan Schwartzman; Bradley Stillman, then of Consumer Federation of America; the staff of Price Waterhouse; Tom Streeter of the University of Vermont; Sanford Ungar, Dean of the School of Communication at American University; John Windhausen of the Competitive Policy Institute; Peter Wissoker of The Guilford Press; Tom Wolzien of Sanford Bernstein; and the staff of American University's Washington College of Law Library.

Contents

FCC Speeches

Communications Policy and the Public Interest

Introduction

When the 1934 Communications Act was passed, no one had a TV set, or a cordless phone, or a computer. By the time the Telecommunications Act of 1996 was passed, comprehensively amending the 1934 Act for the first time, many working Americans were living with faxes, cable TV, email, and voicemail in their homes. The 1996 Act reflected broad shifts in technology use, but even more it reflected shifts in policy approaches. Its shaping showcased the fact that the public interest, endlessly controversial, is also at the center of communications policy. It will continue to be. This book describes the reshaping of the public interest standard in this massive rewrite of the 1934 Communications Act and describes the issues now facing the public in its aftermath.

This book is directed at two related audiences. Scholars and students in communication, government, and sociology have long seen the powerful shaping role of policy in the socially critical business of communications. As well, active citizens and activists in nonprofit organizations, addressing social concerns from poverty to public health to education, have recognized the importance of telecommunications policy and legislation for their concerns.

The quality of public information and discussion on communications issues is increasingly important. In the years just before and after passage of the Act, the issues that it raised and addressed were rarely out of the headlines on the financial pages. They equally rarely, however, made the front pages of newspapers, though, and exceedingly infrequently made TV news. In fact, no media or telecommunications story made the *Tyndall Report*'s Top Ten Stories of 1996. This rarely reflected a deliberate attempt to obscure the issue. It looked pretty obscure to start with, to most editors. Communications policy does not make for high-concept news, fitting neatly into the narratives that implicitly frame top-ten headlines. By and large, the American public perforce ceded the argumentation over terms of the Act to experts.

And yet there is broad social significance in this Act. Communications systems are an essential infrastructure of an information society, one that is increasingly international. Information products are a primary U.S. export, and communications is, according to the Federal Communications Commission (FCC), an $800 billion business today. The American Electronics Association found that in the 1990s, computing and telecommunications sales rose 57 percent, making information technology the largest U.S. industry by 1997 and high tech the largest single manufacturer.

These are not any-old-widget businesses, but the vehicles and instruments of our shared culture. Communications networks map the nation's access to information, resources, and the basic social inclusion that is a prerequisite of citizenship. Mass media, far more visibly and controversially, pervade and shape the culture—both consciously and unconsciously. The way in which they operate also reflects a society's priorities and possibilities. From its origins in the United States, communications policy has been marked by the recognition that communications and culture are intimately linked. That recognition, interpreted differently in different periods, has been carried forward through the phrase "the public interest, convenience and necessity."

The 1996 Act took shape in a period of heightened awareness of the relationship between communications systems and the quality of public, community, and democratic life. It is not merely a matter of finding the right technology, or letting the market work its magic, in order for the citizens of an ever-more-plugged-in culture to reap the benefits of innovation. Even what constitutes a benefit is debatable.

Social philosophers who have explored the failures of a laissez-faire liberalism in a postmodern, just-in-time global context have seen the role of communications as central—and often disturbing. Communications systems break down boundaries of space and time, without necessarily facilitating discourses that matter for civility. In fact, they may exacerbate problems of disconnection, paranoia, and social volatility. For instance, Robert Kuttner, in his *Everything for Sale* (1996), persuasively linked the erosion of civic life with the agenda-setting power of mass media-fed commercial culture. Political theorist Benjamin Barber posed clashing ideologies as grimly linked in *Jihad vs. McWorld* (1995), with communications systems both part of the problem and solutions. They made isolation, confusion, pathological distraction just as possible as any kind of virtual community, Barber argued: "Much of McWorld's strategy for creating global markets depends on a systematic rejection of any genuine consumer autonomy or any costly program variety—deftly coupled, however, with the appearance of infinite variety" (p. 116). As Michael Sandel (1996) put it in *Democracy's Discontent,* satellites, cyberspace, and global markets "link people in distant places without necessarily making them neighbors or fellow citizens or participants in a common venture. Converting networks of communications and interdependence into a public life worth affirming is a moral and political matter, not a technological one" (p. 340). In *Data Smog* (1997), David Shenk vividly described an emerging world of "nichified microcultures," where distracted citizens are plied with news nuggets rather than engaged in a deliberative process.

Widespread information anxiety points to the importance of the frameworks established by government policies on communication. The decisions made by the various and competing actors who shaped the Telecommunications Act of 1996 had and will have vast and unintended consequences. These decisions in turn shape social possibility in the transformatory, unpredictable ways that make social philosophers take notice. They also, of course, have immediate consequences as evident as the sudden rise in the price of pay phones or a changed format in your favorite radio station. These changes, large and small, are under close scrutiny. Intellectuals and advocates played major roles in debates over equity, access, and public accountability during the process of shaping legislation, and they continue to intervene as the Act is implemented.

The book is organized according to the following logic: Chapter 1 offers a broad historical and analytic context for the Act, followed by a synoptic description of the legislative process in Chapter 2. Chapter 3 provides a thematic summary of the basic clauses, as they are organized in the Act itself, explained in terms of the perceived problems the clauses were intended to address. Chapter 4 summarizes the immediate consequences of the passage of the Act, and Chapter 5 addresses its more far-reaching implications for the concept of the public interest. Bibliographic resources include references, an annotated bibliography of analyses of the Act, and a guide to organizations concerned with interpreting the public interest in the Act's implementation. Appendices include an abridgement by Dean Thomas Krattenmaker, of the Act itself the Supreme Court decision on the Communications Decency Act, and relevant documents, including advocacy and policy arguments and regulatory speeches. The Appendices assemble documents that permit a fuller exploration of the Act and its implications. They include, first, the definitive legal documents: the Act, as abridged (for concision only) by Dean Thomas Krattenmaker (Appendix A), and the Supreme Court decision relating to the Communications Decency Act portions of it (Appendix B).

Next are documents that reveal ideological tensions surrounding the Act. Computer Professionals for Social Responsibility's *Serving the Community* (Appendix C) provided at the time a blueprint not only for socially concerned professionals but for Administration officials and government agencies concerned with social equity. It describes in simple language the fundamental idea of open platforms. This principle was also important to the loose coalition of activists on cyberspace and social equity issues who formed the Telecommunications Policy Roundtable (Appendix D). The TPR proposal specifically emphasizes the development of civic spaces and habits. The Progress and Freedom Foundation's manifesto (Appendix E), in sharp contrast, was a libertarian-inflected document arguing against regulation and legislation, and for permitting large incumbents to enter new arenas unfettered. The Technorealist manifesto (Appendix F), without rejecting the advantages of new technology, argued against a utopian belief that cyberspace would in itself bring greater equity or, indeed, improvement in the general quality of life. Appendix G provides, in a progressive activist lawyer's speech to conservatives, a concise description of the need for continued regulatory oversight of thesarea. Appendix H provides, in the remarks of the then-head economist at the FCC, a concise argument for open competition and deregulation; this argument is phrased in terms of wireless services, but it applies to other technological areas as well.

The speeches by chairmen of the FCC that follow (Appendices I, J, and K) track the challenges facing regulators in the wake of the Act. The ambitious schedule put forward by Reed Hundt in 1996 (Appendix I) carefully articulated the emerging notion of the public interest, and the way in which it continues to differ for mass media and telecommunications. His 1997 speech (Appendix J) captures the frustration of regulators with blocking mechanisms used by large players to jockey for position after the Act. Chairman William Kennard's 1998 speech articulates the continuing importance of the notion of universal service, at that moment and afterward an embattled concept.

CHAPTER 1

Background

Telecommunications policy is a calculated government intervention in the structures of businesses that offer communications and media services. The public is endlessly invoked in communications policy, but rarely is it consulted or even defined. Policymakers claim that they do what they do in the name of and for the benefit of the people they represent, who may or may not be consumers of the service. Without this connection to the public, policymakers would have no grounds to intervene in these businesses.

Who is the public that U.S. policy represents, and what is its interest? It might be taken, as early communications and antitrust regulators took it, to be coterminous with the economic health of a capitalist society, associated with social peace and prosperity. This is a definition that, as New Dealers worked it out, effectively made government regulators the representatives of society's interests as well as of the large, stable businesses the government regulators helped to create and maintain. This definition can lead to a ponderous paternalism on the part of bureaucrats, functionaries, and middle managers. It can stall technological innovation and stifle small business.

Another way to see the public is as an agglomeration of consumers, or potential consumers. This is one significance of the 1966 court decision (*Office of Communications, United Church of Christ v. FCC,* 1966) that recognized purchasers of radio and television sets as parties with an interest in FCC proceedings, and which, for the first time, permitted the general public to participate in the FCC's deliberations. While opening the door to much broader (and more politically volatile) participation, this definition can lead to checkbook democracy on a grassroots level, where people participate in

5

society to the extent that they are consumers, and to the extent that they exercise consumer choice. Not only does the definition measure social participation only by purchase, but it also conveniently ignores the social institutional structures within which we all live, and within which consumers make their small choices.

There is also much in communication policy that reaches past traditional economic concerns, whether at the macro- or microlevel, and that reaches into social welfare considerations. Government regulators act as allies of and sometimes protectors of the weak and vulnerable in society. Policies have been made to protect children, the disabled, rural dwellers, the poor; these policies ensure equality of access to a communications technology for everyone, no matter what's in their wallets or on their minds; and these policies further the political promise of free expression. Policies have even attempted to set cultural standards, such as public decency on the airwaves, and have attempted to create cultural spaces, as in the case of public broadcasting.

Each of these social welfare-oriented approaches has a slightly different take on the notion of the public and its relationship to government. Some approaches are blatantly paternalistic, and some respond to the squeaky-wheel version of American politics. But all of them go beyond economic concerns. They indicate, sometimes clumsily, the notion that the public is more than a mass of consumers or the inhabitants of a commercial society, but rather is a social institution important enough to address in nonmarketplace ways. These approaches can easily result in patch-up policies or can be accused of catering to special interests, however vulnerable or worthy those interests may be.

In recent decades, with the rise of deregulation, market liberals who are concerned with policy have basically asserted that the public is roughly the same thing, for the purposes of policymaking, as a vigorous marketplace. They have advocated deregulation, in order to promote an unfettered marketplace. However, in large infrastructure industries, deregulation does not necessarily lead to competition. Even then, these advocates would argue, so long as the sector is vigorous, growing, widely offering more jobs and a greater selection of products and choices, it acts in the public interest.

The equation of public interest with an unregulated marketplace, which has grown to be widely accepted, has resulted in disconnecting social consequences from the cultivation of the marketplace. But the booming electronic media and telecommunications marketplaces inevitably affect cultural habits and have social consequences. Dial-a-porn, Jerry Springer scandal shows, wrong credit rating data spread via the Internet are a few among many of the concerns that have mobilized activists to demand government action. Such concerns are marginalized into a fringe area of policy. A zone of cultural backlash grows, where antipornography, antiviolence, anticensorship, pro-privacy, and anti-hate crimes advocates all sullenly hunker down. Those pioneers of emerging social landscapes find uneasy alliances as often as they carve out new Balkan states of opinion. And inevitably, cultural advocates of all kinds return to policymakers.

This has been a pattern throughout the history of U.S. communications regulation, but it appears ever more boldly as deregulation unleashes new market behaviors and intensifies others. There is a bipolar quality to current communications policies. The passion for regulatory platforms that permit unregulated industries, unbounded by government constraints, vies with the passion for social control over the emerging networks and channels that we plug into each day.

The problem of designing policies appropriate to today's and tomorrow's communications technologies and business environments always comes back to the problem of the public. Back in the days when people would crank a phone to get an operator's attention, the American philosopher John Dewey suggested that the public is not a notion with much life in it, at an individual level, not even when you add individuals up. The public, he argued, is a social creation, quite distinct from governmental organizations that claim to speak in its name, and is also quite apart from the goal of individual freedom. It is the product of relationships that are kept alive in conversation about the consequences of social, political, and economic arrangements we all share (Dewey, 1927).

The public in this sense is something that exists in imagination, in practice, and also in real and virtual space. It is important for people to see themselves as having a public life as much as they have a domestic or a work life. They also need places to have it. As we map ourselves onto various electronic grids, those grids themselves become places where we define ourselves—as consumers, as citizens, and also as members of the public.

Communications policy either encourages or discourages public life, whatever its intent. So, of course, do many other social policies, including electoral practices and educational regimes. But communications structures in many ways map our social connections, and our communications practices express our cultural habits and understandings.

Legal scholar Monroe Price (1995) shows that electronic media regulation has long danced around the question of culture. He argues for policies that recognize the importance of electronic media for establishing and maintaining public spaces. Simply endorsing the competitive marketplace, as if to do so were a value-neutral decision, merely displaces problems.

Within this notion of the public, then, policies make the political culture of a democracy a central priority. This argument accords well with those of political philosophers who argue, as does Sandel (1996), that

> the formative aspect of republican politics requires public spaces. . . . The global media and markets that shape our lives beckon us to a world beyond boundaries and belonging. But the civic resources we need to master these forces, or at least to contend with them, are still to be found in the places and stories, memories and meanings, incidents and identities, that situate use in the world and give our lives their moral particularity. (p. 349)

The revival of what Benjamin Barber (1984) contagiously called "strong democracy"—a more participatory and communitarian political system— requires "constructive civic uses of the new telecommunications technology" (p. 277).

But this approach to the public and the public interest has not been popular within the world of communications regulation. Over the years since the 1927 Radio Act, which was the precursor of the 1934 Communications Act, struggles over the notion of the public interest have inevitably, but often messily and uncomfortably, reflected the relationship between communications and culture. The very principles of economic intervention upon which regulation emerged as a social practice make it hard to see the connection between communication and culture. The First Amendment as it has evolved in the 20th century has also complicated any clear articulation. But tensions and conflicts in policy can often be seen as deriving from the thick and tangled relationship between communications businesses and services, on the one hand, and the expectations and habits of the societies they serve, on the other.

REWRITING THE RULES

The creation of the Telecommunications Act of 1996, which President Bill Clinton signed into law on February 8, 1996, raised to public view issues that are often buried in regulatory procedures, and it showcased questions of the social impact of telecommunications policy.

The Act was designed to create a regulatory platform that would permit broad competition among different kinds of telecommunications service providers, encourage innovation, and recognize rapid technological change. The Act attempts to jump-start an era in which communications industries—and especially networked businesses that offer telephony and related network services—can operate as unregulated competitors rather than as monolithic utilities.

To accomplish this, the legislation rewrote the basic law that governs communications policy from top to bottom. That does not mean that the new law abolishes policies of the past or that it is even very foresightful, much less effective. In its amending of the 1934 Communications Act, the new law sketches out some regulatory principles, creates some possibilities, and proposes a controversial premise of interindustry competition. Its sketches may end up being far different from a workable, regulatory regime. But it is without a doubt the first step in a decisively different regulatory universe for communications.

The law lurched and stumbled into existence, driven forward by a combination of ideological and technological changes to the terms of an existing compact between big business and big government. For two decades before its passage, Congress attempted in a variety of ways to comprehend, foster, and get some social benefit from changing communications technologies. The ensuing law contains within it elements of previous regulatory regimes, and elements of a new one as well.

Its inelegance has a long history. The evolution of electronic communications policy has been a complex, and often ad hoc, process. This process has reflected, in part, the separate, independent development of several kinds of businesses. Each of those businesses, ranging from telephony to radio and television to computing, has evolved with its own logic. Government regulation evolved parochially with each industry, and typically with a powerful allegiance to incumbents (Winston, 1986).

But today, the technologies of telephony, mass media, and computing increasingly cross the borders of their traditional business arenas. Would-be entrepreneurs, within and without central industry positions, increasingly chafe at regulatory regimes designed for a former era and oppose opportunities for others than themselves. Those regimes emerge from a welter of places. They include, at the federal level, Congress, the Federal Communications Commission, the Department of Justice, the Federal Trade Commission, and the Department of Commerce. At the state and local level, Public Service Commissions and Public Utility Commissions have powerful sway over telecommunications, while municipalities have plenty to negotiate with any user of their rights of way, such as cable companies.

This state will continue. Under the new law, multiple jurisdictions remain, and industry rivals go on making the most of leverage won by pitting courts, legislators, and regulators against each other. But industry frustration with lack of clarity about the legality and regulatory structure of emerging technology uses was a powerful push toward the rewrite as it finally emerged.

TECHNOLOGICAL INNOVATION

Changes in the technical possibilities of telecommunications have been dramatic in the last four decades, building on a hefty investment in communications research during and after World War II. Those innovations have also changed the shapes of the industries involved and have introduced new players (Cairncross, 1997).

Technological innovations have brought new services and also have challenged the value of monopoly. *More, bigger,* and *faster* were key words for these changes. These innovations also made increasingly artificial the crafted distinction between common-carriage networks and editor-based mass media. These innovations made it possible to imagine (and even experience) communications networks that had multiple purposes and to imagine spectrum with multiple or shared uses.

Key technical innovations included satellites and digitally based information processing. Satellites permitted, among other things, vastly more efficient, over-the-air, point-to-multipoint transmission of large amounts of information. Satellites turned cable from a small-time, mom-and-pop local business dedicated to improving the television viewer's reception of over-the-air signals into a highly centralized industry featuring local delivery of satellite-delivered signals. Satellites made it economically viable for newspapers to produce regional editions across the nation, using satellite-delivered copy. Satellites generated new mass media services and, indeed, eventually, a new video platform in direct broadcast satellite, or DBS. Satellite access also changed the economics of telephone networks, vastly shrinking the costs of connection and shrinking as well the difference between local and long-distance service.

Digital processing, which is the motor of growth in computing, has been another major disruptive force in the organization of communications industries. The encoding of signals in simple, binary code, allowing computers both to compute and to communicate with great accuracy and speed, has rocked the way we do business in everything from stock trading to shopping for swimsuits and has powerfully affected all telecommunications businesses. It has squeezed and reshaped spectrum, it has multiplied the uses to which we put phones, and it has hosted a new mode of communication, namely, the many-to-many environment of the Internet. It has provided a common electronic language on the spectrum, making the spectrum far more mutable, permitting machines to talk to machines, and blurring the distinction between content and infrastructure on any system.

Perhaps most important, digital processing has changed the very characteristics of communications networks. Rapidly evolving computing that is based on digital processing has made it possible to decentralize networks. Many of the decisions once made in large centralized switches are now made at intermediate stops or even within the consumer's telephone. Along with increased flexibility and the potential to reconfigure the very shape of networks and subnetworks, decentralized digital processing has dramatically increased the amount of intelligence—or the ability to respond to input and take action—in communications networks. This innovation provides a fundamental challenge to the notion of common carriage, or the restriction of network providers to transmission alone, because the clear lines between content and conduit have become muddied. Networks themselves have information, or content, built into them.

Related innovations have greatly, and suddenly, affected the variables of price, speed, and the cost of communication. Fiber optic wires, transmitting digital signals, vastly increased the capacity of wired networks. Compression techniques, ever in refinement, have permitted both increased speed of transmission and also new kinds of transmission. Wireless connections, in combination with wired networks, have permitted cheap, mobile communication in cellular phones as well as in data and even video transmission. Large businesses were the first beneficiaries of these innovations, and the incorporation of these innovations into business practice have driven further development, as well as the appetite for procompetitive policy (Harvey, 1992).

The elements of technological change that pushed toward rewriting the Communications Act were those that made it easy for telecommunications-based services to tap into existing networks and were those that potentially corroded the line between mass media and telecommunications. The first undercut the case for monopoly, and the second blurred regulatory categories. When a broadcaster was able to use part of available spectrum for nonbroadcast services such as paging; when a phone company was tempted out of the common carrier box, maybe even to dream of offering cable service; when a cable network was able to offer phone service or Internet service to its customers, many different stakeholders appeared to redraw the rules. And when business—locally, internationally and virtually—had built telecommunications into its own infrastructures, all large users became invested in the prices and terms of provision of service.

THE POLITICAL PROCESS

The evolution of this rewrite legislation was, however, not primarily understandable as a result of technological innovation that was driving change, although technology transformation was important in it. As described by

Robert Horwitz in his pathbreaking analysis *The Irony of Regulatory Reform* (1989), transformations in regulatory approach can best be seen as a political process. Summarizing the historical process of deregulation in infrastructure industries throughout the past three decades, he notes:

> The reasons are, as usual, a complex mosaic of regulatory, political, economic, legal, and ideological factors. In telecommunications and banking they include technological changes as well. But . . . deregulation is at bottom a *political* phenomenon. Deregulation is basically a story of political movement from regulatory activism to regulatory "reform."
>
> Nonetheless, deregulation *could not have occurred* without these supporting, underlying factors. . . . As a result [of the interplay between economic trends, political organizing, and legal actions], by the mid-1970s regulation came to be held responsible for the fall of American economic productivity. That ideological shift was surprisingly important, especially because it underlay the changing terms in which various political elites conceptualized regulation. (p. 198; emphasis in original)

Thus, the very notion of what regulation is and should be was at stake. Progressive Era federal agencies grew up around antitrust concerns generated by the monopolistic behavior of large national corporations. Such regulation safeguarded interests of small producers from large corporations. New Deal era agencies such as the Federal Communications Communication were mandated to protect and nurture specific industries. Such agencies ostensibly safeguarded the interests of consumers by providing the context in which dependable, affordable services could grow. The stability of this system "of mutual compromises and benefits to major corporations, organized labor, and even consumers" (Horwitz, 1989, p. 17) was irrevocably undermined in the 1960s and 1970s, with dramatic new technological possibilities. That instability was accompanied and facilitated by ideological ferment, in which the basic notion of what regulation—and even government itself—does came under revision.

THE PUBLIC INTEREST:
NEW DEALERS AND STABILITY

The notion of serving the public interest was associated from the start with stable, broadly available commercial communications services, and government was responsible for monitoring socially significant audiences, arenas, and services that the market serves poorly.

The "public interest, convenience and necessity" part of communications law since the 1927 Radio Act, is a phrase of art, and deliberately a loose one. The Supreme Court, in a historic case, called it "a supple instrument to effect congressional desires to 'maintain . . . a grip on the dynamic aspects of radio transmission' " (*Red Lion Broadcasting Co. v. FCC,* 1969). The phrase was a sine qua non for the work of making policy at all. It has been the notorious fudge factor in the FCC's rule making over the years; failure to serve the public interest has been a stick with which to beat recalcitrant operators; it has been a modesty curtain behind which entire changes of regulatory ideology have taken place; it has been the favorite invocation of every stakeholder in the regulatory process (Krasnow, Longley, & Terry, 1982, pp. 17–19).

But while the public interest has been, to put it mildly, malleable, it has been something more than raw material. The term *public interest* is grounded in a notion of governmental responsibility to create conditions for a healthy business that can serve a broad range of consumers. As Thomas Streeter argues so well in *Selling the Air* (1996), the 1934 Communications Act was part of a larger process of institutionalizing "corporate liberalism." Corporate liberalism is a set of regulatory and legal arrangements that makes possible stable, large-scale businesses and complex markets. The creation of monopolies, cartels, and sectors typified by substantial market power was seen as having powerful benefits.

The precedent for the 1927 and 1934 Acts' employment of the phrase "the public interest" had been first established at the state level. There, regulation developed in a close relationship with consolidating forces in a developing industry. That relationship ensured stability of incumbents and profitability, in exchange for dependable service extended throughout the nation (Rowland, 1997a, 1997b). It was an understanding that was widely shared. In 1925, talking about radio, then-Secretary of Commerce Herbert Hoover (an enthusiast for the incipient broadcasting industry) argued, "The ether is a public medium, and its use must be for a public benefit. The use of a radio channel is justified only if there is public benefit" (quoted in Robinson, 1989, p. 9). What he meant was that commercial owners of radio channels should provide services available to "the great body of the listening public" and be susceptible to regulation that would be designed as the activity evolved, in order to protect " the public interest." His language had, as Monroe Price (1995) notes, "a patrician sense of national purpose and national propriety," a "legacy of the great nineteenth-century idea of the gospel of wealth" (p. 161). Sen. Clarence Dill (D-WA), who inserted the phrase "public interest, convenience and necessity" into the 1927 Radio Act, later told then-FCC head Newton Minow that he had wanted to encourage investment in the new technology. His basic concern, in the same patrician mode, was the financial health of the business (Minow, 1995, pp. 67–68). In any case, members of the general public were largely excluded from the shaping of that concept in broadcasting at the FCC, until media reform activists, led by the United Church of Christ, won standing, or the right to go to court, in broadcast license renewal cases, in 1966 (*Office of Communications, United Church of Christ v. FCC,* 1966).

In both telecommunications and in mass media, the 1934 Act drew on the notion of natural monopoly. Building on the 1927 Act, the 1934 Act set forward a scheme to organize the telecommunications sector. The Act ensured that communications services would be commercial rather than governmental. This ran counter to most contemporary national policies. At the same time, the Act established that the communications sector would be heavily regulated, to the end of promoting valuable services as efficiently as possible to the American people. The public, seen as potential consumers, would not be deprived of services by having unviable businesses take up spectrum that belonged to the nation. That scheme organized the sector into two general categories: mass media and common carrier.

MASS MEDIA

Spectrum to be used by mass media would be privately, commercially managed by corporate entities that would act as editors, oriented to local communities. They would control the content of their programming rather than just rent out their spectrum to whoever wanted to program. (Congress was afraid AT&T would become an uncontrollable giant if "toll broadcasting" were permitted.) They would be obligated to consider the "public interest, convenience and necessity" when they programmed, in the sense of providing a broadly commercial service—preferably appealing to entire families.

This principle was asserted in contrast to special interest money-making schemes—for instance, the on-air broadcasts of a doctor who prescribed over the air, with prescriptions filled only by participating pharmacies—and also against highly partisan or propagandistic owner/operators. The excesses of a medical huckster, in 1930, and a religious broadcaster, in 1932, both attracted regulatory ire (Krasnow, 1997; Rowland, 1997b, pp. 384–385; Wollenberg, 1989, p. 67) Broadcasters were "public trustees" of that spectrum they held by license. But they were also speakers with First Amendment rights, and they were not operating an essential service.

Broadcast licensees had, by this structure, remarkable market power. They held a resource that no one else could use. Locally they operated oligopolistically. As programming networks and syndication services developed, these operated oligopolistically at a national level. Regulators discouraged monopoly, vertical integration, and cross-ownership by a variety of rules: limitation on the number of stations that networks could own; limitations on the number of stations a single owner could hold; banning of cross-ownership of newspapers and cable. But they granted broadcasters monopoly control over their slice of the spectrum.

Monopoly spectrum use protected incumbent broadcasters, and they appreciated that fact. From 1927 on, large commercial players had endorsed that model, in exchange for serving "the public interest." It was, of course, a choice to issue monopoly licenses on a local level to commercial enterprises construed as entertainment vehicles. Legislators could have chosen to construct a government-authorized, private service like the BBC, paid for with license fees on home sets; to permit national program services (such as ultimately emerged in the networks serving local stations); to license broadcasters on a range of objectives, including diversity of perspectives or educational objectives (a goal met feebly and as an afterthought). But broadcasters conducted a vigorous campaign for an advertiser-supported medium, within the logic of corporate liberalism that balanced entrepreneurial expansionism with goals of stability and scope.

With monopoly seemingly a natural feature of spectrum licensing, the notion of scarcity was a guiding principle of regulation. Scarcity meant that broadcasters were monopoly editors over spectrum that was both owned by the American people and was also not enough for all interested speakers to speak. Therefore regulators had to make sure that broadcasters used it well. Most basically, they had to use it at all—be commercially viable.

One important, unarticulated underlying assumption was that the programmed ether was a kind of virtual public culture. It was not at all clear how radio, and later TV, services transcended individual expression and consumer entertainment, justifying a permanent government presence monitoring content. This problem became more acute as the notion of a consumer society developed and as television became a pervasive, daily part of American culture. Congress had created a peculiar creature: a First Amendment speaker whose rights were conditioned by the fact of monopoly power and whose voice was that of a ventriloquist for advertisers (Douglas, 1987; Hazlett, 1990; McChesney, 1993; Streeter, 1996).

COMMON CARRIER

Under the 1934 Act, telephony was operated as a utility, a service available to everyone at reasonable rates. This was to be a business of providing access to a network of other people, not a business of programming or providing content.

Economically, monopoly was seen as a necessary efficiency in telephony. With a goal of a transparent, dependable, and affordable network, one set of wires and standard interconnecting equipment were seen as optimal. Having competing companies built competing national wired networks—an "overbuild" scenario—would be wasteful. This was an assumption enthusiastically promoted by AT&T, which went to great lengths to buy other competing phone companies, establish interconnection protocols with others, and eventually to dominate the industry (Friedlander, 1995). AT&T became one of the strongest supporters of a strong FCC, which was the phone company's protector. The federal government, reciprocally, saw a strong AT&T, properly reined in, as the motor of development of a national, universal phone service, as well as guardian of national security interests in communication.

By 1913, telephony was already on its way to being a regulated monopoly, with AT&T gaining government approval for offering most of the nation's telephone service noncompetitively and providing most of the equipment in exchange for price and quality of service regulation, while giving up its telegraphy interests. (Non-AT&T companies serving the remaining fifth of the nation fell under the same principles.) AT&T secured its own equipment manufacturing arm, Western Electric, a vertically integrated arrangement sanctioned by government because it promised standardization and, thus, interconnected "universal" service. In any area, the phone company was a monopoly provider. As monopoly providers of information transportation, telephone operators were banned from providing such content. They were common carriers, barred by law from taking unfair advantage of their control over the network by also offering services on it.

The principal regulatory mechanism was rate-of-return regulation, in which regulators established the amount of allowable profit, the amount of allowable depreciation and investment, and the allocation of subsidies. Central goals of regulators, beyond limiting excess profits, were quality, dependability, and universality of service. Phone companies were to make their services available at "reasonable" rates. Since the phone companies were monopolies that offered a variety of functions and services (e.g., research, equipment, local and long distance transmission, commercial and residential service, emergency access, pay phones), this state of affairs required a complex set of economic evaluations. Regulation of industry pricing under rate-of-return regulation became a huge subset of economic theory and practice (Horwitz, 1989, Ch. 5; Krattenmaker, 1994, p. 463f.; Melody, 1997, pp. 13–17).

Phone companies were also to offer certain qualities of service under their protected status as monopolies. Besides common carriage, consistent quality, and reasonable prices, they were also to offer universal service. The notion of universal service evolved pragmatically, in direct relation to

AT&T's growing hold over the telephone market (Noam, 1997). The term *universal service* itself, like *public interest,* is a term of art. AT&T first used the term, even before the existence of the Communications Act, to mean interconnection to other networks, not service to all customers; its promise was part of a quid pro quo in which the government would not challenge AT&T's dominance in the market. Universal service in the sense of a widely accessible network, as Milton Mueller (1997) and others in a revisionist trend have noted (Friedlander, 1995), developed originally through vigorous competition and through consumer demand, not through government incentives to a monopolist. Those small beginnings, however, became the basis for a national network, eventually consolidated and managed by AT&T. Universal service came to mean, over years of state and federal regulation, connecting each to all, at reasonable and fairly standard prices. Rural and other high-cost service areas, the disabled, and the poor have, over the years, become targeted at-risk populations (Cooper, 1997).

The old AT&T provided for universal service simply by shifting revenues between its different services and divisions, in classic cross-subsidy fashion. Paying customers were charged a little more to cover costs for those whose payments did not cover costs. Local service was underpriced. Long distance and ancillary service prices compensated for the cost of hooking up customers. Because cost allocation was highly political and to some degree arbitrary within the vertically integrated company, it was never clear how much money universal service cross-subsidies entailed.

The universal service policy articulated what has become a reality in the United States, where telephone service is nearly ubiquitous, although it varies most significantly with income (U.S. FCC, 1998e). Ninety-nine percent of households making more than $40,000 a year have a phone, but only 87 percent of those making $10,000 do. Nearly a quarter of all poverty-level households with children have no phone service, and half of female-headed poor households lack dialtone (Cooper, 1998). Universal service subsidies for the poor, often linked to other welfare benefits such as food stamps, are an important, but rarely seen, welfare benefit, reaching around 4.4 million people. Since AT&T was broken up and regional local phone companies inherited the universal service mandate, telephone penetration has basically stayed stable, increasing or decreasing slightly in different years (U.S. FCC, 1998e). The price of telephone service has varied and continues to vary by region and state, but not nearly as much as the difference in cost-of-service provision between, say, a low-rise building in a city and scattered housing in an exurban development. That is because a difficult-to-estimate amount, perhaps as low as 3 percent of revenues, and perhaps much higher in subsidies supports the high-cost investment (Cooper, 1997; Blau, 1997).

Universal service has been, thus, a combination of de facto industrial policy—build out the network—and social welfare. It has been a clear statement that access to communications networks is such a basic part of social life that it is now a necessity. It was incorporated without having to articulate any of this, however. The 1934 Act's overarching purpose, stated in the preamble, was easy to apply toward a universal service mandate: "to make available, so far as possible to all the people of the United States, a rapid, efficient, nation-wide, and world-wide wire and radio communications service with adequate facilities at reasonable charges." It was to the benefit of phone companies operating under rate-of-return regulation to invest handsomely in expanding services, generating new customers while benefiting from many incentives to invest in the network. AT&T, with regulatory approval, raised long-distance prices and used profits from that service to pay for investment in universal service. Universal service was also an important claim of social benefit, which could discourage adoption of a competitive model of service provision.

REGULATORY REFORM

In the political ferment of the 1960s, New Deal-era regulation came under attack by a range of activists who pushed for more and broader public participation in government. The agencies that had fostered large, stable industries were criticized for being "captured" by them, for being protectors of wealthy and stodgy incumbents that were blocking progress. Social activists ranging from environmentalists to community development organizers to third political party proponents pushed for new kinds of regulatory agencies and for greater participation in the traditional ones. They also enthusiastically endorsed new communications technologies, from satellite transmission to cable TV, which expand the range of mass media programming and listener/viewer choice (Horwitz, 1989, Ch. 7).

At the same time, powerful, large corporate interests, expanding in part thanks to an expanding telecommunications network, demanded more, better, and cheaper services. Overlapping in rhetorical style sometimes with the activists, the corporate interests pushed for greater marketplace options and targeted regulatory guardians of monopoly providers as the problem.

MASS MEDIA REFORMS

In mass media, consumer and social issue organizations mobilized in a broad and diverse media reform movement that flourished along with other movements that emerged from the civil rights era. Minorities, women, children's advocates, seniors, organized labor, education advocates, and gays and lesbians, in coalition and separately, identified mass media policy as a site of struggle for equity and access. The United Church of Christ Office of Communication became an important actor. Its head, the Rev. Everett Parker, had seen media as a key institution for the quality of public life in the postwar era, and he led his church into battle in the courts to establish the audience as a First Amendment player and to achieve standing—legal clout—for the general public at the FCC (Cole & Oettinger, 1978; Minow, 1995; Montgomery, 1989).

A Washington, DC-based public-interest-policy community developed around these initiatives. Religious, labor, educational, library, and civil rights institutions tagged communications policy as a concern for their advocates. For more than a decade, until the mid-1980s, a Washington-based group of nonprofit organization leaders and advocates met weekly in Washington, calling themselves "the Good Guys and Gals." They advocated, among other things on behalf of consumer price and quality issues, expansion of the range of expression in media, encouragement of viewer and listener access to media, and encouragement of the development of new uses of technology. These new uses might then act as expanders of viewer and listener choice and also as competitors to incumbents. The Good Guys and Gals supported both structural and content regulation, and their tool was often the threat of a petition to deny a broadcast license upon renewal, using publicly available logbooks to record programming that was aired.

The FCC, wedded to the oligopolistic market structure of the media, developed mitigating structural regulations. These included limiting cross-ownership and concentration of ownership, which permitted viewers and listeners to monitor more easily broadcasters' performance, and preferences for license applicants who were minorities or women, in order to encourage diversity of sources. In the mid-1970s, the FCC responded to rapid trading in broadcast stations, which was seen as weakening owners' relationship with the local community, by prohibiting owners from selling newly purchased stations for three years. The goal was the cultivation of community ties, rather than the use of broadcast stations as trading chips by owners.

The FCC also, controversially, established programming guidelines. Attempts to codify its programming priorities in the mid-1940s had failed. However, courts did affirm the FCC's obligation to examine program quality. In 1943, the Supreme Court ruled that, because of scarcity, the FCC had "the burden of determining the composition of that traffic [i.e., program content]" on the air (quoted in Krasnow, 1997, p. 7). By the 1960s, the FCC let station owners know that they were, among other things, required to ascertain, or discover, local community concerns; to cover public affairs, to air controversial issues, and to do so fairly; to serve constituencies that broadcasters found it less lucrative to serve, such as children; and to provide politicians low-cost time and to air electoral issues fairly. These measures gave social advocates small but significant leverage with broadcasters. Among the most irritating of these regulations to broadcasters were (1) the Fairness Doctrine, requiring broadcasters to air controversial issues, guidelines strongly suggesting that broadcasters air some public affairs, and (2) rules on electoral candidate access to broadcast time (Krattenmaker, 1994, Ch. 5).

Content regulation, or even arm's-length incentives for programming, confronted questions of culture, values, and the ability of symbols to shape reality. These issues of social relationships fit uncomfortably with the terms of the First Amendment, and content regulation could easily become the tool of a censoring bully. The problems surrounding content regulation also pointed, intentionally or not, to the procrustean limits of a public interest concept wherein the public interest was equated, ultimately, with economic viability. State action had designed an economic environment that had become a profound and pervasive element of daily culture, but there were few and weak tools to address the consequences.

However frail programming-related regulation was as a regulatory tool, it was a highly visible and popular political device. Violence and sex in programming were subject areas of perennial fascination. Widespread anxiety about the social effects of mass media also reflected the fact that communications and culture were intimately linked. Children and democracy were good rallying points for politicians, who over decades found good material in electronic media (Rowland, 1983).

Electronic spaces protected from commercial entertainment priorities were also created. These acts implicitly acknowledged the limitations of the commercial model but operated within the terms of it. Public radio and then public TV were both originally envisioned primarily as educational services and were approved and even supported by commercial broadcasters as relief from their own obligations as public trustees as well as safely noncompetitive neighbors on the spectrum. Public radio was placed on FM at a time when the service was experimental and there was no market in receivers. Public TV was placed on UHF at a time when TV dials could not tune to that part of the spectrum (Engelman, 1996). Neither service was imagined, at the outset, as explicitly *public* in the primary way in which the term was used in the 1934 Act—that is, serving the consumer interests of the broad population. Public radio and TV were conceived, effectively, as niche services to address market failures and to pacify vocal subconstituencies (Aufderheide, 1991).

It was the 1967 Public Broadcasting Act, passed at the height of the Johnson administration's Great Society rhetoric and in the flush of changes wrought at the federal level in civil rights, that explicitly labeled a noncommercial cultural service as "public." Both public radio and public TV evolved into significant services with specialty audiences and also important arenas of specifically civic activity. Their cultural presence was limited, however, by ongoing political ambivalence over the value of subsidy for such services (Engelman, 1996).

Cable television, which had been for nearly two decades the blighted, lurking Caliban of video delivery for an FCC committed to protecting broadcasters, benefited from a reformist surge that targeted the hegemony of broadcasters as the problem. A 1972 FCC decision represented a pro-competitive victory. The ruling made cable a viable independent service and extended court judgments for importation of distant and broadcast signals, while also imposing localism and diversity restrictions. Cable won access to the broadcast programs that are still the most-watched programming on cable today and gradually became a serious rival to broadcasters for viewer eyeballs and advertising dollars. Since cable had aspects of a network and aspects of mass media, policymakers struggled over its proper status. A presidential commission, in fact, urged that cable be treated as a common carrier, on the network model. But the issue became moot once cable companies grew to become powerful lobbyists, able to protect their advantage as controllers of content (Aufderheide, 1992; Krattenmaker, 1994, Ch. 2).

By 1984, cable companies had successfully negotiated with municipalities, their most significant opponents, a law that lifted many of the 1972 restrictions (some of which had since been successfully challenged in court anyway). The law asserted that broadcasting was enough of a competitor for cable services that, even though almost all cable companies were monopolies in their areas, most cable systems needed no price regulation.

TELECOM REFORMS

In the 1960s and 1970s, the monopoly provider model of phone service fell apart. Customer premises equipment, or terminal equipment, was gradually and idiosyncratically deregulated. As early as 1955, the FCC had begun loosening the rules barring outsiders from attaching to AT&T's network. This process was precipitated by a company's selling what it called the Hush-a-Phone, or a little plastic cup attachable to the mouthpiece of a phone, to muffle noise. AT&T, closely guarding its monopoly, had insisted that any attachment to its network, even a little plastic mouthpiece, would threaten the integrity of the network. It was a slow beginning; it took another 13 years to clear regulatory permission for electronic attachments, during which advancing technology greatly simplified interconnection.

The network itself was also being opened up. By the 1970s, large corporate users were demanding more and faster phone services, and AT&T was unable to meet the need. In 1969, MCI won the right to attach to the AT&T network in order to offer what then were merely private network services for corporations (set up, for instance, all within one company or between two companies or sites). The decision to permit rival companies to offer limited, corporate service, without being obligated to the universal service requirements of the monopoly provider, was a defining step toward a competitive era. This decision fundamentally challenged the old logic of cross-subsidy. AT&T charged the upstarts with "cream skimming"—taking the high-dollar clients and leaving AT&T with the large, expensive network to service. The next decade of regulatory dispute in telecommunication was driven by conflict between a monopoly and a competitive model of regulation (Horwitz, 1989, Ch. 8).

The culmination of a 1974 antitrust suit, the decree finally rendered in 1982 as the Modification of Final Judgment or MFJ, broke the phone industry into local telephony and long distance. Long distance, including AT&T, was now to be competitive. Local business continued to be a monopoly, mostly run by huge holding companies called Regional Bell Operating Companies (RBOCs), or Baby Bells. The (then) seven RBOCs in turn ran a total of 22 regional, regulated monopoly phone companies. GTE, a local monopoly provider built out of holdings of AT&T's competitors, unlike the Baby Bells, got to offer long distance as well as local service (Coll, 1986).

The breakup posed serious reorganizational challenges. Repricing both long distance and local service was particularly painful, since both prices had been politically rather than economically established. Local prices were artificially low and were kept that way by local regulators, while long distance prices had long subsidized both local and universal service.

DEREGULATION

Rewriting the 1934 Communications Act occurred at the crest of a deregulatory ideological tide. Ideological battles over the value of deregulation created the vocabulary within which change occurred and was understood, although in at least the medium range the outcome was mixed. The debate took place over notions of what the basic terms of business in the relevant industries were, and what the basic job of government was. Central to discussion was the shifting valuation of monopoly and monopoly power.

Deregulatory enthusiasts were galvanized by the policy implications of new technologies. Theorist Ithiel de Sola Pool's *Technologies of Freedom* had, by 1983, articulated the deregulatory argument grounded in technological change:

> Historically, the various media that are now converging have been differently organized and differently treated under the law. The outcome to be feared is that communications in the future may be unnecessarily regulated under the unfree tradition of law that has been applied so far to the electronic media. The clash between print, common carrier, and broadcast models is likely to be a vehement communications policy issue in the next decades. Convergence of modes is upsetting the trifurcated system developed over the past two hundred years, and questions that had seemed to be settled centuries ago are being reopened, unfortunately sometimes not in a libertarian way. (Pool, 1983, p. 7)

By the 1970s, with fully developed economic sectors around electronic media and telecommunications, the naturalness of natural monopoly came to be challenged at several levels—economic, political, ideological—and for a variety of motives. Economists such as George Stigler and Alfred Kahn, economic theorists of law such as Richard Posner, and some regulators, legislators, and judges built elaborate arguments against the protection and regulation of monopoly services (Breyer, 1982; Horwitz, 1989, pp. 198–220). Large corporate users cheered on these efforts, which built upon Carter-era liberals' discontent with old-style regulation. Corporate foundations heavily backed theoretical and empirical research in that vein, building a solid base that was to change the very character of policy intervention (Stefancic & Delgado, 1996; Covington, 1997).

Deregulation advocates argued that conditions now existed in telecommunications for competing networks to establish truly competitive market conditions. This would permit the government to address any social welfare needs directly—for instance by giving out "phone stamps" like food stamps—while also promoting competitive market conditions. Some argued that large, essential services like telecommunications might require what Richard Vietor called "contrived competition" (1994), or highly managed competition among giants. Even so, such a management would better achieve economic vigor than the patrolling of boundaries that were, in any case, increasingly under attack. Libertarian advocates argued that unregulated monopolists, even when exploiting market power, may not do worse than regulators who tended either to work with monopolists or to inevitably worked in a politicized environment that distorts even the benefits of monopoly.

A common rallying point was the goal of getting politics out of an economic process. Deregulatory reformers often saw themselves as the party of David against the Goliath of the entrenched phone company. The public interest, for market liberals both domestically and internationally, came to be associated with deregulated markets, competition, and consumer choice, with many expecting that consumer choice would derive automatically from the freeing of markets (Keane, 1991).

One major site of debate was the traditional public interest obligation of telephone companies to provide universal service. Rethinking universal service was a direct result of the uneasy and unstable mix of regulated and unregulated network policy. The core network, being run by monopoly providers, was still responsible for the integrity of the entire network, including its highest-cost aspects. Meanwhile, other companies were using that network, taking profits, and not sharing the burden.

Was that fair, or tolerable, or even a real problem? Positions ranged from arguing that a more open system would provide for universality without rigging prices, to saying that rigging was probably necessary but should be an explicit social welfare benefit not attached to the internal pricing systems of telecommunications businesses, to arguing that telecommunications businesses needed to build in the mechanisms to ensure universal service not only for social welfare but for the best economic results. Programs such as Lifeline (providing subsidies for the poor in most states) and Linkup (providing rebates on phone installation) were alternatively excoriated as paternalistic welfare and a prop to monopoly or claimed as critical elements of a safety net for the disadvantaged in a modern democracy. Core network businesses portrayed universal service obligations as essential and expensive. If such obligations were not to remain a justification for monopoly, they should at least be shared. Competitors supported arguments that portrayed the universal service policy as poorly managed; poorly located in telecommunications services rather than in a basket of welfare services; or even unnecessary, in an era in which telecommunications services not only were well entrenched but were likely under open market conditions to become quickly cheaper and more accessible (Blau, 1997; Mueller, 1997; Noam, 1993; Sawhney, 1994).

In mass media as well, well-established notions of public interest obligations were challenged on a market-liberal basis, although the range of platforms and passionate identification of voters with particular programming (such as children's or sports programming) tended to complicate discussion. Under attack was the central notion of scarcity. That was the idea that mass media regulation was justified because spectrum was a scarce resource. This was not because broadcast spectrum was getting any more plentiful (although digital technologies among other strategies allowed both for dif-

ferent uses and for more efficient use) but because roughly comparable sub-
stitutes (cable, videocassette, a greater number of independent stations) now
existed. Critics attacked the notion of spectrum monopoly as an artifact of a
mutually convenient and rewarding relationship between big broadcasters
who wanted a protected environment and politicians who wanted control
over the spectrum (Hazlett, 1990). The traditional interpretations of the public interest became, in this formulation, a mere cynical tool of power. Everyone could claim it, and in the end the best politickers would win. As
Krattenmaker and Powe (1994) put it in a definitive summation of this cri-
tique, "In defining the public interest, enforcers tend to be motivated by partisan political goals and by their own program preferences" (p. 144).

The most entrenched beneficiaries of the old regime did not always
agree. In mass media, deregulatory activists often found themselves frustrated by the caution of broadcasters. Broadcasters might argue vociferously
for deregulation or the relaxing of rules pertaining to license renewal, but the
great majority did not want to jeopardize the underpinnings of the licensing
system that accounted for almost all the value of their stations or to forsake
the security of a protected monopoly over their piece of the airwaves. They
were officially sanctioned public trustees, custodians of spectrum for a
vaguely defined public. They valued this protection all the more as they saw
how digital processing and digital compression made it possible to imagine
multiple uses for the spectrum that had previously been fully taken up by
radio or TV transmission. They could imagine themselves as lords of whole
new domains of the spectrum, all under the protection of the trusteeship
umbrella. Sen. Bob Packwood (R-OR), who became a leader on broadcast
deregulation, especially against the Fairness Doctrine, found himself repeatedly (and ineffectively) accusing broadcasters of being spineless.

Meanwhile, politicians from both major political parties catered to
widespread cynicism about the quality and effects of "big government,"
often associating reform with a smaller government role and a larger role for
market forces. Jimmy Carter won election with the claim, later to become
routine, of being a Washington outsider. Both Democrats and Republicans
steered away from perceived liberalism. The probusiness, anti-social welfare
Democratic Leadership Council, crucial to Bill Clinton's eventual election,
was installed in 1985. Deregulation became a rallying cry, associated with
the goal of substituting market behaviors for government social welfare policies. But the term *deregulation* cloaked a range of positions and was often
invoked for changes that were not deregulatory, in fact, but reregulatory—
such as the divestiture of the telephone company.

A global ideological sea change was underway, triggering and matched
by changing economic and political circumstances. Communist regimes col-

lapsed, leaving new governments to design market-based economic structures, often involving the privatization of state-owned telecommunications services (among others). Privatizing and deregulatory policies were sweeping communications policy worldwide, with public service broadcasting under critical scrutiny and nationalized telecommunications utilities under restructuring (Melody, 1997). The U.S. deregulatory move was widely seen internationally as an imperial move to seize the lead in the booming area of informatics and communication (Tunstall, 1986). Liberalization and policy restructuring in France, Japan, and England resulted both in competition and in vertical integration, upping the ante in the United States as well and spurring a movement for legislation to rewrite the 1934 Act (Noam, 1989). "New" technologies became available gambits in a restructuring of communications.

In the process, the public interest was openly articulated as and widely reconstrued to mean an open market environment that could be maintained with a minimum of government interference.

REAGAN AND BEYOND

The election of Ronald Reagan in 1980 was a watershed for deregulatory action, in part because executive appointments to agencies and courts accomplished change that would have been far more difficult to enact in a legislative arena. This of course came to gall national legislators, who not only made it a partisan issue but across party lines saw it as preempting their power. Deregulation became a turbulent political issue. But by the end of the 1980s, the public interest as measured by deregulation, competition, or both had become an established fact both in mass media and telecommunications.

Legislative action to restructure the basic framework of communications law had seemed possible at the end of the Carter era, precipitated by turmoil in telecommunications. AT&T's effort to reinstate a more comfortable monopoly arrangement through legislation in 1976 precipitated an attempt, led by Rep. Van Deerlin (D-CA) starting in 1977, to rewrite the Communications Act in order to permit more competition and to minimize paternalistic regulation. Van Deerlin put forward proposals that involved, among other things, initiating a competitive, low-regulation market in long distance; establishing spectrum fees and broadcast deregulation; and creating a noncommercial program production endowment (U.S. Congress, House of Representatives, 1979). The project also spurred research and open discussion about paradigms, but it ended when Van Deerlin lost the election in 1980. Republican legislators learned well from this experience that omnibus legislation was too hard to pass, because of partisanship, and the conflicting interests of different industries.

The Republican victories in 1980 were not simply a changing of the guard but an aggressive assertion of ideological shift. Marking the change, and to some extent providing a blueprint for it, was the conservative Heritage Foundation's guide to remaking government, *Mandate for Leadership* (Heatherly, 1981). Deregulation was at the center of a kind of holy war in policy: "The extraordinary growth of government . . . has brought mounting costs to society which, in turn, have added to inflationary pressures, reduced productivity, discouraged new investment, and increased bureaucrats' intrusion into everyday life. . . . Regulation threatens to destroy the private competitive free market economy it was originally designed to protect" (p. 697). The document targeted communications as "the next prime target for comprehensive deregulation" (p. 705). It charted an agenda that dictated the focus of regulatory action in the 1980s, and that in large degree was eventually addressed in the 1996 legislation. It called for a stripping back of the FCC's role in radio and cable TV to that of a spectrum traffic cop; for an easing of regulation and license renewal terms for TV; and for opening competition in telecommunications, particularly letting the Baby Bells get into new markets. The Heritage Foundation would maintain this agenda into the 1990s legislative negotiations (Thierer, 1994).

Congressional Democrats blocked omnibus legislation, but the Reagan-appointed FCC took a lead role in changing the regulatory environment in the early 1980s. The FCC moved aggressively from a social equity to an economic efficiency objective. In telecommunications, FCC policy committed itself to regulatory forbearance on competitive principles. Daniel Brenner, who as chief aide to FCC chair Mark Fowler had a large role in implementing strategies designed by Carter appointee Charles Ferris in the late 1970s, saw this shift as responding to and encouraging competition in the telecommunications industry in the absence of legislation.

The FCC argued that it was in fact fulfilling the intent of the 1934 Act by focusing on a company's competitive impact as a deciding factor in whether or not to regulate at all. Its 1980 order on competitive carriers says in part, referring specifically to the purpose of the 1934 Act to offer "a rapid, efficient . . . communication service with adequate facilities at reasonable charges":

> So long as our regulation imposes costs on some firms, and thus on the public, not exceeded by the benefits generated thereby, the provision of communications service by those firms can never be as "efficient" nor can the charges be as "reasonable" as they might be in the absence of such artificial costs.

> It is equally well-established that Section 4(i) of the Act . . . provides us with the statutory basis to enact regulations and adopt policies codifying our view of the public interest. . . . Our experience to date is replete with evidence that competition in the telecommunications industry is a relevant factor in weighing the public interest. (Brenner, 1996, p. 101)

Although the FCC approach was repeatedly challenged in court (and was finally made explicit in the 1996 law to preempt further legal action), it lent weight to the argument that regulation was best conducted when least conducted.

In mass media, the FCC also played a decisive role by deregulating broadcasting, policy by policy, in line with the arguments put forward by FCC head Fowler and Brenner in a pathbreaking 1982 law review article: "Our thesis is that the perception of broadcasters as community trustees," they argued, "should be replaced by a view of broadcasters as marketplace participants. Communications policy should be directed toward maximizing the services the public desires. . . . The public's interest, then, defines the public interest" (Fowler & Brenner, 1982, p. 207).

Fowler and Brenner charged that such scarcity as existed did not merit the trusteeship model, which also was counterproductive. They argued that broadcasters' First Amendment rights stood primary and that where there was any question of listener/viewer rights it should be left to the market, not the government, to decide. They imagined spectrum auctions, sale of licenses, and even free resale as options. In practice, constrained by the Act itself, the FCC proceeded in a more piecemeal manner. It systematically struck down individual structural and content regulations, including some ownership limitations, the requirement to keep logbooks, rules pertaining to program length commercials on children's television, the trafficking (three-year holding) rule, and finally the Fairness Doctrine.

While the FCC was rewriting the concept of the public interest, antitrust lawyers at the Department of Justice were retooling antitrust. The 1982 consent decree had, in the hands of Judge Greene, who administered it, been a cautious foray into telecommunications competition (Coll, 1986). The goal was to limit the monopoly power of companies that had a tight grip on what had become nearly a necessity—dialtone. The ultimate goal of such regulatory architecture was a competitive system, but the phone companies remained common carriers. So long as the phone companies maintained monopoly or significant market power over an essential service, they were to remain under regulatory vigilance.

Antitrust law was key to this kind of regulatory vigilance, but there was a growing body of economists and lawyers who argued that efficiency might produce positive effects that would far outweigh the good of antimonopoly action. The controversy is well caught in a noted article of the time by lawyer and quondam Federal Trade Commissioner Robert Pitofsky. He argued for a tempering of reckless economism, partly in order to avoid "an economy so dominated by a few corporate giants that it will be impossible for the state not to play a more intrusive role in economic affairs" (Pitofsky, 1979, p. 1051), while supporting Chicago and Harvard school economic arguments for economic efficiency as a paramount goal of antitrust.

Not only was there ideological ferment around the concept of antitrust, but shifting technologies led to questions about the very nature of what had been thought of as natural monopoly in telecommunications. Did the logic of the Consent Decree, which kept telephone companies from providing content on their own networks, make sense given the way software was now interpenetrating the network? If competition was allowed into the system, should the providers of the network be excluded from competing? The Department of Justice, burdened with the challenge of administering the breakup of the phone company, cast about for ways to understand telecommunications markets. It commissioned a study that became central to later thinking: Peter Huber's 1987 *The Geodesic Network.*

Huber argued that because computers were now able to perform traditional switching (or linking) functions, switching was becoming decentralized. It was also becoming cheaper and far more flexible and accessible both to potential competitors and to providers of a range of services. The decentralized, geodesic domelike structure would lead to patterns that the old pyramidal switching structure did not have. It would do so in financial as well as in engineering terms:

> The emerging new reality, difficult to accept for those raised in the age of the Pyramid, is that the geodesic network will support both consolidation and competition. Vertical integration and horizontal competition were irreconcilable within a pyramidal network designed to provide universal access, because horizontal traffic hand-offs were prohibitively difficult and expensive. Once traffic was in the network, the only sensible thing to do was to move it up or down, as quickly as possible. But in a world of multi-lateral connectivity and highly dispersed electronic intelligence, integration and competition can coexist. Each supplier can independently provide end-to-end service, and yet suppliers as a group can offer universal access, by providing horizontal links among their networks. The operations of vertically integrated firms fit into the geodesic dome like the slices of an orange. (p. 1.9)

This argument, the immediate precursor of the visions of cyberlibertarians, waved away traditional antitrust concerns of the aggrandizement of monopoly power. Concentration and vertical integration were normal features of this new architecture, the argument said, but their traditional downsides, at least insofar as regulators could cope with them, had now disappeared, thanks to technology. Network technology would drive toward openness, no matter what. This gave proponents of radical deregulation technological an argument in their favor.

At the same time, the newly restructured local telephone companies were pressuring policymakers for freedom to enter other businesses, such as long distance, enhanced services, and video distribution, and the FCC was adapting its rules to promote such experiments. In 1987, the FCC permitted local phone companies to offer some enhanced services if they permitted other information providers nondiscriminatory access to their networks (Open Network Architecture, or ONA). This position was opposed to the basic notion of the MFJ, which restrained monopoly providers to their basic service provision, and it permitted phone companies to cross the line from common carrier to provider of editorial content, and it markedly blurred the line between different regulatory regimes.

But such blurring was now seen as in the public interest, meaning promotion of innovation and a marketplace that could foster a greater range of products. That could even mean giving incumbents an advantage. As a paper by FCC strategist Robert Pepper (1998) put it, the American public stood to get integrated broadband networks sooner or later—that is, pipes carrying all kinds of information, ranging from voice to data to video. Consumers would get those networks sooner and better if phone companies were permitted to own cable businesses and to deliver video. Phone companies needed this option because they insisted it was the necessary incentive for them to invest in high-capacity fiber optic wire. Communications policy blocked the growth of integrated broadband networks in several ways, including the MFJ restrictions, cross-ownership bans, and local franchise requirements for cable.

Deregulation that promoted networks that could promote competition, Pepper argued, would work for the American public, meaning consumers and potential businesspeople, and against the ever-present tendency of incumbents to protect what they had:

> The question for policymakers is how to promote the public interest by permitting new institutional arrangements to develop that will result in the best technological solutions and deployment of new services. The alternative is allowing players to "game the process"—use the regulatory, policy and political processes to thwart potential competitors—resulting in less competition and few, if any, benefits for customers—both consumers and content/information service providers.

In the long-term, integrated broadband network development probably implies the fundamental restructuring of the domestic U.S. telecommunications and mass media industries. . . . This is an unstable environment in which no existing player is guaranteed an outcome. Therefore, the tendency is to protect the past, rather than look forward. If policymakers permit this backward view to prevail, a significant opportunity to advance our telecommunications infrastructure and industries may be lost. (Pepper, 1998, pp. 103, 106)

An investment in flexibility, new entrants, and the strength of the marketplace to answer fast-changing needs with fast-changing technology also drove economic thought around spectrum. As a witty essay by economist Michael Katz (1996) (see Appendix H) on the issue of auctioning the spectrum explains succinctly, many saw government—both because of ignorance and the political process—as far less capable than the market of fostering business in this field. They also saw anything more as outreaching the appropriate grasp of telecommunications policy. The agency's best policy move would be to create clear property rights in the basic commodity of the spectrum.

Opposing deregulation were a variety of forces. Some state-level telecommunications regulators argued that the old system was not actually broken and didn't need fixing. They argued that deregulation would lead to unregulated monopoly with all its negative effects. Consumer organizations focused on telecommunications, including the American Association of Retired Persons, Consumers Union, and Consumer Federation of America, along with the United Church of Christ, and argued that that breakup of the old phone monopoly had to be accompanied by well-informed, data-rich monitoring of the unleashed behemoths to prevent unregulated monopoly and that giants such as the Baby Bells and AT&T needed tight controls. These consumer organizations foresaw erosion of phone penetration, particularly among the poor and disadvantaged, threats to quality of service, rising prices, exploitation of ratepayers for the funding of untested profit-making ventures, and unequal distribution of access to new services. They argued that if costs were shifted to local service it would mean that real social costs—deriving from the sacrifices people would make in order to keep their phone service—would be masked, since those social costs would not show themselves in decreased phone penetration statistics (Aufderheide, 1987). Unions feared the loss of union jobs with the creation of new entities and of nonunionized separate subsidiaries. Most consumer and public interest advocates were deeply skeptical that real competition would in fact emerge in basic telephony.

Remnants of the organizations that had been represented around the table at Good Guys and Gals meetings in the early 1980s in Washington also argued that mass media deregulation would not meet the needs of society's more vulnerable. Organizations that represented consumers, children, listeners, viewers, disabled persons, civil rights, gender rights, and First Amendment issues—broadly grouped under the catchword "public interest organizations"—saw their minor successes in mass media evaporating under the FCC's enthusiastic piecemeal deregulation. At the same time, they found their organizations' resources depleted as an array of social welfare policies came under attack, as regulatory tools were removed, and as charitable contributions became more widely dispersed. They argued that broadcast deregulation would not work to create more diversity in and access to mass media because scarcity in real life continued to exist and broadcasters used their monopoly powers without regard to the impact on the social fabric. They foresaw threats to the ability of citizens to hold local broadcasters accountable, threats to the range of views expressed, threats to the fair showcasing of controversial and electoral issues, and threats to the range of services in vulnerable arenas, for example, children's programming, local public affairs, minority viewpoints. They saw the scope of antitrust law narrowing further with deregulation, while the competition that supposedly would minimize the need for antitrust law was ineffective to truly check monopoly power.

These public interest opponents of mass media deregulation were placed in the difficult position of arguing defensively for a weak public interest standard (Bollier, 1992). Arguments that were procompetition and against government intrusion were not only fashionable but echoed with some of the most traditional values in a commercial, New World society. Arguments that could be construed as endorsing mildly palliative or even ineffective policy positions—for instance, decades of children's advocates' pressure on the FCC, resulting in rules that were no more than suggestions—could not counter arguments that new technologies required new approaches.

Public interest advocates were vulnerable to the charge that they were indulging in old-fashioned paternalism. Such paternalism, their opponents argued, may or may not have been necessary in a former era, but it was merely a benefit to bloated incumbents and a hindrance to most in their own constituencies in an era in which spectrum availability had been opened up, in which competition was newly possible because of cross-platform competition, and in which many channels could now stand where one had stood before. Aggressive advocates of a libertarian or deregulatory position painted public interest advocates as partisans of hapless and undeserving special interests. Deregulatory enthusiasts seized the populist mantle, representing themselves as partisans of freedom from government and social engineers and as partisans for entrepreneurship and competition.

Social advocates, the legatees of regulatory reform in the 1960s, lacked a broad social movement or intensive corporate funding. They found themselves marginalized in the now-heated debate over the redrawing of telecommunications policy.

COMPETITION AND DEREGULATION: FIRST TRIALS

However halting and awkward, the trend toward deregulation and a competitive marketplace had been well-enough established by the end of the 1980s to test its effects. Telecommunications had been liberalized under a traditional antitrust model, with competition in long distance. In a measured assessment of the consequences, veteran regulator and scholar Eli Noam (1995) notes that throughout the 1980s telephone penetration overall gradually increased, in part because some universal service subsidies were maintained. Local service prices increased less quickly than the consumer price index, although benefiting slightly more business users, while long distance prices plummeted. Quality of basic service has stayed constant, although occasional system failures have been alarming. Competitors to AT&T in the long distance market did in fact emerge. Productivity in telecommunications rose while total number of jobs in the largest firms fell. In other words, while the picture was mixed, telecommunications restructuring in fact opened up competition and lowered some prices without wrecking the network, a process that had involved extensive and ongoing regulatory oversight.

In mass media, deregulation had profound effects that are much harder to measure or assess than in basic telephone services, because mass media so pervasively interact with other cultural forces. Broadcast stations were turned, from one moment to another in 1984, into fast-moving properties. Three years after the dropping of the so-called trafficking rule, which had required new owners to wait at least three years before selling a station, half the broadcast stations in the country had been sold, many of them repeatedly, and for escalating, even dazzling prices. In the purchasing fury, groups and chains were favored over smaller purchasers. A new generation of station managers came to the fore, whose eyes were focused not merely on the bottom line but on the next sale. Group and chain broadcast holdings fueled a syndication market that both mass produced and tailored for individual markets headline news services, providing the simulacrum of local news and public affairs programming.

The rapid changeovers, at the height of the stock market boom, triggered other content changes. New owners, eager to boost ratings before another quick sale, fueled a market in salacious, scandalous, and cheap-to-produce programming. "Shock jocks" such as the Greaseman and Howard Stern got their footing as a result of the deregulated marketplace in broadcast stations. After the Fairness Doctrine was suspended in 1987, the lid was off highly opinionated, usually personality or attitude-selling talk shows (Rush Limbaugh's is the most lucrative example). At the same time it became more difficult for groups without advertising budgets to get access to airtime on electoral issues. After the FCC dropped rules on program-length commercials, product-related children's television shows blossomed. Regulatory relaxation assisted the rise of Rupert Murdoch's fourth network, Fox TV, which floated to success on the tried-and-true technique of providing more vulgar, titillating, and cheaper-to-produce programming than its rivals. The shaking up of old network arrangements—along with mergers and purchases in producing and distributing megamedia—spurred the formation of mini-networks, which mostly recycled archival product.

Regulatory relaxation, then, permitted larger-scale broadcasters to compete more vigorously with cable, VCRs, computers, and the demands of work and family, all drawing people away from broadcast TV. While expanding the program production business, it also had widespread, difficult-to-evaluate cultural consequences. As Daniel Brenner, by then a UCLA law professor, told Congress in 1991, "If there has been a decline in TV's quality, the sad truth may be that much of the blame rests with the vigorous competition that was spawned over the last decade. In some ways, competition has led us from the vast wasteland; in other ways, it has made it harder to reclaim it" (U.S. Congress, House of Representatives, 1991).

Those changes brought forth policy backlashes. The aggressive, new kinds of broadcast programming that careened through the culture triggered complaints from the religious Right. The FCC, bowing to an increasingly important Republican constituency, created highly-contested indecency rules. This reintroduced through the back door content regulations that the FCC had booted out, through the front door.

A different kind of backlash was evident in cable. The 1984 legislation had created opportunities for multiple system operators to grow, without constraining prices. Cable remained a monopoly business at the local level. Unsurprisingly, prices rose dramatically. Rising prices and poor service provoked consumers, at the same time that cable penetration passed 50 percent of homes and kept growing. Market liberals argued that cable's expanded offerings were worth the tradeoff, while consumer organizations saw price and quality issues as unambiguous evidence of unacceptable market power (Aufderheide, 1992; Crandall & Furchgott-Roth, 1996).

Consumer organizations such as Consumer Federation of America began to pressure for a return to more traditional cable regulation, which resulted in the 1992 act. Broadcasters enthusiastically supported the reregulation, especially for its insistence on "must-carry." This meant that cable operators were forced either to carry or to negotiate a price for carriage of local broadcast signals (which continue to be cable's most popular programming) on up to a third of their capacity. If they agreed to carriage, the agreement was called "must-carry." If they negotiated payment, it was called "retransmission consent." Either way, it was the very opposite of unregulated marketplace orientation in policy.

These regulatory conflicts in mass media evidenced not only intraindustry clashes but the arena's impact on and sensitivity to cultural habits. The opening up of new programming, with broadcast deregulation, expanded choice but also set in motion furious protests that ranged from outraged conservative religious groups, upset with vulgarity, to angry parents upset with toy commercials thinly disguised as kids' cartoons, to concerned sports fans afraid that their programming might become unavailable on "free" TV. Mass media deregulation and reregulation strengthened big broadcasters and large cable companies but did not redesign the policy platform. Broadcast deregulation made megamedia bigger, and cable deregulation grew multiple-system operators. Cultural turmoil ensued over their various strategies for encouraging viewer and advertiser attention.

ON THE BRINK OF CHANGE

During the Bush administration, ad hoc policy continued to find trouble at the edges of the distinction between common carrier and mass media. A commission to establish standards for high-definition TV was reenergized, as broadcasters began to grasp the threat to land claims at their borders. Broadcasters were watching as nonbroadcast services begged for parts of spectrum adjoining the broadcasters' licensed ranges, and they watched the valuation of such parts of the spectrum soar. High-definition TV was more a concept than a possibility, but it was a justification to Congress and the FCC to acquiesce when broadcasters requested expansion of their spectrum allocations (Brinkley, 1997a). Successfully laying claim to this spectrum allowed broadcasters to imagine and plan for an era in which their business would be interactive, and perhaps even networked, rather than dependent on the transmission of one signal to a large blanket of the population. It also made them very interested in the prospects for multichannel TV.

In networked communication, the lines between regulated and unregulated businesses got more blurry. The FCC passed rules permitting telephone companies to provide video services on a common carrier basis, a policy called video dialtone. This offered the possibility their acquiring multichannel TV business, but, because of continuing common carrier status, the chance to also control programming options was denied them. It was a controversial policy, and one that the Bells argued did not offer enough incentive for them to invest in the uncharted business of cable TV. After all, cable companies controlled their own programming. Anything less would not be a level playing field. Niche-market providers of competitive local phone service to corporations won rules permitting them to co-locate their equipment on monopoly provider property, expanding the challenge to the Bells and further blurring the line between regulated and unregulated provision.

Two decades of conflict over the role of regulation in telecommunications policy, combined with heady and accelerating technological change, created a broad and diffuse set of incentives to restructure the legal framework. The fundamental shift was away from regulated monopoly and toward competition, preferably across traditionally separated business arenas. There was a broad consensus that competition was generally preferable to regulated monopoly. But there was no solid evidence that effective competition was actually possible either in mass media or in telecommunications.

In the late 1980s and early 1990s, the Internet provided a model and a spur to coalesce interests and to provide a vision of how to redraw the policy landscape.

CHAPTER 2

The Shaping
of the 1996 Act

The rewrite of communications law that emerged by early 1996 was driven by the appetite of the Bell legatees to position themselves as central providers of both content and conduit for an information age. To this end, deregulatory ideology and the utopian pronouncements of new tech gurus were extremely useful. The Bells also had many enemies, including potential rivals, potential providers of services that use networks, and potential large users of network services. All these forces supported procompetitive, open market policies that featured liberalization rather than radical deregulation and that invoked the public interest.

Other communications interests, especially broadcasters, capitalized on the legislative moment. Social advocates, sometimes in alliance with corporations, closely monitored the billmaking. But the dynamic of the process, which was extraordinarily messy and convoluted, always returned to the tensions around creating a competitive marketplace out of a monopoly-provider utility service. Distinctions between the vested interests of various stakeholders were often obscured by a highly contagious fascination with the newest networked communication: the Internet.

INTERNET FASHION

In the 1990s, the growth of computer-based networking made it easy for many people to imagine what engineers, lawyers, and nerds had imagined earlier: a paradigm of communication in which the basic architecture of all information services could be a decentralized network. The Internet blossomed as a public and as a consumer phenomenon, between 1991 and 1996, and made communications techno-fashion again. A model of communication that depended on digital encoding of signals sent between computers, often over phone lines, it was a highly visible aspect of the melding of computing, communications, and media that had propelled technological and policy shifts in the 1980s. Its example, and the models of future communications services that its example inspired, had wide-ranging effects and provided the vehicle for legislative change. However, that change occurred subject to the powerful buffetting of fast-changing electoral fortunes and unrelenting corporate pressures.

The Internet's growing popularity created some hints of what a broadly accessible communications network, carrying data and images as well as voice, might mean. It went beyond lumbering gestures of interactivity by cable and phone companies. Such a network could be, in principle, multipurpose. Point to multipoint communication—the mass media model—would become a choice rather than a necessary constraint and feature of the system. The Internet could, theoretically, be equally good at sending and receiving, in any direction, making every user a potential producer as much as a potential consumer. It could be endlessly recombinant and open at any point to new users and service providers who wanted to hook up. It could involve ongoing relationships between groups of people, so that one could imagine those places as virtual neighborhoods.

The Internet demonstrated that network design was important for public policy. As a model of an openly accessible, flexible-use communications network capable of carrying and even retrieving archives worth of voice, data, audio, and video signals, it challenged traditional concepts of both mass media and telephony. If one could imagine posting content—TV programs, books, databases, libraries worth of music—on a digital server and attracting visitors to it, this turned audience hunting into something more like what direct mailers do. The Internet turned anyone into a potential media producer. And it made it easy to imagine the consequences of exclusion from or inclusion among those with access to such a powerful tool.

The Internet challenged traditional assumptions about telephony. Its use of protocols dramatized the way in which software, using a digital language, was increasingly doing the work of hardware. For many people who may never even have understood why they had to choose a long-distance company, the Internet demonstrated the way in which networks could be interrelated rather than unitary, could have multiple uses, and even be sites of entrepreneurship. Far more glamorously than the fax machine (which was arguably a more significant marker in alerting phone companies to the vast shift in the nature of network use), the Internet made many consumers rethink the meaning of the telephone line in their homes. At the same time, of course, the Internet opportunistically capitalized on the existence of a massively regulated, universally accessible telephone network—one whose capacity it was beginning to challenge.

Popular media enthusiastically represented convergence—the multi-purposing of networks that might then variously offer video, data, and voice—and its harbinger figure of the Internet, as a technological revolution. A popular mythology of limitless freedom on the cyberfrontier was fostered and exemplified in the heady rhetoric of *Wired* magazine. Books such as Howard Rheingold's 1994 *Virtual Community,* a captivating account of the on-line service The Well, and high-octane advocacy by journalist John Perry Barlow, ex-Grateful Dead songwriter, popularized the notion of cyberspace as a libertarian frontier. The career of futurist Alvin Toffler was revived. As the computer's image shifted from the mainframe's Big Brother image to that of the personal computer as the little guy's instrument of liberation, so did new entrepreneurial heroes such as Mitch Kapor and Bill Gates arise.

The ecstatic approach to new communications technologies followed in a long tradition of heralding such innovation. Radio, television, and even postal service had, upon their introduction, been celebrated for their potential to make consumers more comfortable, shake up social relations, and even bring world peace (Carey & Quirk, 1989; John, 1995; Smith & Marx, 1994; Streeter, 1992; Winston, 1986). The computer communications revolution brought out an enduring link between technology and spiritual transcendence, resulting in a giddy utopianism (Noble, 1997, Ch. 10). But besides futuristic hyperbole and bombast, this model also provided a vehicle for mobilizing citizen constituencies, launching new corporate projects, and proposing new policy initiatives. It shaped the search for what the Aspen Institute's Charles Firestone (1995) called "the holy paradigm" for communications policy for a new era.

With the possibilities of a new paradigm for communications systems, a loose coalition emerged of consumer, labor, educational, and watch groups around the overlapping goals of social equity, public service, universal service, and access to communications and media. Public interest organizations that had found social welfare rhetoric to be ineffective in arguing against deregulators found themselves working in concert with libertarian computer rights activists and found themselves on the right side of technological progress in arguing for what the Electronic Frontier Foundation dubbed an "open platform" (Bollier, 1993; Computer Professionals for Social Responsibility, 1993; Drake, 1995a; Miller, 1995; Sclove, 1995).

This open model contrasted, at its extreme, with reality. Reality existed in the kind of network model that cable TV had created: top-down, one-to-many, with the controller of the information pipeline also controlling the content sent through the pipeline. Both content and conduit incumbents found appealing this model of content and conduit control, rather than the model of decentralized, universal access.

This passion for control was directly related to widespread panic over the changing terms of doing business among the largest industry players. Dominant communications and media corporations, especially the largest local phone companies, cable companies, and media conglomerates, spent the early 1990s desperately struggling to increase their size and range and to reposition themselves as front-runners in an era of convergence (Bagdikian, 1993; Schiller, 1996; Price & Weinberg, 1996). Bell Atlantic and TCI, when they attempted to merge—a merger eventually inhibited by antitrust regulators and possibly by second thoughts on the part of the companies themselves—claimed to be harbingers of convergence. Phone companies and media companies alike set up experiments in multiple-use wires to the home and aggressively touted a future-is-now rhetoric. They held up themselves as the engines of development of highly expensive infrastructure systems and held up government regulation as a major obstacle to investment.

Policymakers responded to the opportunities created by the widespread sense of regulatory crisis, also invoking new communications technologies. The 1992 Clinton–Gore campaign strategically positioned itself as forward looking on technology issues, making friends in the computer community and handsomely collecting campaign contributions from computing and telecommunications companies in the process. The White House finally installed networked computers, praised the Internet, and promoted Gore's own phrase: "Information Superhighway." The administration worked to associate its friendliness toward new communications technologies with the future, success, productivity, and jobs.

Legislators also found in this new model a rhetorical urgency. Convergence was much invoked during legislative discussion. Convergence, said Rep. Oxley (R-OH), was "at the heart of this reform effort." Sen. Leahy (D-VT) said it was "about time for Congress to update the law to catch up with the new convergence in video, computer and telephone technologies." Sen. Pressler (R-SD), who entered the bill in the Senate in 1995, claimed it would "allow the cable, telephone, computer, broadcasting, and other telecommunications industries more easily to converge and transform themselves." The 1994 Senate bill report argued that the 1934 Act's "provisions are no longer adequate to protect the public interest in a world of competition for telephone services and increasing diversity of media." The 1995 report confidently asserted that "changes in technology and consumer preferences have made the 1934 Act a historical anachronism." Epithets such as "anachronism" and "antique" ricocheted around discussion of this legislation whenever the 1934 Act was invoked (Price & Duffy, 1997).

The model of a ubiquitous, affordable, and flexible network for communications and information, however powerful as a motivator of action, was not as powerful an indicator of the final shape of legislation. In the end—as legal scholars Monroe Price and John Duffy assert—the 1934 law, much disparaged as an anachronism, acted as a remarkably durable scaffolding of the new order (Price & Duffy, 1997, pp. 978–979). But the notion that technological and economic convergence was forcing change figured largely in the process.

MONEY AND MODELS

As the House bill was put forward for a vote in July 1995, Rep. Marcy Kaptur (D-OH) called the process "living proof of what unlimited money can do to buy influence and the Congress of the United States" (U.S. Congress, 104th Congress, 1st Session, 1995, p. H8467). This was, indeed, very big-ticket legislation. The giving came to have price tags high enough that some lobbyists, finding themselves held hostage by hungry campaigners, openly complained about it to *The New Yorker*'s Ken Auletta (1995) while the process was still ongoing. But it turned out to be difficult for any of the policy purchasers to buy outright the policy outcomes they wanted.

The stakes were as large as the businesses involved, and corporate investments in lobbyists and campaign contributions reflected that fact (Lewis, Benes, & O'Brien, 1996, pp. 61–65; McChesney, 1997, p. 42). By the 1990–1992 electoral cycle, playing in multiple legislative arenas, affected communications and electronics industries increased their PAC donations by 17 percent from the previous cycle—and this $9.6 million total from PACs (half of it from local phone companies alone) represented only two thirds of the donations. AT&T was the top corporate PAC contributor in the nation. In 1993–1994, communications and electronics corporate PAC contributions came to $8.7 million, and in 1995–1996 rose again to $11.3 million. Phone utilities continued to make up about half the PAC money; the local phone companies were the largest group of contributors, followed by long-distance and cable companies. Mass media producers, programmers, and distributors have a greater appetite for individual contributions than does the telecommunications sector. (The Center for Responsive Politics's website, at www.crp.org, contains both data and analysis.)

Publishers, TV and movie makers, telecommunications service providers, utilities, telecommunications equipment manufacturers, computer equipment and services, electronics manufacturing and services, and large user groups both paid up and also monitored the progress of the legislation moment by moment. Those with more money probably got more of what they wanted. For instance, in 1995, on a provision that would have slowed down local phone companies' entrance to long-distance markets, the vote was 57 to 43. Long distance companies averaged $6,474 PAC contributions per no vote, and local phone companies paid on average $16,405 in PAC money for their favored yes vote. On a vote that the local phone companies wanted to defeat, the companies paid on average $5,313 per no vote, while long-distance companies paid $2,819 per yes vote. Conclusions are complicated, however, by the fact that sizable PAC money from the same contributors also went to those who were voting against the donors' positions.

By contrast, consumer, religious, minority, disabled, and other constituencies profoundly affected by communications decision making were hardly represented with PAC money, and many advocates on behalf of civil rights, the poor, children, and other vulnerable constituencies found it difficult even to raise telecommunications as a significant social rights and justice issue in the press, in legislators' offices, or at foundations. Foundations on which these constituencies depend for operating funds by and large do not support advocacy work (laws are also restrictive on nonprofit lobbying), and social action organizers who did have advocacy strategies often found media and communications abstruse. They often found that potential commercial allies were also weak. Small-scale radio station owners attempted, for instance, to mobilize resistance to rules permitting concentration of radio station ownership but found themselves outresourced at the National Association of Broadcasters, the more heavyweight of whose members argued for concentration.

This process was entirely typical of the legislative process on financially significant issues in Congress. In fact, communications and electronics contributors only make it to the bottom of the top ten business sectors contributing to Congress. Banking is easily number one. And while numbers were large, they did not balloon nearing passage. After nearly doubling, the National Association of Broadcasters' PAC contributions in fact declined in both election cycles after 1990–1992. Furthermore, the stakeholders reflected a wide variety of often contending interests, fighting with each other through their congressional proxies. These interests also shifted positions. Large newspaper publishers, for instance, initially hostile to electronic publishing, came to fight side by side for joint venture provisions with telephone companies.

In short, lobbyists for communications and mass media interests profoundly influenced, and often drafted, legislation but were in competition with each other and at the mercy of fast-changing political processes, including pressure occasionally brought by nonprofit organizations and coalitions that took advantage of the moment.

INFORMATION SUPERHIGHWAY

By 1992, some key elements of the legislative battles of 1994 and 1995 were in place. Al Gore, who as a senator had used his role on the Science Committee to propose the National Research and Education Network, had introduced the phrase "information superhighway" into public debate. He had built enthusiasm for federal funding for networking by using an analogy with the federal network of interstate roads that his father had promoted as a senator. As enthusiasm for the concept grew, however, major telecommunications interests became alarmed at the idea of federal investment in and control over aspects of telecommunications service. By the time Clinton took office, it was firmly established that the information superhighway would be a private-sector initiative with government encouragement (Lewis, Benes, & O'Brien, 1996, pp. 61–65). That encouragement would come in two areas: the major one of developing government policies friendly to business innovation and competition, and the minor one of using government funds to promote demonstration projects, experiments, and niche social welfare efforts.

The National Telecommunications Information Administration's *NII (National Information Infrastructure): Agenda for Action,* issued in September 1993, articulated that perspective (U.S. Department of Commerce, 1993). It proposed that communications, information, and entertainment would all become part of a universally accessible network of networks, which could be interactive, decentralized, and competitively provided—not top-down and asymmetrical, like mass media. It unequivocally asserted that this potential communications system would be fully private, with government encouragement, legal frameworks, and some consumer protections. Executive telecommunications policy was intended to promote liberalization, so that competitive, corporate investment in the arena would be stimulated, at the same time as safeguards for consumers and the socially vulnerable were kept in place. The Internet itself was transforming into a system of private networks, with National Science Foundation funding gradually reduced and then cut off by 1994 and with private Internet service providers growing rapidly.

The Clinton administration also appointed a traditional antitrust regulator, Reed Hundt, to head the FCC. Although he frankly admitted that he had arrived at the position by being a high-school classmate of Vice President Gore, he developed an agenda that boldly put forward the question of defining the public interest. Facing a divided commission, he consistently and with increasing boldness supported concrete definitions of public trusteeship and responsibilities in mass media, while endorsing competition generally and particularly for telecommunications.

Federal support for emerging networks was in place. But who would develop an information superhighway? Who would have the money, the incentive, the expertise? How could the promising aspects of an integrated network be kept without the risk of having one wire, controlled by one company or (unthinkably) the government, channeling consumers' electronic access to the world? How were large, expensive, wired systems like cable and the much more elaborate, complex and socially essential telephone supposed to become competitive services?

TWO WIRES, RESALE, AND OPEN PLATFORMS

The so-called two-wire solution became a well-articulated position of two powerful incumbent forces: cable companies and local phone companies. Some argued that phone service ought to be made competitive, at least in the first stages, by permitting companies to buy core network access wholesale, and then sell it retail. This was already being done and had been done in launching competitive long-distance service. But resale competition was not a long-range strategy for the dream of an unregulated, competitive marketplace. It required constant regulatory monitoring of prices and behavior. In the long run, true telecommunications competition would require some kind of hardware-to-hardware or facilities-based competition. Unless an end-to-end wireless service emerged—something that at the time still seemed unlikely—this would mean wired overbuilding, or building competing sets of wired networks.

Cable companies positioned themselves as potential competitors to phone companies for integrated network service. The Bells from the late 1980s on consolidated their endorsement of broadband networks—networks that could carry data, audio, and video, as well as voice—and offered themselves to Congress as the potential competitor in the video marketplace. Both cable and local phone companies warned legislators and regulators that they would need a level playing field in regulation. For instance, phone companies responsible for universal service wanted cable telephony to share the responsibility, and cable companies did not want competitors who were not subject to franchises or must-carry rules. As policy scholar William Drake (1995a) summarized it, cable and phone companies effectively told politicians, "Give us more incentives and revenue opportunities or the highway will not get built and you will get the blame" (p. 314).

At the same time, nonprofit stakeholders in the process were developing the notion of "open platform," or networks that could be provided by any number of competitors, because all would share the same standards and terms and would be equally accessible to all. This notion proved a powerful umbrella under which unprecedented alliances between computing organizations and other public interest-oriented groups were formed. These alliances revived and transformed the nearly moribund coalition of organizations concerned with telecommunications policy in Washington, DC.

By spring 1993, organizations ranging from People for the American Way to the public interest law firm Media Access Project to the American Library Association and the National Writers Union had all found roads into the policy process, at the agency, congressional, and executive levels. Legislation concerning privacy and surveillance had triggered sometimes-fractious interactions between public interest-oriented computing organizations, especially Electronic Frontier Foundation (EFF), and other communications-policy organizations, especially the nonprofit Center for Media Education and Taxpayers Assets Project, a Ralph Nader organization.

The EFF's proposal for open platform, for a policy goal of establishing a network of networks that would be universally accessible and symmetrical (equal capacity for sending and receiving), and Computer Professionals for Social Responsibility's call for socially responsive network designs and applications provided a vision. The Telecommunications Policy Roundtable, convened by the Center for Media Education for the first time in May 1993 and, sponsored by all participants, reincarnated the 1980s Good Guys and Gals coalition as a cross-platform coalition for an era of convergence. It featured activists who represented unionized workers in education and writing, librarians, computer professionals, the varied clients of pro bono lawyers on communications issues, consumer activists, children's activists, and representatives of ethnic minority and disabled organizations, among others (Markoff, 1993). Meeting monthly and serving as an informal site to coordinate efforts, it became a vital communications network as legislation developed. Computer Professionals for Social Responsibility and others in the TPR coalition developed a coherent, ambitious vision for a national communications policy in the public interest. Put forward synoptically in the Telecommunications Policy Roundtable principles (see Appendix D) and articulated with elegance in Computer Professionals for Social Responsibility's

Serving the Community (see Appendix C), they included, among main points:

- Universal access (including universal service requirements and anti-redlining provisions);
- promotion of the civic sector (actively encouraging behaviors that promote grassroots-level democratic participation);
- freedom to communicate in a vigorous and diverse information marketplace, while protecting privacy rights;
- use of technologies to make work higher quality and more equitable.

These priorities became touchstone issues in the policy debate. The Twentieth Century Fund's policy analysis, which involved experts in communication, information, and regulation, for instance, featured recommendations that build in those priorities. Those recommendations included considering the needs of noncommercial stakeholders, guaranteeing technically open platforms, and fostering diversity of ownership and expression (Drake, 1995a, pp. 345–378).

The nonprofits' goal of open platform resonated with what large corporations, especially the phone utilities, said in high-visibility public relations efforts, namely, that they were interested in broadband networks for public service, a more responsive electorate, and a better educated youth. For the first time in more than a decade, advocates for nonprofits, disadvantaged social groups, consumers, labor, and education interests could share rhetoric with corporate forces whose commitment would eventually be crucial to any real-world business activity.

Nonprofit participation in policy, discouraged and even ridiculed during the twelve-year period of Republican presidencies, was invited in the early Clinton years. By late 1993, White House staffers were holding liaison meetings with nonprofit organizations in a wide range of sectors, including telecommunications. The White House lent its support to the notion of a public interest conference on superhighway policy. The Benton Foundation, an operating foundation dedicated to helping nonprofit organizations and community activists use new technologies, sponsored the event. Only weeks after an industry summit had been held on information superhighway issues, in March 1994, the Public Interest Summit, titled "Shaping the National Information Infrastructure," was held in Washington, DC. It attracted more than 700 people nationwide, made visible and lent credibility to public interest involvement in the process of building a new policy platform for an era of convergence.

STAKING CLAIMS

Corporate positions on rewrite legislation were articulated, in hearings, briefings, think tanks, and meetings. While negotiations were complicated by overlapping interests of conglomerates, typical positions among the major players and positions were as follows:

Bell Holding Companies and GTE

These companies wanted freedom from the Modified Final Judgment's limitation on new kinds of businesses. They wanted to be able to offer everything from customer premises equipment to long-distance service to video service to Websites and electronic yellow pages, without having to set up separate subsidiaries that would shield ratepayers from the costs of business experiments that fail. They had not only the most to gain but more important, the most to lose. They also had the deepest pockets of any of the major players.

The union to which many local phone company workers belong, the Communications Workers of America, often supported them, particularly on issues of network integrity. The core businesses of local phone companies are heavily unionized, a product of the monopoly era of regulation. Most other telecommunications providers, as well as the separate subsidiaries and new businesses of local phone companies, are aggressively antiunion. The union argued that the phone business is a natural monopoly and that market forces will eventually return us to that state—but without the consumer and worker protection of regulation. The union also opposed separate subsidiaries, for the simple reason that most separate subsidiaries are nonunion.

Large Users, Long-Distance Phone Companies, and Niche Services

These parties shared an interest in connecting at the lowest cost to the core network, among other things to be able to rent phone capacity wholesale (or benefit from lower prices). A big goal, therefore, was requiring incumbents to provide access to unbundled, wholesale phone services. Many shared an interest in restraining Bell competition, by such means as putting conditions on entry into long distance; forcing Bells to operate nondialtone business through separate subsidiaries; and limiting ownership and cross-ownership in electronic publishing and cable businesses. Through the ad hoc No Name Coalition (subsequently the Unity Coalition), they successfully resisted the local phone companies' push to enter new markets unchecked. They developed a minimum set of requirements before Bells could enter long distance. Burglar alarm businesses became a poster child in this effort, as an example of a diversified (some 13,000 companies nationwide, with 130,000 workers and 17 million homes as customers [U.S. Congress, Senate, Committee on Commerce, Science and Transportation, 1995, p. 8]) and burgeoning new growth sector.

This industry coalition also found allies in some consumer advocates, especially Consumers Union and Consumer Federation of America. Consumer groups insisted on Bell entry to new businesses through separate subsidiaries, to protect ratepayers from subsidizing new ventures and to prevent cross-subsidy. They also called for a ban on cross-ownership with cable companies, in order to encourage cable and telephone companies to compete with each other instead of just buying each other and continuing local monopolies.

Cable Operators

Multisystem cable operators, promising to be the "second wire to the home," wanted in exchange to abolish cross-ownership limitations for telephony or broadcast. They also wanted an end to price regulation, arguing that they already faced a competitive video delivery environment, soon to be made more competitive with direct broadcast satellite. They wanted to maintain bottleneck control over consumer choice and resisted standardization of set-top boxes. The set-top boxes would control increased consumer options, especially as cable invested in digital equipment. Cable operators, and especially TCI, wanted them to be proprietary, not a stand-alone, competitively offered, standard product.

Broadcasters

Broadcasters cast themselves as the endangered species of the networked era, as old-fashioned, over-the-air mass media. They argued that "free" broadcasting was such a valuable public resource by this time, the only electronic medium to reach into virtually every home, that Congress should offer broadcasters special protection from new competitors and also turn to broadcasters to develop new technologies. Their top priority was free and exclusive access to adjoining spectrum for digital uses, particularly since the emerging model for spectrum management was auctioning. They argued that the cost and risk of digital transmission required the market protection of that free spectrum. They wanted to abolish concentration of ownership and cross-ownership restrictions, especially for radio but also for TV. They argued that radio advertising was underpriced, financially crippling the medium, because of limits to concentration of ownership. Broadcast television audiences were shrinking, chiseling into broadcaster profits; consolidation and cross-ownership would protect the video medium of the poor, the immigrant, the uncabled.

Computing Interests

Computing interests supported standards setting that would benefit computing, such as open standards for set-top boxes and computer-friendly standards for digital TV. They also opposed defining Internet services as telecommunications services for the purposes of universal service and other obligations of phone providers. They joined anti-Bell forces in wanting to protect from Bell domination the smaller and up-and-coming businesses that use communications networks. They resisted language that would punish Internet behavior as censorship.

Computing-industry-funded organizations such as Electronic Frontier Foundation, as well as organizations such as Computer Professionals for Social Responsibility and the Electronic Privacy Information Center, often articulated key issues in terms of the public interest. When intraindustry disagreements erupted over EFF's negotiations over digital surveillance legislation, EFF cut back to a minimalist agenda. Some departing EFF staffers formed the Center for Democracy and Technology, with a wider funding base that included phone companies but that strongly supported open platform agendas.

Nonprofit organizations thus often found allies in the floating coalition of Bell enemies, and sometimes even with the Bells. But on the mass media side, nonprofits found corporate partnerships hard. They typically opposed provisions permitting concentration of ownership, relaxation of public trusteeship regulation, including licensing oversight; relaxation of cable's price regulation; and cross-ownership provisions. They could sometimes find friends in smaller industry players, which were threatened by mergers, such as network affiliate stations and small radio station owners.

But these players also lacked clout. The shape of the industry was changing most rapidly, through financial, not technical, convergence, as large firms got larger and more multifaceted. Large media conglomerates such as Viacom and Time Warner, interested in cable and broadcast programming and delivery, and very large providers such as TCI, had equally large presences when arguing for concentration and cross-ownership relaxation. They could also argue that the high-stakes, high-cost new network paradigms could only be accomplished by the very rich and powerful.

FIRST DRAFTS

Several attempts to pass legislation failed before 1995, and even then, passage was in doubt up to the last days. The two years preceding passage were crucially important to final passage, however, because the open debates educated many legislators and staffers for the first time on developments that had been the bailiwick of a few policymakers and legislators for decades. In this period, industry stakeholders took sides and formed and reformed alliances.

In 1993, several legislative efforts to devise a new policy platform for telecommunications failed, as did privacy legislation and a bill to promote nonprofit research and small business uses of telecommunications networks. Bills to permit spectrum auctions and to extend FBI surveillance were enacted. Finally, in late 1993, the Clinton administration honed its proposal for a redesign of the 1934 Communications Act. But it was too late to intervene in the political gamesmanship of Congress, where powerful committee heads had already staked out claims, allies, and campaign contributors.

In November 1993, two telecommunications bills were introduced in the House, followed in January 1994 by one in the Senate. Each reflected the concerns and corporate affiliations of their sponsors.

H.R. 3626, sponsored by Jack Brooks (R-TX) and John Dingell (D-MI), reflected their powerful allegiance to entrenched telephone interests. It represented the virtually unimpeded interests of the Bells. Local phone companies were permitted to enter long-distance and other businesses, with some minor impediments, upon the enactment of legislation.

H.R. 3636, sponsored by Ed Markey (D-MA) and Jack Fields (R-TX), strongly reflected well-developed Democratic positions and administration interests. It showcased Rep. Markey's long-term interest in communications issues, relationships with public interest organizations, and association with the Clinton administation. This bill proposed far more stringent limitations on Bell entry into competitive long-distance services, permitted phone companies to offer cable service only on a common carrier model (equal access to all comers), and encouraged the open platform model by asking the FCC to open an inquiry into it. The legislation also let the FCC take the lead in setting policy above states, mandated open (rather than proprietary) technology for equipment that would hook up TV sets to telecommunications services, and protected universal service. In fact, it extended the concept of universal service by mandating price breaks for schools, libraries, and rural hospitals. It also proposed an FCC/National Telecommunications and Information Administration inquiry to promote civic uses of the Internet. The bill both supported broadly competitive telecommunications policy and also the concerns of the public interest activists. H.R. 3636 and 3626 were merged as 3626 and overwhelmingly passed the House (Drake, 1995a; Drake, 1997).

In the Senate, powerful committee chair Ernest Hollings (D-SC), with John Danforth (R-MO), proposed S. 1822, which shared a perspective with that of the Markey–Fields Bill. This bill created stringent requirements for local competition before the Bells could enter long-distance competition. It required evidence of competition at the local level, not mere resale of an incumbent carrier's capacity to a competitor, but head-to-head competition between companies so that each had some of their own equipment (known as facilities-based competition). Bells would have to establish separate subsidiaries for dealing with competitors, for information services, and for manufacturing. The bill limited cross-ownership between cable companies and telephone companies to 5 percent in a shared area of service, in order to encourage competition between services, not just conglomeration. It extended the notion of universal service to enhanced or new "information services," including the Internet, and required telecommunications providers to extend universal service provisions to nonprofit institutions, including K–12 schools, libraries, health care facilities, and museums, including zoos and aquaria. In mass media, an arena that was a special interest of Sen. Hollings, broadcasters were permitted to use new digital spectrum for a broad range of uses, not merely for high-definition TV (U.S. Congress, Senate Committee on Commerce, Science and Transportation [USCSCCST], 1994, passim and pp. 126–128).

PUBLIC LANES AND DECENCY ZONES

S. 1822 also included a clause, incorporating an amendment proposed by Sen. Daniel Inouye (D-HI), that originally reserved 20 percent of all available space on the information superhighway for the public interest. This concept revived the failed Wagner-Hatfield amendment to the 1934 Act, which had reserved 25 percent of the broadcast spectrum for nonprofit uses. Strongly backed by public TV interests, it was proposed and supported by members of the Telecommunications Policy Roundtable as a placeholder for future public communications activity. A "public lane on the information superhighway" became a rallying cry for public interest advocates of all stripes. While it was completely unclear how such a set-aside would be implemented, and who would use it, it was clear that a fifth of available resources would be declared public domain, like public parks or public libraries.

The legislation eventually whittled the set-aside back to 5 percent, and the provision was unlikely ever to have survived final negotiations. Providers of every kind of telecommunications service raised objections about how both to provide the service and to provide interconnection with potential partial competitors. But it was a remarkable precedent and statement about the necessity for a public domain on the frontier in cyberspace. It was especially noteworthy because it employed the notion of "the public" in a way that did not simply equate the public with competition and consumer price and new-product benefits. The 5 percent set-aside linked the promise of open platform or open network architecture to the quality of public life.

Networks with truly open architecture (as determined by the FCC) were exempt, but networks that involved gatekeeping or bottlenecks of some kind would have to make space for nonprofit organizations' "providing educational, informational, cultural, civic, and charitable services to the public" (p. 39). Using precedents, including reserved spectrum for public TV and for DBS, the legislative language justified the set-aside by arguing the following:

> The builders of these new networks will use real public property for laying copper wires, coaxial cable, and fiber optic cable, and use previously unused electromagnetic frequencies. The public has a right to demand compensation in the form of public access to such networks by entities that provide substantial benefits to the public. . . . Second, the U.S. Government has a compelling interest in ensuring that all citizens of the United States have access to a broad and diverse array of communications services, including noncommercial educational, informational, cultural, civic, and charitable services. Such broad access furthers the Government's compelling interests in education, in facilitating widespread public discourse among all citizens, and in improving democratic self-governance. Because citizens now receive a large majority of their information through use of these telecommunications networks, the owners of these networks will become gatekeepers of the information that the public receives. . . . Third, the owners of these telecommunications networks are likely to design their networks so as to maximize the potential profit of such networks. . . . These owners are unlikely to adopt rate structures that will allow access for entities with few financial resources. In particular, entities providing noncommercial educational, informational, cultural, civic, and charitable services are likely to be excluded. . . . By reserving capacity for public users, the legislation provides a public forum for speech without involving the Government in regulating speech content. (USCSCCST, 1994, pp. 13–14)

Finally, the language noted that this measure would effectively reduce government involvement in the lives of citizens: "Many of these entities have historically provided important public services that would otherwise have to be provided by the Government. Ensuring that these nonprofit organizations have access to telecommunications networks at incremental rates is likely to decrease the need for any other government involvement" (USCSCCST, 1994, p. 39).

This approach to public benefit was at dramatic odds with a clause attached at the last moment to S. 1822, a version of the Communications Decency Act. Its presence demonstrated activism by politically sensitive family values groups, including the Family Research Council, the American Center for Law and Justice, and the Christian Coalition. The added amendment, proposed by Sen. James Exon (D-NE), made indecent communication with a minor over the Internet illegal (Cannon, 1996, pp. 52–54). However, it proposed to apply to the Internet standards appropriate for mass media; it took no consideration of the network design of the Internet. It thus so flagrantly misrepresented (or simply misunderstood) the Internet as a communications medium that libertarian digerati came to use it as an example of the dangers of making policy at all in this arena. But it won support from senators who either did not understand the Internet or feared that opponents would say they had voted "for indecency" at election time, or both.

END AND BEGINNING

Incumbent local telephone companies, whose support was a sine qua non, found this legislation entirely unacceptable. John Breaux (D-LA) proposed an enthusiastically pro-Bell bill, S. 2111, opposed by virtually everyone but the local phone companies. The difference between the two bills was a marker of the distance to be traversed by negotiations across industry lines before any rewrite could be sanctioned by the corporations that would be most affected by it.

The fall 1994 electoral season was dominated politically by polls showing that Republicans appeared to be able to win enough seats to control the House of Representatives and win key gubernatorial and local races. The Clinton administration seemed to some Democratic candidates to be part of the problem, and those candidates began to shy away from White House support. Any leverage that the White House had on the legislative process was rapidly eroded. Meanwhile Republicans, led by Sen. Bob Dole (R-KS), adopted a wrecking strategy, so that Democratic-backed legislation of all kinds would not pass. As the election drew near, and it became clear that Republicans would be intransigent in blocking action, Hollings withdrew S. 1822 rather than suffer defeat.

Billmaking in the 104th Congress took place in a highly politicized environment. House of Representatives Majority Leader Newt Gingrich's (R-GA) Progress and Freedom Foundation issued a document intended to recapture the rhetorical and conceptual high ground from the public interest-oriented coalition and to promote a deregulatory telecommunications policy that, coincidentally, was also Bell friendly.

"Cyberspace and the American Dream: A Magna Carta for the Knowledge Age," created by the heterodox political amalgam of Esther Dyson, Alvin Toffler, George Keyworth, and George Gilder (see Appendix E), was written as a manifesto. It is a breathtaking synopsis of cyberutopianism combined with a bold, even simplistic formula for arriving at paradise. It asserted the inexorable arrival of the Third Wave, as the Tofflers have called it— a decentralized postindustrial society organized around information flow. It imagined universal access to a broadband communications network as a central feature of such a society and asserted that universal access derives directly from "reducing [government] barriers to entry and innovation." It specifically endorsed the notion of permitting telephone and cable companies to unite to provide broadband services, rather than forcing them to compete. That way, it argued (along with cable and phone companies), there would be faster, more efficient construction of networks. It announced the end of natural monopoly in communication, and it posited a clear role for government, namely, that it "should focus on removing barriers to competition and massively deregulating the fast-growing telecommunications and computing industries." The manifesto signaled, among other things, a commitment on the part of Republican leadership to Bell support.

While the manifesto was launched in conjunction with a conference that had a grand public display, in congressional committees Republican majorities were going to work quickly. Democratic-backed versions of the bills that had emerged from the 103d Congress were introduced and quietly died. In the House, by May, Commerce Committee Chair Thomas Bliley (R-VA) introduced H.R. 1555, which created stringent conditions for local telephone entry into other businesses.

But on August 4, 1995, a manager's amendment was introduced by House leadership, including Reps. Dingell and Gingrich. A manager's amendment represents the deal arrived at by the party leaders who are coordinating debate on a topic. In this case, it was a deal vastly different from that struck in committee. The amendment boldly flouted that committee's designated responsibility. It dramatically rewrote the bill in favor of the Bell companies. The bill made it much easier and quicker for them to get into other businesses, especially long distance, before having to wait for true, facilities-based competition to emerge. It loosened the rules on the prices that local phone companies could charge potential competitors, in favor of the Bells. It dropped the requirement that phone companies that offered cable would have to do so on a common carrier model. And it excluded universal service language that would guarantee the status quo or extend it. The manager's amendment also included clauses calculated to win support from a range of other interests, including local and state government officials, cable companies, newspaper publishers, power companies, and even minority groups, who were to be beneficiaries of a development fund for small entrepreneurs (U.S. Congress, 104th Congress, 1st Session, 1995, p. H8426-60; Healey, 1995).

The manager's amendment created enormous institutional hostility and spurred heated debate on the floor. In a remarkable parliamentary maneuver, Rep. Markey managed, in the heat of the moment during floor debate, to insert an amendment requiring the V-chip, a filtering device that would monitor violent programming according to a to-be-determined industry rating system, on future TV sets. Nonetheless H.R. 1555 passed quickly in a highly polarized atmosphere as representatives rushed to close business before the end of session.

One rare area of agreement across party and ideological lines was a shared House hostility to the Communications Decency Act (CDA). From Speaker of the House Newt Gingrich to Democratic liberal Ron Wyden (D-OR), there was consensus that Congress should not impose regulation on cyberspace, although the House bill did not actually block the amendment as it was proposed in the Senate (Cannon, 1996, pp. 66–69).

Senate process was more rapid. At the outset of the session, Commerce Committee chair Larry Pressler (R-SD) hurriedly floated a Republican draft of legislation in committee. S. 652 claimed to create "a pro-competitive, de-regulatory national policy framework" for advanced telecommunications and information technologies and services "by opening all telecommunications markets to competition." Despite its language, the bill looked more like a set of boxed gifts to some of the largest, most entrenched elements of media and communications industries, with a special bent toward the Regional Bell Operating Companies, or "Baby Bells." This was hardly surprising. Pressler was one of the bigger individual beneficiaries of campaign contributions in the sector and used the bill as an opportunity to host campaign-contribution breakfasts.

The bill loosened restrictions on Bells' entering long-distance and other businesses. It permitted cable and telephone companies to enter each other's businesses and to merge with each other. Cable companies would be released from rate regulation for any channels other than basic cable, and could move most of their basic channels up to higher prices, with price regulation of any kind abolished with the arrival of a competitor. Broadcasters would get longer, easier-to-renew licenses and expanded national reach, as well as cross-ownership with cable. Existing broadcasters would get digital bandwidth, without limitations. Sen. Exon reintroduced the Communications Decency Act, backed by some religious and child welfare organizations. Internet service providers successfully shifted responsibility away from providers to users and took themselves out of the debate (Drake, 1995a; Cannon, 1996).

The bill's incumbent-friendly pragmatism generated partisan and intraparty conflict. Some Republicans, including Sens. Bob Packwood (R-OR), John McCain (R-AZ), and Bob Dole (R-KS), wanted a much more radically deregulatory line. Spectrum auctions, deregulation of all price regulation, and slashing of universal service were among their demands. On the other side, the administration and particularly Vice President Gore, who had worked hard to reregulate cable, promoted a liberalization model. They wanted to see rate regulation tightened up and cable-telco mergers restrained.

COMPETITION AND PUBLIC SPACES

Nonprofits attacked different features of the bill, to varying effect. The Consumer Federation of America, the American Association of Retired Persons, and Consumers Union, for example, focused on anticompetitive features such as cable-telco cross-ownership and the potential for Bell monopoly power. The checklist for Bell entry to long distance was toughened, and telephone companies were only permitted to own up to 10 percent of cable companies in their local service area. The Center for Media Education, the Media Access Project, the Benton Foundation, and a range of educational organizations, including the National Education Association, among others, attempted to revive the 5 percent set-aside that had been part of S. 1822, without success. The Alliance for Community Media, defending access cable centers, failed to win reserved space for nonprofits on video delivery but did win the requirement for any service that was competing with a local cable company to carry the same amount of access channels—government, educational, and public—as the cable company had to carry. Nonprofits, including the Media Access Project, the Center for Media Education, the Benton Foundation, and the Taxpayers Assets Project, among others, had argued strongly against broadcast concentration and cross-ownership with cable, and the White House urgently expressed their concerns. A 35 percent national ceiling for audience reach was maintained for national television station ownership, although it was entirely removed for radio. Other concentration of broadcast ownership questions were referred to the FCC, to be dealt with later.

The granting of extended spectrum to broadcasters, for digital service, nearly became a deal breaker in the final stages of legislative negotiations. Broadcasters that were menaced by the prospect of nearby spectrum's being gobbled up by potential competitors, including nonbroadcasters' planning for telecommunications uses, claimed that they needed that spectrum. Searching for plausible uses, broadcasters suggested that they pioneer high-definition TV, which Japan was pioneering in analog form. Eventually, U.S. industry stakeholders settled on a digital standard. In order to transmit digital signals, broadcast stations must each invest heavily in new equipment and build tall towers (Brinkley, 1997a; Common Cause, 1997; Schwartzman & Sohn, 1995).

Broadcasters insisted that such investment, for a risky venture that had no proven profit, was a substantial public benefit. Only broadcasters, they argued, were likely to try it, under their relatively protected status as public trustees. But the allocation of large chunks of spectrum to broadcasters not only offended nonprofits but also conservatives, free marketers, and libertarians who wanted spectrum to be auctioned and, some even argued, unlabelled for particular kinds of use. Discovering this issue at the last moment, then-presidential candidate and senator Bob Dole denounced it as "corporate welfare."

UNIVERSAL SERVICE

Universal service became a rallying cry around which many facets of the coalition could coalesce and in which library and education interests had a particularly large stake. Cyber-rights and First Amendment activists targeted the CDA, and Sen. Leahy with supporters introduced an alternative amendment that called for a mere study of the general problem.

Universal service became a point of intense negotiation, both for pocketbook and ideological reasons. Universal service subsidies, which spread out unequal costs of service geographically and demographically, account for billions of dollars—the exact figures ever in dispute—of phone business revenues (Noam, 1997). Once created by internal cross-subsidies, universal service subsidies had become largely a contribution of long-distance carriers to local service providers, included in their access charges or payments to local companies to hook up to their customers. Competition in local as well as long-distance service would require redesigning access charges, and deciding who would contribute what to the maintenance of universal service (Blau, 1997). Deregulatory activists challenged the very notion of the need for subsidy, especially in such a well-developed network. They and others argued that if subsidies were necessary, they should be provided out of general revenues, not made part of the cost of doing telecommunications business.

But there were many more political and social pressures to continue universal service subsidies. Public interest advocates argued persuasively that universal service made excellent economic as well as social and political sense, building inclusion into growth that made the service more economically attractive and limiting the dangers of a social divide along informational lines. Furthermore, incumbent phone companies still liked having the subsidy funds. Local and national regulators and politicians did not relish announcing cuts of existing services for vulnerable and/or highly vocal populations. Especially those legislators with rural constituencies, which had long benefited from price-averaging and other subsidies that made rural access on par with urban access, found a cause in universal service.

Library organizations, especially the American Library Association, and organizations representing K–12 educational interests dramatically developed a coalition, EdLiNC, that promoted not merely universal service provisions but an expansion of the entire notion. Not only should basic service be "affordable," the coalition argued, since income is the most important variable in access to phone service, but what constituted basic service should change. With improved technologies, low-cost access to a broad range of telecommunications services should be extended specifically to key social institutions such as schools, libraries, and medical facilities. Universal service was aggressively reconceived as a major mechanism to address equity of access to information technologies (Noam, 1997, p. 961).

This argument found political support. The House and Senate committees concerned with telecommunications were weighted toward rural and Western representatives, whose constituencies had historically benefited from universal service policies that favored rural and high-cost areas. Responding to advocates' concerns and proposals, as well as constituency demands and committee support, Sens. Olympia Snowe (R-ME) and John D. Rockefeller (D-WV) introduced an amendment that became a significant innovation in communications policy. Their amendment stipulated lower rates and access to advanced services for libraries, K–12 schools, and rural health care facilities.

Some stakeholders, including long-distance, cable companies, and Internet service providers, disputed definitions of those responsible for paying into the fund. Incumbent local phone companies were concerned about covering the cost of maintaining the network in a competitive environment. The real cost of stand-alone local phone service, after all—stripped of access charges and internal subsidies, such as those provided by call waiting and conference calls—had never been established. Regarding libraries, schools, and rural health care facilities, there was dispute over how large a contribution this would involve and whether there would or should be consideration of training, terminal equipment, software, and evaluation. Furthermore, states historically manage most of the universal subsidy issues, and this bill was federal legislation. In order to reach consensus, critical issues of authority, definition, and pricing were consigned to a state–federal committee to be convened by the FCC and to bodies the FCC would then create.

The Snowe–Rockefeller–Exon–Kerrey amendment became part of the law, during the week of frenetic floor debate before passage. Participants were limited to schools, libraries, and rural health care facilities, excluding, among others, nonprofits (such as museums and community organizations) and urban health care facilities for the poor. Training, software, and other interface tools were excluded. No one knew how much money would be involved or exactly where it would come from. But the amendment extended universal service institutionally. This was a policy innovation, which created a small but significant precedent for the notion of public domains and spaces in the telecommunications future. It also became a testing ground for the compatibility of universal service requirements and a competitive telecommunications environment.

CONFERENCE

The vociferous, contentious demands for a purer deregulatory bill by Gingrich, McCain, Dole, and others failed to result in action. The major deregulatory objectors either were looking more for sound bites than results (Dole was running for president and McCain was eyeing a future presidential bid) or lacked close enough working relationships with industry players to achieve results. Both the House bill, passed in August, and S. 652, which passed in June, both by wide majorities, underwent major surgery in conference. Specific concerns were addressed, from a variety of perspectives. Ameritech, which already had a burglar alarm business, was exempted from the clauses restricting Bells from entry into the service, which hooks up to phone lines. Small towns and cable companies' demands to be exempted from restrictions against cable-telco buyouts were answered, by permitting buyouts for areas with populations under 50,000.

One of the surprises was an entirely new service, Open Video Service. This made it possible for a telephone company, and also possibly a cable company, to offer almost regulation-free video services if it kept two-thirds of the channels open to all comers, as a common carrier. This clause superseded the video dialtone option for phone companies, an option that was already legally embattled, and addressed concerns of Republicans that the bill was still too heavily regulatory (Healey, 1995; Robinson, 1997).

The White House, still in close communication with a range of nonprofit organizations, put its weight behind some clauses regarded as key for consumers and civic action organizations, even threatening to veto the legislation (Drake, 1995a, p. 344; Telecommunications reform, 1996, p. 13; The year the government, 1995). The process was removed from the larger body of conferees, and Vice President Gore and key leaders met to cut deals. By December 20, Gore triumphantly declared victory, but the next day the deal fell apart. House Republicans were particularly exercised, both about shortcutting the process and also about the prospect of Clinton and Gore's taking credit for a bipartisan process. By December 31, however, the conferees pledged to return to work and emerged with a final version on February 1.

Partly as a result of Democratic and nonprofit pressure, the Department of Justice's approval was required, via the FCC, for local telephone company entry into long distance, providing more antitrust oversight than before. The ban on newspaper–electronic media cross-ownership was maintained. Deregulation of cable pricing on higher tiers was postponed. Conflict over foreign ownership provisions—the bill had relaxed restrictions on foreign ownership—resulted in letting the restrictions stand (Carney, 1995).

Conferees, none of whom included the most vociferous anti-CDA legislators, let stand the CDA. They also, however, included the Cox–Wyden amendment—which denounced the CDA but still permitted it. The final version also included clauses encouraging telecommunications and mass media providers to make service accessible to the disabled, so long as it was not financially burdensome; encouraging small-business participation; and protecting consumers from privacy violations by competing telecommunications firms forced to share information such as phone numbers and billing addresses.

By the time the bill emerged from conference and the president signed it on February 8, 1996, it had introduced new terms into an overlapping set of powerful industries in turmoil. Waxing pragmatic, the president praised the bill as a tool to "strengthen our economy, our society, our families, and our democracy" (U.S. Congress, House of Representatives, 1997, p. 228-4).

While wrapping itself around existing realities of money and power, the bill had also introduced fundamental change. It had, most importantly, introduced competition into the local loop and thus staked a claim for a long-term goal of an unregulated marketplace in telecommunications services. Its passage demonstrated the power of incumbency, the messiness of the legislative process, the volatility of the industries involved, and the strength of noneconomic factors.

CHAPTER 3

Overview of the Act

The Telemmunications Act of 1996 as it was finally passed (P.L. No. 104-104, 110 Stat. 56 [1996]; U.S. Congress, House of Representatives, Committee on Commerce, 1997; www.thomas.loc.gov; www.fcc.gov; and see Bibliographic Resources) was then integrated into the text of the 1934 Communications Act (U.S.C. 47; See Appendix A for an abridged version). It established the terms for competition within local telephony, for a range of telecommunications services, for competitive video services provision, and for expansion of broadcast services.

It also encoded an emerging understanding of the role of regulation and its relationship to infrastructural industries. That understanding boldly equated the public interest with a competitive economic environment, in which consumer and producer desires and needs can be matched efficiently in the marketplace, not structured by regulators. However, regulatory vigilance was plainly in evidence for the transition, and the *status quo ante* touchstones of public interest—respectively, universal service and public trusteeship—remained present.

The law, reflecting its history of conflicts and compromises, emerged as far less radical a redrawing of the regulatory platform than many had anticipated. It did not aggressively design an "information superhighway" of technical convergence. Rather it addressed the challenge of crossing technical delivery platforms at the edges. Wired telephony stayed in the center of the telecommunications picture. At the same time that it mandated competition in telecommunications, the law committed the field to continued, elaborate regulation through cross-subsidy arrangements. The current lead agency on communications policy issues, the FCC, was given a crucial and central role, partly because legislators tended to resolve ambiguity conflicts among themselves by saying that the FCC would figure out how to make it work.

In the area of mass media, the Act endorsed concentration, conglomeration, and vertical integration. It also shifted emphasis in public trusteeship dramatically by relaxing regulatory restrictions on ownership and further relaxing regulatory oversight on license renewal.

The Act is a large forest, with many, many trees. But some general objectives are met, and some overarching changes are clearly established. It also follows tradition in its organization. The text of the law is organized in the same general way that the 1934 Act is. Since it amended the 1934 Act, maintaining this logic has a practical value, permitting clauses to be merged into existing categories. The 1996 Act first addresses telecommunications issues, then mass media issues—first in broadcasting, then in cable. It then proceeds to address implementation issues and introduces new regulatory features regarding obscenity, indecency, and violence on both telecommunications and media services.

The solutions that this law proposes for communications policy respond to formulations of the problem that were, in the course of the legislative process, part of great debate. That is why, in this overview of the basic relation to the legislation, the revisions to communications law are described in terms of the problem they are designed to solve. Assessments of the effectiveness of this law in coming years will be based on whether they solve those problems and on whether those were the problems that needed solving.

The core challenge of the rewrite is how to encourage competition in traditionally monopoly-based communication networking, while also preserving the vitality of established industry sectors and feeding the strength of U.S.-based communications businesses in an increasingly competitive international environment. This challenge demonstrates remarkable continuity with the past. It maintains an industry-specific regulatory focus, a commitment to the existing shape of the industries in question, and a firm understanding of policy as linked to the U.S. position in world trade. It makes the American public, and public life itself, a derivative of the vigor and appetites of large business.

A secondary challenge of the law is how to manage a range of social and economic dysfunctions, given this first priority. This makes the state, and the regulated businesses involved, guardians of the socially vulnerable, whether they are people or values.

TITLE I: TELECOMMUNICATIONS SERVICES

The telecommunications segment of the law takes first steps toward competition in basic phone services. It does so by, at least in the short and medium range, expanding the amount and scope of regulation. Competition in this case thus creates greater regulatory complexity. It eliminates uncertainty at one level. But it introduces whole new realms of uncertainty in implementation.

In Title I, the Act makes the definitive break with the tradition of regulated monopoly in phone service. It lays out the basic terms of competition in phone services, especially local dialtone service and long distance. The major obstacles to launching competition occur at the point where any competing service must interconnect with existing, or incumbent, local telephone service providers. The law puts the FCC in charge of working out many of the rules for interconnection, sometimes in conjunction with the states, but leaves ambiguous where the buck really stops with respect to pricing decisions. This fudging at the legislative level made for much trouble later, as affected corporations took their problems with jurisdiction to the courts. The law also leaves to the states, through the state regulatory bodies known as Public Service and Public Utility Commissions, many of the details of implementing universal service and pricing provisions for telecommunications service providers.

The law in this section addresses three general problems, among its many clauses:

1. How will any prospective competitor for local telecommunications service get into this previously closed market? How exactly will competitors negotiate with the incumbent local phone company?

Local phone companies, the great majority of them inheritors of the old Bell system, have built and maintain, rehabilitate, and innovate on gigantic physical networks of cables and wires. Legislators perceived that there were no competitors ready to build or run entire networks that could provide head-to-head competition by using their own equipment—what is called facilities-based competition. They reasoned that facilities-based competition would emerge, but that the first phase of competition is probably simple resale, or renting the basic capacity from the incumbent phone company at a discount and reselling it. Even if facilities-based competitors develop, they would still need at least to connect with incumbent phone companies in order to link their customers to each other.

The law requires local phone companies to resell their services at wholesale rates and also in piecemeal (or unbundled) form, thus permitting potential rivals to offer selected services. It leaves to the FCC and to states (in an unclear formulation) the determination of what price is fair for resale. It also requires the states to let customers use their familiar phone numbers even when switching local services (number portability), to let customers get a competitor's services without dialing extra access numbers (dialing parity), and to work out payment arrangements for each competitor's part of a shared call. It gives small and rural phone companies some protection from competition. But it generally says that if someone is willing to enter the marketplace and compete with an incumbent local phone company, the local phone company has to let that competitor use one or more of its own facilities. The law includes pay phones, which historically had been the responsibility of the local monopoly phone company (Lipschitz, 1996).

This provision reflects a broad consensus that competition in local service is both possible and desirable. There is real contention, however, over whether full-fledged, facilities-based competition will ever be a reality, and whether potential rivals really want to offer competitive residential phone service, since corporate service is more lucrative. The first stages, or the testing ground, for any kind of competition depend on finding a pricing strategy for wholesale rental or resale. That pricing strategy should provide incentives for owners of key aspects of the network to continue to invest in it and keep it working well, while also make it possible for a renter to make a profit. The strategy should not provide so much of an incentive to competitors that nobody wants to build facilities-based competition either. Furthermore, all the parties have to accept the pricing arrangements, and they have not. Incumbent phone companies have successfully challenged the FCC's right to set default prices and have delayed the challenge of local competition.

The solution for a transition to open telecommunications markets is here one of highly regulated competition.

2. What happens to universal service in a competitive regime? If more than one company is providing local phone service, who then sustains the existing subsidy that makes sure that everyone—even the poor, rural dwellers, and nonprofit institutions such as schools—gets access to a phone, and that basic service prices stay more or less the same for subscribers with very different costs of provision?

The law settles, for the moment, the vigorous debate on whether telecommunications pricing should include social welfare subsidies. It sides with subsidy, a position particularly popular with legislators from rural areas, which have long been beneficiaries of such subsidies, but also with many social welfare advocates. The law basically affirms the mechanism of subsidizing marginal participation by raising revenues within the telecommunications network, but asks for more transparency in the way the mechanism is run.

Universal service subsidies will now be collected from telecommunications providers, and not from users of that service such as Internet service providers. (Ambiguities in the law about what constitutes "telecommunications providers" reflect an inability to come to consensus in legislative process, leaving the door open for much regulatory and legal negotiation later.) Any telecommunications carrier that services high-cost areas, schools, or libraries can withdraw funds to give them their discounts.

Universal service is an explicit principle for the first time in law, since up until then the entrenched policy was sustained only by the general wording in the preamble of the 1934 Act. The Act declares that its meaning will change as telecommunications services evolve; we may eventually regard Internet access, caller ID, and/or full-motion video as "basic." It makes clear that when calculating costs, telecommunications companies must include competitive services in estimating the cost of their networks, so that universal service charges end up being "no more than a reasonable share" of the cost of the network. It orders the FCC to appoint a joint board of federal and state regulators and consumer advocates to write new rules for a universal service fund that all local telecommunications providers would contribute to and draw on. That fund should make sure everyone in the nation gets "just, reasonable, and affordable rates," with equal access to "advanced" telecommunications and information services and with the same basic rates whether they live in the city or the country (where it costs more because of lower population density). Schools, libraries, and rural health care facilities get priority treatment for access to advanced telecommunications services and get reduced rates (Cooper, 1997; www.fcc.gov).

These clauses increase the size and importance of this existing subsidy program, as well as maintain the principle of cross-subsidy into what was promoted as an open market paradigm. The explicit charge of "affordable" is new and, while clarifying an assumption in the 1934 Act's preamble, also adds a definitional challenge. The inclusion of nonprofit institutions—schools, health care, libraries—is a historic breakthrough. The charge to reexamine the very notion of "basic" offers opportunities to adjust subsidies to changing technical realities and also depends on the ability of affected constituencies to organize and lobby effectively. At the same time, the law mandates that the subsidy be made explicit; the conference report sharply notes that "any support mechanism continued or created under the new section 254 should be explicit, rather than implicit as many support mechanisms are today" (U.S. Congress, House of Representatives, Committee on Commerce, 1995, p. 131). Expanding the size and importance of the subsidy, while making explicit the transfers—a requirement for a competitive environment—guaranteed a highly visible, ongoing argument over payment arrangements.

Big winners (and dogged proponents, in the legislative process) in the institutional provision were K–12 schools and libraries. Among the big losers were colleges and universities, whose libraries are not covered by the definition; community organizations; urban health care providers; and cultural institutions.

3. In a competitive universe, the formerly-monopoly local phone companies can and must compete, both for local and for long distance service, as well as for new services (such as Internet provision and interactive services such as proposed services that would electronically monitor and regulate a household's energy use, and burglar alarms, which depend on telephone connections). How are these huge, well-capitalized companies to compete in ways that will not just swamp competition?

The law lets Bell phone companies get into long-distance phone service immediately, everywhere but in their own territory. The law does not prohibit the largest non-Bell local phone service provider, GTE, from long distance; GTE was already offering long-distance service when the Act was passed. Outside their own regions Bells can offer local and long distance and can even offer them together.

Within their own regions, Bells must first let competitors into the market and must show the FCC they have complied. This is called the "competitive checklist," and it includes such elements as giving the competitor access to network elements, poles and ducts, 911 services, and white pages directory. Then they have to set up a separated affiliate to offer long-distance service, in order to protect against cross-subsidizing. Once they face competitors in their own regions, they can finally get back into manufacturing. They had been banned from manufacturing since the AT&T breakup. If they set up separated affiliates, those affiliates can go into manufacturing without waiting. They can also set up separated affiliates to offer voicemail, email, or data transmission services in their own regions, and they may go into joint ventures in electronic publishing.

Generally, the law encourages Bell Operating Companies to compete right away in other regions. In the area of burglar alarms, a thriving grassroots business that depends on hookups to telephone systems, Bells have to wait several years before they can enter the market, so as not to swamp existing businesses. Ameritech is exempted because that company already had a burglar alarm business. The law permits the Bells to expand their operations within their own regions, after competition is established and within some accounting guidelines that are intended to ensure that ratepayer resources (payments for basic service) are applied to basic service and not used to float new ventures. The Bells, like their competitors, can become vertically integrated, full-service providers of telecommunications transmission and content provision, once there is viable competition.

These conditions all attempt to balance the interests of consumers, potential rivals, and incumbent local phone companies in the areas of most-attractive first-stage competition. Clauses intended to provide a handicap for new competitors and to rein in the former monopolists' ability to skew the game all have significant exemptions and offer substantial leeway for interpretation. Key issues for such a scheme are pricing models and jurisdiction of regulators. The legislation leaves both issues ambiguous.

TITLE II: BROADCAST SERVICES

The law gives broadcasters greater powers of concentration and cross-ownership, greater security in the holding of their licenses, and more spectrum. It also maintains their public trustee obligations but does not specify or extend them. The largest single change of kind in this section is permitting cross-ownership of broadcast and cable systems.

The section unabashedly reflects the core argument of the largest broadcasting interests: that they were an endangered species in the emerging world of competitive communications. In the law, broadcasters successfully maintained the privileges of an old order—preservation of monopoly control over spectrum—while claiming to be potential players in a competitive environment.

The law does change rules extensively within existing categories, with long-term implications for the shape of the broadcast industry. It addresses perceived problems in the following areas:

1. How can the nation promote digital TV service, given that providing such a service over-the-air means technological innovation and redesign, reallocation of the spectrum, and a massive investment in new hardware at all levels?

It is not in the least clear that the nation's progress depends on getting digital TV, but it has become one of the coat hooks upon which promises of convergence are hung. Rewarding broadcasters for building the new service, the law permits them—pending a congressional revisiting of the issue, which was later made perfunctorily—to add more spectrum on to their existing licensed spectrum, so long as it is used for digital broadcast. Mostly it is taken away from low-power TV license holders, land mobile services, and other small broadcasters, most of whom held their licenses on a second-class or temporary basis.

The broadcasters get the use of the spectrum for free. In order to use it, however, each station will have to spend millions to outfit itself for digital transmission. Even if broadcasters use the spectrum to transmit high-definition images—something large industry players such as Fox, Sinclair, and ABC began to question immediately after passage—broadcasters do not have to use all the new spectrum to do that. If they want to use some of the spectrum for other things, such as pay TV or data transmission, they will have to pay a fee of some kind, to be determined later (for instance, equal to what such spectrum might bring in at auction). The law specifically maintains a station's public trustee obligations for broadcasting activities. For nonbroadcast activities such as paging and data services on the digital spectrum, broadcasters will have to pay a fee for use, to be determined by the FCC. What constitutes the public interest in broadcast programming will be defined and enforced at the level of the FCC. In October 1997 a presidential advisory commission was formed to provide some guidelines for enforcement. There was widespread skepticism about its effectiveness, given that broadcasters had secured the essential, which was the spectrum allocation.

The expectation in the law is that today's analog spectrum will be returned, once we all own digital TV sets to receive signals sent on the digitally indicated spectrum. However, in 1997 Congress permitted broadcasters to hang on to the spectrum for what will almost certainly prove to be many years, perhaps indefinitely. Congress did this by delaying return of the analog spectrum until a hypothetical moment when digital viewership exceeds 85 percent.

The law thus entrusts the future of digital TV to station owners, giving the spectrum to them just as the 1934 Act did—for free, in return for unspecified public trustee obligations. The public interest is equated, here, with the development of a commercial digital TV service.

2. How can broadcasting—once the only electronic medium available to consumers in their home and the only electronic medium that reaches all Americans daily and for free—be strengthened and kept competitive in an era of competition from videocassettes, cable, and DBS?

In order, as is spelled out in the House Conference Report, "to preserve and to promote the competitiveness of over-the-air broadcast stations" (U.S. Congress, House of Representatives, Conference Committee, 1996, p. 11) by increasing their size and ability to control the market, the law dramatically loosens strictures on concentration of ownership, both for radio and for TV. It also shrinks public trusteeship obligations further by making it even easier to keep a license.

Radio, up to that time the least concentrated and most locally rooted electronic medium and the one with the cheapest advertising rates by far, had all national ownership restrictions removed. Broadcasters had argued that the very viability of radio was threatened by the low advertising rates and that owners were too poor to program creatively.

The law here permits consolidation, to improve the health of the radio industry. Local ownership restrictions are relaxed, according to the size of the market, basically so that one owner cannot own more than half the radio stations in any one place.

In TV, a single owner may now buy stations that reach up to 35 percent of the national audience. In the 50 largest markets, it is now legal to own more than one TV station or a radio and a TV station. It is now also possible to own a TV station and a cable TV system in the same place. The law also permits the ownership of more than one network (except for the biggest existing networks) and cross-ownership of cable systems and TV networks.

The law virtually guarantees license renewal, providing almost complete protection of broadcasters from public scrutiny and from enforcement of public trustee obligations. It extends licensing from five years (TV) and seven (radio) to eight years and bans comparative renewal proceedings in the first round. This means that no one can challenge an incumbent's license unless the FCC has already found the licensee unfit. Furthermore, the FCC can no longer find licensees unfit because of failure of public trusteeship.

The one clause that runs counter to the easier-licensing logic is, predictably, about the perennial hot button of violence. The law requires broadcasters to append to license renewals any written comments from listeners or viewers about violent programming.

These provisions continue an aggressive trend in deregulating broadcasting without changing the terms of basic broadcast policy. The law charges the FCC with continuing the trend by reassessing its ownership rules every two years to see if any more of them can be relaxed or abolished. The broadcast provisions give broadcasters greater security in their most valuable possession: the license. The quid pro quo for continued operations is continued financial viability under the same public interest obligations as before and provision of high-definition TV on some portion of the newly available spectrum.

TITLE III: CABLE

Cable rules in the Act feature solutions in two major areas: deregulation of existing cable, particularly around rates, and the creation of incentives for establishing cross-platform competition among services (cable into tele-phony, phone companies into video service). Cable rules thus attempt both to lower the levels of regulation for incumbents and to increase competition across platforms.

The law does not change cable's regulatory platform. Cable is still treated as an editor, a gatekeeper of programming, with a variety of public interest obligations ranging from required carriage of local broadcast signals to franchise obligations imposed by local authorities. The law strongly favors existing large cable companies over smaller cable companies and is against consumer pressure for rate surveillance. It permits network busi-nesses to enter the cable environment as traditional mass media players, thus extending the top-down, mass media model to networked services. The law also does not create any further protection for access cable channels—the cable channels for governmental, educational, and public use that are often required in municipal franchises. The law, however, requires any cable com-petitors to offer the same channels as a local cable company must.

Within this context, the cable title addresses problems generally phraseable as the following:

1. Cable was once the only multichannel video service in town. But multisystem owner cable companies now exist in a more competitive climate thanks to DBS, videocassettes, the possibility of pay services over digital broadcast spectrum, and the prospect of telephone company appetite for video service delivery. How can cable companies be freed from rate regula-tion that limits their ability to test what the market will bear?

The law's cable provisions demonstrate, both in conception and execu-tion, a qualified victory for major cable interests that had pushed for deregu-lation. Cable's regulatory history has been particularly messy, with enduring tensions between local and federal regulation. Legislation in 1984 had lim-ited localities' jurisdiction without abolishing cable's need to secure a local contract or franchise. It had limited the FCC's role in price regulation by declaring that "effective competition" (triggering deregulation of rates) existed if there were network TV channels in the area. When rates soared and angry consumers protested, cable legislation in 1992 basically declared that effective competition could only be seen as coming from another com-plete cable system in the area, a very rare situation. Consumer groups were pleased, and deregulators made gloomy, by the tightening of price regulation (Aufderheide, 1992; Crandall & Furchgott-Roth, 1996; Krattenmaker, 1994, p. 321).

This part of the law presumes at least the beginnings of a competitive marketplace in multichannel video delivery and shows great optimism about the eagerness of phone companies to get into video delivery. It relaxes rate regulation consistently in ways that benefit large existing cable companies, and sometimes in ways that encourage other very large players, such as phone companies, to compete for the same business. It provides that all rate regulation of any cable channels, except for programming on the basic tier (broadcast channels and government, educational and public access channels), is to disappear by March 31, 1999. (Immediately upon passage, however, legislators began talking about postponing that date.) "Effective competition," triggering rate deregulation of the basic tier, exists once anyone uses a local phone company's network to offer a new video delivery service, even before it attracts any customers. The law also relaxes regulation for cable operators attempting to compete with niche video providers such as SMATV ("small antenna TV" or companies privately wiring buildings) and for very small operators. The law is unclear on whether cable companies' offerings of enhanced, interactive, or dedicated program services—gambling, data transmission, or something else—are subject to local, state, or federal regulations for more traditional cable programming.

The law does not, however, change some significant constraints on cable operators. For instance, cable operators still either must carry, on a third of their channel capacity, if necessary, local broadcast signals or must (if the broadcaster is not willing to settle for free carriage) negotiate a payment. Broadcasters had made "must-carry" a major concern, but cable operators had not chosen to fight it, thinking (erroneously, in the end) that the issue would be settled in their favor in court.

Finally, cable companies that own programming as well as systems must offer their programs to competitors for fair prices. This extends provisions in the 1992 act that encourage competition with cable, by making sure that DBS and other competitors have access to programming.

Cable continues to operate in a highly regulated environment, although the law substantially relaxes rate regulation. This is a powerful benefit for incumbents.

2. How can the nation create incentives for a real competitor to cable— one that also offers a wire to the home, with the same kinds of capabilities?

The two-wire solution is evident here. The law establishes terms for rivalry on today's cable model, rather than H.R. 3626's more ambitious one, of a common carrier model for telephone-based providers of video or other "video dialtone" models—or the still more ambitious ideal of an interconnected, open platform for any networked communication with governmental incentives for the building of a broadband network. The law presumes that phone companies want to compete with cable companies for video delivery, something that phone companies strongly indicated they did. Rejecting video dialtone after 1993, Bell Atlantic and other phone companies had mounted challenges to cross-ownership provisions and had strongly argued that they required some control over programming to make the risky new venture safely profitable for them (U.S. Congress, House of Representatives, Committee on Commerce, 1995, p. 16).

The law explicitly permits phone companies to offer video programming, in which case they become subject to cable regulation for that business. But any company, including a phone company, that offers wireless video services is not to be regulated as a cable operator, any more than DBS operators are.

During the conference process, a new, hybrid kind of video service was invented, superseding the video dialtone whose limitations the phone companies were contesting in court. Responding to Republican deregulatory pressure, this new service represented a more phone company-friendly version of the video dialtone that the FCC had controversially approved a few months before (Ross, 1996): Open Video Systems (OVS). Any company, including cable and phone companies, could offer customers a package of subscription video that is exempt from rate regulation, if two-thirds of the system is open to outside, independent programmers. Therefore, OVS would be a hybrid between a common carrier arrangement (such as video dialtone had been envisioned) and a programmed service such as cable operators offer, without many of the entangling regulations of either. It would not require a local franchise, as cable does, nor be subject to rate regulation, and it would be free of the rules banning common carriers from carrying their own programming. However, OVS could not favor its own programs over competitors' programs, either in program packages made available to consumers or in the way that the delivery system is arranged. OVS indicated, among other things, rejection of common carriage as a regulatory strategy, in favor of vertically integrated service provision (Noam, 1997, p. 971).

3. How can cable companies be given incentives for facilities-based competition in basic phone service?

Just as phone companies were seen as the most likely competitors with cable companies for video delivery, cable companies were seen as the most likely "wired" competitors for local phone companies. This presumes that cable companies actually wanted to compete with phone companies, something they strongly indicated they did (Anstrom, 1995).

The law attempts to provide incentives for cable companies to enter local phone service. It provides that any telecommunications service that cable companies offer is exempt from state and local regulation of the cable company. Such services will not, in other words, be double regulated, both as phone and cable providers. For instance, franchise agreements with a municipality can only apply to the programming part of the cable business. This removes substantial decision-making authority from localities, a shift that has since been contested.

4. How can consumers be protected from having cable and phone companies gang up on them in a single market? or, How can facilities-based competition rather than conglomeration or simple buy-outs be encouraged?

The danger in the two-wire scenario, as consumer advocates phrased it, was the prospect of "making love, not war." What if phone and cable companies, unleashed to do competitive battle, instead decided to team up for monopoly advantage? Thus, the 1996 law discourages, except in situations that are considered economically unviable, exploiting one network for several functions, if there is no rival network. Reinforcing antitrust laws, the law bans mergers, joint ventures, and greater-than-10-percent investments between cable and phone companies that serve the same market.

There are, however, an impressive number of exceptions, which, taken together, encourage competition among existing large players and do not encourage new entrants. For instance, phone companies can buy into cable companies that challenge a major player in an area, if that new company is not itself part of one of the big cable companies. Since received wisdom is that the business is one of the large players, this tendency does not contradict the goal of competition. The law also provides that in small rural communities cross-ownership is permitted, presuming that the market may be too small for facilities-based competition. The FCC may also issue waivers, based on the economic situation.

Although there is substantial wiggle room, the law discourages cable and telephone operators from offering joint services.

TITLE IV: REGULATORY REFORM

This title is the heart of the Act as ideological architecture of a new era in communication policy. Even so, it follows on 20 years of policy evolution in practice, and its decisiveness is limited. The problem it addresses can be stated as follows:

What is the appropriate role for regulation, which in this arena historically is intended to compensate for the failures of the marketplace in services
and industries that are noncompetitive, in an emerging competitive marketplace?

The title puts into law a policy that has been evolving in regulatory practice over the past two decades, with much contestation in the courts. That
policy is of forbearance, or opting not to conduct or enforce regulation that
interferes with the public interest. The FCC has repeatedly and unambigu-
ously identified the public interest as being a competitive or a procompetitive
environment. This policy, which courts repeatedly have found in violation of
congressional intent, is now, finally, congressional intent. In Sec. 401, the
law explicitly equates competitive environment and public interest: "If the
Commission determines that such forbearance will promote competition
among providers of telecommunications services, that determination may be
the basis for a Commission finding that forbearance is in the public interest."

The entire title, however, applies only to telecommunications services,
not to mass media, and—at least temporarily—not to two central telecommunications policies. Interconnection rules, governing how competitors
hook up to incumbent phone companies, and rules governing Bell entry to
long distance—both of which are essential to delimiting Bell market power
in competitive telephony—are exempt from forbearance. These are two
examples of the challenge of adapting regulation to a competitive environment that does not yet exist.

The FCC must, in applying any regulation, decide that consumers will
not be harmed. But its basic concern must be whether forbearance would
promote competitive market conditions. Any industry actor can ask for forbearance, and the FCC has to respond within the year. Furthermore, the FCC
must, starting in 1998, review its entire body of telecommunications services
regulation and assess it under a public interest standard defined as promoting
a competitive marketplace.

Among other things, this is the most explicit definition of the public
interest, convenience, and necessity ever made in the law. It also puts a very
precise definition on the role of the regulator. That role is to substitute as dis-
creetly as possible for a competitive marketplace, to promote competition,
and to phase itself out. However, other titles of the law implicitly commit the
FCC to extensive and continued monitoring and maintenance of competition
among very large firms with many reasons to like market power. Furthermore, the law as a whole commits telecommunications policy to an order
that requires much management of competition.

The biggest issue is left unresolved in the forbearance clause: What policies work to make an environment competitive, and with what kind of com-

petition? Deregulation, as incumbents learned in the course of making this law, can work powerfully in favor of those with market power.

TITLE V: OBSCENITY AND VIOLENCE

This title vividly demonstrates the bipolar quality of communications policy as deregulation and competition-oriented ideologies have evolved and communications options have multiplied. This title demonstrates the reappearance of value issues and content control, within a regulatory context that otherwise promotes aggressive competition for listener, viewer, and customer.

Subtitle A: Obscene, Harassing, and Wrongful Utilization of Telecommunications Facilities (Communications Decency Act of 1996)

Subtitle A, most of which the Supreme Court found unconstitutional in July 1997 (see Appendix B), became the most well-publicized aspect of the law by the time it was passed, possibly because it dealt with both sex and the Internet. Senatorial support possibly rested on the familiar reason that elected officials do not like to be seen (especially by their opponents) voting for pornography, and also undoubtedly from senatorial ignorance of the medium (Corn-Revere, 1996; Cannon, 1996). It addresses the following perceived challenge:

How can innocents, particularly youngsters, be protected from obscene and indecent interactions as networked communication becomes not just one-to-one but many-to-many?

The law bases its remedy on communications law that bans obscene or harassing phone calls and makes it a crime to use "a telecommunications device" (including Internet communications, which go over phone lines) to make an obscene, indecent, or harassing phone call or to make an indecent communication to a minor. The subtitle attempts to distinguish Internet service providers (ISPs) such as America Online from individuals making obscenity or indecency available. It also reemphasizes existing law by requiring cable operators to block all programming that the subscriber did not opt for, upon request, and also requires any multichannel video program distributor (such as DBS, MMDS, SMATV) also to block or scramble sexually explicit programming.

There were so many problems with this subtitle, ranging from definitions of broad terms such as "lewd" to questions of appropriate state action given the technology to national enforcement of a globally interconnected medium, that subtitle C specified expediting legal action resulting from it.

Subtitle B: Violence

After three decades of congressional handwringing over the social implications of TV violence (Rowland, 1983), this subtitle offers a sort of solution. The problem as addressed is as follows:

TV violence, we know, has powerful, negative social effects. How can government limit those effects without violating the First Amendment?

The law attempts to use emerging digital technology to address the perceived problem, a long-time concern of liberal Democrats and an administration cause. The law requires the FCC first to create a rating system if the industry fails to do so within a year, and it then requires the FCC to set standards for and to require TV sets to include a chip that can receive signals labeling shows with ratings.

This approach is philosophically opposite from the approach in Subtitle A. Rather than criminalize certain kinds of transmission and access, this approach uses filtering technology to enhance consumer choice. Of course the technology in question did not exist yet when the law was passed. Furthermore, the filtering technology is merely intended to block certain kinds of programming that is defined as socially negative. It is not conceived as a broadly flexible tool to give TV viewers more choice in programming, for instance, by being able to identify and select programming on any content basis they may choose. This amount of consumer choice is a prospect dreaded by programmers generally and broadcasters in particular, because it relinquishes some of broadcasters' power to control viewer behavior.

The viability of the technology was less in question at the time than the value of proposing a solution to a problem that many voters could understand (as opposed to the arcana of much of the law). The choice of technique reflects inchoate but pervasive public discontent with mass media as a social force, existing First Amendment law, and the vulnerability of legislators on issues of morality and social values in media.

These subtitles are peculiar and revealing contradictions to the logic, such as it is, of the rest of the law. The bulk of the law's provisions, for better and worse, are designed to encourage large existing corporate sectors to accept and engage in competition of some variety. But these subtitles invite content regulation back into communications law. Out of the vast range of social behaviors represented in electronic media and telecommunications, these subtitles select predictable arenas for state action: sexual and violent expression.

These subtitles can be seen as symptoms of social backlash against the very precepts of deregulation, open competition, and aggressive innovation that the rest of the law promotes (sometimes more in name than in deed). These subtitles may be evidence, albeit indirect, of profound social anxiety as predictable context evaporates in communications and mass media. The subtitles certainly do not testify to coherent policy approaches, or even successful ones.

Both remedies ignore the basic realities of the technologies that they affect. The CDA does not take into account the realities of the Internet as a storage and retrieval vehicle and many-to-many distributor. The V-chip provision narrowly targets one kind of behavior (although it is a behavior immensely difficult to rate usefully), limiting its spur to new filtering technologies to one issue. Both remedies also ineffectively intervene in industry economics. The CDA jeopardizes Internet service providers without solving the problem it attempts to address, and the V-chip runs afoul of broadcasters' deep dislike for viewer choice. Finally, both remedies involve elaborate initial and continued government involvement.

This oscillation between the relaxing of rules governing the conduct of large corporate players, and the micromanagement of offensive image, reference, and conduct could become a pattern that reveals a fundamental weakness of the liberalization strategy.

TITLE VI: EFFECT ON OTHER LAWS

This title coordinates the law technically with existing law and policy related to telephony. It specifically replaces the terms of the Modified Final Judgment, as it evolved, of the consent decree breaking up AT&T.

TITLE VII: MISCELLANEOUS PROVISIONS

Among many other things, including privacy rules governing information that competitive phone service providers have to share about their customers, this title addresses several perceived special needs categories. Generally, these provisions address a problem phraseable as follows:

How can the law encourage socially important goals—participation of new players and small entrepreneurs, use of new technology in schools, and telemedicine—that the market is likely not to address?

This section also demonstrates ideological inconsistency in the law. Moreover, it shows how lawmaking is a public process, susceptible to influence and change, a process that is not necessarily logical or equally or elegantly responsive to all members of the public.

For instance, the law creates the Telecommunications Development Fund (TDF). This fund will be fueled with what could end up to be real money from interest on escrowed bids for spectrum auctions, to loan money to small businesses and to conduct relevant research and analysis. The TDF emerged as a new item in manager's amendment to H.R.1555 (U.S. Congress, 104th Congress, 1st Session, 1995, H8448). The amendment was, as expected, controversial. Some civil rights advocates understand the TDF as a preemptive gesture toward ethnic minority caucuses, a quid pro quo for support. Recent court decisions had ruled out mechanisms that would explicitly use affirmative action mechanisms, but the TDF was promoted as a benefit to ethnic minorities.

Other special clauses include the formal constitution of the National Education Technology Funding Corporation, which had already existed, as a private nonprofit corporation to facilitate advanced communications technology in educational institutions and to channel relevant funds or other assistance from private or public institutions and agencies. Unlike the TDF, it has no designated source of income. The law also orders a report on the state of and possibilities for advanced communications technologies in medicine ("tele-medicine"), and also mandates consideration of access for the disabled to communications technologies, wherever it does not represent an economic burden.

These clauses indicate multiple rhetorical and ideological approaches to communications policy, as well as constituency pressure.

CONCLUSION

The Telecommunications Act of 1996 destroys the legal basis for protected monopoly in telecommunications, while providing many areas of negotiation and comfort zones for incumbents. In mass media, the law does not change the policy framework in principle and gives substantial new protections to the largest players in both broadcast and cable without demanding any renewed or increased public obligation or accountability.

It boldly articulates, at long last, the principle that a competitive environment is equated with the public interest, is convenient, and is a necessity, and is to be facilitated by deregulation. But many of the clauses then contradict the principle: universal service, protected space for small entrepreneurs, the Communications Decency Act, the V-chip. In mass media, the law anoints broadcasters as the agents of over-the-air innovation and grants them a continued privileged position among mass media providers. The massive and ongoing task of managing transition is assigned to the FCC, an agency for which deregulatory ideologues have long expressed contempt as being a tool of major industry interests. But the Act does not authoritatively give the FCC control over national policy, since the bulk of phone regulation continues to happen at the state level.

CHAPTER 4

After the Act

The Telecommunications Act of 1996 received enormous publicity, upon passage, for two of its more anomalous features: the Communications Decency Act (CDA) and the V-Chip. That lopsided coverage had its logic, of course. These were features that connected with readers', viewers', and listeners' anxieties. Professional and legal opinion in the wake of the Act focused on the telephony provisions and was one of resigned acceptance. Across ideological lines, scholars and lawyers agreed that the process had been strongly influenced by incumbents, but that first steps had been taken toward a competitive environment in basic telecommunications services (see Annotated Guide to Analyses of the Act in Bibliographic Resources).

Those steps were slow and halting in the first two years. Industry reaction, over the course of the first 18 months, demonstrated the power of incumbency. Where the Act permitted or mandated basic change, as in competition in basic telecommunications services, incumbents fought cleverly, consistently, and effectively to secure market advantage. Where the Act maintained or reinforced existing trends, as in mass media concentration of ownership, industry action was swift. Such patterns, as Brian Winston's history of communications technology development *Misunderstanding Media* (1986) shows, have a long tradition.

Implementation of the complex Act's many provisions provided a host of venues where competition could be waylaid. In particular, the interests of incumbents intersected with an ongoing tussle between state and federal regulators, one that emerged in a variety of court battles. Implementation also demonstrated the importance of nonindustry forces in shaping policy. In the months following the Act's passage, the CDA was overturned, ratings standards were established for TV, and universal service provisions were established. In each of these areas, nonprofit groups, cyberspace activists, and civil liberties organizations played key roles.

Two years after the Act, the communications landscape was the most different from the way it had been two years before the Act in that utopian visions of converged-yet-competitive technology were gone. Communications corporations were larger than ever, but rarely more competitive with each other. There were pockets of savage competition, as the cutthroat business of wireless telephony showed, dotting a telecommunications landscape largely dominated by familiar players. At the same time, investors were pouring money into selected aspects of the field, especially those that catered to large, corporate users; those that maintained market power, and those that could freshen the dream of convergence. The largest industry players saw advantages in getting even larger and in positioning themselves eventually to offer full-service communications.

THAT MALLEABLE DEFINITION

From the outset, the FCC, as the lead agency implementing the Act, grappled with the definition of public interest. In a speech outlining and agenda for 1997 (see Appendix I), FCC chairman Reed Hundt signaled clearly that spurring competition and making public interest obligations in mass media concrete were and would be twin goals.The FCC should, he said, "guarantee that necessary public benefits from communications are distributed fairly and efficiently" by two major mechanisms: "(a) competition, and where that doesn't work completely or equitably, (b) proactive social policies structured to be sustainable in a competitive environment." It was not surprising, he said, that telephony incumbents fought so hard to maintain privilege, but it was crucial to find incentives for competition.

In mass media, Hundt supported flexibility in spectrum use, to stimulate the market, but also insisted on "establishing clear, specific, quantified public interest obligations that, like covenants or easements on real estate, remain with the spectrum licenses." In broadcasting, he suggested one way of allocating spectrum would be to favor applications to offer political, educational, minority and "other valuable programming that the market demonstrably does not generate in sufficient amounts."

Hundt argued that government played a crucial role in assuring nonmarket social benefits from telecommunications industries. In universal service, he noted that the schools provision as developed by Joint Board recommendations "articulate a visionary social contact between the communications industry and the public." He heralded the FCC's new rules enforcing the Children's Television Act of 1990. He cautioned, however, that continued success would require citizen mobilizing, with the FCC taking responsibility "to make our public information initiatives meaningful." He celebrated the concept of reserved spectrum for civic activities, including electoral information that could become part of campaign finance reform. In short, Hundt supported regulatory activism within a procompetitive environment: "The government should step in with precise rules that fine-tune and redirect the powerful engine of the marketplace." Hundt maintained this position consistently, but with increasing resistance within the FCC, until his departure in fall 1997. Besides internal resistance, he also faced vociferous lobbies, especially from incumbents and judges who sided with them.

Hundt's genial successor, Bill Kennard, arrived with great optimism, declaring victory in implementing the 1996 Act but pledging to encourage competition in phone service while making universal service's promises pay out. "Competition is important only if it serves to build communities," he told consumer advocates (Kennard, 1998, in Appendix K). But he presided over an FCC even less interested in fine-tuning the marketplace. One of the new arrivals, Michael Powell, after five months expressed great doubt about employing the public interest language for social or communal ends. He employed, he told American Bar Association lawyers, five criteria on public interest standards, each of which discouraged any proregulatory activism: "(1) Does the Commission have the authority to do what is asked; (2) Even if it does, is it nonetheless better to leave the matter to Congress or await more specific instruction; (3) Is the issue best addressed by a State agency or another Federal agency; (4) Should we address the matter at all; and (5) Would any action we take violate the Constitution." He argued that, given the FCC's resources, rapid change in the field, and the need to respect jurisdictional boundaries, caution and narrowly targeted objectives should be used (U.S. FCC, 1998e). The FCC's basic obligations to enforce the public interest continued, in the aftermath of passage, to be ideologically contentious.

PRICES

In the immediate aftermath of the 1996 act, there was little appetite for head-to-head competition, and prices reflected this fact. Prices for consumers, advertisers, and purchasers of media systems rose immediately after the Act, one indication of continuing or increased market power.

Prices in telephone and cable service in the first two years also reflected the benefits of incumbency. Local phone rates rose after the Act, with added requests by Baby Bells to further increase charges for basic service, although long-distance rates continued to decline with competition (U.S., Federal Communications Commission [FCC], 1998e). Pay phone rates rose predictably, as approved in the legislation, with incumbents in the forefront of price rises. Cable prices rose three times higher than inflation in 1996, and four times faster than inflation in 1997, according to the FCC (Kimmelman, 1997b, p. 1; Farhi, 1998). The changes were not attributable to a rise in program prices but were linked to cable's continuing market power (Lieberman, 1998). Broadcast advertising revenues, an indicator of market power created by increased concentration of ownership, increased 12 percent in 1996 (U.S. FCC, 1998a, p. 57).

JOBS

The legislation had been promoted as a jobs bill, something that would create a platform for a competitive, expanded, 21st-century workforce. The short-range effect in telecommunications was the downsizing of large corporations that merged, however, as well as the expansion of nonunionized jobs. While the total number of jobs available in the sector appeared to stay about the same, they were less likely to be jobs with security and benefits and less likely to be unionized (Communications Workers, 1997). The dominant employers in telecommunications, the Bells, aggressively downsized after passage of the Act, anticipating competition that did not, in fact, develop as anticipated (Batt & Keefe, 1998). This followed a trend in telecommunications from the moment of telephone divestiture, when the majority of workers, and an unusually high proportion of the female workforce in particular, had been unionized. Throughout the 1990s, unionization levels had declined, and inequality of incomes between unionized and nonunionized workers had risen significantly (Batt & Strausser, 1997).

Whether this trend was seen as a temporary phenomenon of transition toward a higher-productivity global economy or as a harbinger of more grueling working conditions in the competitive environment, shifted according to ideological perspective (McKinsey Global Institute, 1993; Miller, 1996, pp. 346–373). But in the short run, the trends were inhospitable to the currently employed workers and were unstable for new applicants.

COMPETITION IN LOCAL TELEPHONY: RESALE PROBLEMS AND PRIVATE NETWORKS

Negotiations in the legislative process centered on making telephony of all kinds broadly competitive. The great stumbling block was the transition toward competition from the core networks still controlled by Bell companies. In the end, the conferees declared victory by leaving the actual terms vague. Those ambiguities left potential competitors—especially the local phone companies—rewarded more for stalling than acting.

Although facilities-based competition, between rival hardware services, was a long-range model, legislators expected the first stage of competition to take place through competitors' renting core network capacity, or resale. Everything then depended on the wholesale price. The law had left unclear the role of states in establishing and monitoring that price, and had left to regulators the job of establishing it.

The FCC had to set default guidelines for the mechanisms of interconnection, or the ways in which competitors would rent, hook up with, and share information and services with local phone companies. The FCC accomplished this monumental task within the first year—although, *The Washington Post* reported, electric bills for the agency offices tripled as staffers stayed long into the night and worked weekends for months (Mills, 1997a). But local phone companies immediately challenged parts of the FCC's interpretation, which they found too favorable to competitors, and won a highly controversial, court-ordered stay of the interconnection order (Landler, 1996; Mills, 1997c) on the grounds that the FCC did not have the authority to set the terms in the way in which it had (Chen, 1997, p. 862).

Few competitors were able to challenge local phone companies in local residential service, and fewer still may actually have wanted to. In two years after the Act's passage, investment in competitive local exchange carriers (CLECs) soared, and access lines controlled by the CLECs rose impressively. But their business was almost entirely corporate and urban. By early 1998, they controlled perhaps 1 percent of local lines. Those lines, however, represented about 3 percent of local phone revenues, a fact that reveals why competitors like the business side of phone service (U.S. FCC, 1998b).

The dominant long-distance companies, regarded as the most likely competitors for local service, publicly announced that they were not interested in resale. As WorldCom concluded negotiations to merge with MCI, its chief executive, in a candid moment that he later regretted, suggested that MCI would focus only on more-dependable and high-profit business clients for projected local service. AT&T tried several routes to offering local service, including an abortive attempt to merge with Bell holding company SBC, signaling among other things AT&T's frustration with other ways to enter local markets. AT&T announced it would no longer pursue local residential customers, arguing that the incentives were not big enough, and MCI admitted the same. AT&T purchased one of the most successful providers of competitive local phone service to corporations, Teleport, giving it a way around its resale problems, but continuing to focus only on the corporate market (Keller, 1997; Mills, 1997a, 1997c; Young, 1998).

Rare attempts at competitive, residential service revealed the clumsiness of new competitors, as well as incumbent intransigence and foot-dragging (Keller, 1998). In October 1997, the California-based Utility Consumers' Action Network released a report describing horrific local consumer problems. Sample complaints included being disconnected from one service provider days before a competitive service provider supplied hookup; being told erroneously that a competitor would not provide 911 service; being billed incorrectly; and being subjected to complex, noncomparable pricing schemes (Fraser, 1997, p. 5).

Some doubted that local phone service would ever become truly competitive. Consumer Federation of America economist Mark Cooper, long dubious of the proposition, commented that if AT&T needed to merge with SBC in order to get access to local markets, "then the entire theory of the 1996 law is wrong. I defy you to find a lawmaker who will tell you they voted for three companies to divide up the whole country" (Mills, 1997a).

COMPETITION IN LONG DISTANCE: CHECKING THE LIST

Incumbent local phone companies' entrance into long distance was permitted only when competitive local service came into existence. The FCC interpreted, as prescribed in the law, the "checklist" that incumbent local phone companies were required to meet before they could enter long-distance service. It created a stiff interpretation of the guideline requirements in response to Ameritech's petition to enter the Michigan market, noting ways in which the local phone company was dragging its feet in permitting local competition (www.fcc.gov; Mills, 1997d). The FCC also rejected other Bell requests to enter the long-distance markets, although state regulators would have agreed to them.

Local phone companies argued that delays were due in part to sabotage by dominant long-distance incumbents A&T, MCI, and Sprint. They claimed that long-distance companies were encouraging the FCC to set the bar too high and were also refusing to compete as a tactic to keep the Bells out of their markets (Cauley, 1997). Phone companies challenged so many FCC decisions—as well as state-level ones—that Commission chairman Reed Hundt likened the legal mess to the *Jarndyce v. Jarndyce* lawsuit in Charles Dickens's *Bleak House* (Hundt, 1997, in Appendix J).

CABLE TELEPHONY: TWO WIRES?

During the shaping of legislation, the great hope for pioneering the "two-wire" solution to competition had been cable companies. However, major cable companies backed away from diversified services immediately after passage. In fall 1996, Time Warner announced it was withdrawing from telephony on its cable systems, and it pulled the plug on its ambitious experiment in converged, interactive wired service provision in Orlando, Florida. Interactive enhanced services were abandoned as well. At the same time, the largest cable MSO, TCI, facing falling stock prices, delayed plans to offer Internet services in order to concentrate on its core business of cable television delivery. A year later, it still only had Internet demonstration projects (Robichaux, 1997, p. 1). But enhanced services offered a potential way out of head-to-head competition with the phone companies. Leo Hindery, president of TCI, told investors in 1998 that TCI had no interest in providing telephone service as it was regulated under the 1996 Act, calling the Act "a fraud on the country" for promising cable/telco competition, because continued regulation and its ambiguities was too burdensome. TCI would look to telephony over the Internet, which was still unregulated as a telecommunications service (Anonymous, 1998).

The viability of cross-platform competition at all came under scrutiny (Garnham, 1996). A Clinton administration official told *Columbia Journalism Review*'s Neil Hickey bitterly (and under guarantee of anonymity) that staffers had known that cross-platform competition was a "lie": "Everybody in Washington so badly wanted this to happen that they didn't ask the cable and phone companies: 'How much is this going to cost you? How do you plan to finance the crushing costs? How will you conduct a business about which you now know nothing?' " (Hickey, 1997, p. 27).

VIDEO FROM THE PHONE COMPANY

A complementary goal to telecommunications competition was competition in video delivery services, with phone companies permitted to offer video services. This goal was also overshadowed by industry retrenchment and incumbent intransigence in the aftermath of the Act. Incumbent local telephone companies by and large showed only tentative interest in providing video services—a business that involved acumen they did not have. Content was a particularly weak point. Two telephone company partnerships to produce and package programming—Tele-TV and Americast—essentially collapsed within the first two years (U.S. FCC, 1998a, pp. 71–72). In its annual survey of cable competitiveness, the FCC noted that two years after passage of the Act, the local phone companies had a competitive presence only in a small number of markets. Some of the companies had opted for providing the service via "wireless cable" (MMDS), thus avoiding the high cost of "the last mile" into the consumer's home. Other companies had bought cable franchises inside and outside their own regions, creating in several dozen communities the potential for competition. Almost none of the companies had chosen the OVS option, which requires a provider to keep two-thirds of the system available to other programmers. But along with the gingerly experiments, major industry players drastically downsized or sold their investment in each of these routes to video delivery within the first two years (pp. 66–69).

The hesitancy and cutbacks also undercut the growth of related competitors. "Wireless cable" (MMDS) operators had anticipated partnering with local phone companies to deliver video services, expanding their limited channel capacity and introducing new services. But when NYNEX/Bell Atlantic and PacTel, legatees of Tele-TV and pioneers of video delivery partnership, abandoned the strategy to concentrate on their core businesses, the decision put the struggling wireless cable business into panic (Colman, 1997a). Both phone and wireless companies blamed cable companies for maintaining market power over programming, an increasingly important element in a business that was already strongly marked by horizontal integration (Waterman, 1995). In fall 1997, Ameritech New Media, a subsidiary of Midwestern Baby Bell Ameritech, a local phone company that had invested substantially in video delivery, testified at a congressional hearing that cable companies demanded exclusive contracts with outside suppliers, making it impossible for new entrants to compete (Albiniak, 1997a, p. 20).

OTHER VIDEO COMPETITORS

Satellite, or DTH (direct-to-home), video providers faced many of the same problems. Major cable interests, including TCI, purchased interests in satellite-delivered video companies and jointly worked to control access to sports programming. When News Corp. tried to buy into DBS company Echostar— a move that would have created a viable competitor to cable—major cable interests, especially TCI and Time Warner, succeeded in derailing the deal, among other things by brandishing the power to pull Fox programming from cable systems. Potential competitors also found they could not get access to programming, even when not directly controlled by large cable companies, because those large companies exercised the monopoly power derived from their horizontal integration. DirecTV told the FCC that Comcast, which by law must offer its own, satellite-transmitted programming to competitors, was instead transmitting via microwave in order to evade the legal obligation and keep DirecTV from competing with its cable systems (Colman, 1997b). By early 1998, satellite-delivered multichannel video controlled less than 10 percent of the market, with prospects for slow growth (U.S. FCC, 1998b, p. 58).

Two years after the Act's passage, the FCC calculated that old-fashioned cable still had 87 percent of the market share for local video service, making it far overqualified for designation of "highly concentrated" (U.S. FCC, 1998a, p. 76).

CONVERGENCE FOR WHAT AND FOR WHOM?

Technical convergence, the handy hook for so much discussion during the shaping of legislation, was not much in evidence directly afterward, either on the part of incumbents or upstarts. It was, however, a node of active investment. It was not necessarily a trend that would lead to head-to-head competition (Madden, 1997).

The experience of upstart RCN, a company with utility involvement offering bundled services—voice, video, and data—was disturbing evidence of the power of incumbents in both camps. Testifying before the FCC, RCN's CEO, Mike Mahoney, charged that closing a deal with local phone companies for resale—even at 100 percent of retail—sometimes proved impossible. Cable companies, he said, were no better. Multiple system operators could raise prices in noncompeting areas to cover low prices in competing areas, for instance, and some programming available to cable customers was difficult or even impossible to get (Mahoney, 1998).

Cox, a large cable multiple system operator among its other media holdings, was a rare case of a cable company that invested in offering local telephony as well as data and video services, using its cable infrastructure and connecting to the local phone company. Although it did win interconnection agreements in several states, it found the negotiations slow going and clouded by ongoing litigation. Cox vice president Alex Netchvolodoff told the FCC that one carrier had simply changed codes that had been agreed upon, giving Cox customers busy signals. Nonetheless, Cox had invested several billion dollars in building out a full-service network in several targeted geographic areas and eventually expected success (Netchvolodoff, 1998).

Both cable and phone companies had eagerly expressed interest in entering broadband services provision, and they did, positioning themselves as well to be full-service providers. Phone companies began experimenting with digitally enhanced, phone-line-based, fast Internet access through what were called xDSL technologies, and cable companies launched cable modem-access services. But market analysts noted that, even in the same markets, they were unlikely to go head to head for the same customers, since phone-provided broadband appealed to business customers, and cable modem-driven cable services were pitched at residential users (Madden, 1998).

Convergence could also mean enhanced market power. Long-distance company WorldCom's 1997 purchase of America Online's Internet backbone, which had already incorporated CompuServe's backbone, for instance, positioned WorldCom as a gatekeeper in cyberspace, an arena of control made more significant still by WorldCom's purchase of MCI in fall 1997 (Wilke, Gruley, & Lipin, 1997). Microsoft's purchase of cable interests in Comcast, in order to provide "Web TV" or audiovisual and interactive services via the TV set, raised the prospect of extending the computing company's enormous control into new regions. Concern over its extension into the Internet were revived by antitrust lawyers at the Department of Justice in fall 1997 (Wilke & Gruley, 1997).

TOWARD *KEIRETSU*

The convergence much more in evidence was financial. The Act had encouraged cross-ownership and concentration of ownership, in an atmosphere in which, industry participants assured legislators at hearings, size mattered. Only large players could attract the investment capital needed to take new risks. This occurred at a time when mergers and acquisitions had changed the face of most major industries. The value of merger deals generally, according to Securities Data Corp., rose steadily in the United States from at least $100 billion in 1991 to more than $700 billion in 1997 (Smart, 1997, p. A10). Antitrust theorists had moved toward efficiency as a primary goal, away from a suspicion of size and even vertical integration in itself.

In the months following the Act, mergers and buyouts multiplied. In 1997 alone, $154 billion in media and telecommunications deals was recorded in the following categories, according to Paul Kagan Associates research (Mermigas, 1998a), *telephone,* $90 million; *radio,* $8.3 billion; *TV station deals,* $9.3 billion; and *entertainment and media networks,* $22 billion.

These deals were largely triggered by the changing terms of the Act but often were taken as indications of attempts to build protection against competition. Mergers both consolidated like interests and also created conglomerates and vertically integrated, or at least multifaceted, media and communications corporations.

Leading long-distance providers, panicky about the prospect of local phone company entry, eagerly pursued strategies they believed would protect them. Among the most popular were mergers, which had already begun before passage. These mergers evidenced a variety of agendas: to unite some version of local and long-distance service (AT&T and McCaw, AT&T's failed attempt to merge with the already-merged SBC, AT&T and Teleport), to dominate enhanced services markets (WorldCom-UUNet-MFS); to attain global scope (the ultimately failed attempt to unite British Telecom and MCI); or all of them (WorldCom and MCI) (Price Waterhouse, 1996; Lipin & Keller, 1997; Mills, 1997a).

In mass media, the law permitted broadcasters to consolidate ownership. Total TV and station sales almost doubled between 1995 and 1996. The biggest short-range prize was radio, where national concentration limits had been lifted entirely. Virtually overnight, an industry marked by relative diversity of ownership and formats, and low advertising rates, became highly concentrated. Within a year and a half, more than a quarter of U.S. radio stations had been sold at least once. Radio stock prices rose 80 percent in 1997, reflecting the new market power of group owners. The FCC calculated that two years after the Act the number of owners of radio stations had declined nearly 12 percent, while the number of commercial radio stations had increased 2.5 percent (U.S. FCC, 1997b; U.S. FCC, 1998c).

Group owners increased, and the largest increased the most. The most concentrated, promising the greatest control over advertising and the largest economies of scale, looked the best to investors in this market. While the radio market as a whole was up 10 percent in 1997 over 1996, Evergreen, one of the most greatly consolidated, rose 21 percent (Rathbun, 1997). Westinghouse and Chancellor Media had come to control about half the advertising market in radio in five major U.S. cities, including New York, Los Angeles, and Chicago, prompting such concern from advertisers that the Department of Justice ruled that in some cases market control could not exceed 40 percent, and dedicated several attorneys to monitor radio owners' advertising practices (Shapiro, 1997).

Rising stock prices in broadcasting, insecurity about the structure of communications businesses in the future, and relaxation of cross-ownership rules fueled the pace of mergers. Media conglomerates were attempting to assemble integrated operations that would build in control over all aspects of products and minimize risk in distribution. Throughout the 1990s, this trend had fed on itself (Price & Weinberg, 1996). In 1991, total media merger figures were $14 billion. They rose to $90 billion in 1995, before exploding in 1996. Megadeals such as Disney's purchase of ABC, Westinghouse–CBS–Infinity, and Turner–Time Warner rocked the industry, while less well known names—Sinclair, Belo, Seagram's—won or consolidated major holdings. (Woodhull & Snyder, 1996; Miller, 1996; Price Waterhouse, 1996)

In this environment, the largest cable interests grew larger and more vertically integrated. TCI, theretofore the largest force in cable, consolidated further, purchasing 33 percent of sixth-largest MSO Cablevision systems. By June 1997, according to *Broadcasting & Cable,* the top 25 cable MSOs composed 88 percent of the industry, and the top 10 accounted for 75 percent. Time Warner and TCI together, and with interlaced directorates, controlled at least half the cable systems in the country. Key program services, such as TBS, CNN, Discovery Channel, ESPN, HBO, and Cinemax, were owned by cable companies. The cable industry leaders could thus control what viewers saw and what producers could raise money to produce, both by controlling access to national audiences through cable systems and by their allegiances to the program services in which they held equity (Waterman & Weiss, 1997).

By the end of 1997, the merger fever had cooled somewhat among the largest players. It was, market analysts suggested, being replaced by strategic partnerships (Mermigas, 1998a). The Japanese *keiretsu,* an informal set of alliances among corporations in related industries, became a model to evoke the elaborate relationships thus cultivated among megamedia corporations. Veteran media journalist Ken Auletta noted that TCI, News Corp., GE/NBC, Time Warner, Disney/ABC, and Miscrosoft all have interests in cable, media production, Internet content and conduit, home video, and sports teams. Most had interests in broadcasting, print, and telephone and wireless communications. These multiple interests also led them to form complex, temporary alliances with other similar entities. Most of these corporations had larger or smaller partnerships with each other (Auletta, 1997).

Such alliances could be expected to dull interest in head-to-head competition. TCI has been the pioneer of this architecture: a joint venture with News Corp here, part ownership of Time Warner there, and a lead role in the five megacorporation coalition that owns satellite video provider Primestar. In positioning itself as a gatekeeper for the interactive TV era, via a TV set-top box, TCI developed partnering deals with set-top box manufacturer General Instrument Corporation, software designer Microsoft, financial service provider Bank of America, Ticketmaster, and a host of other interested parties (Mermigas, 1998b).

BIGGER, BETTER?

This concentration and conglomeration did not in fact create conditions to take high-cost new risks. This was most boldly displayed in broadcasting, where merger fever was most heated. Having won control of new electromagnetic real estate in the law, permitting them to expand spectrum use for digital broadcasting, broadcasters faced the challenge of how to deploy it.

The prospect of spending millions of dollars per station to install necessary equipment—even finding the technicians who could accomplish it—suddenly appeared daunting. The FCC also insisted that broadcasters use some of the spectrum for high-definition TV, as had originally been envisioned. Industry leaders, including Disney/ABC, floated the proposition that they might simply use the spectrum to provide more variety of services, and perhaps experiment with limited interactivity. FCC chair Hundt suggested that several stations might band together and, by offering multichannel TV, challenge local cable services. Many broadcasters appeared not to be ready to restructure their business plans for new services in a new communications paradigm, although they would eventually have to make investments in order to hold on to the spectrum (Pope, 1997; Albiniak, 1997b).

SCARCITY AGAIN

The rapid consolidation of mass media corporations after the Telecommunications Act of 1996 did little to undercut the most traditional justification for public trustee obligations and public interest regulation in mass media. That justification was scarcity, the lack of general access to airwaves, and the lack of diverse perspectives on them.

During the passage of H.R. 1555, Rep. Markey (D-MA) had warned of "communications cannibalism" and "digital Darwinism," where the largest media entities could stifle the democratic process (U.S. Congress, House of Representatives, Committee on Commerce, 1995, p. 109). Digital Darwinism proceeded rapidly after passage of the Act. Scarcity seemed even more present than ever. In radio, shrinking ownership did not appear statistically to shrink the variety of radio formats since, the FCC found, the purchasers pursued format diversification (U.S. FCC, 1997b; U.S. FCC, 1998c), within the established range of commercial formats.

Diversification did not necessarily reflect social diversity. It certainly raised the price of experimentation and encouraged new lows of commercialism. For instance, Disney/ABC purchased a small alternative and community-oriented music station in Minneapolis, Rev105, adding to its two other holdings in the area, and replaced it with hard rock. Low-budget business infomercial programming sprouted after passage of the Act, in which broadcast programming, created as long-form advertisements, was aired with only intermittent announcements about its lack of editorial autonomy. Chancellor Media, a large multistation owner, daringly chose this format for one of its stations in the very home of regulation, Washington, DC (Farhi, 1998b, p. 13). Such close links between program content and advertiser interest had resulted, in the 1930s, in FCC actions in the public interest.

In broadcasting, diversity also did not necessarily mean a range of information on local issues of public importance. In an early 1998 study, 40 commercial television stations in five big city and small-town markets were surveyed. The study found that more than a third of the stations offered no local news at all. In three markets, not a single station offered any local public affairs programming. Far less than 1 percent of the programming over a two-week period was devoted to local public affairs, almost none of it in prime time (Benton Foundation & Media Access Project, 1998).

Integrated media companies took advantage of built-in synergies, which created restlessness among those outside the gates. Major Hollywood producers complained that "broadcasting's prime real estate is increasingly locked up by in-house production and deal-driven alliances struck by corporate behemoths like Disney/ABC, Fox and NBC" (Littleton, 1997). Disney's refusal to show commercials for a rival's animated feature film *Anastasia* on some ABC TV shows, the proliferation of mentions of Disneyland on ABC sitcoms, and the appearance of Disney-related stars on an expensive, Disney-backed stunt episode intended to rescue the Disney-produced sitcom *Ellen* from declining ratings on ABC all drew media fire, which in its turn demonstrated widespread suspicion of centralized control over mass media.

Broadcast station ownership became even less ethnically diverse than before passage of the Act, which came fast upon the elimination of special tax advantages for sale to a minority owner. "Minority ownership is melting away," said Larry Irving, head of the Department of Commerce's National Telecommunications and Information Administration in 1997 (Hatch, 1997). The Minority Media and Telecommunications Council estimated that minority ownership had declined 15 percent after passage of the Act. Bob Johnson, owner of Black Entertainment Television, made the connection between ownership and diversity, from an African American perspective. Media concentration had proceeded, he argued, at the expense of smaller, minority entrepreneurs. As well, he claimed, such concentration encourages irresponsibility and renewed government intrusion: "When you remove the publisher/editor from the newspaper, the publisher/editor from the radio or TV station, you get media companies of a tremendous size and a dwindling of a commitment to some of the fundamentals of media ownership and publishing. Government becomes your countervailing weight, [that countervailing weight is] not necessarily your competitor next door" (Johnson, 1997).

Space for new programs and for public service programming was even scarce in the multichannel environment (Barnhart, 1996), with niche services squeezed out by vertically integrated megamedia (Dempsey, 1997). Diversity of viewpoints was also at issue, especially viewpoints disagreeing with owners, if anecdotal evidence was any hint. Steve Brill, founder-owner of a variety of legal publications and cable program service Court TV, claimed that once Time Warner became a partner in Court TV, one of Time Warner Executives told him to kill a story on a Federal Trade Commission official lest it affect the FTC review of the Turner–Time Warner merger. Brill also mentioned, in an outraged, leaked memo to Levin, two other cases in which Time Warner had told Brill to stay away from stories sensitive to Time Warner (Kurtz, 1997). That kind of problem became a reason for a regular column in *Columbia Journalism Review,* called "Synergy Watch."

Cable's public service contribution, C-SPAN, continued to be at the mercy of TCI, which over the last few years had been cutting back on the service. Even after TCI's new president promised space on all TCI systems within three years, C-SPAN head Brian Lamb could still say that space on systems was C-SPAN's biggest problem and the reason that its proposed C-SPANs 3, 4, and 5 had been put on hold (West & Brown, 1997).

Neither new technologies nor ostensibly competition-oriented legislation had managed to retire the scarcity claim. Months after the Act was passed, a crucial court decision, *Time Warner v. FCC* (93 F. 3d 957 [D.C. Cir. 1996]) reinforced the scarcity doctrine, saying that both the broadcaster's and the public's First Amendment rights must be balanced in regulation, because of the continuing scarcity of spectrum (p. 975).

A GLASS HALF . . .

The highly imperfect business profile of communications industries in the months following passage of the Act drew a variety of explanations. For ideological deregulators, the weak evidence of head-to-head competition was evidence of the dead weight of ongoing regulation restraining innovation and entrepreneurship (McAvoy, 1996). Insider Peter Huber, an early champion of the notion that networked technologies would drive toward open access and competition, defended the notion that we are still at the beginning. Given that real obstacles were not in the marketplace but in the political architecture of regulation, which had created the very incumbents that were now creating the problem, it was good that the Act was whittling away at it, however awkwardly (Huber, 1997). Consumer defenders such as Gene Kimmelman at Consumers Union believed that old and familiar monopolists were taking advantage of regulatory relaxation and lack of clarity in a new process and that structural and price regulation and antitrust vigilance were urgently necessary (Kimmelman, 1997b).

SOCIAL WELFARE

The Act's procompetitive measures had been bulwarked—or contradicted, depending on the perspective—with measures protecting constituencies that ranged from the disabled to rural residents to small entrepreneurs. In the months following passage, these provisions became sites of furious policy activity. In the area where the greatest dollars and biggest incumbents were involved—universal service—the struggles to set the terms of implementation were particularly complex and frustrating.

Civic advocates, many continuing to work within the vision of the Telecommunications Policy Roundtable, participated in these processes. Sentiments often cut across traditional ideological or party lines, demonstrating a general concern about the cultural impact of unleashing new commercial and technological forces in communications. As usual, advocates on social equity and on children's and consumer issues worked at a tremendous economic disadvantage. For instance, in telecommunications, where the American Library Association had an immediate interest in implementing universal service discounts, the American Library Association estimated that by mid-1996 alone it had directly spent $126,000 for lobbying and employed two lobbyists, contrasting sharply with local and long-distance companies, which together registered 97 lobbyists and directly spent $24 million in the same period. The Bells and GTE spent $16 million and employed 60 lobbyists, roughly double the long-distance companies (www.ala.org/oitp/usrfacts.html). Nonetheless, nonindustry positions often carried surprising weight.

INTERNET AND INDECENCY

The Communications Decency Act (CDA) was a highly visible target of public concern. Within hours of the president's signing of the legislation, Websites throughout cyberspace went to black backgrounds, to signal protest, and lawsuits were filed. The amendment had succeeded in offending across ideological lines, from conservative to liberal (Corn-Revere, 1996; Cannon, 1996).

Two overlapping coalitions brought individual suits, which the courts consolidated. One group, organized around free expression issues, was led by the American Civil Liberties Union and by a variety of cyberrights organizations including the Electronic Privacy Information Center. The other, featuring companies from the computing industry, and including civil liberties groups such as Media Access Project and the Center for Democracy and Technology, made slightly different First Amendment challenges to two specific provisions in the law and undertook to educate the judges about networked communication. The lawsuits challenged two specific provisions in District Court, which criminalized sending obscene, indecent, or offense messages to a minor, and won a stay. The Court found the clauses to be overbroad and vague. Following the fast-track process written into the law, the Supreme Court acted by June 1997 to decide against the two crucial clauses.

The decision was a clear victory for those who argued the distinctiveness of cyberspace and for those who argued First Amendment issues. The Court argued that the Internet had never been subject to broadcast-type regulation, that it is inherently not as invasive as mass media and is not subject to scarcity logic. It also portrayed the law as chilling free speech (see Appendix B for text of the Supreme Court decision).

However inappropriate the Exon amendment's methods, problems following upon the Internet's very accessibility—exploitation of customer databases, cyberfraud, alarmist misinformation, among others—are only likely to grow with Internet use. Issues of children's access to inappropriate materials, especially commercial messages for adult products such as tobacco and liquor, became the object of FTC concern, partly in response to the Center for Media Education's research on children and online services (U.S. FTC, 1996; Center for Media Education, 1997). State laws similar to the CDA were promptly introduced, and congressional initiatives began a vigorous debate on filtering software and its accuracy. These issues are being monitored by freedom of expression and cyberrights activists, who developed coalition strength around the CDA (see Resources for Active Citizens).

TV VIOLENCE

Television program ratings became a high-visibility drama in the 18 months following passage of the Act. The law gave the industry a year to come up with ratings that could then be used in a filtering chip, the so-called V-chip, to be installed in future TV sets. Producers, programmers, and broadcasters tended to see TV ratings as a First Amendment infringement, and as, at least potentially, bad for business. They feared that if viewers would set their TV sets to exclude whole chunks of programming, their advertising revenues would be in jeopardy. Industry leaders quickly agreed to back a version of the Motion Picture Association of America's age-based movie ratings. Children's advocates from left, right, and center all found the proposal unacceptable because, they argued, it does not give enough information to provide a useful selection mechanism. If PG (parental guidance) now covers four fifths of the film industry, they reasoned, all of prime time could be blanketed by the same kind of generality. Industry representatives, spurred by V-chip supporter Markey, organized through the Motion Picture Association of America and led by veteran lobbyist Jack Valenti, negotiated with children's advocates and related concerned organizations in 1996, without budging on age-based ratings (Browning, 1997, p. 1689).

President Clinton endorsed the age-based ratings as a step forward, but 27 children's advocate organizations and Rep. Markey immediately denounced the ratings. Among others, the National PTA, the American Psychological Association, the American Academy of Pediatrics, the National Education Association, and the Center for Media Education came out against the ratings. The Senate Commerce Committee held a hearing showcasing the views of the children's advocate organizations. Legislators began introducing bills to force the industry to rate for content, which Valenti portrayed as a First Amendment attack. When House telecommunications Subcommittee chair Rep. Billy Tauzin (R-LA) held a hearing in Peoria, Illinois, and parents also expressed their outrage at the inadequacies of age-based ratings, the industry began to reach out to advocates again. Representatives from the Center for Media Education, the PTA, National Education Association, the American Psychiatric Association, and American Medical Association met in secret, with surprise backing from Vice President Gore, and emerged with an agreement for a content-based ratings system, signed by most of the industry (minus NBC) and most of the advocates (minus the American Psychiatric Association) (Browning, 1997, pp. 1690–1691). Added to age-based ratings would be V (violence), S (sex), L (language), D (suggestive dialog), and FV (fantasy violence for kids' programs). The FCC finally approved the ratings in March 1998.

The struggle toward consensus had demonstrated a broad public engagement with and concern about mass media quality and consumer control and a wide public enthusiasm for consumer and viewer choice.

UNIVERSAL SERVICE

Perhaps the most significant social-regulation element of the 1996 Act was the change in universal service. It involved billions of dollars and represented an important precedent. This was of passionate interest to a wide range of groups. There were more than 200 filers in the first round, many of them nonprofits (Cooper, 1997), mounting to nearly 1,000 by the end (www.ala.org/oitp/usrfacts.html). The FCC staff read more than 200,000 pages of comments in the first round (U.S. FCC, 1997b, p. 6). Nonprofit concern was broad. Among the filers included on just one of the joint filings were People for the American Way, Alliance for Community Media, Alliance for Communications Democracy, Benton Foundation, Center for Media Education, League of United Latin American Citizens, Minority Media and Telecommunications Council, National Council of La Raza, and National Rainbow Coalition.

Industry representatives were most interested in the mechanisms for collecting and disbursing the money. Nonprofits were most interested in the definition of universal service and in measures used to determine discounts. Many organizations, particularly regulatory bodies, advocated leaving maximal discretion to the states. As usual, incumbents and competitors created the greatest noise. Although there were differences among major players, generally issues and stakes were seen in this way (see summaries of filings at www.benton.org):

Local phone companies. The major players mostly wanted long-distance companies to continue to be the primary contributors to the fund. Costs should take into consideration the players' existing investment in physical plant and should be assessed according to their estimates. In particular, they wanted federally mandated universal funds to cover what they estimated to be extremely high costs in rural areas.

Wireless/cellular. They wanted all telecommunications providers to pay in, and any telecommunications provider willing to offer universal service to be able to take from the fund.

Major long-distance providers. They wanted to ensure that incumbent phone companies would not be able to use universal service funds to shore up their position. They wanted to drop or reduce drastically the charges they pay to local phone companies to hook up—some of which charges are used for universal service. They wanted all telecommunications providers, not just long-distance companies, to pay into the universal service fund, and they wanted costs to be calculated without including existing investment. MCI wanted to get a dollar figure for the value of the subsidy and have states provide it to the carriers. GTE, which has long-distance as well as local phone service, suggested creating a surcharge related to all end user transactions.

Competitive telecommunications providers, including cable companies, and large users. They wanted all providers to pay into the fund, they wanted any that were interested in providing the service to be able to withdraw from it, and they wanted eligible services to be tightly defined and circumscribed.

Computing. Computing businesses with Internet interests wanted advanced services to be included in the definition of universal service.

Schools and libraries. They focused on calculation of discounts, to make sure that filing would not be burdensome and that the neediest institutions got the greatest help and to make sure that advanced communications services were included in the definition of universal service.

Consumer groups. They wanted to ensure that local phone rates would not increase and that phone companies would not use universal service funds to pay for investment they would otherwise make. They also wanted a clear definition of affordable, which would take into consideration how burdensome costs that still might be paid would be on a poor person's budget.

Netizens and advocates for civic and civil rights organizations. They wanted advanced telecommunications services (e.g., Internet) to be covered under universal service obligations. As well, they were concerned about special needs groups and about an expansive definition of universal service for institutional sites for digital access.

Unions. Different unions reflected their members' specific concerns. Communications Workers of America (CWA) was most concerned about the long-term health of the core network, as competitors challenged incumbent phone companies. CWA argued that all providers using the core network and thus benefiting from universal service—including Internet service providers—should pay into the fund. Communications Workers of America also advocated including advanced services in the definition. The American Federation of Teachers was most concerned about getting advanced telecommunications into the definition and also advocated costing that did not include sunk costs.

In May 1997, the FCC adopted rules on universal service provisions and also on regulated pricing mechanisms that affect universal service (price caps and access charges) (U.S. FCC, 1997a). Only telecommunications providers offering interstate services had to contribute to the fund, including non-common carrier long-distance providers. Pay phone providers were also included. At the same time, the charges that long-distance companies were required to pay to local phone companies were reduced, and local phone charges levied on consumers stayed the same. Any common carrier that offered all the services within the definition could withdraw from the fund. Costs for high-cost areas would not include sunk costs for existing plant. In terms of payments in and out, this altered the status quo ante without changing key aspects of the basic structure. Long distance continued, in this way, to subsidize local access to phone service, something that displeased major long-distance providers. Incumbent local phone companies were not pleased either, since they were not permitted to include long-range, sunk investment and only could claim federal universal service money for a portion of their high-cost service, including in rural areas.

The rules put into motion the conflict between competition and maintenance of the core network. They extended the subsidy programs for the poor to all states and territories. The FCC limited the definition for individual users to touch-tone, voice-grade services, thus supporting access to advanced services but not the services themselves.

The rules also established the terms for schools, libraries, and rural health care facilities. There was to be $2.25 billion per year for schools and libraries. Rural health care providers receive up to $400 million. Schools and libraries could now get discounts on all telecommunications services (long distance, local, call waiting, cell phones), on Internet access, and internal connections to hook up to the Internet. Training, teaching materials, and terminal equipment were to be the school's affair. Services had to be provided by a telecommunications entity, a requirement that excluded Internet service providers and providers of private networks, which would be considered equipment rather than service. Discounts ranged from 20 to 90 percent, depending on poverty level, as measured by school lunch eligibility.

The rules were immediately challenged. Local phone companies, led by SBC and GTE, unsuccessfully appealed the FCC decision in June 1997, charging that the FCC did not have authority to create and oversee the universal service fund. The legal quarrel registered not merely intransigence but conflict among current and potential telecommunications firms over the terms of redistribution (Chen, 1997, p. 866). The issues sparking continued conflict included the following:

- Was all this money necessary? Were incumbents delivering services inefficiently or even padding the bill? Was the subsidy process hiding the real costs of such discounted services?
- Had the FCC created a large enough pool of money when it lowered access charges of long-distance providers and then told them to pay other charges? Would the quality of basic network services be impaired, or the price raised?
- Was it fair for providers of service that did not pay into the fund to withdraw from it, or for contributions and withdrawals to be unbalanced?

• Would the highest cost service provision be covered, especially if the states would have to provide for the bulk of the payment?

The rulemaking then led to new challenges. States had to establish their own universal service rules in order to get federally mandated benefits, and schools and libraries had to submit plans for use to the Universal Service Administration Company. Each of these activities involved new potential coalitions of users, institutional and residential, and new potential uses as well. Nonprofits, including major consumer organizations such as American Association of Retired Persons and Consumers Union, as well as the Center for Media Education (American Association of Retired Persons, 1995; Center for Media Education, 1996), began targeting state Public Utility and Public Service Commissions on universal service issues. Libraries and related organizations, such as the 37 national organizations mobilized as EdLiNC to pressure for universal service provisions during passage of the Act, began working with localities to ensure that schools and libraries would and could use the new provisions (Benton Foundation and Libraries for the Future, 1997; www.ala.org/oitp and www.ala.org/edlinc). The National Telecommunications and Information Administration, among other agencies, offered information on discounts (www.ntia.doc.gov/opadhome/uniserve).

Contention surrounding the issue continued to grow. In the Senate, Sen. John McCain (R-AZ) used the high-visibility issue as a vehicle to discredit the Act, challenging the universal service provision itself and charging the FCC with overstepping its boundaries. Consumer advocate Gene Kimmelman at Consumers Union called the program a "train wreck waiting to happen," because of the high rates that long-distance companies were charging consumers in the name of universal service.

Subsidies worked awkwardly in a procompetitive environment, generating much intraindustry conflict over the anticompetitive possibilities of subsidy. Raising the price of local phone service seemed inevitable, once internal cross-subsidies were jeopardized by the prospect of competitors' being able to offer specialized services. Externalizing the subsidies was politically volatile. The universal service provision registered unresolved questions among stakeholders about the social and political implications of procompetitive policy.

DIGITAL SPECTRUM AND PUBLIC INTEREST

In broadcasting, the Act had put its seal of approval on the old regime of public trusteeship. It further had entrusted broadcasters with the future of digital TV, without specifying how broadcasters would exercise their public trusteeship on that new spectrum. It left the FCC to specify any particular obligations that broadcasters would have. Broadcasters by and large took the attitude they had honed during legislative debate: they would serve the public by offering a broadly available service and by investing in digital broadcasting.

Reed Hundt's FCC took seriously the need to define the new public interest obligations of broadcast trustees beyond that level. Upon the FCC's adoption of rules on digital TV spectrum on April 3, 1997, Hundt personally stressed two areas: a set-aside of capacity for "public interest purposes" and free airtime for politicians. The second suggestion became more prominent as campaign finance reform developed and threatened to tar the Democratic administration. In late 1997, the president's Advisory Commission on Public Interest Obligations of Digital TV, with 21 members from unions, networked communications corporations, ethnic organizations, disability rights groups, and the public interest media law firm Media Access Project, was formed to make recommendations on obligations for digital spectrum (Brinkley, 1997b). But the recommendations would have to be implemented by the FCC, and powerful legislators from both parties strongly rebuked the new FCC head, Bill Kennard, even for suggesting opening an inquiry on free time for political campaigns (McConnell, 1998).

OTHER SOCIAL POLICIES

The Telecommunications Development Fund, designed to promote small business and sold to African-American and other ethnic constituencies as a prominorities project, established its board, with input from a range of civil rights organizations. The scope of its funding would depend on the market in spectrum auctions. Proposals for ways to improve access to mass media for the disabled were developed, but implementation depended on the appetite of providers to invest in and adopt them.

SUCCESS OR FAILURE?

Two years after passage of the Act, there was far less head-to-head competition than had been touted before its passage. Residential consumers were not seeing more choice in former monopolies such as cable and local phone service. Very large media firms had become much larger, without either offering new commercial services or expanding their social obligations. But billions of investor dollars had been pumped into the sector, the U.S. example had been held up internationally as a model, and niche competitors had blossomed. Communications networks continued to function with a high degree of accuracy.

The problems that surfaced immediately upon the Act's passage demonstrated the centrality of the political process and the guiding role of policy in establishing new market conditions for communications, media, and information services. Incumbents and powerful interests showed a keen awareness of the political process in maintaining their position. So did such stakeholders as entrepreneurs, workers, consumers, and advocates for more vulnerable members of society. Procompetitive objectives sometimes warred with antiregulatory objectives. The simple clarity of forbearance was not borne out in the business of crafting new rules of the game.

The law had changed the terms of doing business in the area but had not established any consistent zone of responsibility for the social effects of the communications processes that these businesses put in motion. The result was, and promised to continue to be, political ferment.

CHAPTER 5

The Public Interest
beyond the Act

The Telecommunications Act of 1996 ensures that some kind of competitive telecommunications environment will emerge. But it is still not clear what kind of environment that will be, or what its advantages will be for social equity, democratic relationships, and the civil culture of a pluralist society. The Act ratifies long-developing trends toward a competitive marketplace, vertically integrated corporations, and a minimalist regulatory stance. It does not create a policy framework that resolves conflicts arising from a competitive environment, as the universal service debate demonstrates. It also raises questions about the capacity of government regulators to monitor uncompetitive behavior among the giants who are now unleashed.

If the most basic objectives of the 1996 Act are accomplished, then defining and acting upon the public interest in telecommunications become even more complicated, more contentious, and more public than ever before. FCC chairman Reed Hundt recognized this. As he put it succinctly on the eve of his departure from the Commission,

> The primary job of the FCC Chairman historically was to give licenses to the airwaves to a limited group of folk and to rig markets so none would ever do poorly. The good reason was to permit the firms to do well economically; the bad effect was a closed, oligopolized market with little diversity of viewpoint.
>
> The primary job now ought to be the opposite: introduce risk and reward to all sectors of the communications business.

The problem then is how to promote noncommercial purposes—such as conducting civic debate about political issues or educating kids—without simply relying on a cozy partnership between government and a tiny group of media magnates. (Hundt, 1997)

That last problem has no easy answers. The preceding six decades had established no clear precedent about what noncommercial functions or social objectives are appropriate for government attention in communications policy. Instead, that history established that such concerns would be dealt with after the fact, accommodated at the margins, or made the subject of endless and ongoing debate.

An even larger problem, in today's environment, is finding a social site to discuss and decide what constitutes a socially valuable "noncommercial purpose" and how it should be provided for. This is a challenge that is as much about social networks, education, expectation and background knowledge as it is about available spaces in which to have conversations. It is a challenge that is addressed by omission—as it largely has been in the past—in the communications policy elaborated by the 1996 Act.

The emerging communications landscape is thus, unsurprisingly, impoverished in public sites or even noncommercial arenas of any kind. For instance, in the Act, public TV is simply treated as another broadcaster, potentially benefitting from digital spectrum (but not required to contribute to the quality of public life in any way as a result). Cable access channels that already exist are recognized but not encouraged or given a more general mandate. Schools, libraries, and rural health care facilities are given modest and oblique encouragement to build public relationships through a universal service provision that facilitates their access to advanced communications technologies. That provision sets aside nothing for equipment, teacher training, investment in community education, or civic activities that might make use of such networks.

There are no subsidies here, of course, for programming, production, or content creation associated with civic, community, or democratic behaviors and relationships. And there are no likely sources elsewhere in cultural policy. Such subsidy is being stripped away throughout the society. The National Endowments for the Humanities and Arts are both on the endangered species lists. Even the Department of Commerce's grants for demonstration nonprofit-sector projects in distributed networking (the so-called TIIAP, or Telecommunications and Information Infrastructure Assistance Program, grants) are held hostage to congressional whim. To the extent that there are economic benefits to the society from the changing terms of communications businesses, the largesse is thus carefully protected from falling upon the ground of daily political life. The notion of a protected electronic commons has been quashed, by corporations aspiring to be at once the shapers of culture and the delivery systems of it.

The sheer abundance of communications options is unlikely to lead, in itself, to formations of electronic commonses. The promise that burgeoning communications systems will create an abundance of access, making governmentally protected spaces and activities unnecessary, turns out to be hollow as the electronic universe expands. It is not merely that corporations that are developing new services are striving to develop proprietary gates and pathways through that electronic universe. In order to make use of any such common or public spaces, people have to have something to say, someone to talk to, and something that can happen. They need habits, knowledge, history, resources.

A minitest of the opportunities provided by open space was initiated when the FCC addressed the problem of using space set aside for noncommercial purposes on DBS. This was an issue raised in the 1992 Cable Act, then set aside because of legal action for several years. Finally, in 1997, there was, hypothetically, space for noncommercial and public purposes available on direct broadcast satellite services. Who, the FCC basically asked, wanted to use such space, and for what? Viable takers were few. The two entities with ready programming appropriate for the channel—a consortium of universities, and public TV—were long-time recipients of various kinds of public subsidy (Aufderheide, 1998).

At the same time, informational and communications abundance increases in the commercial sphere, often feeding social polarization. Broad discontent and unease does not stop, for lack of ways and places to resolve it. It gets expressed in clumsy policy. The bipolar approach to communications policy sets up a dynamic that pushes for new solutions. The deregulatory era may thus lead to renewed governmental intrusion. It may also create conditions for renewed civic activism around communications, as incoherent discontent is articulated and channeled. The quality of a new wave of regulatory reform will depend on the vitality, diversity, and vision of such civic activism.

Ironically, civic activism may be essential to the success of a much-vaunted competitive business environment. The principle of forbearance, so central to the regulatory logic of the Act, not only assumes the vitality of marketplace forces but implies a vital and active civic sector as a concomitant of functioning markets. And yet that sector is starved of resources.

Government will also continue to be a crucial tool of transition, as Gigi Sohn, executive director of Media Access Project, told an audience at the libertarian Cato Institute:

Government can play a constructive role in making markets work better, thereby lessening the need for government involvement in the future, and, in particular, obviating intrusive content-based regulation. It can do so by ensuring that all Americans have access to the tools that are becoming more and more central to education, the economy, social interaction, First Amendment values and democracy. And it can do so by making more competitive markets than are currently dominated by entrenched monopolies. (Sohn, 1997, Appendix G)

Predictable cries of outrage at media concentration were common after passage of the Act, especially from journalists (Hickey, 1997; Schechter, 1997) and academics (Barnouw et al., 1997; McChesney, 1997). The Media and Democracy Congresses of 1996 and 1997 featured vigorous denunciations of media fat cats by left-wing journalists, and at Cultural Environment Movement meetings speakers denounced commercialism in media as a kind of pollution.

But far harder for media activists, noted consultant David Bollier, was finding "a coherent, positive *vision* that can help mobilize and unify diverse nonprofit players," in comparison with the "intellectually respectable, highly marketable consumerist and entertainment-oriented vision of the new media" put forward in the corporate world. What was needed was a "sovereign citizen vision" of community and civic life supported crucially by a web of accessible electronic pathways and services. To do that, he argued, there needed to be more, larger, more committed and visible constituencies than civic advocates had been able to mobilize for anything other than consumer price issues (Bollier, 1997).

That "sovereign citizen vision" must also be imagined, discussed, nurtured, and experimented with. It is not a single, resolved-focus image, after all, but a practice in which contending views are exercised, not always comfortably. Identifying that practice as significant and valuable is a process that in itself requires resources, as a project by the Civil Rights Project, Inc.— parent organization to a variety of media projects, including the historic *Eyes on the Prize* public TV series—recognized. Researchers, foundation staff, and representatives of civil rights organizations have been invited to consider communications policy as a civil rights issue. As project coordinator Mark Lloyd put it, "The communications policy debate is a debate about the nature of our democracy. It is a debate about who gets to speak, and for what price, and to whom." He has called for organizations across the social action spectrum to consider a new civil rights agenda, to include such rights as the right to speak, to information, to service, to economic opportunity, privacy and "meaningful participation in the political process" (Lloyd, 1997, pp. 9–10).

In cyberspace, the giddy utopianism of pre-1996 has yielded to far more practical discussion, some of it occurring under the rubric of technorealism (see Appendix F). A clutch of likeminded cyberpundits, exasperated by widespread political naivete in the computing communities, produced a manifesto that included these tenets:

- Technologies are not neutral.
- The Internet is revolutionary, but not utopian.
- Government has an important role to play in the electronic frontier.
- Wiring the schools will not save them.
- The public owns the airwaves; the public should benefit from their use.

"It is foolish," wrote the authors, "to say that the public has no sovereignty over what an errant citizen or fraudulent corporation does online. As the representative of the people and the guardian of democratic values, the state has the right and responsibility to help integrate cyberspace and conventional society."

Technology standards and privacy issues, for example, are too important to be entrusted to the marketplace alone. Competing software firms have little interest in preserving the open standards that are essential to a fully functioning interactive network. Markets encourage innovation, but they do not necessarily insure the public interest (see Appendix F). This perspective on the inevitable interrelationships between civic involvement, government regulation, and new communications technology opportunities opens the door for a stakeholders' debate on the evolving meaning of the public interest. It directly challenges the position that converging technologies sweep away the logic of earlier regulatory regimes. Instead it requires assessing problems and finding solutions as technologies and the corporate structures that promote them develop.

Advocates of civil society, concerned with communications policy, will have their hands full in coming years. It will be crucial to assess the viability of the association between the public interest and a competitive environment in communications policy. Is competition truly developing? Does it strengthen the economy and workers' and consumers' options within it? Is that competition also fostering or permitting democratic behaviors, public life, and mutual respect? It will also be important to use, even if in demonstration projects, emerging communications to foster habits and relationships of civil society. Systems that have already become the lifeblood of global business surely have applications for vital democratic practices in the global community. Finally, it will be important to promote policies that pay for such experiments in public practice.

The passage and implementation of the legislation revising the platform for U.S. communications policy has demonstrated a continuing and even increased need for social participation on familiar issues of industry structure. It has demonstrated a continuing need for regulators to monitor performance by media corporations of their public obligations. Finally, it has shown the growing importance of the complicated fact that communications systems transmit not merely information but culture.

BIBLIOGRAPHIC
RESOURCES

References

Albiniak, P. (1997a, September 29). Cable competitors demand access to cable programming. *Broadcasting and Cable,* pp. 19–20.

Albiniak, P. (1997b, September 29). Consumer groups call for cable rate cap, ownership overhaul. *Broadcasting and Cable,* p. 15.

American Association of Retired Persons. (1995). *A guide to deregulation and competition in the electric and telecommunications industries.* Washington, DC: Author.

Anonymous. (1998, March 16). In brief. *Broadcasting and Cable,* p. 92.

Anstrom, D. (1995, March 21). *National Cable Television Association testimony before the Committee on Commerce, Science and Transportation, U.S. Senate.* Washington, DC: National Cable Television Association.

Aufderheide, P. (1987). Universal service: Telephone policy in the public interest. *Journal of Communication, 37*(1), 81–96.

Aufderheide, P. (1991). Public television and the public sphere. *Critical Studies in Mass Communication, 8*(2), 168–183.

Aufderheide, P. (1992). Cable television and the public interest. *Journal of Communication, 42*(1), 52–65.

Aufderheide, P. (1998). The public interest in new communications services: The DBS debate. In A. Calabrese & J.-C. Burgelman (Eds.), *Communication, citizenship and social policy: Re-thinking the limits of the welfare state.* Lanham, MD: Rowman & Littlefield.

Auletta, K. (1995, June 5). Pay per views. *The New Yorker,* pp. 51–57.

Auletta, K. (1997, October 20). American keiretsu. *The New Yorker,* pp. 225–227.

Bagdikian, B. (1993). *The media monopoly.* New York: Oxford University Press.

Barber, B. (1984). *Strong democracy.* Berkeley: University of California Press.

Barber, B. (1995). *Jihad vs. McWorld.* New York: Times Books.

Barnhart, A. (1996, December 23). Cable, cable everywhere but not a thing to watch. *New York Times,* p. D7.

Barnouw, E., et al. (1997). *Conglomerates and the media.* New York: New Press.

Batt, R., & Keefe, J. (1998, April 15). *Human resource and employment practices in telecommunications services, 1980–1998* (Report to the New American Realities Committee, National Planning Association). Unpublished manuscript.

Batt, R., & Strausser, M. (1997). Labor market outcomes of deregulation in telecommunications services. *Proceedings of the Fiftieth Annual Meeting of the Industrial Relations Research Association,* January 3–5, Chicago, IL. Madison, WI: IRRA Series.

Benton Foundation and Libraries for the Future. (1997). *Local places, global connections: Libraries in the digital age.* Washington, DC: Benton Foundation.

Benton Foundation and Media Access Project. (1998, April). *What's local about local broadcasting?* Washington, DC: Authors.

Blau, A. (1997). A high wire act in a highly wired world: Universal service and the Telecommunications Act of 1996. In H. Kubicek, W. Dutton, & R. Williams (Eds.), *The social shaping of information superhighways: European and American roads to the information society* (pp. 247–264). New York: St. Martin's.

Bollier, D. (1992, May 29). *The rise and fall of the media reform movement—and some suggestions for its resurrection.* Washington, DC: Essential Information.

Bollier, D. (1993, July/August). The information superhighway: Roadmap for renewed public purpose. *Tikkun,* pp. 20–22, 89–90.

Bollier, D. (1997). *Reinventing democratic culture in an age of electronic networks.* Chicago: John D. and Catherine T. MacArthur Foundation.

Bolter, W., McConnaughey, J., & Kelsey, F. (1990). *Telecommunications policy for the 1990s and beyond.* London: Sharpe.

Brenner, D. (1996). *Law and regulation of common carriers in the communications industry.* Boulder, CO: Westview.

Breyer, S. (1982). *Regulation and its reform.* Cambridge, MA: Harvard University Press.

Brinkley, J. (1997a). *Defining vision: The battle for the future of television.* New York: Harcourt Brace.

Brinkley, J. (1997b, October 23). Panel to consider new rules for digital TV broadcasters. *New York Times,* p. D8.

Browning, G. (1997, August 23). No oscar for Jack. *National Journal,* pp. 1688–1691.

Cairncross, F. (1997). *The death of distance: How the communications revolution will change our lives.* Boston: Harvard Business School Press.

Cannon, R. (1996). The legislative history of Senator Exon's Communications Decency Act: Regulating barbarians on the information superhighway. *Federal Communications Law Journal, 49*(1), 51–59.

Carey, J., & Quirk, J. (1989). The mythos of the electronic revolution. In J. Carey, *Communication as culture* (pp. 113–147). New York: Unwin Hyman.

Carney, D. (1995, December 23). Spate of squabbles leaves bill's fate still uncertain. *Congressional Quarterly Weekly Report,* p. 3881.

Cauley, L. (1997, December 15). Genuine competition in local phone service is a long distance off. *Wall Street Journal,* pp. A1, A10.

Center for Media Education. (1996). *Connecting children to the future: A telecommunications policy guide for child advocates.* Washington, DC: Author.

Center for Media Education. (1997, Winter). ABSOLUTe Web: Tobacco and alcohol industries launch into cyberspace. *InfoActive,* pp. 1–16.

Chen, J. (1997). The legal process and political economy of telecommunications reform. *Columbia Law Review, 97*(4), 835–873.

Cole, B., & Oettinger, M. (1978). *Reluctant regulators: The FCC and the broadcast audience.* Reading, MA: Addison-Wesley.

Coll, S. (1986). *Deal of the century: The breakup of AT&T.* New York: Atheneum.

Colman, P. (1997a, September 29). DirecTV complains to FCC about Comcast. *Broadcasting and Cable,* p. 68.

Colman, P. (1997b, June 23). Wireless regroups after tough year. *Broadcasting and Cable,* p. 58.

Common Cause. (1997, August). Your master's voice. *Wired,* pp. 45–48, 164–165.

Communications Workers of America. (1997). *Prospects for employment in competitive local telephone markets.* Washington, DC: Author.

Computer Professionals for Social Responsibility. (1993). *Serving the community: A public interest vision of the national information infrastructure.* Washington, DC: Author.

Cooper, M. (1997). *Universal service: A historical perspective and policies for the 21st century.* Washington, DC: Benton Foundation and Consumer Federation of America.

Cooper, M. (1998). *Ensuring telephone access in the digital age.* Washington, DC: Center for Media Education.

Corn-Revere, R. (1996). New age comstockery. *CommLaw Conspectus: Journal of Communications Law and Policy, 4,* 173–187.

Covington, S. (1997). *Moving a public policy agenda: The strategic philanthropy of conservative foundations.* Washington, DC: National Committee for Responsive Philanthropy.

Crandall, R. (1997). Are we deregulating telephone services? Think again. *Policy Brief, 13,* 6–9. Washington, DC: Brookings Institution.

Crandall, R., & Furchgott-Roth, H. (1996). *Cable TV: Regulation or competition?* Washington, DC: Brookings Institution.

Crandall, R., & Waverman, L. (1995). *Talk is cheap: The promise of regulatory reform in North American telecommunications.* Washington, DC: Brookings Institution.

Dempsey, J. (1997, February 17–23). Cable ops caught in nets. *Variety,* pp. 1, 84.

Dewey, J. (1983). *The public and its problems.* Athens, OH: Swallow Press.

Douglas, S. (1987). *Inventing American broadcasting, 1899–1922.* Baltimore, MD: Johns Hopkins University Press.

Drake, W. (1995a). The national information infrastructure debate: Issues, interests, and the congressional process. In W. Drake (Ed.), *The new information infrastructure: Strategies for U.S. policy* (pp. 305–344). New York: Twentieth Century Fund Press.

Drake, W. (Ed.). (1995b). *The new information infrastructure: Strategies for U.S. policy.* New York: Twentieth Century Fund Press.

Drake, W. (1997). Public interest groups and the Telecommunications Act of 1996. In H. Kubicek, W. Dutton, & R. Williams (Eds.), *The social shaping of information superhighways: European and American roads to the information society* (pp. 173–198). New York: St. Martin's.

Dyson, E., Gilder, G., Keyworth, G., & Toffler, A. (1994, August). *Cyberspace and the American dream: A Magna Carta for the Knowledge Age.* Washington, DC: Progress and Freedom Foundation.

Engelman, R. (1996). *Public radio and television in America.* Thousand Oaks, CA: Sage.

Farhi, P. (1998a, February 21). Paying the price for cable TV. *Washington Post,* pp. H1, H2.

Farhi, P. (1998b, April 6). The business of investor infomercials. Washington Business section, *Washington Post,* pp. 12–14.

Ferris, C. D., Lloyd, F. W., & Symons, H. J. (1996). *Guidebook to the Telecommunications Act of 1996.* New York: Matthew Bender.

Firestone, C. (1995). The search for the holy paradigm: Regulating the information infrastructure in the 21st century. In G. Turin et al. (Eds.), *The changing nature of telecommunications/information infrastructure* (pp. 34–62). Washington, DC: National Academy Press.

Fowler, M., & Brenner, D. (1982). A marketplace approach to broadcast regulation. *Texas Law Review, 60,* 207–257.

Fraser, B. (1997, October 14). *Local telephone competition: Dysfunctional and disconnected.* San Diego, CA: Utility Consumers' Action Network.

Friedlander, A. (1995). *Natural monopoly and universal service.* Reston, VA: Corporation for National Research Initiatives.

Garnham, N. (1996). Constraints on multimedia convergence. In W. Dutton (Ed.), *Information and communication technologies: Visions and realities* (pp. 103–119). New York: Oxford University Press.

Gomery, D. (1996). Mass media merger mania. *American Journalism Review, 18*(9), p. 46.

Hammond, A. (1997). The Telecommunications Act of 1996: Codifying the digital divide. *Federal Communications Law Journal, 50*(1), 179–216.

Hatch, D. (1997, September 15). Minority ownership slips again. *Electronic Media,* p. 44.

Harvey, D. (1992). *The condition of postmodernity.* Cambridge: Blackwell.

Hazlett, T. (1990). The rationality of U.S. regulation of the broadcast spectrum. *Journal of Law and Economics, 23*(1), 133–176.

Head, S. (1996, February 29). The new, ruthless economy. *The New York Review of Books,* pp. 47–52.

Healey, J. (1995, December 16). Telecommunications: Leaders' last-minute additions offer morsels for everyone—almost. *Congressional Quarterly Weekly Report,* p. 2348.

Heatherly, C. L. (Ed.). (1981). *Mandate for leadership.* Washington, DC: Heritage Foundation.

Hickey, N. (1997, January/February). So big: The Telecommunications Act at Year One. *Columbia Journalism Review,* pp. 23–32.

Horwitz, R. B. (1989). *The irony of regulatory reform.* New York: Oxford University Press.

Huber, P. (1987). *The geodesic network.* Washington, DC: U.S. Government Printing Office.

Huber, P. (1997). *Law and disorder in cyberspace: Abolish the FCC and let common law rule the telecosm.* New York: Oxford University Press.

Huber, P., Kellogg, M., & Thorne, J. (1995). *Federal broadband law.* Boston: Little, Brown.

Huber, P., Kellogg, M., & Thorne, J. (1996). *The Telecommunications Act of 1996: Special report.* Boston: Little, Brown.

Hundt, R. (1997, September 23). Yale Law School 1997 Dean's Lecture Series. www.fcc.gov.

John, R. (1995). *Spreading the news: The American postal system from Franklin to Morse.* Cambridge, MA: Harvard University Press.

Johnson, B. (1997, May 19). The First Amendment speech you've never heard before. *Broadcasting and Cable,* pp. 22–24.

Katz, M. L. (1996). Interview with an umpire. In Institute for Information Studies (Ed.), *Annual review: The emerging world of wireless communications* (pp. 1–20). Washington, DC: Aspen Institute and Nortel North America.

Keane, J. (1991). *The media and democracy.* Cambridge, MA: Polity/Blackwell.

Keller, J. (1997, June 11). For AT&T, building local service is tough job. *Wall Street Journal,* p. B1.

Keller, J. (1998, April 17.) It's hard not to notice phone service leaves a lot to be desired. *Wall Street Journal,* pp. A1, A6.

Kimmelman, G. (1997a, March 19). Testimony before the Subcommittee on Communications, Committee on Commerce, Science and Transportation, U.S. Senate. Washington, DC: Consumers Union.

Kimmelman, G. (1997b, September 24). *Testimony before the Committee on the Judiciary, U.S. House of Representatives, on the state of competition in the cable television industry.* Washington, DC: Consumers Union.

Krasnow, E. (1997, October 22). *The "public interest" standard: The elusive search for the Holy Grail.* Briefing paper prepared for the Advisory Committee on Public Interest Obligations of Digital Television Broadcasters. Retrieved March 12, 1998 from http://www.ntia.doc.gov/pubintadvcom/ictntg/krasnow. htm.

Krasnow, E., Longley, L., & Terry, H. (1982). *The politics of broadcast regulation* (3rd ed.). New York: St. Martins.

Krattenmaker, T. (1994). *Telecommunications law and policy.* Durham, NC: Carolina Academic Press.

Krattenmaker, T. (1996). The Telecommunications Act of 1996. *Connecticut Law Review, 29,* 123–173.

Krattenmaker, T., & Powe, L., Jr. (1994). *Regulating broadcasting programming.* London and Washington, DC: MIT Press and American Enterprise Institute Press.

Kuttner, R. (1996). *Everything for sale.* New York: Knopf.

Kurtz, H. (1997, July 10). Time Warner, sitting on the news? *Washington Post,* p. B1.

Landler, M. (1996, October 16). U.S. appeals panel delays rules allowing full phone competition. *New York Times,* pp. D1, D10.

Lewis, C., Benes, A., & O'Brien, M. (1996). *The buying of the president.* New York: Avon.

Lieberman, D. (1998, March 16). Rate hikes: Justified by costs or a raw deal? *USA Today,* p. 3B.

Libraries for the Future. (1997, October). *The library advocates guide to telecommunications.* New York: Author.

Liebowitz, S. J., & Margolis, S. E. (1996). Should technology choice be a concern of antitrust policy? *Harvard Journal of Law and Technology, 9*(2), 283–318.

Lipin, S., & Keller, J. (1997, October 2). WorldCom's MCI bid alters playing field for telecom industry. *Wall Street Journal,* p. B8.

Lipschitz, B. (1996). Payphone deregulation under the Telecommunications Act of 1996. *Media Law and Policy Bulletin, 5*(2), 13–16.

Littleton, C. (1997, June 2). Wakeup call for DreamWorks. *Broadcasting and Cable,* p. 11.

Lloyd, M. (1997, May 13). *Communications policy is a civil rights issue.* Washington, DC: Civil Rights Telecommunications Forum.

Madden, A. (1997, November). Industry briefing: Telecommunications as you know it is dead. *Red Herring,* pp. 59–69.

Madden, A. (1998, March). Pipe dreams. *Red Herring,* pp. 47–49.

Mahoney, M. (1998, January 29). Testimony. In U.S. Federal Communication Commission, *En banc hearing on the state of local competition.* Washington, DC: Federal Communication Commission.

Maney, K. (1995). *Megamedia shakeout: The inside story of the leaders and the losers in the exploding communications industry.* New York: Wiley.

Markoff, J. (1993, October 26). New coalition to seek a public data highway. *New York Times,* p. D2.

McAvoy, P. (1996). *The failure of antitrust and regulation to establish competition in long distance telephone services.* Cambridge, MA: MIT Press; Washington, DC: AEI Press.

McChesney, R. (1993). *Telecommunications, mass media and democracy.* New York: Oxford University Press.

McChesney, R. (1997). *Corporate media and the threat to democracy.* New York: Seven Stories Press.

McConnell, C. (1998, March 30). Kennard calls time-out on free airtime. *Braodcasting and Cable,* p. 14.

McKinsey Global Institute. (1993). *Manufacturing productivity.* McKinsey and Company.

Melody, W. (1997). *Telecom reform: Principles, policies and regulatory practices.* Lyngby, Denmark: Technical University of Denmark.

Mermigas, D. (1998a, March 16). Complexion of media deals changing. *Electronic Media,* p. 3.

Mermigas, D. (1998b, April 20). Malone: Sculpting TCI's future. *Electronic Media,* pp. 1, 36, 37.

Miller, M. (Ed.). (1996, June 3). National entertainment state [special issue]. *The Nation.*

Miller, S. (1995). *Civilizing cyberspace: Policy, power, and the information superhighway.* Reading, MA: Addison-Wesley.

Mills, M. (1997a, June 1). Hanging up on competition? *Washington Post,* p. H1.

Mills, M. (1997b, July 19). Court overrules FCC on phone rate rules. *Washington Post,* p. C1.

Mills, M. (1997c, August 20). Leaving long-distance dangling. *Washington Post,* p. D9.

Mills, M. (1997d, December 19). AT&T Corp. halts effort to sell local residential phone service. *Washington Post,* p. C1.

Mills, M., & Farhi, P. (1997, Jan. 19). This is a free market? The Telecommunications Act so far: Higher prices, fewer benefits. *Washington Post,* p. H1.

Minow, N. (1995). *Abandoned in the wasteland: Children, television, and the First Amendment.* New York: Hill and Wang.

Montgomery, K. (1989). *Target: Primetime.* New York: Oxford University Press.

Mueller, M. (1997). *Universal service: Competition, interconnection, and monopoly in the making of the American telephone system.* Cambridge, MA: MIT Press; Washington, DC: AEI Press.

National Research Council. (1995). *The Changing nature of telecommunications/information infrastructure.* Washington, DC: National Academy Press.

Netchvolodoff, A. (1998, January 29). Testimony. In U.S. Federal Communications Commission, *En banc hearing on state of local competition.* Washington, DC: Federal Communications Commission.

Noam, E. (1989). International telecommunications in transition. In R. Crandall & K. Flamm (Eds.), *Changing the rules: Technological change, international competition, and regulation in communications* (pp. 257–297). Washington, DC: Brookings Institution.

Noam, E. (1993). *NetTrans Accounts: Reforming the financial support system for universal service in telecommunications* [Manuscript posted on the World Wide Web]. Washington, DC: Benton Foundation. Retrieved November 16, 1997 from the World Wide Web: http://www.benton.org.

Noam, E. (1995). Beyond telecommunicatons liberalizations: Past performance, present hype, and future direction. In W. Drake (Ed.), *The new information infrastructure: Strategies for U.S. policy* (pp. 31–54). New York: Twentieth Century Fund Press.

Noam, E. (1997). Will universal service and common carriage survive the Telecommunications Act of 1996? *Columbia Law Review, 97*(4), 955–975.

Noam, E., & Cutler, C. (1994). Freedom of expression and the 1992 Cable Act: An introduction. *Hastings Communications and Entertainment Law Journal 17,* 1–16.

Noble, D. (1997). *The religion of technology.* New York: Knopf.

Office of Communication of the United Church v. FCC, 359 F.2d 994 (DC Cir., 1996).

Paglin, M. (Ed.). (1989). *A legislative history of the Communications Act of 1934.* New York: Oxford University Press.

Pepper, R. M. (1988, November). *Through the looking glass: Integrated broadband networks, regulatory policy and institutional change.* OPP Working Paper Series No. 24. Washington, DC: Federal Communications Commission.

Pitofsky, R. (1979). The political content of antitrust. *University of Pennsylvania Law Review, 127,* 1051–1081.

Pool, I. (1983). *Technologies of freedom.* Cambridge: Belknap Press of Harvard University Press.

Pope, K. (1997, August 13). High-definition TV is dealt a setback. *Wall Street Journal,* p. B5.

Price, M. (1995). *Television, the public sphere, and national identity.* New York: Oxford University Press.

Price, M., & Duffy, J. (1997). Technological change and doctrinal persistence: Telecommunications reform in Congress and the court. *Columbia Law Review, 97*(4), 976–1015.

Price, M., & Weinberg, J. (1996). United States (2). In V. MacLeod (Ed.), *Media ownership and control in the age of convergence* (pp. 265–278). London: International Institute of Communications.

Price Waterhouse. (1996). *EMC technology forecast 1997.* Menlo Park, CA: Price Waterhouse World Firm Services.

Rathbun, E. (1997, August 11). Station-rich owners get richer. *Broadcasting and Cable,* pp. 31–32.

Rattner, S. (1996). A golden age of competition. *Media Studies Journal, 10*(2–3), 7–14.

Red Herring Tech 250. (1997, June). *Red Herring,* p. 120.

Red Lion Broadcasting Co. v. FCC, 395 U.S. 367, 89 S.C.T. 179 (1969).

Rheingold, H. (1994). *The virtual community: Homesteading on the electronic frontier.* Reading, MA: Addison-Wesley.

Robichaux, M. (1997, January 2). Malone says TCI push into phones, Internet isn't working for now. *Wall Street Journal,* p. 1.

Robinson, G. (1989). The Federal Communications Act: An essay on origins and regulatory purpose. In M. D. Paglin (Ed.), *A Legislative History of the Communications Act of 1934* (pp. 3–24). New York: Oxford University Press.

Ross, S. (1996). When the wires cross: Ensuring diversity in the era of video dialtone. *Communications Law and Policy, 1*(1), 65–97.

Rowland, W. (1983). *The politics of TV violence: Policy uses of communication research.* Beverly Hills, CA: Sage.

Rowland, W. (1997a). The meaning of "the public interest" in communications policy, Part I: Its origins in state and federal regulation. *Communication Law and Policy, 2*(3), 309–328.

Rowland, W. (1997b). The meaning of "the public interest" in communications policy, Part II: Its implementation in early broadcast law and regulation. *Communication Law and Policy, 2*(4), 363–396.

Sandel, M. (1996). *Democracy's discontent: America in search of a public philosophy.* London: Belknap Press of Harvard University Press.

Sawhney, H. (1994). Universal service: Prosaic motives and great ideals. *Journal of Broadcasting and Electronic Media, 38*(4), 375–395.

Schechter, D. (1997). *The more you watch the less you know.* New York: Seven Stories Press.

Schiller, H. (1996). United States (1). In V. MacLeod (Ed.), *Media ownership and control in the age of convergence* (pp. 249–264). London: International Institute of Communications.

Schwartzman, A., & Sohn, G. (1995, October). *Pretty pictures or pretty profits: Issues and options for the public interest and nonprofit communities in the digital broadcasting debate.* Washington, DC: Media Access Project.

Sclove, R. (1995). *Democracy and technology.* New York: Guilford Press.

Shapiro, E. (1997, September 18). A wave of buyouts has radio industry beaming with success. *Wall Street Journal,* p. 1.

Shenk, D. (1997). *Data smog: Surviving the information glut.* San Francisco: HarperEdge.

Smart, T. (1997, October 27). Big mergers get bigger in the '90s. *Washington Post,* pp. A1, A10.

Smith, M. R., & Marx, L. (Eds.). (1994). *Does technology drive history? The dilemma of technological determinism.* Cambridge, MA: MIT Press.

Smith, R. L. (1970, May 18). The wired nation. *Nation,* pp. 582–606.

Sohn, G. (1997, September 12). *Why government is the solution, and not the problem* [Speech at Cato Institute]. Washington, DC: Media Access Project.

Stefancic, J., & Delgado, R. (1996). *No mercy: How conservative think tanks and foundations changed America's social agenda.* Philadelphia: Temple University Press.

Sterling, C. (1997). Understanding the Telecommunications Act of 1996. *Federal Communications Law Journal, 49*(2), 509–515.

Streeter, T. (1992). Blue skies and strange bedfellows: The discourse of cable television. In L. Spigel & M. Curtin (Eds.), *The revolution wasn't televised: Sixties television and social conflict* (pp. 221–242). New York: Routledge.

Streeter, T. (1996). *Selling the air.* Chicago: University of Chicago Press.

Telecommunications reform: Regulating the information superhighway. (1996). *Congressional Digest, 75*(1), 1–13.

Thierer, A. (1994). *A policy maker's guide to deregulating telecommunications: Heritage talking points.* Washington, DC: Heritage Foundation.

Tunstall, J. (1986). *Communications deregulation: The unleashing of America's communications industry.* New York: Basil Blackwell.

U.S. Congress, House of Representatives. (1979). *To establish certain requirements relating to interstate and foreign telecommunications, and for other purposes* (96th Congress, 1st Session, H.R. 3333). Washington, DC: U.S. Government Printing Office.

U.S. Congress, House of Representatives, Committee on Commerce. (1997, January). *Compilation of selected acts within the jurisdiction of the Committee on Commerce* (105th Congress, 1st Session). Washington, DC: U.S. Government Printing Office.

U.S. Congress, House of Representatives, Committee on Energy and Commerce. (1991). *Public interest in broadcasting* (102d Congress, 1st Session, 102-52). Washington, DC: U.S. Government Printing Office.

U.S. Congress, House of Representatives, Committee on Commerce. (1995, July 24). *Telecommunications Act of 1996* (House Report 104-204). Washington, DC: U.S. Government Printing Office.

U.S. Congress, House of Representatives, Conference Committee. (1996, January 31). *Telecommunications Act of 1996* (House Report 104-458). Washington, DC: U.S. Government Printing Office.

U.S. Congress, 104th Congress, 1st Session. (1995, August 4). *Congressional Record, 141*(129), H8425–H8507.

U.S. Congress, Senate, Committee on Commerce, Science and Transportation. (1994, September 12). *Communications Act of 1994* (103d Congress, 2d Session, Report 103-367). Washington, DC: U.S. Government Printing Office.

U.S. Congress, Senate, Committee on Commerce, Science and Transportation. (1995, March 30). *Telecommunications Competition and Deregulation Act of 1995* (104d Congress, 1st session, Report 104-23). Washington, DC: U.S. Government Printing Office.

U.S. Congress, Senate, Committee on the Judiciary. (1995, May 3). *Antitrust issues in telecommunications legislation* (104th Congress, 1st session, Senate Hearing 104-725 on S. 652). Washington, DC: U.S. Government Printing Office.

U.S. Department of Commerce, Information Infrastructure Task Force. (1993, September 15). *The national information infrastructure.* Washington, DC: Department of Commerce.

U.S. Federal Communications Commission. (1997a, May 7). *Commission implements Telecom Act's universal service provisions.* Washington, DC: Author.

U.S. Federal Communications Commission. (1997b). *Staff report on the broadcast radio industry: Mass media bureau, policy and rules division.* Washington, DC: Author.

U.S. Federal Communications Commission. (1998a, January 13). *Annual Assessment of the Status of Competition in Markets for the Delivery of Video Programming* (Fourth Annual Report, CS Docket No. 97-141). Washington, DC: Author.

U.S. Federal Communications Commission. (1998b, January 29). *En Banc hearing on state of local competition.* Washington, DC: Author.

U.S. Federal Communications Commission. (1998c, March 13.) *Review of the radio industry, 1997: Mass media bureau, policy and rules division.* Washington, DC: Author.

U.S. Federal Communications Commission. (1998d, April 5). *The public interest standard: A new regulator's search for enlightenment* (Speech by Michael K. Powell, Commissioner, before the American Bar Association, 17th Annual Legal Forum on Communications Law, Las Vegas, NV). Washington, DC: Author.

U.S. Federal Communications Commission. (1998e, January 22). *Statistics of Communications Common Carriers, 1996/1997.* Washington, DC: U.S. Government Printing Office.

U.S. Federal Trade Commission. (1996, December). *Staff report: Public workshop on consumer privacy on the Global Information Infrastructure.* Washington, DC: Author.

Vietor, R. (1994). *Contrived competition: Regulation and deregulation in America.* Cambridge, MA: Belknap Press of Harvard University Press.

Waterman, D. (1995, April). Vertical integration and program access in the cable television industry. *Federal Communications Law Journal, 47,* 511–534.

Waterman, D., & Weiss, A. (1997). *Vertical integration in cable television* (AEI Studies in Telecommunications Deregulation). Cambridge, MA: MIT Press.

West, D., & Brown, S. (1997, July 21). America's town crier. *Broadcasting and Cable,* pp. 70–74.

Wilke, J., & Gruley, B. (1997, October 22). Is antitrust relevant in this digital age? Watch Microsoft's case. *Wall Street Journal,* p. 1.

Wilke, J., Gruley, B., & Lipin, S. (1997, November 12). Slow approval of WorldCom deal likely. *Wall Street Journal,* p. A2.

Winston, B. (1986). *Misunderstanding media.* Cambridge: Harvard University Press.

Wollenberg, J. R. (1989). The FCC as arbiter of the public interest, convenience and necessity. In M. D. Paglin (Ed.), *A legislative history of the Communications Act of 1934* (pp. 61–78). New York: Oxford University Press.

Woodhull, N. J., & Snyder, R. (Eds.). (1996). Media mergers [special issue]. *Media Studies Journal, 10*(2–3).

Young, S. (1998, January 23). MCI cancels plan to resell local service. *Wall Street Journal,* p. A10.

The year the government made way for competition. (1995). *FCC Report, 14*(26).

Annotated Guide
to Analyses of the Act,
1996–1997

Becker, L. E., Jr. (1996). Comments on "The Telecommunications Act of 1996," by Thomas G. Krattenmaker. *Connecticut Law Review, 29,* 175–185.

The author argues that communications systems are the lifeblood of a democracy and that we need to consider the need for affirmative goals such as common ground and universal access in setting regulatory goals.

Benton Foundation. (1996). *The Telecommunications Act of 1996 and the changing communications landscape.* Washington, DC: Author.

This work is an overview of the sections of the Act reflecting public interest coalition concerns, including universal service, antitrust, digital TV and public interest obligations, cable rates, and First Amendment concerns. Benton's Communications Policy Project director Andrew Blau argues for nonprofit involvement in implementation: "The key issues that will determine whether this Act advances the public interest are still up for grabs." The Benton Foundation also has other and continuously updated resources on the Act and implementation on its Website.

Benton Foundation. (1997, June). *What's at stake 2.* Washington, DC: Author.

This resource is a large-format, 15-page guide, including graphs, tables and graphics, to public interest initiatives in networking and new communications technologies, including, on pages 4–5, "The Telecom environment: Implementing the

Telecommunications Act of 1996," describing ongoing rulemakings and other sites of intervention.

Cannon, R. (1996). The legislative history of Senator Exon's Communications Decency Act: Regulating barbarians on the information superhighway. *Federal Communications Law Journal, 49*(1), 51–59.

This article is a critical summary of the history and a three-pronged analysis (feasibility, First Amendment, necessity) of the highly contested section of the Act that bans obscene and indecent transmissions on a telecommunications-based network to children and that was later found unconstitutional. The author finds a combination of ignorance, public opinion currying, and inflammatory but unreliable evidence behind the support for the measure.

Center for Media Education. (1996). *Connecting children to the future: A telecommunications policy guide for child advocates.* Washington, DC: Author.

This 40-page guide gives citizen activists tools to understand (1) opportunities in networked, digital-era communications, (2) changes in implementation of universal service as a result of the 1996 Act, and (3) the importance of state-level organizing at public utility (or service) commissions.

Chen, J. (1997). The legal process and political economy of telecommunications reform. *Columbia Law Review, 97*(4), 835–873.

The author describes evolution of the Act as shaped by "client politics, institutional stagnation and reform, imperfect economic competition, and technological innovation." He sees the Act's initiating another era in regulation, "the Age of Anticipation" (of competition), not the end of regulation.

Corn-Revere, R. (1996). New age comstockery. *CommLaw Conspectus: Journal of Communications Law and Policy, 4,* 173–187.

This article contains a harsh criticism of the Communications Decency Act as a retrograde and inappropriate form of censorship, threatening to "lobotomize the Internet."

Geller, H. (1996). The 1996 Telecom Act: Cutting the competitive Gordian Knot. *Connecticut Law Review, 29,* 205–215.

This venerable policy maker and communications lawyer effectively summarizes long-standing positions of his, arguing that the creation of rules for a competitive environment is positive; that universal service provisions should be funded from the general treasury, not from telecommunications carriers; and that spectrum fees dedicated to a public telecommunications endowment should be substituted for broadcast licensing and trusteeship obligations.

Hammond, A. (1997). The Telecommunications Act of 1996: Codifying the digital divide. *Federal Communications Law Journal, 50*(1), 179–216.

The author argues that the Act acknowledges the "digital divide," or social inequity reflected in unequal access to telecommunications and computing resources, especially with universal service provisions. However, legal stalling maneuvers threaten even this limited strategy, within a law that primarily puts its faith in market mechanisms. The law's outright failures to address inequity include the lack of electronic redlining provisions (which would prohibit discrimination in basic service provision) and the exclusion, in its universal service provision, of community-based organizations and urban healthcare facilities for the poor.

Hazlett, T. (1996). Explaining the Telecommunications Act of 1996: Comment on Thomas G. Krattenmaker. *Connecticut Law Review, 29,* 217–242.

This veteran and militant supporter of deregulation argues that the law, albeit only the start of an extended process, succeeds in opening competition in telecommunications (although in ways that continue and even extend elaborate regulation, and likely not providing enough incentives for competitors) but merely continues and further ratifies the cozy deal between broadcasters and politicians. He believes that the law resulted from intertwined political, economic, and regulatory processes and made incumbent telephone companies eager for permission to compete, cable companies willing to accept phone competition in order to get out of rate regulation and willing to promote the V-chip in order to hobble broadcasters, and broadcasters eager for more monopoly spectrum in order to increase their options in a changing environment.

Huber, P., Kellogg, M., & Thorne, J. (1996). *The Telecommunications Act of 1996: Special report.* Boston: Little, Brown.

This analysis is from the authors of *Federal Broadband Law* and from one of the architects of phone provisions, Peter Huber, and is thorough, detailed, opinionated, and readable. The authors deplore ways in which the law continues the previous regulatory regime, which they argue is riddled with inconsistencies, provides incentives not to compete, and intrudes upon corporate and individual rights. They, however, celebrate the death of the AT&T consent decree, the opening of competition in local phone service, and the prospect of Bell competition in other services. They see broadcast provisions as lowering unnecessary regulations on broadcasters and encouraging broadcasters to get into multichannel services.

Kelter, R., & Weston, B. J. (1995). *A guide to deregulation and competition in the electric and telecommunications industries.* Washington, DC: American Association of Retired Persons.

This is a crisp, clear, layman's overview of consumer concerns in the creation of competitive environment for telecommunications services, produced by one of the leading organizations at the state level. The basic position is that: "reduced regulation can lead to higher basic service rates and lower service quality, especially in the absence of effective competition. Consumers must be protected by either regulation or effective competition."

Krattenmaker, T. (1996). The Telecommunications Act of 1996. *Connecticut Law Review, 29*, 123–173; and Krattenmaker, T. (1996). Responses. *Connecticut Law Review, 29*, 373–390.

This is a brisk and bold summary of the Act and its legal and regulatory context, from a vigorous proponent of regulatory liberalization and a marketplace definition of the public interest. From that perspective, the author finds the Act largely a disappointment, both in telecommunications and broadcasting. However, he finds sections "good," "bad," and "ugly" according to whether they minimize regulatory intrusion and promote competition.

Levy, L. (1996). Not with a bang but a whimper: Broadcast license renewal and the Telecommunications Act of 1996. *Connecticut Law Review, 29*, 243–287.

The author argues that the FCC by abandoning comparative renewal of broadcast licenses is implicitly abandoning the pretense of selecting the best applicant to serve the public interest; that this is in line with a 25-year history of the FCC's attempting to minimize or eliminate this requirement; that it indicates an ideological shift; and that some standards, perhaps quantitative and at least specific, should apply to broadcasters that are still public trustees.

McFadden, D. B. (1997). Antitrust and communications: Changes after the Telecommunications Act of 1996. *Federal Communications Law Journal, 49*(2), 457–472.

The author argues that the Act makes antitrust law particularly important, since it creates conditions for mergers and other corporate behaviors that could trigger antitrust issues and since the law explicitly removes traditional insulation from antitrust enforcement that came with FCC oversight. As well, FCC's preemption of state telecommunications regulation may be challenged constitutionally.

Meyerson, M. I. (1997). Ideas of the marketplace: A guide to the 1996 Telecommunications Act. *Federal Communications Law Journal, 49*(2), 251–288.

This is a title-by-title summary with a short commentary, drawing in part on author's extensive knowledge of cable law and First Amendment issues. The author sees the law as fundamentally redesigning the policy landscape by introducing competitive models, but not diminishing the role of regulators. Major problem areas of the immediate future for the author are (1) dangers of monopoly power from major players and incumbents and (2) diminishing intramedia competition.

Miller, S. (1995). *Civilizing cyberspace: Policy, power, and the information super-highway.* Reading, MA: Addison-Wesley.

This is an analysis of policy issues around the National Information Infrastructure, written at the time at the Telecommunications Act was the centerpiece of policy formation. The author, aligned with what he calls the "progressive communitarians, or grassroots progressives," argues that the legislation encourages incumbent conglomerates and ideologically favors corporate conservatives.

Mills, M., & Farhi, P. (1997, January 19). This is a free market? The Telecommunications Act so far: Higher prices, fewer benefits. *Washington Post,* p. H1.

Two of the most well-informed observers of the process of shaping this legislation succinctly assess the immediate consequences—concentration and vertical integration without the benefits of competition—of the Telecommunications Act of 1996 and create a chart of winners (investment bankers, Murdoch, Malone, dish owners, parents, GTE, pay phone companies) and losers (consumers, Sen. Pressler, overworked FCC bureaucrats).

Noam, E. (1997). Will universal service and common carriage survive the Telecommunications Act of 1996? *Columbia Law Review 97*(4), 955–975.

The author argues that under the regime established by the Act, universal service will endure and expand, perhaps with even greater political backing. Meanwhile common carriage appears to be receding with competition, replaced with the value of interconnection. Even so, equity considerations may require a rule that the author calls "third part neutrality," permitting a carrier to discriminate among customers but not among its customers' customers.

Price, M., & Duffy, J. (1997). Technological change and doctrinal persistence: Telecommunications reform in Congress and the court. *Columbia Law Review, 97*(4), 976–1015.

In assessing the claims of technological imperatives for legal decisions, the authors find the Act "bold in word, but incremental in deed." The incrementalism, the authors argue, is a result of an effort by "existing sectors to preserve market share or prevent market erosion." Among examples is the law's treatment of telephone company entry into video programming, and especially Open Video Service.

Read, W., & Weiner, R. (1997). FCC reform: Governing requires a new standard. *Federal Communications Law Journal, 49*(2), 289–324.

The authors argue that a new public interest standard is needed for an era in which regulation is minimized to enhance competition. The public interest must be defended vigorously by giving the FCC antitrust monitoring and enforcement as part of its public interest responsibility.

Robinson, G. (1996). The "new" Communications Act: A second opinion. *Connecticut Law Review, 29,* 289–329.

The author sees the Act as an achievement in coherent and procompetitive policy making on the telecommunications side, while reverting to flawed tradition in its broadcasting segments (in order, according to him, to protect a "declining industry"). He would prefer instituting spectrum auctions or other ways of ensuring flexible, efficient use of spectrum. While celebrating a competitive model, he notes it appears to require an ever-mounting quantity of regulation. He decries a universal service policy that does not make explicit the social goals to be reached.

Robinson, G. (1997). The new video competition: Dances with regulators. *Columbia Law Review, 97*(4), 1016–1047.

The author analyzes the Open Video Service provision of the Act, with FCC implementation, as a partial and inadequate approach to stimulating video program service competition. There are still substantial regulatory obligations, he argues, that inhibit the use of Open Video Service, as well as substantial ambiguity in interpretation that has led to legal wrangling.

Rosario, P., & Kohler, M. (1996). The Telecommunications Act of 1996: A state perspective. *Connecticut Law Review, 29,* 331–351.

The authors describe preemption of state authority in provisions that spur telecommunications competition, protect universal service, and deregulate cable rates. These areas are narrow, they argue; states maintain substantial arenas of control and should be looked upon as important arenas of regulatory innovation in an emerging competitive era.

Sidak, J., & Spulber, D. (1997). The tragedy of the telecommons: Government pricing of unbundled network elements under the Telecommunications Act of 1996. *Columbia Law Review, 97*(4), 1081–1161.

The authors argue that the FCC's approach to pricing competitive access to "unbundled network elements" is unfair to incumbents and may not cover future investment in basic network components. They propose an alternative pricing system.

Spitzer, M. (1996). Dean Krattenmaker's road not taken: The political economy of broadcasting in the Telecommunications Act of 1996. *Connecticut Law Review, 29,* 353–372.

The author charges that, just as the 1934 rules for broadcasters constituted a cynical, mutually beneficial arrangement for broadcasters (secure monopoly) and politicians (a tamed information source friendly to incumbents), the 1996 regulations continue the good deal, for the same reasons of mutual benefit.

Telecommunications reform: Regulating the information superhighway. (1996). *Congressional Digest, 75*(1), 1–13.

This article is a dependable journalistic overview of issues in the final stages of congressional action.

Wiley, R. (1996). *Communications Law 1996: Vol. 2. The Telecommunications Act of 1996.* New York: Practising Law Institute.

The author gives a positive assessment of the law as a first step toward lessening government regulation and encouraging competition. A succinct, discursive assessment basically follows the structure of the Act. The author articulates the competition-among-giants argument, suggesting that consumers may benefit.

Resources
for Active Citizens

Alliance for Community Media   www.alliancecom.org
666 11th Street NW, #806
Washington, DC 20001
Phone: (202) 393-2650
Fax: (202) 393-2653

Representing hundreds of cable access centers nationwide, the Alliance for Community Media follows the interests of its members in the implementation of the Act, including Open Video System requirements to honor any existing public, educational, or governmental access obligations of a competing cable provider.

American Library Association   www.alawash.org
ALA Washington Office
1301 Pennsylvania Avenue NW, #403
Washington, DC 20004-1701
Phone: (202) 628-8410
       (800) 941-8478 (toll-free)
Fax: (202) 628-8419

The American Library Association tracks universal service, censorship, and privacy issues, among other issues of central importance to librarians; its home page has information on its own efforts and links to other sites on these issues.

Benton Foundation   www.benton.org
1 Farragut Square South NW, 12th Floor
Washington, DC 20006

Phone: (202) 638-5770
Fax: (202) 638-5771

The operating foundation, dedicated to helping nonprofit organizations use communications technologies to promote democratic behaviors and grassroots organizing, maintains a website that archives much valuable research on public interest and nonprofit-oriented issues in communications policy and focuses particularly on implementation of the Act. Its links page is an impressive guide to groups and resources on communications policy.

Blumenfeld and Cohen Technology   www.technologylaw.com
Law Group

This law group maintains an excellent page on the Act, with a hypertext index, summary of the law, and related issues, including congressional and administration speeches.

Center for Democracy and Technology   www.cdt.org
634 Eye Street NW, Suite 1100
Washington, DC 20006
Phone: (202) 637-9800
Fax: (202) 637-0968
Email: info@cdt.org

This nonprofit, which grew out of organizing on public interest issues on the Telecommunications Act, works on policies that advance constitutional civil liberties and democratic values in new computer and communications technologies. An instrumental plaintiff in the effort to repeal the Communications Decency Act (CDA), it was a prime mover in the anti-CDA coalition Citizens Internet Empowerment Coalition (www.ciec.org), which includes associations of universities, libraries, civil rights (Media Access Project), and cyberrights organizations.

Center for Media Education   www.cme.org
2120 L Street NW, #200
Washington, DC 20037
Phone: (202) 331-7833
Fax: (202) 331-7841
Email: cme@cme.org

This organization, dedicated to fostering telecommunications policy making in the public interest, researches, advocates, and monitors Telecommunications Act–related issues ranging from universal service implementation to privacy and censorship issues in cyberspace to the public interest obligations of broadcasters.

Center for Responsive Politics   www.crp.org
320 19th Street NW, Suite 700

Washington, DC 20036
Phone: (202) 857-0044
Fax: (202) 857-7809

This nonprofit tracks and analyzes lobbying and campaign contributions, including those from telecommunications and mass media organizations, at the level of individual, committee, and party, and has produced several analyses linking contributions of telecommunications-related businesses and legislative votes in regard to the Act.

Consumer Federation of America
1424 16th Street NW
Washington, DC 20036
Phone: (202) 387-6121

This coalition of consumer organizations, representing more than 30 million U.S. consumers, has been a leading monitor of antitrust tendencies and defender of consumers against monopolistic pricing and service standards. It continues to monitor the pocketbook effects of the Telecommunications Act of 1996.

Consumer Project on Technology   www.cptech.org
Center for the Study of Responsive Law
PO Box 19367
Washington, DC 20036
Phone: (202) 387-8030
Fax: (202) 234-5176
Email: love@cpt.org

Founded by Ralph Nader, the Consumer Project on Technology features telecommunications among its concerns. Issues include public accountability, copyright, access, open policy process, and media concentration. The website has much information on media concentration gathered at the time the Telecommunications Act was debated and enacted.

Consumers Union   www.consumerreports.org
101 Truman Avenue
Yonkers, NY 10703-1057
Phone: (914) 378-2904 (Education Services)
        (800) 234-1645 (Subscriptions; toll-free)
        (800) 272-0722 (Books; toll-free)
Fax: (914) 378-2900

The publisher of *Consumer Reports* maintains a close eye on antitrust issues and consumer pricing issues generally related to implementation of the Telecommunications Act and procedures initiating competition.

Electronic Frontier Foundation   www.eff.org
1550 Bryant Street, Suite 725
San Francisco, CA 94103-4832
Phone: (415) 436 9333
Fax: (415) 436 9993
Email: ask@eff.org

This foundation, fueled by profits from the computing sector and dedicated to freedom of expression in new communications technologies, was influential in the shaping of the law on cyber issues, opposed the Communications Decency Act, and was active in the legal process following passage of the Act. It continues to track and intervene on issues of civil liberties in cyberspace.

Electronic Privacy Information Center   www.epic.org
666 Pennsylvania Avenue SE, #301
Washington, DC 20003
Phone: (202) 544-9240
Fax: (202) 547-5482

This public interest research organization, dedicated to protecting privacy and constitutional rights in cyberspace, was active in declaring the Communications Decency Act unconstitutional and continues to track privacy and free speech issues.

Federal Communications Commission   www.fcc.gov
1919 M Street NW
Washington, DC 20554
Phone: (202) 418-0200
       (202) 418-2555 (TTY)
       (888) 225-5322 (toll-free)
Fax: (202) 418-0232
       (202) 418-2830 (Fax on Demand)

The FCC has on its website a page devoted to the Telecommunications Act and ensuing FCC-related actions.

Government Printing Office   www.access.gpo.gov
Phone: (202) 512-1530
       (888) 293-6498 (toll-free)
Fax: (202) 512-1262
Email: gpoaccess@gpo.gov

This website permits retrieval of a wide variety of documents relating to the Telecommunications Act of 1996.

Internet Telecommunications Project   www.cais.net/cannon
Robert Cannon, President

2358 North Vernon Street
Arlington, VA 22207
Email: cannon@dc.net

Cannon's particular focus is Internet and privacy issues, and his website has a useful Internet Policy and Law Links page.

Kansas Corporation Commission   www.kcc.state.ks.us
1500 SW Arrowhead Road
Topeka, KS 66604
Phone: (785) 271-3140

The Kansas utility regulation body's website has a valuable set of links to other state utility regulators, as well as to national organizations of regulators and to national bodies.

Neil J. Lehto   Pages.prodigy.com/YXSC98A
Municipal Cable Television
   and Telecommunications Franchising,
   Regulation, Negotiation, Litigation
   & Legal Consulting
O'Reilly, Rancilio, Nitz,
   Andrews & Turnbull, P.C.
12900 Hall Road, Suite 350
Sterling Heights, MI 48313-1151
Phone: (810) 726-1000
Fax: (810) 726-1560

Site includes news, archives, and links to sites on municipal franchising and cable aspects of implementation of the Telecommunications Act of 1996, including an emphasis on public, educational, and government access channels.

Libraries for the Future   www.lff.org
121 West 27th Street, #1102
New York, NY 10001
Phone: (800) 542-1918
Fax: (212) 352-2342
Email: lff@lff.org

This nonprofit, dedicated to preserving public libraries in a digital era, provides briefing documents and guides, such as *The Library Advocates Guide to Telecommunications* (October 1997), on their website as well as hard copy; Libraries for the Future also hosts fora on communications policy issues related to the implementation of the Act and cultivates the National Library Advocacy Network.

Media Access Project   www.mediaaccess.org
1707 L Street NW, Suite 400

Washington, DC 20036
Phone: (202) 232-4300

This public interest media law firm, an active participant in the shaping of the legislation, plays an ongoing role in issues of implementing the Telecommunications Act of 1996.

NetAction   www.netaction.org
601 Van Ness Avenue, #631
San Francisco, CA 94102
Phone: (415) 775-8674
Fax: (415) 673-3813
Email: audrie@netaction.org

NetAction focuses on access and equity issues on the Internet, mounting grass-roots citizen action campaigns and coalitions that link cyberspace activists with grassroots organizations. On the first anniversary of the Telecommunications Act of 1996, NetAction and the Center for Educational Priorities (CEP), cosponsored a month-long protest of the Act's failure to benefit consumers, creating a website on the Act's aftermath, archived at www.cep.org/protest.html.

People for the American Way Action Fund   www.pfaw.org
2000 M Street, #400
Washington, DC 20036
Phone: (202) 467-4999
Fax: (202) 293-2672

This nonprofit, 300,000-plus member organization, which generally defends "fundamental American values, including opportunity, equal justice under the law, and individual liberty," monitors public interest provisions of the Act and cyberrights issues in the public interest, including public interest demonstration projects. After vigorously participating in lawsuits to declare the Communications Decency Act unconstitutional, it has monitored implementation of the universal service provisions, public interest obligations of broadcasters that offer digital TV, and Internet rating and blocking issues.

Telecommunications Resources on the Internet   http://china.si.umich.edu/
                                               telecom/telecom-info.html.

Assembled by University of Michigan Professor Jeffrey MacKie-Mason (jmm@umich.edu) and Juan Riveros, the website contains more than 5,000 links in more than a dozen categories and is constantly updated.

United States Congress   thomas.loc.gov

This site provides texts and digests of legislation, as well as committee and conference reports.

United States Telephone Association www.usta.org
1401 H Street NW, Suite 600
Washington, DC 20005-2164
Phone: (202) 326-7300
Fax: (202) 326-7333

This trade association for major local phone companies summarizes key legislation, including the Telecommunications Act of 1996, tracks regulatory initiatives, and provides the association's perspective on current policy issues.

Wisconsin Public Libraries www.dpi.state.wi.us/dpi/dlcl/pld/
Wisconsin Department of Public Instruction telact.html
State Division for Libraries
  and Community Learning
125 S. Webster Street
Madison, WI 53707-7841
Phone: (608) 266-2127
Fax: (608) 267-1052

Maintains an excellent web page on public interest issues in the Telecommunications Act, with links to many useful sites and focus on educational and nonprofit uses of networked communication.

Wiley, Rein and Fielding wrf.ljx.com/pub
1776 K Street NW
Washington, DC 20006
Phone: (202) 429-7000
Fax: (202) 429-7049

This leading law firm maintains a website with a clause-by-clause breakdown of the Telecommunications Act of 1996, as well as analysis of the Act and related proceedings.

APPENDICES

Government Documents

APPENDIX A

TELECOMMUNICATIONS ACT OF 1996*

Abridged by
Dean Thomas Krattenmaker

SECTION 1. SHORT TITLE; REFERENCES.

(a) **Short Title**— This Act may be cited as the "Telecommunications Act of 1996."

(b) **References**— Except as otherwise expressly provided, whenever in this Act an amendment or repeal is expressed in terms of an amendment to, or repeal of, a section or other provision, the reference shall be considered to be made to a section or other provision of the Communications Act of 1934 (47 U.S.C. 151 et seq.).

SEC. 3. DEFINITIONS.

(a) **Additional Definitions**— Section 3 (47 U.S.C. 153) is amended—(2) by adding at the end thereof the following:

(38) **Customer Premises Equipment**— The term "customer premises equipment" means equipment employed on the premises of a person (other than a carrier) to originate, route, or terminate telecommunications.

(39) **Dialing Parity**— The term "dialing parity" means that a person that is not an affiliate of a local exchange carrier is able to provide telecommunications services in such a manner that customers have the ability to route automatically, without the use of any access code, their telecommunications to the telecommunications services provider of the customer's desig-

---

*[Ed.] This is a heavily edited version of the Act, designed to make it easier to read. Most omissions are not indicated. Copyright © 1996 Connecticut Law Review. Reprinted by permission.

nation from among 2 or more telecommunications services providers (including such local exchange carrier).

(40) **Exchange Access**— The term "exchange access" means the offering of access to telephone exchange services or facilities for the purpose of the origination or termination of telephone toll services.

(41) **Information Service**— The term "information service" means the offering of a capability for generating, acquiring, storing, transforming, processing, retrieving, utilizing, or making available information via telecommunications, and includes electronic publishing, but does not include any use of any such capability for the management, control, or operation of a telecommunications system or the management of a telecommunications service.

(44) **Local Exchange Carrier**— The term "local exchange carrier" means any person that is engaged in the provision of telephone exchange service or exchange access. Such term does not include a person insofar as such person is engaged in the provision of a commercial mobile service under section 332(c), except to the extent that the Commission finds that such service should be included in the definition of such term.

(46) **Number Portability**— The term "number portability" means the ability of users of telecommunications services to retain, at the same location, existing telecommunications numbers without impairment of quality, reliability, or convenience when switching from one telecommunications carrier to another.

(48) **Telecommunications**— The term "telecommunications" means the transmission, between or among points specified by the user, of information of the user's choosing, without change in the form or content of the information as sent and received.

(49) **Telecommunications Carrier**— The term telecommunications services . . . A telecommunications carrier shall be treated as a common carrier under this Act only to the extent that it providing telecommunication services . . .

(50) **Telecommunications Equipment**— The term "telecommunications equipment" means equipment, other than customer premises equipment, used by a carrier to provide telecommunications services, and includes software integral to such equipment (including upgrades).

(51) **Telecommunications Service**— The term "telecommunications service" means the offering of telecommunications for a fee directly to the public, or to such classes of users as to be effectively available directly to the public, regardless of the facilities used.

TITLE I—TELECOMMUNICATIONS SERVICES
SUBTITLE A—TELECOMMUNICATIONS SERVICES
SEC. 101. ESTABLISHMENT OF PART II OF TITLE II.

(a) **Amendment**— Title II is amended by inserting after section 229 (47 U.S.C. 229) the following new part:

PART II—DEVELOPMENT OF COMPETITIVE MARKETS
SEC. 251. INTERCONNECTION.

(a) **General Duty of Telecommunications Carriers**— Each telecommunications carrier has the duty—

   (1) to interconnect directly or indirectly with the facilities and equipment of other telecommunications carriers; and

   (2) not to install network features, functions, or capabilities that do not comply with the guidelines and standards established pursuant to section 255 or 256.

(b) **Obligations of All Local Exchange Carriers**— Each local exchange carrier has the following duties:

   (1) **Resale**— The duty not to prohibit, and not to impose unreasonable or discriminatory conditions or limitations on, the resale of its telecommunications services.

   (2) **Number Portability**— The duty to provide, to the extent technically feasible, number portability in accordance with requirements prescribed by the Commission.

   (3) **Dialing Parity**— The duty to provide dialing parity to competing providers of telephone exchange service and telephone toll service, and the duty to permit all such providers to have nondiscriminatory access to telephone numbers, operator services, directory assistance, and directory listing, with no unreasonable dialing delays.

   (4) **Access to Rights-of-way**— The duty to afford access to the poles, ducts, conduits, and rights-of-way of such carrier to competing providers of telecommunications services on rates, terms, and conditions that are consistent with section 224.

   (5) **Reciprocal Compensation**— The duty to establish reciprocal compensation arrangements for the transport and termination of telecommunications.

(c) **Additional Obligations of Incumbent Local Exchange Carriers**— In addition to the duties contained in subsection (b), each incumbent local exchange carrier has the following duties:

   (1) **Duty to Negotiate**— The duty to negotiate in good faith in accordance with section 252 the particular terms and conditions of agreements to fulfill the duties described in paragraphs (1) through (5) of subsection (b) and this subsection. The requesting telecommunications carrier also has the duty to negotiate in good faith the terms and conditions of such agreements.

   (2) **Interconnection**— The duty to provide, for the facilities and equipment of any requesting telecommunications carrier, interconnection with the local exchange carrier's network—

      (A) for the transmission and routing of telephone exchange service and exchange access;

      (B) at any technically feasible point within the carrier's network;

      (C) that is at least equal in quality to that provided by the local exchange carrier to itself or to any subsidiary, affiliate, or any other party to which the carrier provides interconnection; and

(D) on rates, terms, and conditions that are just, reasonable, and nondiscriminatory.

(3) **Unbundled Access**— The duty to provide, to any requesting telecommunications carrier for the provision of a telecommunications service, nondiscriminatory access to network elements on an unbundled basis at any technically feasible point on rates, terms, and conditions that are just reasonable, and nondiscriminatory. An incumbent local exchange carrier shall provide such unbundled network elements in a manner that allows requesting carriers to combine such elements in order to provide such telecommunications service.

(4) **Resale**— The duty—

(A) to offer for resale at wholesale rates any telecommunications service that the carrier provides at retail to subscribers who are not telecommunications carriers; and

(B) not to prohibit, and not to impose unreasonable or discriminatory conditions or limitations on, the resale of such telecommunications service, except that a State commission may, consistent with regulations prescribed by the Commission under this section, prohibit a reseller that obtains at wholesale rates a telecommunications service that is available at retail only to a category of subscribers from offering such service to a different category of subscribers.

(5) **Notice of Changes**— The duty to provide reasonable public notice of changes in the information necessary for the transmission and routing of services using that local exchange carrier's facilities or networks, as well as of any other changes that would affect the interoperability of those facilities and networks.

(6) **Collocation**— The duty to provide, on rates, terms, and conditions that are just, reasonable, and nondiscriminatory, for physical collocation of equipment necessary for interconnection or access to unbundled network elements at the premises of the local exchange carrier, except that the carrier may provide for virtual collocation if the local exchange carrier demonstrates to the State commission that physical collocation is not practical for technical reasons or because of space limitations.

(e) **Numbering Administration**—

(1) **Commission Authority and Jurisdiction**— The Commission shall create or designate one or more impartial entities to administer telecommunications numbering and to make such numbers available on an equitable basis.

(g) **Continued Enforcement of Exchange Access and Interconnection Requirements**— On and after the date of enactment of the Telecommunications Act of 1996, each local exchange carrier, to the extent that it provides wireline services, shall provide exchange access, information access, and exchange services for such access to interexchange carriers and information service providers in accordance with the same equal access and nondiscriminatory interconnection restrictions and obligations (including receipt of compensation) that apply to such carrier on the date immediately preceding the date of enactment of the Telecommunications Act of 1996 under any court order, consent decree, or regulation, order, or policy of the Commission, until such restrictions and obligations are explicitly superseded by regulations prescribed by the Commission after such date of enactment.

(h) **Definition of Incumbent Local Exchange Carrier**—
   (1) **Definition**— For purposes of this section, the term "incumbent local exchange carrier" means, with respect to an area, the local exchange carrier that—
      (A) on the date of enactment of the Telecommunications Act of 1996, provided telephone exchange service in such area.

SEC. 252. PROCEDURES FOR NEGOTIATION, ARBITRATION, AND APPROVAL OF AGREEMENTS.

(a) **Agreements Arrived at Through Negotiations**—
   (1) **Voluntary Negotiations**— Upon receiving a request for interconnection, services, or network elements pursuant to section 251, an incumbent local exchange carrier may negotiate and enter into a binding agreement with the requesting telecommunications carrier or carriers without regard to the standards set forth in subsections (b) and (c) of section 251. The agreement shall include a detailed schedule of itemized charges for interconnection and each service or network element included in the agreement. The agreement . . . shall be submitted to the State commission under subsection (e) of this section.
   (2) **Mediation**— Any party negotiating an agreement under this section may, at any point in the negotiation, ask a State commission to participate in the negotiation and to mediate any differences arising in the course of the negotiation.

(b) **Agreement Arrived at Through Compulsory Arbitration**—
   (1) **Arbitration**— During the period from the 135th to the 160th day (inclusive) after the date on which an incumbent local exchange carrier receives a request for negotiation under this section, the carrier or any other party to the negotiation may petition a State commission to arbitrate any open issues.
   (4) **Action by State Commission**—
      (C) The State commission shall resolve each issue set forth in the petition and the response, if any, by imposing appropriate conditions as required to implement subsection (c) upon the parties to the agreement, and shall conclude the resolution of any unresolved issues not later than 9 months after the date on which the local exchange carrier received the request under this section.

(c) **Standards for Arbitration**— In resolving by arbitration under subsection (b) any open issues and imposing conditions upon the parties to the agreement, a State commission shall—

(1) ensure that such resolution and conditions meet the requirements of section 251, including the regulations prescribed by the Commission pursuant to section 251;

(2) establish any rates for interconnection, services, or network elements according to subsection (d); and

(3) provide a schedule for implementation of the terms and conditions by the parties to the agreement.

(d) **Pricing Standards—**

(1) **Interconnection and Network Element Charges—** Determinations by a State commission of the just and reasonable rate for the interconnection of facilities and equipment for purposes of subsection (c)(2) of section 251, and the just and reasonable rate for network elements for purposes of subsection (c)(3) of such section—

(A) shall be—

(i) based on the cost (determined without reference to a rate-of-return or other rate-based proceeding) of providing the interconnection or network element (whichever is applicable), and

(ii) nondiscriminatory, and

(B) may include a reasonable profit.

(3) **Wholesale Prices for Telecommunications Services—** For the purposes of section 251(c)(4), a State commission shall determine wholesale rates on the basis of retail rates charged to subscribers for the telecommunications service requested, excluding the portion thereof attributable to any marketing, billing, collection, and other costs that will be avoided by the local exchange carrier.

(e) **Approval by State Commission—**

(1) **Approval Required—** Any interconnection agreement adopted by negotiation or arbitration shall be submitted for approval to the State commission. A State commission to which an agreement is submitted shall approve or reject the agreement, with written findings as to any deficiencies.

(2) **Grounds for Rejection—** The State commission may only reject—

(A) an agreement (or any portion thereof) adopted by negotiation under subsection (a) if it finds that—

(i) the agreement (or portion thereof) discriminates against a telecommunications carrier not a party to the agreement; or

(ii) the implementation of such agreement or portion is not consistent with the public interest, convenience, and necessity; or

(B) an agreement (or any portion thereof) adopted by arbitration under subsection (b) if it finds that the agreement does not meet the requirements of section 251, including the regulations prescribed by the Commission pursuant to section 251, or the standards set forth in subsection (d) of this section.

(5) **Commission to Act if State Will Not Act**— If a State commission fails to act to carry out its responsibility under this section in any proceeding or other matter under this section, then the Commission shall issue an order preempting the State commission's jurisdiction of that proceeding or matter within 90 days after being notified (or taking notice) of such failure, and shall assume the responsibility of the State commission under this section with respect to the proceeding or matter and act for the State commission.

(f) **Statements of Generally Available Terms**—

(1) **In General**— A Bell operating company may prepare and file with a State commission a statement of the terms and conditions that such company generally offers within that State to comply with the requirements of section 251 and the regulations thereunder and the standards applicable under this section.

(2) **State Commission Review**— A State commission may not approve such statement unless such statement complies with subsection (d) of this section and section 251 and the regulations thereunder. Except as provided in section 253, nothing in this section shall prohibit a State commission from establishing or enforcing other requirements of State law in its review of such statement, including requiring compliance with intrastate telecommunications service quality standards or requirements.

(h) **Filing Required**— A State commission shall make a copy of each agreement approved under subsection (e) and each statement approved under subsection (f) available for public inspection and copying within 10 days after the agreement or statement is approved.

(i) **Availability to Other Telecommunications Carriers**— A local exchange carrier shall make available any interconnection, service, or network element provided under an agreement approved under this section to which it is a party to any other requesting telecommunications carrier upon the same terms and conditions as those provided in the agreement.

(j) **Definition of Incumbent Local Exchange Carrier**— For purposes of this section, the term "incumbent local exchange carrier" has the meaning provided in section 251(h).

SEC. 253. REMOVAL OF BARRIERS TO ENTRY.

(a) **In General**— No State or local statute or regulation, or other State or local legal requirement, may prohibit or have the effect of prohibiting the ability of any entity to provide any interstate or intrastate telecommunications service.

(b) **State Regulatory Authority**— Nothing in this section shall affect the ability of a State to impose, on a competitively neutral basis and consistent with section 254, requirements necessary to preserve and advance universal service, protect the public safety and welfare, ensure the continued quality of telecommunications services, and safeguard the rights of consumers.

(c) **State and Local Government Authority—** Nothing in this section affects the authority of a State or local government to manage the public rights-of-way or to require fair and reasonable compensation from telecommunications providers, on a competitively neutral and nondiscriminatory basis, for use of public rights-of-way on a nondiscriminatory basis.

(d) **Preemption—** If, after notice and an opportunity for public comment, the Commission determines that a State or local government has permitted or imposed any statute, regulation, or legal requirement that violates subsection (a) or (b), the Commission shall preempt the enforcement of such statute, regulation, or legal requirement to the extent necessary to correct such violation or inconsistency.

SEC. 254. UNIVERSAL SERVICE

(a) **Procedures to Review Universal Service Requirements—**
  (1) **Federal–State Joint Board on Universal Service—** Within one month after the date of enactment of the Telecommunications Act of 1996,the Commission shall institute and refer to a Federal-State Joint Board under section 410(c) a proceeding to recommend changes to any of its regulations in order to implement sections 214(e) and this section, including the definition of the services that are supported by Federal universal service support mechanisms and a specific timetable for completion of such recommendations.
  (2) **Commission Action—** The Commission shall initiate a single proceeding to implement the recommendations from the Joint Board required by paragraph (1). The rules established by such proceeding shall include a definition of the services that are supported by Federal universal service support mechanisms and a specific timetable for implementation.

(b) **Universal Service Principles—** The Joint Board and the Commission shall base policies for the preservation and advancement of universal service on the following principles:
  (1) **Quality and Rates—** Quality services should be available at just, reasonable, and affordable rates.
  (2) **Access to Advanced Services—** Access to advanced telecommunications and information services should be provided in all regions of the Nation.
  (3) **Access in Rural and High Cost Areas—** Consumers in all regions of the Nation, including low-income consumers and those in rural, insular, and high cost areas, should have access to telecommunications and information services, including interexchange services and advanced telecommunications and information services, that are reasonably comparable to those services provided in urban areas and that are available at rates that are reasonably comparable to rates charged for similar services in urban areas.
  (4) **Equitable and Nondiscriminatory Contributions—** All providers of tele-

communications services should make an equitable and nondiscriminatory contribution to the preservation and advancement of universal service.

(5) **Specific and Predictable Support Mechanisms**— There should be specific, predictable and sufficient Federal and State mechanisms to preserve and advance universal service.

(6) **Access to Advanced Telecommunications Services for Schools, Health Care, and Libraries**— Elementary and secondary schools and classrooms, health care providers, and libraries should have access to advanced telecommunications services as described in subsection (h).

(7) **Additional Principles**— Such other principles as the Joint Board and the Commission determine are necessary and appropriate for the protection of the public interest, convenience, and necessity and are consistent with this Act.

(c) **Definition**—

(1) **In General**— Universal service is an evolving level of telecommunications services that the Commission shall establish periodically under this section, taking into account advances in telecommunications and information technologies and services. The Joint Board in recommending, and the Commission in establishing, the definition of the services that are supported by Federal universal service support mechanisms shall consider the extent to which such telecommunications services—

(A) are essential to education, public health, or public safety;

(B) have, through the operation of market choices by customers, been subscribed to by a substantial majority of residential customers;

(C) are being deployed in public telecommunications networks by telecommunications carriers; and

(D) are consistent with the public interest, convenience, and necessity.

(3) **Special Services**— In addition to the services included in the definition of universal service under paragraph (1), the Commission may designate additional services for such support mechanisms for schools, libraries, and health care providers for the purposes of subsection (h).

(d) **Telecommunications Carrier Contribution**— Every telecommunications carrier that provides interstate telecommunications services shall contribute, on an equitable and nondiscriminatory basis, to the specific, predictable, and advance universal service. The Commission may exempt a carrier or class of carriers from this requirement if the carrier's telecommunications activities are limited to such an extent that the level of such carrier's contribution to the preservation and advancement of universal service would be de minimis. Any other provider of interstate telecommunications may be required to contribute to the preservation and advancement of universal service if the public interest so requires.

(e) **Universal Service Support**— After the date on which Commission regulations implementing this section take effect, only an eligible telecommunications carrier designated under section 214(e) shall be eligible to receive specific Federal universal service support. A carrier that receives such support shall use that support only for the provision, maintenance, and upgrading of facilities and services for which the support is intended.

(f) **State Authority**— A State may adopt regulations not inconsistent with the Commission's rules to preserve and advance universal service. Every telecommunications carrier that provides intrastate telecommunications services shall contribute, on an equitable and nondiscriminatory basis, in a manner determined by the State to the preservation and advancement of universal service in that State.

(g) **Interexchange and Interstate Services**— The Commission shall adopt rules to require that the rates charged by providers of interexchange telecommunications services to subscribers in rural and high cost areas shall be no higher than the rates charged by each such provider to its subscribers in urban areas. Such rules shall also require that a provider of interstate interexchange telecommunications services shall provide such services to its subscribers in each State at rates no higher than the rates charged to its subscribers in any other State.

(h) **Telecommunications Services for Certain Providers**—
   (1) **In General**—
      (B) **Educational Providers and Libraries**— All telecommunications carriers serving a geographic area shall, upon a bona fide request for any of its services that are within the definition of universal service under subsection (c)(3), provide such services to elementary schools, secondary schools, and libraries for educational purposes at rates less than the amounts charged for similar services to other parties. The discount shall be an amount that the Commission, with respect to interstate services, and the States, with respect to intrastate services, determine is appropriate and necessary to ensure affordable access to and use of such services by such entities.
   (2) **Advanced Services**— The Commission shall establish competitively neutral rules—
      (A) to enhance, to the extent technically feasible and economically reasonable, access to advanced telecommunications and information services for all public and nonprofit elementary and secondary school classrooms, health care providers, and libraries; and
      (B) to define the circumstances under which a telecommunications carrier may be required to connect its network to such public institutional telecommunications users.
   (3) **Terms and Conditions**— Telecommunications services and network capacity provided to a public institutional telecommunications user under this subsection may not be sold, resold, or otherwise transferred by such user in consideration for money or any other thing of value.

(i) **Consumer Protection**— The Commission and the States should ensure that universal service is available at rates that are just, reasonable, and affordable.

SEC. 255. ACCESS BY PERSONS WITH DISABILITIES.

(b) **Manufacturing**— A manufacturer of telecommunications equipment or customer premises equipment shall ensure that the equipment is designed, developed, and fabricated to be accessible to and usable by individuals with disabilities, if readily achievable.

(c) **Telecommunications Services**— A provider of telecommunications service shall ensure that the service is accessible to and usable by individuals with disabilities, if readily achievable.

(d) **Compatibility**— Whenever the requirements of subsections (b) and (c) are not readily achievable, such a manufacturer or provider shall ensure that the equipment or service is compatible with existing peripheral devices or specialized customer premises equipment commonly used by individuals with disabilities to achieve access, if readily achievable.

SEC. 257. MARKET ENTRY BARRIERS PROCEEDING.

(a) **Elimination of Barriers**— Within 15 months after the date of enactment of the Telecommunications Act of 1996,the Commission shall complete a proceeding for the purpose of identifying and eliminating, by regulations pursuant to its authority under this Act (other than this section), market entry barriers for entrepreneurs and other small businesses in the provision and ownership of telecommunications services and information services, or in the provision of parts or services to providers of telecommunications services and information services.

(b) **National Policy**— In carrying out subsection (a), the Commission shall seek to promote the policies and purposes of this Act favoring diversity of media voices, vigorous economic competition, technological advancement, and promotion of the public interest, convenience, and necessity.

(c) **Periodic Review**— Every 3 years following the completion of the proceeding required by subsection (a), the Commission shall review and report to Congress on—

 (1) any regulations prescribed to eliminate barriers within its jurisdiction that are identified under subsection (a) and that can be prescribed consistent with the public interest, convenience, and necessity; and

 (2) the statutory barriers identified under subsection (a) that the Commission recommends be eliminated, consistent with the public interest, convenience, and necessity.

SEC. 259. INFRASTRUCTURE SHARING.

(a) **Regulations Required**— The Commission shall prescribe regulations that require incumbent local exchange carriers (as defined in section 251(h)) to make available to any qualifying carrier such public switched network infrastructure, technology, information, and telecommunications facilities and functions as may be requested by such qualifying carrier for the purpose of enabling such qualifying carrier to provide telecommunications services, or to provide access to information services, in the service area in which such qualifying carrier has requested and obtained designation as an eligible telecommunications carrier.

(b) **Terms and Conditions of Regulations**— The regulations prescribed by the Commission pursuant to this section shall—

    (1) not require a local exchange carrier to which this section applies to take any action that is economically unreasonable or that is contrary to the public interest;

    (2) permit, but shall not require, the joint ownership or operation of public switched network infrastructure and services by or among such local exchange carrier and a qualifying carrier;

    (3) ensure that such local exchange carrier will not be treated by the Commission or any State as a common carrier for hire or as offering common carrier services with respect to any infrastructure, technology, information, facilities, or functions made available to a qualifying carrier in accordance with regulations issued pursuant to this section;

    (4) ensure that such local exchange carrier makes such infrastructure, technology, information, facilities, or functions available to a qualifying carrier on just and reasonable terms and conditions that permit such qualifying carrier to fully benefit from the economies of scale and scope of such local exchange carrier, as determined in accordance with guidelines prescribed by the Commission in regulations issued pursuant to this section;

    (5) establish conditions that promote cooperation between local exchange carriers to which this section applies and qualifying carriers;

    (6) not require a local exchange carrier to which this section applies to engage in any infrastructure sharing agreement for any services or access which are to be provided or offered to consumers by the qualifying carrier in such local exchange carrier's telephone exchange area; and

    (7) require that such local exchange carrier file with the Commission or State for public inspection, any tariffs, contracts, or other arrangements showing the rates, terms, and conditions under which such carrier is making available public switched network infrastructure and functions under this section.

(c) **Information Concerning Deployment of New Services and Equipment**— A local exchange carrier to which this section applies that has entered into an infrastructure sharing agreement under this section shall provide to each party to such agreement timely information on the planned deployment of telecommunications services and equipment, including any software or upgrades of software integral to the use or operation of such telecommunications equipment.

(d) **Definition**— For purposes of this section, the term "qualifying carrier" means a telecommunications carrier that—

(1) lacks economies of scale or scope, as determined in accordance with regulations prescribed by the Commission pursuant to this section; and

(2) offers telephone exchange service, exchange access, and any other service that is included in universal service, to all consumers without preference throughout the service area for which such carrier has been designated as an eligible telecommunications carrier.

SUBTITLE B—SPECIAL PROVISIONS CONCERNING BELL OPERATING COMPANIES
SEC. 151. BELL OPERATING COMPANY PROVISIONS.

(a) **Establishment of Part III of Title II**— Title II is amended by adding at the end of part II (as added by section 101) the following new part:

PART III—SPECIAL PROVISIONS CONCERNING BELL OPERATING COMPANIES
SEC. 271. BELL OPERATING COMPANY ENTRY INTO INTERLATA SERVICES.

(a) **General Limitation**— Neither a Bell operating company, nor any affiliate of a Bell operating company, may provide interLATA services except as provided in this section.

(b) **InterLATA Services to Which this Section Applies**—

(1) **In-region Services**— A Bell operating company, or any affiliate of that Bell operating company, may provide interLATA services originating in any of its in-region States (as defined in subsection (i)) if the Commission approves the application of such company for such State under subsection (d)(3).

(2) **Out-of-region Services**— A Bell operating company, or any affiliate of that Bell operating company, may provide interLATA services originating outside its in-region States after the date of enactment of the Telecommunications Act of 1996, subject to subsection (j).

(4) **Termination**— Nothing in this section prohibits a Bell operating company or any of its affiliates from providing termination for interLATA services, subject to subsection (j).

(c) **Requirements for Providing Certain In-region InterLATA Services**—

(1) **Agreement or Statement**— A Bell operating company meets the requirements of this paragraph if it meets the requirements of subparagraph (A) or subparagraph (B) of this paragraph for each State for which the authorization is sought.

(A) **Presence of a Facilities-based Competitor**— A Bell operating company meets the requirements of this subparagraph if it has entered into one or more binding agreements that have been approved under section 252 specifying the terms and conditions under which the Bell operating company is providing access and interconnection to its network facilities for the network facilities of one or more unaffiliated competing providers of telephone exchange service to residential and business Subscribers.

(B) **Failure to Request Access**— A Bell operating company meets the requirements of this subparagraph if, after 10 months after the date of enactment of the Telecommunications Act of 1996,no such provider has requested the access and interconnection described in subparagraph (A) . . . and a statement of the terms and conditions that the company generally offers to provide such access and interconnection has been approved or permitted to take effect by the State commission under section 252(f).

(2) **Specific Interconnection Requirements—**

(A) **Agreement Required**— A Bell operating company meets the requirements of this paragraph if, within the State for which the authorization is sought—

(i) (I) such company is providing access and interconnection pursuant to one or more agreements described in paragraph (1)(A), or
(II) such company is generally offering access and interconnection pursuant to a statement described in paragraph (1)(B), and

(ii) such access and interconnection meets the requirements of subparagraph (B) of this paragraph.

(B) **Competitive Checklist**— Access or interconnection provided or generally offered by a Bell operating company to other telecommunications carriers meets the requirements of this subparagraph if such access and interconnection includes each of the following:

(i) Interconnection in accordance with the requirements of sections 251(c)(2) and 252(d)(1).

(ii) Nondiscriminatory access to network elements in accordance with the requirements of sections 251(c)(3) and 252(d)(1).

(iii) Nondiscriminatory access to the poles, ducts, conduits, and rights-of-way owned or controlled by the Bell operating company at just and reasonable rates in accordance with the requirements of section 224.

(iv) Local loop transmission from the central office to the customer's premises, unbundled from local switching or other services.

(v) Local transport from the trunk side of a wireline local exchange carrier switch unbundled from switching or other services.

(vi) Local switching unbundled from transport, local loop transmission, or other services.

(vii) Nondiscriminatory access to—

(I) 911 and E911 services;
(II) directory assistance services to allow the other carrier's customers to obtain telephone numbers; and
(III) operator call completion services.

(viii) White pages directory listings for customers of the other carrier's telephone exchange service.

(ix) Until the date by which telecommunications numbering administration guidelines, plan, or rules are established, nondiscriminatory access to telephone numbers for assignment to the other carrier's telephone exchange service customers. After that date, compliance with such guidelines, plan, or rules.

(x) Nondiscriminatory access to databases and associated signaling necessary for call routing and completion.

(xi) Until the date by which the Commission issues regulations pursuant to section 251 to require number portability, interim telecommunications number portability through remote call forwarding, direct inward dialing trunks, or other comparable arrangements, with as little impairment of functioning, quality, reliability, and convenience as possible. After that date, full compliance with such regulations.

(xii) Nondiscriminatory access to such services or information as are necessary to allow the requesting carrier to implement local dialing parity in accordance with the requirements of section 251(b)(3).

(xiii) Reciprocal compensation arrangements in accordance with the requirements of section 252(d)(2).

(xiv) Telecommunications services are available for resale in accordance with the requirements of sections 251(c)(4) and 252(d)(3).

(d) **Administrative Provisions—**

(1) **Application to Commission—** On and after the date of enactment of the Telecommunications Act of 1996, a Bell operating company or its affiliate may apply to the Commission for authorization to provide interLATA services originating in any in-region State. The application shall identify each State for which the authorization is sought.

(2) **Consultation—**

(A) **Consultation with the Attorney General—** Before making any determination under this subsection, the Commission shall consult with the Attorney General. The Attorney General shall provide to the Commission an evaluation of the application using any standard the Attorney General considers appropriate. The Commission shall give substantial weight to the Attorney General's evaluation, but such evaluation shall not have any preclusive effect on any Commission decision under paragraph (3).

(B) **Consultation with State Commissions—** Before making any determination under this subsection, the Commission shall consult with the State commission of any State that is the subject of the application in order to verify the compliance of the Bell operating company with the requirements of subsection (c).

(3) **Determination—** Not later than 90 days after receiving an application under paragraph (1), the Commission shall issue a written determination approving

or denying the authorization requested in the application for each State. The
Commission shall not approve the authorization requested in an application
submitted under paragraph (1) unless it finds that—

(A) the petitioning Bell operating company has met the requirements of subsection (c)(1) and—

   (i)   with respect to access and interconnection provided pursuant to sub-
         section (c)(1)(A), has fully implemented the competitive checklist in
         subsection (c)(2)(B); or

   (ii) with respect to access and interconnection generally offered pursuant
         to a statement under subsection (c)(1)(B), such statement offers all of
         the items included in the competitive checklist in subsection (c)(2)(B);

(B) the requested authorization will be carried out in accordance with the
requirements of section 272; and

(C) the requested authorization is consistent with the public interest, convenience, and necessity.

(4) **Limitation on Commission**— The Commission may not, by rule or otherwise, limit or extend the terms used in the competitive checklist set forth in
subsection (c)(2)(B).

SEC. 272. SEPARATE AFFILIATE; SAFEGUARDS.

(a) **Separate Affiliate Required for Competitive Activities**—

(1) **In General**— A Bell operating company (including any affiliate) which is a
local exchange carrier that is subject to the requirements of section 251(c)
may not provide any service described in paragraph (2) unless it provides
that service through one or more affiliates that—

(A) are separate from any operating company entity that is subject to the
requirements of section 251(c); and

(B) meet the requirements of subsection (b).

(2) **Services for Which a Separate Affiliate Is Required**— The services for
which a separate affiliate is required by paragraph (1) are:

(A) Manufacturing activities (as defined in section 273(h)).

(B) Origination of interLATA telecommunications services, other than—

   (ii) out-of-region services described in section 271(b)(2); or

(C) InterLATA information services, other than electronic publishing (as
defined in section 274(h)) and alarm monitoring services (as defined in
section 275(e)).

(b) **Structural and Transactional Requirements**— The separate affiliate required
by this section—

(1) shall operate independently from the Bell operating company;

(2) shall maintain books, records, and accounts in the manner prescribed by the

Commission which shall be separate from the books, records, and accounts maintained by the Bell operating company of which it is an affiliate;

(3) shall have separate officers, directors, and employees from the Bell operating company of which it is an affiliate;

(4) may not obtain credit under any arrangement that would permit a creditor, upon default, to have recourse to the assets of the Bell operating company; and

(5) shall conduct all transactions with the Bell operating company of which it is an affiliate on an arm's length basis with any such transactions reduced to writing and available for public inspection.

(c) **Nondiscrimination Safeguards—** In its dealings with its affiliate described in subsection (a), a Bell operating company—

(1) may not discriminate between that company or affiliate and any other entity in the provision or procurement of goods, services, facilities, and information, or in the establishment of standards; and

(2) shall account for all transactions with an affiliate described in subsection (a) in accordance with accounting principles designated or approved by the Commission.

(d) **Biennial Audit—**

(1) **General Requirement—** A company required to operate a separate affiliate under this section shall obtain and pay for a joint Federal/State audit every 2 years conducted by an independent auditor to determine whether such company has complied with this section and the regulations promulgated under this section.

(e) **Fulfillment of Certain Requests—** A Bell operating company and an affiliate that is subject to the requirements of section 251(c)—

(1) shall fulfill any requests from an unaffiliated entity for telephone exchange service and exchange access within a period no longer than the period in which it provides such telephone exchange service and exchange access to itself or to its affiliates;

(2) shall not provide any facilities, services, or information concerning its provision of exchange access to the affiliate described in subsection (a) unless such facilities, services, or information are made available to other providers of interLATA services in that market on the same terms and conditions;

(3) shall charge the affiliate described in subsection (a), or impute to itself (if using the access for its provision of its own services), an amount for access to its telephone exchange service and exchange access that is no less than the amount charged to any unaffiliated interexchange carriers for such service; and

(4) may provide any interLATA or intraLATA facilities or services to its interLATA affiliate if such services or facilities are made available to all car-

riers at the same rates and on the same terms and conditions, and so long as the costs are appropriately allocated.

(f) **Sunset**—

(1) **Manufacturing and Long Distance**— The provisions of this section (other than subsection (e)) shall cease to apply with respect to the manufacturing activities or the interLATA telecommunications services of a Bell operating company 3 years after the date such Bell operating company or any Bell operating company affiliate is authorized to provide interLATA telecommunications services under section 271(d), unless the Commission extends such 3-year period by rule or order.

(2) **InterLATA Information Services**— The provisions of this section (other than subsection (e)) shall cease to apply with respect to the interLATA information services of a Bell operating company 4 years after the date of enactment of the Telecommunications Act of 1996, unless the Commission extends such 4-year period by rule or order.

SEC. 273. MANUFACTURING BY BELL OPERATING COMPANIES.

(a) **Authorization**— A Bell operating company may manufacture and provide telecommunications equipment, and manufacture customer premises equipment, if the Commission authorizes that Bell operating company or any Bell operating company affiliate to provide interLATA services under section 271(d), subject to the requirements of this section and the regulations prescribed thereunder.

(c) **Information Requirements**—

(1) **Information on Protocols and Technical Requirements**— Each Bell operating company shall, in accordance with regulations prescribed by the Commission, maintain and file with the Commission full and complete information with respect to the protocols and technical requirements for connection with and use of its telephone exchange service facilities.

(4) **Planning Information**— Each Bell operating company shall provide, to interconnecting carriers providing telephone exchange service, timely information on the planned deployment of telecommunications equipment.

(d) **Manufacturing Limitations for Standard-setting Organizations**—

(3) **Manufacturing Safeguards**— (A) Any entity which certifies telecommunications equipment or customer premises equipment manufactured by an unaffiliated entity shall only manufacture a particular class of telecommunications equipment or customer premises equipment for which it is undertaking or has undertaken, during the previous 18 months, certification activity for such class of equipment through a separate affiliate.

(C) Such entity that certifies such equipment shall—

(i)   not discriminate in favor of its manufacturing affiliate in the establishment of standards, generic requirements, or product certification;

(ii)   not disclose to the manufacturing affiliate any proprietary information that has been received at any time from an unaffiliated manufacturer, unless authorized in writing by the owner of the information; and

(iii)   not permit any employee engaged in product certification for telecommunications equipment or customer premises equipment to engage jointly in sales or marketing of any such equipment with the affiliated manufacturer.

(4) **Standard-setting Entities**— Any entity that is not an accredited standards development organization and that establishes industry-wide standards for telecommunications equipment or customer premises equipment, or industry-wide generic network requirements for such equipment, or that certifies telecommunications equipment or customer premises equipment manufactured by an unaffiliated entity, shall—

(A)   establish and publish any industry-wide standard for, industry-wide generic requirement for, or any substantial modification of an existing industry-wide standard or industry-wide generic requirement for, telecommunications equipment or customer premises equipment only in compliance with the following procedure—

(i)   such entity shall issue a public notice of its consideration of a proposed industry-wide standard or industry-wide generic requirement;

(ii)   such entity shall issue a public invitation to interested industry parties to fund and participate in such efforts on a reasonable and nondiscriminatory basis, administered in such a manner as not to unreasonably exclude any interested industry party;

(iii)   such entity shall publish a text for comment by such parties as have agreed to participate in the process pursuant to clause (ii), provide such parties a full opportunity to submit comments, and respond to comments from such parties; and

(iv)   such entity shall publish a final text of the industry-wide standard or industry-wide generic requirement, including the comments in their entirety, of any funding party which requests to have its comments so published;

(B)   engage in product certification for telecommunications equipment or customer premises equipment manufactured by unaffiliated entities only if—

(i)   such activity is performed pursuant to published criteria;

(ii)   such activity is performed pursuant to auditable criteria; and

(iii)   such activity is performed pursuant to available industry-accepted testing methods and standards, where applicable, unless otherwise agreed upon by the parties funding and performing such activity;

(C)   not undertake any actions to monopolize or attempt to monopolize the market for such services; and

(D) not preferentially treat its own telecommunications equipment or customer premises equipment, or that of its affiliate, over that of any other entity.

(6) **Sunset**— The requirements of paragraphs (3) and (4) shall terminate for the particular relevant activity when the Commission determines that there are alternative sources of industry-wide standards, industry-wide generic requirements, or product certification for a particular class of telecommunications equipment or customer premises equipment available in the United States. Alternative sources shall be deemed to exist when such sources provide commercially viable alternatives that are providing such services to customers.

(8) **Definitions**— For purposes of this subsection:

(B) The term "generic requirement" means a description of acceptable product attributes for use by local exchange carriers in establishing product specifications for the purchase of telecommunications equipment, customer premises equipment, and software integral thereto.

(C) The term "industry-wide" means activities funded by or performed on behalf of local exchange carriers for use in providing wireline telephone exchange service whose combined total of deployed access lines in the United States constitutes at least 30 percent of all access lines deployed by telecommunications carriers in the United States as of the date of enactment of the Telecommunications Act of 1996.

(D) The term "certification" means any technical process whereby a party determines whether a product, for use by more than one local exchange carrier, conforms with the specified requirements pertaining to such product.

(E) The term "accredited standards development organization" means an entity composed of industry members which has been accredited by an institution vested with the responsibility for standards accreditation by the industry.

(e) **Bell Operating Company Equipment Procurement and Sales**—

(1) **Nondiscrimination Standards for Manufacturing**— In the procurement or awarding of supply contracts for telecommunications equipment, a Bell operating company, or any entity acting on its behalf, for the duration of the requirement for a separate subsidiary including manufacturing under this Act—

(A) shall consider such equipment, produced or supplied by unrelated persons; and

(B) may not discriminate in favor of equipment produced or supplied by an affiliate or related person.

(2) **Procurement Standards**— Each Bell operating company or any entity acting on its behalf shall make procurement decisions and award all supply contracts for equipment, services, and software on the basis of an objective assessment of price, quality, delivery, and other commercial factors.

(3) **Network Planning and Design**— A Bell operating company shall, to the extent consistent with the antitrust laws, engage in joint network planning and design with local exchange carriers operating in the same area of interest.

(4) **Sales Restrictions**— Neither a Bell operating company engaged in manufacturing nor a manufacturing affiliate of such a company shall restrict sales to any local exchange carrier of telecommunications equipment, including software integral to the operation of such equipment and related upgrades.

SEC. 274. ELECTRONIC PUBLISHING BY BELL OPERATING COMPANIES.

(a) **Limitations**— No Bell operating company or any affiliate may engage in the provision of electronic publishing that is disseminated by means of such Bell operating company's or any of its affiliates' basic telephone service, except that nothing in this section shall prohibit a separated affiliate or electronic publishing joint venture operated in accordance with this section from engaging in the provision of electronic publishing.

(b) **Separated Affiliate or Electronic Publishing Joint Venture Requirements**— A separated affiliate or electronic publishing joint venture shall be operated independently from the Bell operating company. Such separated affiliate or joint venture and the Bell operating company with which it is affiliated shall—

(1) maintain separate books, records, and accounts and prepare separate financial statements;

(3) carry out transactions

  (A) in a manner consistent with such independence,

  (B) pursuant to written contracts or tariffs that are filed with the Commission and made publicly available, and

  (C) in a manner that is auditable in accordance with generally accepted auditing standards;

(6) not use for the marketing of any product or service of the separated affiliate or joint venture, the name, trademarks, or service marks of an existing Bell operating company except for names, trademarks, or service marks that are owned by the entity that owns or controls the Bell operating company;

(c) **Joint Marketing**—

(1) **In General**— Except as provided in paragraph (2)—

  (A) a Bell operating company shall not carry out any promotion, marketing, sales, or advertising for or in conjunction with a separated affiliate; and

  (B) a Bell operating company shall not carry out any promotion, marketing, sales, or advertising for or in conjunction with an affiliate that is related to the provision of electronic publishing.

(2) **Permissible Joint Activities**—

(A) **Joint Telemarketing**— A Bell operating company may provide inbound telemarketing or referral services related to the provision of electronic publishing for a separated affiliate, electronic publishing joint venture, affiliate, or unaffiliated electronic publisher: Provided, That if such services are provided to a separated affiliate, electronic publishing joint venture, or affiliate, such services shall be made available to all electronic publishers on request, on nondiscriminatory terms.

(B) **Teaming Arrangements**— A Bell operating company may engage in nondiscriminatory teaming or business arrangements to engage in electronic publishing with any separated affiliate or with any other electronic publisher if

  (i) the Bell operating company only provides facilities, services, and basic telephone service information as authorized by this section, and

  (ii) the Bell operating company does not own such teaming or business arrangement.

(C) **Electronic Publishing Joint Ventures**— A Bell operating company or affiliate may participate on a nonexclusive basis in electronic publishing joint ventures with entities that are not a Bell operating company, affiliate, or separated affiliate to provide electronic publishing services, if the Bell operating company or affiliate has not more than a 50 percent direct or indirect equity interest (or the equivalent thereof) or the right to more than 50 percent of the gross revenues under a revenue sharing or royalty agreement in any electronic publishing joint venture.

(d) **Bell Operating Company Requirement**— A Bell operating company under common ownership or control with a separated affiliate or electronic publishing joint venture shall provide network access and interconnections for basic telephone service to electronic publishers at just and reasonable rates that are tariffed (so long as rates for such services are subject to regulation) and that are not higher on a per-unit basis than those charged for such services to any other electronic publisher or any separated affiliate engaged in electronic publishing.

(g) **Effective Dates**—

  (1) **Transition**— Any electronic publishing service being offered to the public by a Bell operating company or affiliate on the date of enactment of the Telecommunications Act of 1996 shall have one year from such date of enactment to comply with the requirements of this section.

  (2) **Sunset**— The provisions of this section shall not apply to conduct occurring after 4 years after the date of enactment of the Telecommunications Act of 1996.

(h) **Definition of Electronic Publishing**—

  (1) **In General**— The term "electronic publishing" means the dissemination, provision, publication, or sale to an unaffiliated entity or person, of any one or more of the following: news (including sports); entertainment (other than

interactive games); business, financial, legal, consumer, or credit materials; editorials, columns, or features; advertising; photos or images; archival or research material; legal notices or public records; scientific, educational, instructional, technical, professional, trade, or other literary materials; or other like or similar information.

(2) **Exceptions**— The term "electronic publishing" shall not include the following services:

(A) Information access, as that term is defined by the AT&T Consent Decree.

(B) The transmission of information as a common carrier.

(C) The transmission of information as part of a gateway to an information service that does not involve the generation or alteration of the content of information, including data transmission, address translation, protocol conversion, billing management, introductory information content, and navigational systems that enable users to access electronic publishing services, which do not affect the presentation of such electronic publishing services to users.

(D) Voice storage and retrieval services, including voice messaging and electronic mail services.

(E) Data processing or transaction processing services that do not involve the generation or alteration of the content of information.

(I) The provision of directory assistance that provides names, addresses, and telephone numbers and does not include advertising.

(J) Caller identification services.

(M) Any other network service of a type that is like or similar to these network services and that does not involve the generation or alteration of the content of information.

(O) Video programming or full motion video entertainment on demand.

SEC. 275. ALARM MONITORING SERVICES.

(a) **Delayed Entry into Alarm Monitoring**—

(1) **Prohibition**— No Bell operating company or affiliate thereof shall engage in the provision of alarm monitoring services before the date which is 5 years after the date of enactment of the Telecommunications Act of 1996.

(b) **Nondiscrimination**— An incumbent local exchange carrier (as defined in section 251(h)) engaged in the provision of alarm monitoring services shall—

(1) provide nonaffiliated entities, upon reasonable request, with the network services it provides to its own alarm monitoring operations, on nondiscriminatory terms and conditions; and

(2) not subsidize its alarm monitoring services either directly or indirectly from telephone exchange service operations.

TITLE II—BROADCAST SERVICES
SEC. 201. BROADCAST SPECTRUM FLEXIBILITY.

Title III is amended by inserting after section 335 (47 U.S.C. 335) the following new section:

SEC. 336. BROADCAST SPECTRUM FLEXIBILITY.

(a) **Commission Action**— If the Commission determines to issue additional licenses for advanced television services, the Commission—

    (1) should limit the initial eligibility for such licenses to persons that, as of the date of such issuance, are licensed to operate a television broadcast station or hold a permit to construct such a station (or both); and

    (2) shall adopt regulations that allow the holders of such licenses to offer such ancillary or supplementary services on designated frequencies as may be consistent with the public interest, convenience, and necessity.

(c) **Recovery of License**— If the Commission grants a license for advanced television services to a person that, as of the date of such issuance, is licensed to operate a television broadcast station or holds a permit to construct such a station (or both), the Commission shall, as a condition of such license, require that either the additional license or the original license held by the licensee be surrendered to the Commission for reallocation or reassignment (or both) pursuant to Commission regulation.

(d) **Public Interest Requirement**— Nothing in this section shall be construed as relieving a television broadcasting station from its obligation to serve the public interest, convenience, and necessity. In the Commission's review of any application for renewal of a broadcast license for a television station that provides ancillary or supplementary services, the television licensee shall establish that all of its program services on the existing or advanced television spectrum are in the public interest.

(e) **Fees**—

    (1) **Services to Which Fees Apply**— If the regulations prescribed pursuant to subsection (a) permit a licensee to offer ancillary or supplementary services on a designated frequency—

        (A) for which the payment of a subscription fee is required in order to receive such services, or

        (B) for which the licensee directly or indirectly receives compensation from a third party in return for transmitting material furnished by such third party (other than commercial advertisements used to support broadcasting for which a subscription fee is not required), the Commission shall establish a program to assess and collect from the licensee for such designated frequency an annual fee or other schedule or method of payment that promotes the objectives described in subparagraphs (A) and (B) of paragraph (2).

(2) **Collection of Fees**— The program required by paragraph (1) shall—

   (A) be designed

   (i) to recover for the public a portion of the value of the public spectrum resource made available for such commercial use, and

   (ii) to avoid unjust enrichment through the method employed to permit such uses of that resource; and

   (B) recover for the public an amount that, to the extent feasible, equals but does not exceed (over the term of the license) the amount that would have been recovered had such services been licensed pursuant to the provisions of section 309(j) of this Act and the Commission's regulations thereunder.

(f) **Evaluation**— Within 10 years after the date the Commission first issues additional licenses for advanced television services, the Commission shall conduct an evaluation of the advanced television services program. Such evaluation shall include—

(1) an assessment of the willingness of consumers to purchase the television receivers necessary to receive broadcasts of advanced television services;

(2) an assessment of alternative uses, including public safety use, of the frequencies used for such broadcasts; and

(3) the extent to which the Commission has been or will be able to reduce the amount of spectrum assigned to licensees.

SEC. 202. BROADCAST OWNERSHIP.

(a) **National Radio Station Ownership Rule Changes Required**— The Commission shall modify its regulations by eliminating any provisions limiting the number of AM or FM broadcast stations which may be owned or controlled by one entity nationally.

(b) **Local Radio Diversity**—

   (1) **Applicable Caps**— The Commission shall revise its regulations to provide that—

   (A) in a radio market with 45 or more commercial radio stations, a party may own, operate, or control up to 8 commercial radio stations, not more than 5 of which are in the same service (AM or FM);

   (B) in a radio market with between 30 and 44 (inclusive) commercial radio stations, a party may own, operate, or control up to 7 commercial radio stations, not more than 4 of which are in the same service (AM or FM);

   (C) in a radio market with between 15 and 29 (inclusive) commercial radio stations, a party may own, operate, or control up to 6 commercial radio stations, not more than 4 of which are in the same service (AM or FM); and

(D) in a radio market with 14 or fewer commercial radio stations, a party may own, operate, or control up to 5 commercial radio stations, not more than 3 of which are in the same service (AM or FM), except that a party may not own, operate, or control more than 50 percent of the stations in such market.

(2) **Exception**— Notwithstanding any limitation authorized by this subsection, the Commission may permit a person or entity to own, operate, or control, or have a cognizable interest in, radio broadcast stations if the Commission determines that such ownership, operation, control, or interest will result in an increase in the number of radio broadcast stations in operation.

(c) **Television Ownership Limitations**—

(1) **National Ownership Limitations**— The Commission shall modify its rules for multiple ownership set forth in its regulations—

(A) by eliminating the restrictions on the number of television stations that a person or entity may directly or indirectly own, operate, or control, or have a cognizable interest in, nationwide; and

(B) by increasing the national audience reach limitation for television stations to 35 percent.

(2) **Local Ownership Limitations**— The Commission shall conduct a rule-making proceeding to determine whether to retain, modify, or eliminate its limitations on the number of television stations that a person or entity may own, operate, or control, or have a cognizable interest in, within the same television market.

(f) **Cable Cross Ownership**—

(1) **Elimination of Restrictions**— The Commission shall revise its regulations to permit a person or entity to own or control a network of broadcast stations and a cable system.

(2) **Safeguards Against Discrimination**— The Commission shall revise such regulations if necessary to ensure carriage, channel positioning, and nondiscriminatory treatment of nonaffiliated broadcast stations by a cable system described in paragraph (1).

(g) **Local Marketing Agreements**— Nothing in this section shall be construed to prohibit the origination, continuation, or renewal of any television local marketing agreement that is in compliance with the regulations of the Commission.

(h) **Further Commission Review**— The Commission shall review its rules adopted pursuant to this section and all of its ownership rules biennially . . . and shall determine whether any of such rules are necessary in the public interest as the result of competition. The Commission shall repeal or modify any regulation it determines to be no longer in the public interest.

(i) **Elimination of Statutory Restriction**— Section 613(a) (47 U.S.C. 533(a)) is amended—

(1) by striking paragraph (1) [which prohibited telephone companies to operate cable systems in their service area].

SEC. 203. TERM OF LICENSES.

Section 307(c) (47 U.S.C. 307(c)) is amended to read as follows:

(c) **Terms of Licenses—**
  (1) **Initial and Renewal Licenses—** Each license granted for the operation of a broadcasting station shall be for a term of not to exceed 8 years. Upon application therefore, a renewal of such license may be granted from time to time for a term of not to exceed 8 years from the date of expiration of the preceding license, if the Commission finds that public interest, convenience, and necessity would be served thereby.

SEC. 204. BROADCAST LICENSE RENEWAL PROCEDURES.

(a) **Renewal Procedures—**
  (1) **Amendment—** Section 309 (47 U.S.C. 309) is amended by adding at the end thereof the following new subsection:
(k) **Broadcast Station Renewal Procedures—**
  (1) **Standards for Renewal—** If the licensee of a broadcast station submits an application to the Commission for renewal of such license, the Commission shall grant the application if it finds, with respect to that station, during the preceding term of its license—
    (A) the station has served the public interest, convenience, and necessity;
    (B) there have been no serious violations by the licensee of this Act or the rules and regulations of the Commission; and
    (C) there have been no other violations by the licensee of this Act or the rules and regulations of the Commission which, taken together, would constitute a pattern of abuse.
  (2) **Consequence of Failure to Meet Standard—** If any licensee of a broadcast station fails to meet the requirements of this subsection, the Commission may deny the application for renewal . . . or grant such application on terms and conditions as are appropriate, including renewal for a term less than the maximum otherwise permitted.
  (4) **Competitor Consideration Prohibited—** In making the determinations specified in paragraph (1) or (2), the Commission shall not consider whether the public interest, convenience, and necessity might be served by the grant of a license to a person other than the renewal applicant.
(b) **Summary of Complaints on Violent Programming—** Section 308 (47 U.S.C. 308) is amended by adding at the end the following new subsection:

(d) **Summary of Complaints**— Each applicant for the renewal of a commercial or noncommercial television license shall attach as an exhibit to the application a summary of written comments and suggestions received from the public and maintained by the licensee (in accordance with Commission regulations) that comment on the applicant's programming, if any, and that are characterized by the commentor as constituting violent programming.

TITLE III—CABLE SERVICES
SEC. 301. CABLE ACT REFORM.

(b) **Rate Deregulation**—
  (1) **Upper Tier Regulation**— Section 623(c) (47 U.S.C. 543(c)) is amended—
    (C) by striking paragraph (3) and inserting the following . . . :
      (4) **Sunset of Upper Tier Rate Regulation**— This subsection shall not apply to cable programming services provided after March 31, 1999.
  (2) **Sunset of Uniform Rate Structure in Markets with Effective Competition**— Section 623(d) (47 U.S.C. 543(d)) is amended by adding at the end thereof the following: This subsection does not apply to (1) a cable operator with respect to the provision of cable service over its cable system in any geographic area in which the video programming services offered by the operator in that area are subject to effective competition, or (2) any video programming offered on a per channel or per program basis.
  (3) **Effective Competition**— Section 623(l)(1) (47 U.S.C. 543(l)(1)) is amended—
    (C) by adding at the end the following:
    (D) a local exchange carrier or its affiliate (or any multichannel video programming distributor using the facilities of such carrier or its affiliate) offers video programming services directly to subscribers by any means (other than direct-to-home satellite services) in the franchise area of an unaffiliated cable operator which is providing cable service in that franchise area, but only if the video programming services so offered in that area are comparable to the video programming services provided by the unaffiliated cable operator in that area.

SEC. 302. CABLE SERVICE PROVIDED
BY TELEPHONE COMPANIES.

(a) **Provisions for Regulation of Cable Service Provided by Telephone Companies**— Title VI (47 U.S.C. 521 et seq.) is amended by adding at the end the following new part:

PART V—VIDEO PROGRAMMING SERVICES PROVIDED BY TELEPHONE COMPANIES
SEC. 651. REGULATORY TREATMENT OF VIDEO PROGRAMMING SERVICES.

(a) **Limitations on Cable Regulation—**

    (1) **Radio-based Systems—** To the extent that a common carrier (or any other person) is providing video programming to subscribers using radio communication, such carrier (or other person) shall be subject to the requirements of title III and section 652, but shall not otherwise be subject to the requirements of this title.

    (2) **Common Carriage of Video Traffic—** To the extent that a common carrier is providing transmission of video programming on a common carrier basis, such carrier shall be subject to the requirements of title II and section 652, but shall not otherwise be subject to the requirements of this title.

    (3) **Cable Systems and Open Video Systems—** To the extent that a common carrier is providing video programming to its subscribers in any manner other than that described in paragraphs (1) and (2)—

        (A) such carrier shall be subject to the requirements of this title, unless such programming is provided by means of an open video system for which the Commission has approved a certification under section 653; or

        (B) if such programming is provided by means of an open video system for which the Commission has approved a certification under section 653, such carrier shall be subject to the requirements of this part, but shall be subject to parts I through IV of this title only as provided in 653(c).

(b) **Limitations on Interconnection Obligations—** A local exchange carrier that provides cable service through an open video system or a cable system shall not be required, pursuant to title II of this Act, to make capacity available on a nondiscriminatory basis to any other person for the provision of cable service directly to subscribers.

SEC. 652. PROHIBITION ON BUY OUTS.

(a) **Acquisitions by Carriers—** No local exchange carrier . . . may acquire more than a 10 percent financial interest, or any management interest, in any cable operator providing cable service within the local exchange carrier's telephone service area.

(b) **Acquisitions by Cable Operators—** No cable operator . . . may acquire more than a 10 percent financial interest, or any management interest, in any local exchange carrier providing telephone exchange service within such cable operator's franchise area.

(c) **Joint Ventures—** A local exchange carrier and a cable operator whose telephone service area and cable franchise area, respectively, are in the same market may not enter into any joint venture or partnership to provide video programming directly to subscribers or to provide telecommunications services within such market.

(d) **Exceptions**— [Several sub-sub-sections provide exemptions for certain rural systems, for certain competitive cable systems, and for certain small cable systems. The FCC is also granted limited authority to waive the requirements of (a), (b), and (c).]

SEC. 653. ESTABLISHMENT OF OPEN VIDEO SYSTEMS.

(a) **Open Video Systems**—

(1) **Certificates of Compliance**— A local exchange carrier may provide cable service to its cable service subscribers in its telephone service area through an open video system that complies with this section. To the extent permitted by such regulations as the Commission may prescribe consistent with the public interest, convenience, and necessity, an operator of a cable system or any other person may provide video programming through an open video system that complies with this section.

(b) **Commission Actions**—

(1) **Regulations Required**— The Commission shall prescribe regulations that—

(A) except as required pursuant to section 611, 614, or 615, prohibit an operator of an open video system from discriminating among video programming providers with regard to carriage on its open video system, and ensure that the rates, terms, and conditions for such carriage are just and reasonable, and are not unjustly or unreasonably discriminatory;

(B) if demand exceeds the channel capacity of the open video system, prohibit an operator of an open video system and its affiliates from selecting the video programming services for carriage on more than one-third of the activated channel capacity on such system, but nothing in this subparagraph shall be construed to limit the number of channels that the carrier and its affiliates may offer to provide directly to subscribers;

(D) extend to the distribution of video programming over open video systems the Commission's regulations concerning sports exclusivity, network nonduplication, and syndicated exclusivity; and

(E)(i) prohibit an operator of an open video system from unreasonably discriminating in favor of the operator or its affiliates with regard to material or information (including advertising) provided by the operator to subscribers for the purposes of selecting programming on the open video system, or in the way such material or information is presented to subscribers; and

(iv) prohibit an operator of an open video system from omitting television broadcast stations or other unaffiliated video programming services carried on such system from any navigational device, guide, or menu.

(c) **Reduced Regulatory Burdens for Open Video Systems—**

    (1) **In General—** Any provision that applies to a cable operator under—

        (A) sections 613 (other than subsection (a) thereof), 616, 623(f), 628, 631, and 634 of this title, shall apply,

        (B) sections 611, 614, and 615 of this title, and section 325 of title III, shall apply in accordance with the regulations prescribed under paragraph (2), and

        (C) sections 612 and 617, and parts III and IV (other than sections 623(f), 628, 631, and 634), of this title shall not apply, to any operator of an open video system for which the Commission has approved a certification under this section.

    (2) **Implementation—**

        (B) **Fees—** An operator of an open video system under this part may be subject to the payment of fees on the gross revenues of the operator for the provision of cable service imposed by a local franchising authority or other governmental entity, in lieu of the franchise fees permitted under section 622. The rate at which such fees are imposed shall not exceed the rate at which franchise fees are imposed on any cable operator transmitting video programming in the franchise area.

    (4) **Treatment as Cable Operator—** Nothing in this Act precludes a video programming provider making use of an open video system from being treated as an operator of a cable system for purposes of section 111 of title 17, United States Code.

(b) **Conforming and Technical Amendments—**

    (1) **Repeal—** Subsection (b) of section 613 (47 U.S.C. 533(b)) [which banned telephone company provision of cable television] is repealed.

    (3) **Termination of Video-dialtone Regulations—** The Commission's regulations and policies with respect to video dialtone requirements issued in CC Docket No. 87-266 shall cease to be effective on the date of enactment of this Act. This paragraph shall not be construed to require the termination of any video-dialtone system that the Commission has approved before the date of enactment of this Act.

TITLE IV—REGULATORY REFORM
SEC. 401. REGULATORY FORBEARANCE.

Title I is amended by inserting after section 9 (47 U.S.C. 159) the following new section:

SEC. 10. COMPETITION IN PROVISION OF TELECOMMUNICATIONS SERVICE.

(a) **Regulatory Flexibility**— Notwithstanding section 332(c)(1)(A) of this Act, the Commission shall forbear from applying any regulation or any provision of this Act to a telecommunications carrier or telecommunications service, or class of telecommunications carriers or telecommunications services, in any or some of its or their geographic markets, if the Commission determines that—

(1) enforcement of such regulation or provision is not necessary to ensure that the charges, practices, classifications, or regulations by, for, or in connection with that telecommunications carrier or telecommunications service are just and reasonable and are not unjustly or unreasonably discriminatory;

(2) enforcement of such regulation or provision is not necessary for the protection of consumers; and

(3) forbearance from applying such provision or regulation is consistent with the public interest.

(b) **Competitive Effect to Be Weighed**— If the Commission determines that forbearance will promote competition among providers of telecommunications services, that determination may be the basis for a Commission finding that forbearance is in the public interest.

(e) **State Enforcement after Commission Forbearance**— A State commission may not continue to apply or enforce any provision of this Act that the Commission has determined to forbear from applying under subsection (a).

SEC. 402. BIENNIAL REVIEW OF REGULATIONS; REGULATORY RELIEF.

(a) **Biennial Review**— Title I is amended by inserting after section 10 (as added by section 401) the following new section:

SEC. 11. REGULATORY REFORM.

(a) **Biennial Review of Regulations**— In every even-numbered year (beginning with 1998), the Commission—

(1) shall review all regulations issued under this Act in effect at the time of the review that apply to the operations or activities of any provider of telecommunications service; and

(2) shall determine whether any such regulation is no longer necessary in the public interest as the result of meaningful economic competition between providers of such service.

(b) **Effect of Determination**— The Commission shall repeal or modify any regulation it determines to be no longer necessary in the public interest.

TITLE V—OBSCENITY AND VIOLENCE
SUBTITLE A—OBSCENE, HARASSING, AND WRONGFUL UTILIZATION OF TELECOMMUNICATIONS FACILITIES

SEC. 501. SHORT TITLE.

This title may be cited as the "Communications Decency Act of 1996."

SEC. 502. OBSCENE OR HARASSING USE OF TELECOMMUNICATIONS FACILITIES UNDER THE COMMUNICATIONS ACT OF 1934.

Section 223 (47 U.S.C. 223) is amended—
    (1) by striking subsection (a) and inserting in lieu thereof:
(a) Whoever—
    (1) in interstate or foreign communications—
        (A) by means of a telecommunications device knowingly—
            (i)   makes, creates, or solicits, and
            (ii)   initiates the transmission of, any comment, request, suggestion, proposal, image, or other communication which is obscene, lewd, lascivious, filthy, or indecent, with intent to annoy, abuse, threaten, or harass another person;
        (B) by means of a telecommunications device knowingly—
            (i)   makes, creates, or solicits, and
            (ii)   initiates the transmission of, any comment, request, suggestion, proposal, image, or other communication which is obscene or indecent, knowing that the recipient of the communication is under 18 years of age, regardless of whether the maker of such communication placed the call or initiated the communication;
        (C) makes a telephone call or utilizes a telecommunications device, whether or not conversation or communication ensues, without disclosing his identity and with intent to annoy, abuse, threaten, or harass any person at the called number or who receives the communications;
        (D)   makes or causes the telephone of another repeatedly or continuously to ring, with intent to harass any person at the called number; or
        (E) makes repeated telephone calls or repeatedly initiates communication with a telecommunications device, during which conversation or commu-

nication ensues, solely to harass any person at the called number or who receives the communication; or

(2) knowingly permits any telecommunications facility under his control to be used for any activity prohibited by paragraph (1) with the intent that it be used for such activity, shall be fined under title 18, United States Code, or imprisoned not more than two years, or both.; and

(2) by adding at the end the following new subsections:

(d) Whoever—

    (1) in interstate or foreign communications knowingly—

        (A) uses an interactive computer service to send to a specific person or persons under 18 years of age, or

        (B) uses any interactive computer service to display in a manner available to a person under 18 years of age, any comment, request, suggestion, proposal, image, or other communication that, in context, depicts or describes, in terms patently offensive as measured by contemporary community standards, sexual or excretory activities or organs, regardless of whether the user of such service placed the call or initiated the communication; or

    (2) knowingly permits any telecommunications facility under such person's control to be used for an activity prohibited by paragraph (1) with the intent that it be used for such activity, shall be fined under title 18, United States Code, or imprisoned not more than two years, or both.

(e) In addition to any other defenses available by law:

    (1) No person shall be held to have violated subsection (a) or (d) solely for providing access or connection to or from a facility, system, or network not under that person's control, including transmission, downloading, intermediate storage, access software, or other related capabilities that are incidental to providing such access or connection that does not include the creation of the content of the communication.

    (2) The defenses provided by paragraph (1) of this subsection shall not be applicable to a person who is a conspirator with an entity actively involved in the creation or knowing distribution of communications that violate this section, or who knowingly advertises the availability of such communications.

    (3) The defenses provided in paragraph (1) of this subsection shall not be applicable to a person who provides access or connection to a facility, system, or network engaged in the violation of this section that is owned or controlled by such person.

    (4) No employer shall be held liable under this section for the actions of an employee or agent unless the employee's or agent's conduct is within the scope of his or her employment or agency and the employer (A) having knowledge of such conduct, authorizes or ratifies such conduct, or (B) recklessly disregards such conduct.

    (5) It is a defense to a prosecution under subsection (a)(1)(B) or (d), or under subsection (a)(2) with respect to the use of a facility for an activity under subsection (a)(1)(B) that a person—

(A) has taken, in good faith, reasonable, effective, and appropriate actions under the circumstances to restrict or prevent access by minors to a communication specified in such subsections, which may involve any appropriate measures to restrict minors from such communications, including any method which is feasible under available technology; or

(B) has restricted access to such communication by requiring use of a verified credit card, debit account, adult access code, or adult personal identification number.

(6) The Commission may describe measures which are reasonable, effective, and appropriate to restrict access to prohibited communications under subsection (d). Nothing in this section authorizes the Commission to enforce, or is intended to provide the Commission with the authority to approve, sanction, or permit, the use of such measures. The Commission shall have no enforcement authority over the failure to utilize such measures. The Commission shall not endorse specific products relating to such measures. The use of such measures shall be admitted as evidence of good faith efforts for purposes of paragraph (5) in any action arising under subsection (d). Nothing in this section shall be construed to treat interactive computer services as common carriers or telecommunications carriers.

SEC. 504. SCRAMBLING OF CABLE CHANNELS FOR NONSUBSCRIBERS.

Part IV of title VI (47 U.S.C. 551 et seq.) is amended by adding at the end the following:

SEC. 640. SCRAMBLING OF CABLE CHANNELS FOR NONSUBSCRIBERS.

(a) **Subscriber Request**— Upon request by a cable service subscriber, a cable operator shall, without charge, fully scramble or otherwise fully block the audio and video programming of each channel carrying such programming so that one not a subscriber does not receive it.

SEC. 505. SCRAMBLING OF SEXUALLY EXPLICIT ADULT VIDEO SERVICE PROGRAMMING.

Part IV of title VI (47 U.S.C. 551 et seq.), as amended by this Act, is further amended by adding at the end the following:

SEC. 641. SCRAMBLING OF SEXUALLY EXPLICIT ADULT VIDEO SERVICE PROGRAMMING.

(a) **Requirement**— In providing sexually explicit adult programming or other programming that is indecent on any channel of its service primarily dedicated to sexually-oriented programming, a multichannel video programming distributor shall fully scramble or otherwise fully block the video and audio portion of such channel so that one not a subscriber to such channel or programming does not receive it.

(b) **Implementation**— Until a multichannel video programming distributor complies with the requirement set forth in subsection (a), the distributor shall limit the access of children to the programming referred to in that subsection by not providing such programming during the hours of the day (as determined by the Commission) when a significant number of children are likely to view it.

SEC. 506. CABLE OPERATOR REFUSAL TO CARRY CERTAIN PROGRAMS.

(a) **Public, Educational, and Governmental Channels**— Section 611(e) (4 7 U.S.C. 531(e)) is amended by inserting before the period the following: except a cable operator may refuse to transmit any public access program or portion of a public access program which contains obscenity, indecency, or nudity.

(b) **Cable Channels for Commercial Use**— Section 612(c)(2) (47 U.S.C. 532(c)(2)) is amended by striking "an operator" and inserting "a cable operator may refuse to transmit any leased access program or portion of a leased access program which contains obscenity, indecency, or nudity and."

SEC. 509. ONLINE FAMILY EMPOWERMENT.

Title II of the Communications Act of 1934 (47 U.S.C. 201 et seq.) is amended by adding at the end the following new section:

SEC. 230. PROTECTION FOR PRIVATE BLOCKING AND SCREENING OF OFFENSIVE MATERIAL.

(c) Protection for "Good Samaritan" Blocking and Screening of Offensive Material—

    (1) **Treatment of Publisher or Speaker**— No provider or user of an interactive computer service shall be treated as the publisher or speaker of any information provided by another information content provider.

(2) **Civil Liability**— No provider or user of an interactive computer service shall be held liable on account of—
  (A) any action voluntarily taken in good faith to restrict access to or availability of material that the provider or user considers to be obscene, lewd, lascivious, filthy, excessively violent, harassing, or otherwise objectionable, whether or not such material is constitutionally protected; or
  (B) any action taken to enable or make available to information content providers or others the technical means to restrict access to material described in paragraph (1).

SUBTITLE B—VIOLENCE
SEC. 551. PARENTAL CHOICE IN TELEVISION PROGRAMMING.

(a) **Findings**— The Congress makes the following findings:
  (1) Television influences children's perception of the values and behavior that are common and acceptable in society.
  (2) Television station operators, cable television system operators, and video programmers should follow practices in connection with video programming that take into consideration that television broadcast and cable programming has established a uniquely pervasive presence in the lives of American children.
  (3) The average American child is exposed to 25 hours of television each week and some children are exposed to as much as 11 hours of television a day.
  (4) Studies have shown that children exposed to violent video programming at a young age have a higher tendency for violent and aggressive behavior later in life than children not so exposed, and that children exposed to violent video programming are prone to assume that acts of violence are acceptable behavior.
  (5) Children in the United States are, on average, exposed to an estimated 8,000 murders and 100,000 acts of violence on television by the time the child completes elementary school.
  (6) Studies indicate that children are affected by the pervasiveness and casual treatment of sexual material on television, eroding the ability of parents to develop responsible attitudes and behavior in their children.
  (7) Parents express grave concern over violent and sexual video programming and strongly support technology that would give them greater control to block video programming in the home that they consider harmful to their children.
  (8) There is a compelling governmental interest in empowering parents to limit the negative influences of video programming that is harmful to children.

(9) Providing parents with timely information about the nature of upcoming video programming and with the technological tools that allow them easily to block violent, sexual, or other programming that they believe harmful to their children is a nonintrusive and narrowly tailored means of achieving that compelling governmental interest.

(b) **Establishment of Television Rating Code—**

(1) **Amendment—** Section 303 (47 U.S.C. 303) is amended by adding at the end the following:

(w) Prescribe—

(1)   on the basis of recommendations from an advisory committee established by the Commission in accordance with section 551(b)(2) of the Telecommunications Act of 1996, guidelines and recommended procedures for the identification and rating of video programming that contains sexual, violent, or other indecent material about which parents should be informed before it is displayed to children: Provided: That nothing in this paragraph shall be construed to authorize any rating of video programming on the basis of its political or religious content; and

(2)   with respect to any video programming that has been rated, and in consultation with the television industry, rules requiring distributors of such video programming to transmit such rating to permit parents to block the display of video programming that they have determined is inappropriate for their children.

(2) **Advisory Committee Requirements—** In establishing an advisory committee for purposes of the amendment made by paragraph (1) of this subsection, the Commission shall—

(A) ensure that such committee is composed of parents, television broadcasters, television programming producers, cable operators, appropriate public interest groups, and other interested individuals from the private sector and is fairly balanced in terms of political affiliation, the points of view represented, and the functions to be performed by the committee.

(c) **Requirement for Manufacture of Televisions That Block Programs—** Section 303 (47 U.S.C. 303), as amended by subsection (a), is further amended by adding at the end the following:

(x) Require, in the case of an apparatus designed to receive television signals that are shipped in interstate commerce or manufactured in the United States and that have a picture screen 13 inches or greater in size (measured diagonally), that such apparatus be equipped with a feature designed to enable viewers to block display of all programs with a common rating, except as otherwise permitted by regulations pursuant to section 330(c)(4).

(e) **Applicability and Effective Dates—**

(1) **Applicability of Rating Provision—** The amendment made by subsection (b) of this section shall take effect 1 year after the date of enactment of this Act, but only if the Commission determines, in consultation with appropriate public interest groups and interested individuals from the private sector, that distributors of video programming have not, by such date—

(A) established voluntary rules for rating video programming that contains sexual, violent, or other indecent material about which parents should be informed before it is displayed to children, and such rules are acceptable to the Commission; and

(B) agreed voluntarily to broadcast signals that contain ratings of such programming.

TITLE VI—EFFECT ON OTHER LAWS
SEC. 601. APPLICABILITY OF CONSENT DECREES AND OTHER LAW.

(a) **Applicability of Amendments to Future Conduct—**

(1) **AT&T Consent Decree—** Any conduct or activity that was, before the date of enactment of this Act, subject to any restriction or obligation imposed by the AT&T Consent Decree shall, on and after such date, be subject to the restrictions and obligations imposed by the Communications Act of 1934 as amended by this Act and shall not be subject to the restrictions and the obligations imposed by such Consent Decree.

TITLE VII—MISCELLANEOUS PROVISIONS
SEC. 703. POLE ATTACHMENTS.

Section 224 (47 U.S.C. 224) is amended—

(1) in subsection (a)(1), by striking the first sentence and inserting the following: "The term "utility" means any person who is a local exchange carrier or an electric, gas, water, steam, or other public utility, and who owns or controls poles, ducts, conduits, or rights-of-way used, in whole or in part, for any wire communications.";

(7) by adding at the end thereof the following:

(e)(1) The Commission shall, no later than 2 years after the date of enactment of the Telecommunications Act of 1996, prescribe regulations in accordance with this subsection to govern the charges for pole attachments used by telecommunications carriers to provide telecommunications services, when the parties fail to resolve a dispute over such charges. Such regulations shall ensure that a utility charges just, reasonable, and nondiscriminatory rates for pole attachments.

(f)(1) A utility shall provide a cable television system or any telecommunications carrier with nondiscriminatory access to any pole, duct, conduit, or right-of-way owned or controlled by it.

(2) Notwithstanding paragraph (1), a utility providing electric service may deny a cable television system or any telecommunications carrier access to its poles, ducts, conduits, or rights-of-way, on a non-discriminatory basis where there is insufficient capacity and for reasons of safety, reliability and generally applicable engineering purposes.

APPENDIX B

U.S. SUPREME COURT
SYLLABUS

RENO, ATTORNEY GENERAL OF THE UNITED STATES, et al. v. AMERICAN CIVIL LIBERTIES UNION et al.

Appeal from the United States District Court for the Eastern District of Pennsylvania

No. 96-511.
Argued March 19, 1997
Decided June 26, 1997

Two provisions of the Communications Decency Act of 1996 (CDA or Act) seek to protect minors from harmful material on the Internet, an international network of inter-connected computers that enables millions of people to communicate with one another in "cyberspace" and to access vast amounts of information from around the world. Title 47 U.S.C.A. §223(a)(1)(B)(ii) (Supp. 1997) criminalizes the "knowing" transmission of "obscene or indecent" messages to any recipient under 18 years of age. Section 223(d) prohibits the "knowin[g]" sending or displaying to a person under 18 of any message "that, in context, depicts or describes, in terms patently offensive as measured by contemporary community standards, sexual or excretory activities or organs." Affirmative defenses are provided for those who take "good faith, . . . effective . . . actions" to restrict access by minors to the prohibited communications, §223(e)(5)(A), and those who restrict such access by requiring certain designated forms of age proof,

NOTE: *Where it is feasible, a syllabus (headnote) will be released, as is being done in connection with this case, at the time the opinion is issued. The syllabus constitutes no part of the opinion of the Court but has been prepared by the Reporter of Decisions for the convenience of the reader. See United States v. Detroit Timber & Lumber Co., 200 U.S. 321, 337.*

such as a verified credit card or an adult identification number, §223(e)(5)(B). A number of plaintiffs filed suit challenging the constitutionality of §§223(a)(1) and 223(d). After making extensive findings of fact, a three judge District Court convened pursuant to the Act entered a preliminary injunction against enforcement of both challenged provisions. The court's judgment enjoins the Government from enforcing §223(a)(1)(B)'s prohibitions insofar as they relate to "indecent" communications, but expressly preserves the Government's right to investigate and prosecute the obscenity or child pornography activities prohibited therein. The injunction against enforcement of §223(d) is unqualified because that section contains no separate reference to obscenity or child pornography. The Government appealed to this Court under the Act's special review provisions, arguing that the District Court erred in holding that the CDA violated both the First Amendment because it is overbroad and the Fifth Amendment because it is vague.

Held: The CDA's "indecent transmission" and "patently offensive display" provisions abridge "the freedom of speech" protected by the First Amendment. Pp. 17–40.

(a) Although the CDA's vagueness is relevant to the First Amendment overbreadth inquiry, the judgment should be affirmed without reaching the Fifth Amendment issue. P. 17.

(b) A close look at the precedents relied on by the Government—Ginsberg v. New York, 390 U.S. 629; FCC v. Pacifica Foundation, 438 U.S. 726; and Renton v. Playtime Theatres, Inc., 475 U.S. 41—raises, rather than relieves, doubts about the CDA's constitutionality. The CDA differs from the various laws and orders upheld in those cases in many ways, including that it does not allow parents to consent to their children's use of restricted materials; is not limited to commercial transactions; fails to provide any definition of "indecent" and omits any requirement that "patently offensive" material lack socially redeeming value; neither limits its broad categorical prohibitions to particular times nor bases them on an evaluation by an agency familiar with the medium's unique characteristics; is punitive; applies to a medium that, unlike radio, receives full First Amendment protection; and cannot be properly analyzed as a form of time, place, and manner regulation because it is a content based blanket restriction on speech. These precedents, then, do not require the Court to uphold the CDA and are fully consistent with the application of the most stringent review of its provisions. Pp. 17–21.

(c) The special factors recognized in some of the Court's cases as justifying regulation of the broadcast media—the history of extensive government regulation of broadcasting, see, e.g., Red Lion Broadcasting Co. v. FCC, 395 U.S. 367, 399-400; the scarcity of available frequencies at its inception, see, e.g., Turner Broadcasting System, Inc. v. FCC, 512 U.S. 622, 637-638; and its "invasive" nature, see Sable Communications of Cal., Inc. v. FCC, 492 U.S. 115, 128—are not present in cyberspace. Thus, these cases provide no basis for qualifying the level of First Amendment scrutiny that should be applied to the Internet. Pp. 22–24.

(d) Regardless of whether the CDA is so vague that it violates the Fifth Amendment, the many ambiguities concerning the scope of its coverage render it problematic for First Amendment purposes. For instance, its use of the undefined terms "indecent" and "patently offensive" will provoke uncertainty among speakers about how the two standards relate to each other and just what they mean. The vagueness of such a content based regulation, see, e.g., Gentile v. State Bar of Nev., 501 U.S. 1030, coupled with its increased deterrent effect as a criminal statute, see, e.g., Dombrowski v. Pfister, 380 U.S. 479, raise special First Amendment concerns because of its obvious chilling effect on free speech. Contrary to the Government's argument, the CDA is not saved from vagueness by the fact that its "patently offensive" standard repeats the second part of the three prong obscenity test set forth in Miller v. California, 413 U.S. 15, 24. The second Miller prong reduces the inherent vagueness of its own "patently offensive" term by requiring that the proscribed material be "specifically defined by the applicable state law." In addition, the CDA applies only to "sexual conduct," whereas, the CDA prohibition extends also to "excretory activities" and "organs" of both a sexual and excretory nature. Each of Miller's other two prongs also critically limits the uncertain sweep of the obscenity definition. Just because a definition including three limitations is not vague, it does not follow that one of those limitations, standing alone, is not vague. The CDA's vagueness undermines the likelihood that it has been carefully tailored to the congressional goal of protecting minors from potentially harmful materials. Pp. 24–28.

(e) The CDA lacks the precision that the First Amendment requires when a statute regulates the content of speech. Although the Government has an interest in protecting children from potentially harmful materials, see, e.g., Ginsberg, 390 U.S., at 639, the CDA pursues that interest by suppressing a large amount of speech that adults have a constitutional right to send and receive, see, e.g., Sable, supra, at 126. Its breadth is wholly unprecedented. The CDA's burden on adult speech is unacceptable if less restrictive alternatives would be at least as effective in achieving the Act's legitimate purposes. See, e.g., Sable, 492 U.S., at 126. The Government has not proved otherwise. On the other hand, the District Court found that currently available user based software suggests that a reasonably effective method by which parents can prevent their children from accessing material which the parents believe is inappropriate will soon be widely available. Moreover, the arguments in this Court referred to possible alternatives such as requiring that indecent material be "tagged" to facilitate parental control, making exceptions for messages with artistic or educational value, providing some tolerance for parental choice, and regulating some portions of the Internet differently than others. Particularly in the light of the absence of any detailed congressional findings, or even hearings addressing the CDA's special problems, the Court is persuaded that the CDA is not narrowly tailored. Pp. 28–33.

(f) The Government's three additional arguments for sustaining the CDA's affirmative prohibitions are rejected. First, the contention that the Act is constitutional because it leaves open ample "alternative channels" of communication is unpersuasive because the CDA regulates speech on the basis of its content, so that a "time, place, and manner" analysis is inapplicable. See, e.g., Consolidated Edison Co. of N. Y. v. Public Serv. Comm'n of N. Y., 447 U.S. 530, 536. Second, the assertion that the CDA's "knowledge" and "specific person" requirements significantly restrict its permissible application to communications to persons the sender knows to be under 18 is untenable, given that most Internet forums are open to all comers and that even the strongest reading of the "specific person" requirement would confer broad powers of censorship, in the form of a "heckler's veto," upon any opponent of indecent speech. Finally, there is no textual support for the submission that material having scientific, educational, or other redeeming social value will necessarily fall outside the CDA's prohibitions. Pp. 33–35.

(g) The §223(e)(5) defenses do not constitute the sort of "narrow tailoring" that   would save the CDA. The Government's argument that transmitters may take protective "good faith actio[n]" by "tagging" their indecent communications in a way that would indicate their contents, thus permitting recipients to block their reception with appropriate software, is illusory, given the requirement that such action be "effective": The proposed screening software does not currently exist, but, even if it did, there would be no way of knowing whether a potential recipient would actually block the encoded material. The Government also failed to prove that §223(b)(5)'s verification defense would significantly reduce the CDA's heavy burden on adult speech. Although such verification is actually being used by some commercial providers of sexually explicit material, the District Court's findings indicate that it is not economically feasible for most noncommercial speakers. Pp. 35–37.

(h) The Government's argument that this Court should preserve the CDA's constitutionality by honoring its severability clause, §608, and by construing nonseverable terms narrowly, is acceptable in only one respect. Because obscene speech may be banned totally, see Miller, supra, at 18, and §223(a)'s restriction of "obscene" material enjoys a textual manifestation separate from that for "indecent" material, the Court can sever the term "or indecent" from the statute, leaving the rest of §223(a) standing. Pp. 37–39.

(i) The Government's argument that its "significant" interest in fostering the Internet's growth provides an independent basis for upholding the CDA's constitutionality is singularly unpersuasive. The dramatic expansion of this new forum contradicts the factual basis underlying this contention: that the unregulated availability of "indecent" and "patently offensive" material is driving people away from the Internet. P. 40.

929 F. Supp. 824, affirmed.

Stevens, J., delivered the opinion of the Court, in which Scalia, Kennedy, Souter, Thomas, Ginsburg, and Breyer, JJ., joined. O'Connor, J., filed an opinion concurring in the judgment in part and dissenting in part, in which Rehnquist, C. J., joined.

JANET RENO, ATTORNEY GENERAL OF THE UNITED STATES, et al., APPELLANTS v. AMERICAN CIVIL LIBERTIES UNION et al.

On Appeal from the United States District Court for the Eastern District of Pennsylvania

No. 96-511
[June 26, 1997]

Justice Stevens delivered the opinion of the Court.

At issue is the constitutionality of two statutory provisions enacted to protect minors from "indecent" and "patently offensive" communications on the Internet. Notwithstanding the legitimacy and importance of the congressional goal of protecting children from harmful materials, we agree with the three judge District Court that the statute abridges "the freedom of speech" protected by the First Amendment.[1]

The District Court made extensive findings of fact, most of which were based on a detailed stipulation prepared by the parties. See 929 F. Supp. 824, 830–849 (ED Pa. 1996).[2] The findings describe the character and the dimensions of the Internet, the availability sexually explicit material in that medium, and the problems confronting age verification for recipients of Internet communications. Because those findings provide the underpinnings for the legal issues, we begin with a summary of the undisputed facts.

THE INTERNET

The Internet is an international network of interconnected computers. It is the outgrowth of what began in 1969 as a military program called "ARPANET," [3] which was designed to enable computers operated by the military, defense contractors, and universities conducting defense related research to communicate with one another by redundant channels even if some portions of the network were damaged in a war. While the ARPANET no longer exists, it provided an example for the development of a number of civilian networks that, eventually linking with each other, now enable tens of millions of people to communicate with one another and to access vast amounts of information from around the world. The Internet is "a unique and wholly new medium of worldwide human communication."[4]

The Internet has experienced "extraordinary growth."[5] The number of "host" computers—those that store information and relay communications—increased from about 300 in 1981 to approximately 9,400,000 by the time of the trial in 1996. Roughly 60% of these hosts are located in the United States. About 40 million people used the Internet at the time of trial, a number that is expected to mushroom to 200 million by 1999.

Individuals can obtain access to the Internet from many different sources, generally hosts themselves or entities with a host affiliation. Most colleges and universities provide access for their students and faculty; many corporations provide their employees with access through an office network; many communities and local libraries provide free access; and an increasing number of storefront "computer coffee shops" provide access for a small hourly fee. Several major national "online services" such as America Online, CompuServe, the Microsoft Network, and Prodigy offer access to their own extensive proprietary networks as well as a link to the much larger resources of the Internet. These commercial online services had almost 12 million individual subscribers at the time of trial.

Anyone with access to the Internet may take advantage of a wide variety of communication and information retrieval methods. These methods are constantly evolving and difficult to categorize precisely. But, as presently constituted, those most relevant to this case are electronic mail ("e mail"), automatic mailing list services ("mail exploders," sometimes referred to as "listservs"), "newsgroups," "chat rooms," and the "World Wide Web." All of these methods can be used to transmit text; most can transmit sound, pictures, and moving video images. Taken together, these tools constitute a unique medium—known to its users as "cyberspace"—located in no particular geographical location but available to anyone, anywhere in the world, with access to the Internet.

E mail enables an individual to send an electronic message—generally akin to a note or letter—to another individual or to a group of addressees. The message is generally stored electronically, sometimes waiting for the recipient to check her "mailbox" and sometimes making its receipt known through some type of prompt. A mail exploder is a sort of e mail group. Subscribers can send messages to a common e mail address, which then forwards the message to the group's other subscribers. Newsgroups also serve groups of regular participants, but these postings may be read by others as well. There are thousands of such groups, each serving to foster an exchange of information or opinion on a particular topic running the gamut from, say, the music of Wagner to Balkan politics to AIDS prevention to the Chicago Bulls. About 100,000 new messages are posted every day. In most newsgroups, postings are automatically purged at regular intervals. In addition to posting a message that can be read later, two or more individuals wishing to communicate more immediately can enter a chat room to engage in real time dialogue—in other words, by typing messages to one another that appear almost immediately on the others' computer screens. The District Court found that at any given time "tens of thousands of users are engaging in conversations on a huge range of subjects."[6] It is "no exaggeration to conclude that the content on the Internet is as diverse as human thought."[7]

The best known category of communication over the Internet is the World Wide Web, which allows users to search for and retrieve information stored in remote computers, as well as, in some cases, to communicate back to designated sites. In concrete terms, the Web consists of a vast number of documents stored in different computers all over the world. Some of these documents are simply files containing information. However, more elaborate documents, commonly known as Web "pages," are also prevalent. Each has its own address—rather like a telephone number."[8] Web pages frequently contain information and sometimes allow the viewer to communicate with the page's (or "site's") author. They generally also contain "links" to other documents created by that site's author or to other (generally) related sites. Typically, the links are either blue or underlined text—sometimes images.

Navigating the Web is relatively straightforward. A user may either type the address of a known page or enter one or more keywords into a commercial "search engine" in an effort to locate sites on a subject of interest. A particular Web page may contain the information sought by the "surfer," or, through its links, it may be an avenue to other documents located anywhere on the Internet. Users generally explore a given Web page, or move to another, by clicking a computer "mouse" on one of the page's icons or links. Access to most Web pages is freely available, but some allow access only to those who have purchased the right from a commercial provider. The Web is thus comparable, from the readers' viewpoint, to both a vast library including millions of readily available and indexed publications and a sprawling mall offering goods and services.

From the publishers' point of view, it constitutes a vast platform from which to address and hear from a world wide audience of millions of readers, viewers, researchers, and buyers. Any person or organization with a computer connected to the Internet can "publish" information. Publishers include government agencies, educational institutions, commercial entities, advocacy groups, and individuals.[9] Publishers may either make their material available to the entire pool of Internet users, or confine access to a selected group, such as those willing to pay for the privilege. "No single organization controls any membership in the Web, nor is there any centralized point from which individual Web sites or services can be blocked from the Web."[10]

SEXUALLY EXPLICIT MATERIAL

Sexually explicit material on the Internet includes text, pictures, and chat and "extends from the modestly titillating to the hardest core."[11] These files are created, named, and posted in the same manner as material that is not sexually explicit, and may be accessed either deliberately or unintentionally during the course of an imprecise search. "Once a provider posts its content on the Internet, it cannot prevent that content from entering any community."[12] Thus, for example,

> "when the UCR/California Museum of Photography posts to its Web site nudes by Edward Weston and Robert Mapplethorpe to announce that its new exhibit will travel to Baltimore and New York City, those images are available not only in Los Angeles, Baltimore, and New York City, but also in Cincinnati, Mobile, or Beijing—wherever Internet users live. Similarly, the safer sex instructions that Critical Path posts to its Web site, written in street language so that the teenage receiver can understand them, are available not just in Philadelphia, but also in Provo and Prague."[13]

Some of the communications over the Internet that originate in foreign countries are also sexually explicit.[14]

Though such material is widely available, users seldom encounter such content accidentally. "A document's title or a description of the document will usually appear before the document itself . . . and in many cases the user will receive detailed information about a site's content before he or she need take the step to access the document. Almost all sexually explicit images are preceded by warnings as to the content."[15] For that reason, the "odds are slim" that a user would enter a sexually explicit site by accident.[16] Unlike communications received by radio or television, "the receipt of information on the Internet requires a series of affirmative steps more deliberate and directed than merely turning a dial. A child requires some sophistication and some ability to read to retrieve material and thereby to use the Internet unattended."[17]

Systems have been developed to help parents control the material that may be available on a home computer with Internet access. A system may either limit a computer's access to an approved list of sources that have been identified as containing no adult material, it may block designated inappropriate sites, or it may attempt to block messages containing identifiable objectionable features. "Although parental control software currently can screen for certain suggestive words or for known sexually explicit sites, it cannot now screen for sexually explicit images."[18] Nevertheless, the evidence indicates that "a reasonably effective method by which parents can prevent their children from accessing sexually explicit and other material which parents may believe is inappropriate for their children will soon be available."[19]

AGE VERIFICATION

The problem of age verification differs for different uses of the Internet. The District Court categorically determined that there "is no effective way to determine the identity or the age of a user who is accessing material through e mail, mail exploders, newsgroups or chat rooms."[20] The Government offered no evidence that there was a reliable way to screen recipients and participants in such fora for age. Moreover, even if it were technologically feasible to block minors' access to newsgroups and chat rooms containing discussions of art, politics or other subjects that potentially elicit "indecent" or "patently offensive" contributions, it would not be possible to block their access to that material and "still allow them access to the remaining content, even if the overwhelming majority of that content was not indecent."[21]

Technology exists by which an operator of a Web site may condition access on the verification of requested information such as a credit card number or an adult password. Credit card verification is only feasible, however, either in connection with a commercial transaction in which the card is used, or by payment to verification agency. Using credit card possession as a surrogate for proof of age would impose costs on non commercial Web sites that would require many of them to shut down. For that reason, at the time of the trial, credit card verification was "effectively unavailable to a substantial number of Internet content providers." Id., at 846 (finding 102). Moreover, the imposition of such a requirement "would completely bar adults who do not have a credit card and lack the resources to obtain one from accessing any blocked material."[22]

Commercial pornographic sites that charge their users for access have assigned them passwords as a method of age verification. The record does not contain any evidence concerning the reliability of these technologies. Even if passwords are effective for commercial purveyors of indecent material, the District Court found that an adult password requirement would impose significant burdens on noncommercial sites, both because they would discourage users from accessing their sites and because the cost of creating and maintaining such screening systems would be "beyond their reach."[23]

In sum, the District Court found:

"Even if credit card verification or adult password verification were implemented, the Government presented no testimony as to how such systems could ensure that the user of the password or credit card is in fact over 18. The burdens imposed by credit card verification and adult password verification systems make them effectively unavailable to a substantial number of Internet content providers." Ibid. (finding 107).

The Telecommunications Act of 1996, Pub. L. 104-104, 110 Stat. 56, was an unusually important legislative enactment. As stated on the first of its 103 pages, its primary purpose was to reduce regulation and encourage "the rapid deployment of new telecommunications technologies." The major components of the statute have nothing to do with the Internet; they were designed to promote competition in the local telephone service market, the multichannel video market, and the market for over the air broadcasting. The Act includes seven Titles, six of which are the product of extensive committee hearings and the subject of discussion in Reports prepared by Committees of the Senate and the House of Representatives. By contrast, Title V—known as the "Communications Decency Act of 1996" (CDA)—contains provisions that were either added in executive committee after the hearings were concluded or as amendments offered during floor debate on the legislation. An amendment offered in the Senate was the source of the two statutory provisions challenged in this case.[24] They are informally described as the "indecent transmission" provision and the "patently offensive display" provision.[25]

The first, 47 U.S.C.A. §223(a) (Supp. 1997), prohibits the knowing transmission of obscene or indecent messages to any recipient under 18 years of age. It provides in pertinent part:

"(a) Whoever—
    "(1) in interstate or foreign communications—
       . . . . .
      "(B) by means of a telecommunications device knowingly—
        "(i)   makes, creates, or solicits, and
        "(ii) initiates the transmission of any comment, request, suggestion, proposal, image, or other communication which is obscene or indecent, knowing that the recipient of the communication is under 18 years of age, regardless of whether the maker of such communication placed the call or initiated the communication;
       . . . . .
    "(2) knowingly permits any telecommunications facility under his control to be used for any activity prohibited by paragraph (1) with the intent that it be used for such activity shall be fined under Title 18, or imprisoned not more than two years, or both."

The second provision, §223(d), prohibits the knowing sending or displaying of patently offensive messages in a manner that is available to a person under 18 years of age. It provides:

"(d) Whoever—
　"(1) in interstate or foreign communications knowingly—
　　"(A) uses an interactive computer service to send to a specific person or persons under 18 years of age, or
　　"(B) uses any interactive computer service to display in a manner available to a person under 18 years of age any comment, request, suggestion, proposal, image, or other communication that, in context, depicts or describes, in terms patently offensive measured by contemporary community standards, sexual or excretory activities or organs, regardless of whether the user of such service placed the call or initiated the communication; or
　"(2) knowingly permits any telecommunications facility under such person's control to be used for an activity prohibited by paragraph (1) with the intent that it be used for such activity shall be fined under Title 18, or imprisoned not more than two years, or both."

The breadth of these prohibitions is qualified by two affirmative defenses. See §223(e)(5).[26] One covers those who take "good faith, reasonable, effective, and appropriate actions" to restrict access by minors to the prohibited communications. §223(e)(5)(A). The other covers those who restrict access to covered material by requiring certain designated forms of age proof, such as a verified credit card or an adult identification number or code. §223(e)(5)(B).

On February 8, 1996, immediately after the President signed the statute, 20 plaintiffs[27] filed suit against the Attorney General of the United States and the Department of Justice challenging the constitutionality of §§223(a)(1) and 223(d). A week later, based on his conclusion that the term "indecent" was too vague to provide the basis for a criminal prosecution, District Judge Buckwalter entered a temporary restraining order against enforcement of §223(a)(1)(B)(ii) insofar as it applies to indecent communications. A second suit was then filed by 27 additional plaintiffs,[28] the two cases were consolidated, and a three judge District Court was convened pursuant to §561 of the Act.[29] After an evidentiary hearing, that Court entered a preliminary injunction against enforcement of both of the challenged provisions. Each of the three judges wrote a separate opinion, but their judgment was unanimous.

Chief Judge Sloviter doubted the strength of the Government's interest in regulating "the vast range of online material covered or potentially covered by the CDA," but acknowledged that the interest was "compelling" with respect to some of that material. 929 F. Supp., at 853. She concluded, nonetheless, that the statute "sweeps more broadly than necessary and thereby chills the expression of adults" and that the terms "patently offensive" and "indecent" were "inherently vague." Id., at 854. She also determined that the affirmative defenses were not "technologically or economically feasible for most providers," specifically considering and rejecting an argument that providers could avoid liability by "tagging" their material in a manner that would allow potential readers to screen out unwanted transmissions. Id., at 856. Chief Judge Sloviter also rejected the Government's suggestion that the scope of the statute could be narrowed by construing it to apply only to commercial pornographers. Id., at 854–855.

Judge Buckwalter concluded that the word "indecent" in §223(a)(1)(B) and the terms "patently offensive" and "in context" in §223(d)(1) were so vague that criminal enforcement of either section would violate the "fundamental constitutional principle" of "simple fairness," id., at 861, and the specific protections of the First and Fifth Amendments, id., at 858. He found no statutory basis for the Government's argument that the challenged provisions would be applied only to "pornographic" materials, noting that, unlike obscenity, "indecency has not been defined to exclude works of serious literary, artistic, political or scientific value." Id., at 863. Moreover, the Government's claim that the work must be considered patently offensive "in context" was itself vague because the relevant context might "refer to, among other things, the nature of the communication as a whole, the time of day it was conveyed, the medium used, the identity of the speaker, or whether or not it is accompanied by appropriate warnings." Id., at 864. He believed that the unique nature of the Internet aggravated the vagueness of the statute. Id., at 865, n. 9.

Judge Dalzell's review of "the special attributes of Internet communication" disclosed by the evidence convinced him that the First Amendment denies Congress the power to regulate the content of protected speech on the Internet. Id., at 867. His opinion explained at length why he believed the Act would abridge significant protected speech, particularly by noncommercial speakers, while "[p]erversely, commercial pornographers would remain relatively unaffected." Id., at 879. He construed our cases as requiring a "medium specific" approach to the analysis of the regulation of mass communication, id., at 873, and concluded that the Internet—as "the most participatory form of mass speech yet developed," id., at 883—is entitled to "the highest protection from governmental intrusion," ibid.[30]

The judgment of the District Court enjoins the Government from enforcing the prohibitions in §223(a)(1)(B) insofar as they relate to "indecent" communications, but expressly preserves the Government's right to investigate and prosecute the obscenity or child pornography activities prohibited therein. The injunction against enforcement of §§223(d)(1) and (2) is unqualified because those provisions contain no separate reference to obscenity or child pornography.

The Government appealed under the Act's special review provisions, §561, 110 Stat. 142–143, and we noted probable jurisdiction, see 519 U.S. _____ (1996). In its appeal, the Government argues that the District Court erred in holding that the CDA violated both the First Amendment because it is overbroad and the Fifth Amendment because it is vague. While we discuss the vagueness of the CDA because of its relevance to the First Amendment overbreadth inquiry, we conclude that the judgment should be affirmed without reaching the Fifth Amendment issue. We begin our analysis by reviewing the principal authorities on which the Government relies. Then, after describing the overbreadth of the CDA, we consider the Government's specific contentions, including its submission that we save portions of the statute either by sever-ance or by fashioning judicial limitations on the scope of its coverage.

In arguing for reversal, the Government contends that the CDA is plainly con-stitutional under three four prior decisions: (1) Ginsberg v. New York, 390 U.S. 629 (1968); (2) FCC v. Pacifica Foundation, 438 U.S. 726 (1978); and (3) Renton v. Playtime Theatres, Inc., 475 U.S. 41 (1986). A close look at these cases, however, raises—rather than relieves—doubts concerning the constitutionality of the CDA.

In Ginsberg, we upheld the constitutionality of a New York statute that prohib-ited selling to minors under 17 years of age material that was considered obscene as to them even if not obscene as to adults. We rejected the defendant's broad submis-sion that "the scope of the constitutional freedom of expression secured to a citizen to read or see material concerned with sex cannot be made to depend on whether the citizen is an adult or a minor." 390 U.S., at 636. In rejecting that contention, we relied not only on the State's independent interest in the well being of its youth, but also on our consistent recognition of the principle that "the parents' claim to author-ity in their own household to direct the rearing of their children is basic in the struc-ture of our society."[31] In four important respects, the statute upheld in Ginsberg was narrower than the CDA. First, we noted in Ginsberg that "the prohibition against sales to minors does not bar parents who so desire from purchasing the magazines for their children." Id., at 639. Under the CDA, by contrast, neither the parents' con-sent—nor even their participation—in the communication would avoid the applica-tion of the statute.[32] Second, the New York statute applied only to commercial trans-actions, id., at 647, whereas the CDA contains no such limitation. Third, the New York statute cabined its definition of material that is harmful to minors with the requirement that it be "utterly without redeeming social importance for minors." Id., at 646. The CDA fails to provide us with any definition of the term "indecent" as used in §223(a)(1) and, importantly, omits any requirement that the "patently offen-sive" material covered by §223(d) lack serious literary, artistic, political, or scien-tific value. Fourth, the New York statute defined a minor as a person under the age of 17, whereas the CDA, in applying to all those under 18 years, includes an additional year of those nearest majority.

In Pacifica, we upheld a declaratory order of the Federal Communications Commission, holding that the broadcast of a recording of a 12-minute monologue entitled "Filthy Words" that had previously been delivered to a live audience "could have been the subject of administrative sanctions." 438 U.S., at 730 (internal quota-tions omitted). The Commission had found that the repetitive use of certain words referring to excretory or sexual activities or organs "in an afternoon broadcast when children are in the audience was patently offensive" and concluded that the mono-logue was indecent "as broadcast." Id., at 735. The respondent did not quarrel with the finding that the afternoon broadcast was patently offensive, but contended that it was not "indecent" within the meaning of the relevant statutes because it contained no prurient appeal. After rejecting respondent's statutory arguments, we confronted its two constitutional arguments: (1) that the Commission's construction of its authority to ban indecent speech was so broad that its order had to be set aside even if the broadcast at issue was unprotected; and (2) that since the recording was not obscene, the First Amendment forbade any abridgement of the right to broadcast it on the radio.

In the portion of the lead opinion not joined by Justices Powell and Blackmun, the plurality stated that the First Amendment does not prohibit all governmental regulation that depends on the content of speech. Id., at 742–743. Accordingly, the availability of constitutional protection for a vulgar and offensive monologue that was not obscene depended on the context of the broadcast. Id., at 744–748. Relying on the premise that "of all forms of communication" broadcasting had received the most limited First Amendment protection, id., at 748–749, the Court concluded that the ease with which children may obtain access to broadcasts, "coupled with the concerns recognized in Ginsberg," justified special treatment of indecent broadcasting. Id., at 749–750.

As with the New York statute at issue in Ginsberg, there are significant differences between the order upheld in Pacifica and the CDA. First, the order in Pacifica, issued by an agency that had been regulating radio stations for decades, targeted a specific broadcast that represented a rather dramatic departure from traditional program content in order to designate when—rather than whether—it would be permissible to air such a program in that particular medium. The CDA's broad categorical prohibitions are not limited to particular times and are not dependent on any evaluation by an agency familiar with the unique characteristics of the Internet. Second, unlike the CDA, the Commission's declaratory order was not punitive; we expressly refused to decide whether the indecent broadcast "would justify a criminal prosecution." Id., at 750. Finally, the Commission's order applied to a medium which as a matter of history had "received the most limited First Amendment protection," id., at 748, in large part because warnings could not adequately protect the listener from unexpected program content. The Internet, however, has no comparable history. Moreover, the District Court found that the risk of encountering indecent material by accident is remote because a series of affirmative steps is required to access specific material.

In Renton, we upheld a zoning ordinance that kept adult movie theatres out of residential neighborhoods. The ordinance was aimed, not at the content of the films shown in the theaters, but rather at the "secondary effects"—such as crime and deteriorating property values—that these theaters fostered: " 'It is th[e] secondary effect which these zoning ordinances attempt to avoid, not the dissemination of "offensive" speech.' " 475 U.S., at 49 (quoting Young v. American Mini Theatres, Inc., 427 U.S. 50, 71, n. 34 (1976)). According to the Government, the CDA is constitutional because it constitutes a sort of "cyberzoning" on the Internet. But the CDA applies broadly to the entire universe of cyberspace. And the purpose of the CDA is to protect children from the primary effects of "indecent" and "patently offensive" speech, rather than any "secondary" effect of such speech. Thus, the CDA is a content based blanket restriction on speech, and, as such, cannot be "properly analyzed as a form of time, place, and manner regulation." 475 U.S., at 46. See also Boos v. Barry, 485 U.S. 312, 321 (1988) ("Regulations that focus on the direct impact of speech on its audience" are not properly analyzed under Renton); Forsyth County v. Nationalist Movement, 505 U.S. 123, 134 (1992) ("Listeners' reaction to speech is not a content neutral basis for regulation").

These precedents, then, surely do not require us to uphold the CDA and are fully consistent with the application of the most stringent review of its provisions.

In Southeastern Promotions, Ltd. v. Conrad, 420 U.S. 546, 557 (1975), we observed that "[e]ach medium of expression . . . may present its own problems." Thus, some of our cases have recognized special justifications for regulation of the broadcast media that are not applicable to other speakers, see Red Lion Broadcasting Co. v. FCC, 395 U.S. 367 (1969); FCC v. Pacifica Foundation, 438 U.S. 726 (1978). In these cases, the Court relied on the history of extensive government regulation of the broadcast medium, see, e.g., Red Lion, 395 U.S., at 399-400; the scarcity of available frequencies at its inception, see, e.g., Turner Broadcasting System, Inc. v. FCC, 512 U.S. 622, 637-638 (1994); and its "invasive" nature, see Sable Communications of Cal., Inc. v. FCC, 492 U.S. 115, 128 (1989).

Those factors are not present in cyberspace. Neither before nor after the enactment of the CDA have the vast democratic fora of the Internet been subject to the type of government supervision and regulation that has attended the broadcast industry.[33] Moreover, the Internet is not as "invasive" as radio or television. The District Court specifically found that "[c]ommunications over the Internet do not 'invade' an individual's home or appear on one's computer screen unbidden. Users seldom encounter content 'by accident.' " 929 F. Supp., at 844 (finding 88). It also found that "[a]lmost all sexually explicit images are preceded by warnings as to the content," and cited testimony that " 'odds are slim' that a user would come across a sexually explicit sight by accident." Ibid.

We distinguished Pacifica in Sable, 492 U.S., at 128, on just this basis. In Sable, a company engaged in the business of offering sexually oriented prerecorded telephone messages (popularly known as "dial a porn") challenged the constitutionality of an amendment to the Communications Act that imposed a blanket prohibition on indecent as well as obscene interstate commercial telephone messages. We held that the statute was constitutional insofar as it applied to obscene messages but invalid as applied to indecent messages. In attempting to justify the complete ban and criminalization of indecent commercial telephone messages, the Government relied on Pacifica, arguing that the ban was necessary to prevent children from gaining access to such messages. We agreed that "there is a compelling interest in protecting the physical and psychological well being of minors" which extended to shielding them from indecent messages that are not obscene by adult standards, 492 U.S., at 126, but distinguished our "emphatically narrow holding" in Pacifica because it did not involve a complete ban and because it involved a different medium of communication, id., at 127. We explained that "the dial it medium requires the listener to take affirmative steps to receive the communication." Id., at 127–128.

"Placing a telephone call," we continued, "is not the same as turning on a radio and being taken by surprise by an indecent message." Id., at 128.

Finally, unlike the conditions that prevailed when Congress first authorized regulation of the broadcast spectrum, the Internet can hardly be considered a "scarce" expressive commodity. It provides relatively unlimited, low cost capacity for communication of all kinds. The Government estimates that "[a]s many as 40 million people use the Internet today, and that figure is expected to grow to 200 million by 1999."[34] This dynamic, multifaceted category of communication includes not only traditional print and news services, but also audio, video, and still images, as well as interactive, real time dialogue. Through the use of chat rooms, any person with a phone line can become a town crier with a voice that resonates farther than it could from any soapbox. Through the use of Web pages, mail exploders, and newsgroups, the same individual can become a pamphleteer. As the District Court found, "the content on the Internet is as diverse as human thought." 929 F. Supp., at 842 (finding 74). We agree with its conclusion that our cases provide no basis for qualifying the level of First Amendment scrutiny that should be applied to this medium.

Regardless of whether the CDA is so vague that it violates the Fifth Amendment, the many ambiguities concerning the scope of its coverage render it problematic for purposes of the First Amendment. For instance, each of the two parts of the CDA uses a different linguistic form. The first uses the word "indecent," 47 U.S.C.A. §223(a) (Supp. 1997), while the second speaks of material that "in context, depicts or describes, in terms patently offensive as measured by contemporary community standards, sexual or excretory activities or organs," §223(d). Given the absence of a definition of either term,[35] this difference in language will provoke uncertainty among speakers about how the two standards relate to each other[36] and just what they mean.[37] Could a speaker confidently assume that a serious discussion about birth control practices, homosexuality, the First Amendment issues raised by the Appendix to our Pacifica opinion, or the consequences of prison rape would not violate the CDA? This uncertainty undermines the likelihood that the CDA has been carefully tailored to the congressional goal of protecting minors from potentially harmful materials.

The vagueness of the CDA is a matter of special concern for two reasons. First, the CDA is a content based regulation of speech. The vagueness of such a regulation raises special First Amendment concerns because of its obvious chilling effect on free speech. See, e.g., Gentile v. State Bar of Nev., 501 U.S. 1030, 1048-1051 (1991). Second, the CDA is a criminal statute. In addition to the opprobrium and stigma of a criminal conviction, the CDA threatens violators with penalties including up to two years in prison for each act of violation. The severity of criminal sanctions may well cause speakers to remain silent rather than communicate even arguably unlawful words, ideas, and images. See, e.g., Dombrowski v. Pfister, 380 U.S. 479, 494 (1965). As a practical matter, this increased deterrent effect, coupled with the "risk of discriminatory enforcement" of vague regulations, poses greater First Amendment concerns than those implicated by the civil regulation reviewed in Denver Area Ed. Telecommunications Consortium, Inc. v. FCC, 518 U.S. _____ (1996).

The Government argues that the statute is no more vague than the obscenity standard this Court established in Miller v. California, 413 U.S. 15 (1973). But that is not so. In Miller, this Court reviewed a criminal conviction against a commercial vendor who mailed brochures containing pictures of sexually explicit activities to individuals who had not requested such materials. Id., at 18. Having struggled for some time to establish a definition of obscenity, we set forth in Miller the test for obscenity that controls to this day:

"(a) whether the average person, applying contemporary community standards would find that the work, taken as a whole, appeals to the prurient interest; (b) whether the work depicts or describes, in a patently offensive way, sexual conduct specifically defined by the applicable state law; and (c) whether the work, taken as a whole, lacks serious literary, artistic, political, or scientific value." Id., at 24 (internal quotation marks and citations omitted).

Because the CDA's "patently offensive" standard (and, we assume arguendo, its synonymous "indecent" standard) is one part of the three prong Miller test, the Government reasons, it cannot be unconstitutionally vague.

The Government's assertion is incorrect as a matter of fact. The second prong of the Miller test—the purportedly analogous standard—contains a critical requirement that is omitted from the CDA: that the proscribed material be "specifically defined by the applicable state law." This requirement reduces the vagueness inherent in the open ended term "patently offensive" as used in the CDA. Moreover, the Miller definition is limited to "sexual conduct," whereas the CDA extends also to include (1) "excretory activities" as well as (2) "organs" of both a sexual and excretory nature.

The Government's reasoning is also flawed. Just because a definition including three limitations is not vague, it does not follow that one of those limitations, standing by itself, is not vague.[38] Each of Miller's additional two prongs—(1) that, taken as a whole, the material appeal to the "prurient" interest, and (2) that it "lac[k] serious literary, artistic, political, or scientific value"—critically limits the uncertain sweep of the obscenity definition. The second requirement is particularly important because, unlike the "patently offensive" and "prurient interest" criteria, it is not judged by contemporary community standards. See Pope v. Illinois, 481 U.S. 497, 500 (1987). This "societal value" requirement, absent in the CDA, allows appellate courts to impose some limitations and regularity on the definition by setting, as a matter of law, a national floor for socially redeeming value. The Government's contention that courts will be able to give such legal limitations to the CDA's standards is belied by Miller's own rationale for having juries determine whether material is "patently offensive" according to community standards: that such questions are essentially ones of fact.[39]

In contrast to Miller and our other previous cases, the CDA thus presents a greater threat of censoring speech that, in fact, falls outside the statute's scope. Given the vague contours of the coverage of the statute, it unquestionably silences some speakers whose messages would be entitled to constitutional protection. That danger provides further reason for insisting that the statute not be overly broad. The CDA's burden on protected speech cannot be justified if it could be avoided by a more carefully drafted statute.

We are persuaded that the CDA lacks the precision that the First Amendment requires when a statute regulates the content of speech. In order to deny minors access to potentially harmful speech, the CDA effectively suppresses a large amount of speech that adults have a constitutional right to receive and to address to one another. That burden on adult speech is unacceptable if less restrictive alternatives would be at least as effective in achieving the legitimate purpose that the statute was enacted to serve.

In evaluating the free speech rights of adults, we have made it perfectly clear that "[s]exual expression which is indecent but not obscene is protected by the First Amendment." Sable, 492 U.S., at 126. See also Carey v. Population Services Int'l, 431 U.S. 678, 701 (1977) ("[W]here obscenity is not involved, we have consistently held that the fact that protected speech may be offensive to some does not justify its suppression"). Indeed, Pacifica itself admonished that "the fact that society may find speech offensive is not a sufficient reason for suppressing it." 438 U.S., at 745.

It is true that we have repeatedly recognized the governmental interest in protecting children from harmful materials. See Ginsberg, 390 U.S., at 639; Pacifica, 438 U.S., at 749. But that interest does not justify an unnecessarily broad suppression of speech addressed to adults. As we have explained, the Government may not "reduc[e] the adult population . . . to . . . only what is fit for children." Denver, 518 U.S., at _____ (slip op., at 29) (internal quotation marks omitted) (quoting Sable, 492 U.S., at 128).[40] "[R]egardless of the strength of the government's interest" in protecting children, "[t]he level of discourse reaching a mailbox simply cannot be limited to that which would be suitable for a sandbox." Bolger v. Youngs Drug Products Corp., 463 U.S. 60, 74-75 (1983).

The District Court was correct to conclude that the CDA effectively resembles the ban on "dial a porn" invalidated in Sable. 929 F. Supp., at 854. In Sable, 492 U.S., at 129, this Court rejected the argument that we should defer to the congressional judgment that nothing less than a total ban would be effective in preventing enterprising youngsters from gaining access to indecent communications. Sable thus made clear that the mere fact that a statutory regulation of speech was enacted for the important purpose of protecting children from exposure to sexually explicit material does not foreclose inquiry into its validity.[41] As we pointed out last Term, that inquiry embodies an "over arching commitment" to make sure that Congress has designed its statute to accomplish its purpose "without imposing an unnecessarily great restriction on speech." Denver, 518 U.S., at _____ (slip op., at 11).

In arguing that the CDA does not so diminish adult communication, the Government relies on the incorrect factual premise that prohibiting a transmission whenever it is known that one of its recipients is a minor would not interfere with adult to adult communication. The findings of the District Court make clear that this premise is untenable.

Given the size of the potential audience for most messages, in the absence of a viable age verification process, the sender must be charged with knowing that one or more minors will likely view it. Knowledge that, for instance, one or more members of a 100 person chat group will be minor—and therefore that it would be a crime to send the group an indecent message—would surely burden communication among adults.[42]

The District Court found that at the time of trial existing technology did not include any effective method for a sender to prevent minors from obtaining access to its communications on the Internet without also denying access to adults. The Court found no effective way to determine the age of a user who is accessing material through e mail, mail exploders, newsgroups, or chat rooms. 929 F. Supp., at 845 (findings 90–94). As a practical matter, the Court also found that it would be prohibitively expensive for noncommercial—as well as some commercial—speakers who have Web sites to verify that their users are adults. Id., at 845–848 (findings 95–116).[43] These limitations must inevitably curtail a significant amount of adult communication on the Internet. By contrast, the District Court found that "[d]espite its limitations, currently available user based software suggests that a reasonably effective method by which parents can prevent their children from accessing sexually explicit and other material which parents may believe is inappropriate for their children will soon be widely available." Id., at 842 (finding 73).

The breadth of the CDA's coverage is wholly unprecedented. Unlike the regulations upheld in Ginsberg and Pacifica, the scope of the CDA is not limited to commercial speech or commercial entities. Its open ended prohibitions embrace all nonprofit entities and individuals posting indecent messages or displaying them on their own computers in the presence of minors. The general,undefined terms "indecent" and "patently offensive" cover large amounts of nonpornographic material with serious educational or other value.[44] Moreover, the "community standards" criterion as applied to the Internet means that any communication available to a nation wide audience will be judged by the standards of the community most likely to be offended by the message.[45] The regulated subject matter includes any of the seven "dirty words" used in the Pacifica monologue, the use of which the Government's expert acknowledged could constitute a felony. See Olsen Test., Tr. Vol. V, 53:16-54:10. It may also extend to discussions about prison rape or safe sexual practices, artistic images that include nude subjects, and arguably the card catalogue of the Carnegie Library.

For the purposes of our decision, we need neither accept nor reject the Government's submission that the First Amendment does not forbid a blanket prohibition on all "indecent" and "patently offensive" messages communicated to a 17 year old—no matter how much value the message may contain and regardless of parental approval. It is at least clear that the strength of the Government's interest in protecting minors is not equally strong throughout the coverage of this broad statute. Under the CDA, a parent allowing her 17 year old to use the family computer to obtain information on the Internet that she, in her parental judgment, deems appropriate could face a lengthy prison term. See 47 U.S.C.A. §223(a)(2) (Supp. 1997). Similarly, a parent who sent his 17 year old college freshman information on birth control via e mail could be incarcerated even though neither he, his child, nor anyone in their home community, found the material "indecent" or "patently offensive," if the college town's community thought otherwise.

The breadth of this content based restriction of speech imposes an especially heavy burden on the Government to explain why a less restrictive provision would not be as effective as the CDA. It has not done so. The arguments in this Court have referred to possible alternatives such as requiring that indecent material be "tagged" in a way that facilitates parental control of material coming into their homes, making exceptions for messages with artistic or educational value, providing some tolerance for parental choice, and regulating some portions of the Internet—such as commercial web sites—differently than others, such as chat rooms. Particularly in the light of the absence of any detailed findings by the Congress, or even hearings addressing the special problems of the CDA, we are persuaded that the CDA is not narrowly tailored if that requirement has any meaning at all.

In an attempt to curtail the CDA's facial overbreadth, the Government advances three additional arguments for sustaining the Act's affirmative prohibitions: (1) that the CDA is constitutional because it leaves open ample "alternative channels" of communication; (2) that the plain meaning of the Act's "knowledge" and "specific person" requirement significantly restricts its permissible applications; and (3) that the Act's prohibitions are "almost always" limited to material lacking redeeming social value.

The Government first contends that, even though the CDA effectively censors discourse on many of the Internet's modalities—such as chat groups, newsgroups, and mail exploders—it is nonetheless constitutional because it provides a "reasonable opportunity" for speakers to engage in the restricted speech on the World Wide Web. Brief for Appellants 39. This argument is unpersuasive because the CDA regulates speech on the basis of its content. A "time, place, and manner" analysis is therefore inapplicable. See Consolidated Edison Co. of N.Y. v. Public Serv. Comm'n of N.Y., 447 U.S. 530, 536 (1980). It is thus immaterial whether such speech would be feasible on the Web (which, as the Government's own expert acknowledged, would cost up to $10,000 if the speaker's interests were not accommodated by an existing Web site, not including costs for database management and age verification). The Government's position is equivalent to arguing that a statute could ban leaflets on certain subjects as long as individuals are free to publish books. In invalidating a number of laws that banned leafletting on the streets regardless of their content—we explained that "one is not to have the exercise of his liberty of expression in appropriate places abridged on the plea that it may be exercised in some other place." Schneider v. State (Town of Irvington), 308 U.S. 147, 163 (1939).

The Government also asserts that the "knowledge" requirement of both §§223(a) and (d), especially when coupled with the "specific child" element found in §223(d), saves the CDA from overbreadth. Because both sections prohibit the dissemination of indecent messages only to persons known to be under 18, the Government argues, it does not require transmitters to "refrain from communicating indecent material to adults; they need only refrain from disseminating such materials to persons they know to be under 18." Brief for Appellants 24. This argument ignores the fact that most Internet fora—including chat rooms, newsgroups, mail exploders, and the Web—are open to all comers. The Government's assertion that the knowledge requirement somehow protects the communications of adults is therefore untenable. Even the strongest reading of the "specific person" requirement of §223(d) cannot save the statute. It would confer broad powers of censorship, in the form of a "heckler's veto," upon any opponent of indecent speech who might simply log on and inform the would be discoursers that his 17 year old child—a "specific person . . . under 18 years of age," 47 U.S.C.A. §223(d)(1)(A) (Supp. 1997)—would be present.

Finally, we find no textual support for the Government's submission that material having scientific, educational, or other redeeming social value will necessarily fall outside the CDA's "patently offensive" and "indecent" prohibitions. See also n. 37, supra.

The Government's three remaining arguments focus on the defenses provided in §223(e)(5).[46] First, relying on the "good faith, reasonable, effective, and appropriate actions" provision, the Government suggests that "tagging" provides a defense that saves the constitutionality of the Act. The suggestion assumes that transmitters may encode their indecent communications in a way that would indicate their contents, thus permitting recipients to block their reception with appropriate software. It is the requirement that the good faith action must be "effective" that makes this defense illusory. The Government recognizes that its proposed screening software does not currently exist. Even if it did, there is no way to know whether a potential recipient will actually block the encoded material. Without the impossible knowledge that every guardian in America is screening for the "tag," the transmitter could not reasonably rely on its action to be "effective."

For its second and third arguments concerning defenses—which we can consider together—the Government relies on the latter half of §223(e)(5), which applies when the transmitter has restricted access by requiring use of a verified credit card or adult identification. Such verification is not only technologically available but actually is used by commercial providers of sexually explicit material. These providers, therefore, would be protected by the defense. Under the findings of the District Court, however, it is not economically feasible for most noncommercial speakers to employ such verification. Accordingly, this defense would not significantly narrow the statute's burden on noncommercial speech. Even with respect to the commercial pornographers that would be protected by the defense, the Government failed to adduce any evidence that these verification techniques actually preclude minors from posing as adults.[47] Given that the risk of criminal sanctions "hovers over each content provider, like the proverbial sword of Damocles,"[48] the District Court correctly refused to rely on unproven future technology to save the statute. The Government thus failed to prove that the proffered defense would significantly reduce the heavy burden on adult speech produced by the prohibition on offensive displays.

We agree with the District Court's conclusion that the CDA places an unacceptably heavy burden on protected speech, and that the defenses do not constitute the sort of "narrow tailoring" that will save an otherwise patently invalid unconstitutional provision. In Sable, 492 U.S., at 127, we remarked that the speech restriction at issue there amounted to " 'burn[ing] the house to roast the pig.' " The CDA, casting a far darker shadow over free speech, threatens to torch a large segment of the Internet community.

At oral argument, the Government relied heavily on its ultimate fall back position: If this Court should conclude that the CDA is insufficiently tailored, it urged, we should save the statute's constitutionality by honoring the severability clause, see 47 U.S.C. § 608 and construing nonseverable terms narrowly. In only one respect is this argument acceptable.

A severability clause requires textual provisions that can be severed. We will follow §608's guidance by leaving constitutional textual elements of the statute intact in the one place where they are, in fact, severable. The "indecency" provision, 47 U.S.C.A. §223(a) (Supp. 1997), applies to "any comment, request, suggestion, proposal, image, or other communication which is obscene or indecent." Appellees do not challenge the application of the statute to obscene speech, which, they acknowledge, can be banned totally because it enjoys no First Amendment protection. See Miller, 413 U.S., at 18. As set forth by the statute, the restriction of "obscene" material enjoys a textual manifestation separate from that for "indecent" material, which we have held unconstitutional. Therefore, we will sever the term "or indecent" from the statute, leaving the rest of §223(a) standing. In no other respect, however, can §223(a) or §223(d) be saved by such a textual surgery.

The Government also draws on an additional, less traditional aspect of the CDA's severability clause, 47 U.S.C., §608, which asks any reviewing court that holds the statute facially unconstitutional not to invalidate the CDA in application to "other persons or circumstances" that might be constitutionally permissible. It further invokes this Court's admonition that, absent "countervailing considerations," a statute should "be declared invalid to the extent it reaches too far, but otherwise left intact." Brockett v. Spokane Arcades, Inc., 472 U.S. 491, 503–504 (1985). There are two flaws in this argument.

First, the statute that grants our jurisdiction for this expedited review, 47 U.S.C.A. §561 (Supp. 1997), limits that jurisdictional grant to actions challenging the CDA "on its face." Consistent with §561, the plaintiffs who brought this suit and the three judge panel that decided it treated it as a facial challenge. We have no authority, in this particular posture, to convert this litigation into an "as applied" challenge. Nor, given the vast array of plaintiffs, the range of their expressive activities, and the vagueness of the statute, would it be practicable to limit our holding to a judicially defined set of specific applications.

Second, one of the "countervailing considerations" mentioned in Brockett is present here. In considering a facial challenge, this Court may impose a limiting construction on a statute only if it is "readily susceptible" to such a construction. Virginia v. American Bookseller's Assn., Inc., 484 U.S. 383, 397 (1988). See also Erznoznik v. Jacksonville, 422 U.S. 205, 216 (1975) ("readily subject" to narrowing construction). The open ended character of the CDA provides no guidance whatever for limiting its coverage.

This case is therefore unlike those in which we have construed a statute narrowly because the text or other source of congressional intent identified a clear line that this Court could draw. Cf., e.g., Brockett, 472 U.S., at 504–505 (invalidating obscenity statute only to the extent that word "lust" was actually or effectively excised from statute); United States v. Grace, 461 U.S. 171, 180–183 (1983) (invalidating federal statute banning expressive displays only insofar as it extended to public sidewalks when clear line could be drawn between sidewalks and other grounds that comported with congressional purpose of protecting the building, grounds, and people therein). Rather, our decision in United States v. Treasury Employees, 513 U.S. 454, 479, n. 26 (1995), is applicable. In that case, we declined to "dra[w] one or more lines between categories of speech covered by an overly broad statute, when Congress has sent inconsistent signals as to where the new line or lines should be drawn" because doing so "involves a far more serious invasion of the legislative domain."[49] This Court "will not rewrite a . . . law to conform it to constitutional requirements." American Booksellers, 484 U.S., at 397.[50]

In this Court, though not in the District Court, the Government asserts that—in addition to its interest in protecting children—its "[e]qually significant" interest in fostering the growth of the Internet provides an independent basis for upholding the constitutionality of the CDA. Brief for Appellants 19. The Government apparently assumes that the unregulated availability of "indecent" and "patently offensive" material on the Internet is driving countless citizens away from the medium because of the risk of exposing themselves or their children to harmful material.

We find this argument singularly unpersuasive. The dramatic expansion of this new marketplace of ideas contradicts the factual basis of this contention. The record demonstrates that the growth of the Internet has been and continues to be phenomenal. As a matter of constitutional tradition, in the absence of evidence to the contrary, we presume that governmental regulation of the content of speech is more likely to interfere with the free exchange of ideas than to encourage it. The interest in encouraging freedom of expression in a democratic society outweighs any theoretical but unproven benefit of censorship.

For the foregoing reasons, the judgment of the district court is affirmed.

It is so ordered.

JANET RENO, ATTORNEY GENERAL OF THE UNITED STATES, et al., APPELLANTS v. AMERICAN CIVIL LIBERTIES UNION et al.

On Appeal from the United States District Court for the Eastern District of Pennsylvania

No. 96-511
[June 26, 1997]

Justice O'Connor, with whom The Chief Justice joins, concurring in the judgment in part and dissenting in part.

I write separately to explain why I view the Communications Decency Act of 1996 (CDA) as little more than an attempt by Congress to create "adult zones" on the Internet. Our precedent indicates that the creation of such zones can be constitutionally sound. Despite the soundness of its purpose, however, portions of the CDA are unconstitutional because they stray from the blueprint our prior cases have developed for constructing a "zoning law" that passes constitutional muster.

Appellees bring a facial challenge to three provisions of the CDA. The first, which the Court describes as the "indecency transmission" provision, makes it a crime to knowingly transmit an obscene or indecent message or image to a person the sender knows is under 18 years old. 47 U.S.C.A. §223(a)(1)(B) (May 1996 Supp.). What the Court classifies as a single " 'patently offensive display' " provision, see ante, at 11, is in reality two separate provisions. The first of these makes it a crime to knowingly send a patently offensive message or image to a specific person under the age of 18 ("specific person" provision). §223(d)(1)(A). The second criminalizes the display of patently offensive messages or images "in a[ny] manner available" to minors ("display" provision). §223(d)(1)(B). None of these provisions purports to keep indecent (or patently offensive) material away from adults, who have a First Amendment right to obtain this speech. Sable Communications of Cal., Inc. v. FCC, 492 U.S. 115, 126 (1989) ("Sexual expression which is indecent but not obscene is protected by the First Amendment"). Thus, the undeniable purpose of the CDA is to segregate indecent material on the Internet into certain areas that minors cannot access. See S. Conf. Rep. No. 104-230, p. 189 (1996) (CDA imposes "access restrictions . . . to protect minors from exposure to indecent material").

The creation of "adult zones" is by no means a novel concept. States have long denied minors access to certain establishments frequented by adults.[1] States have also denied minors access to speech deemed to be "harmful to minors."[2] The Court has previously sustained such zoning laws, but only if they respect the First Amendment rights of adults and minors. That into say, a zoning law is valid if (i) it does not unduly restrict adult access to the material; and (ii) minors have no First Amendment right to read or view the banned material. As applied to the Internet as it exists in 1997, the "display" provision and some applications of the "indecency transmission" and "specific person" provisions fail to adhere to the first of these limiting principles by restricting adults' access to protected materials in certain circumstances. Unlike the Court, however, I would invalidate the provisions only in those circumstances.

Our cases make clear that a "zoning" law is valid only if adults are still able to obtain the regulated speech. If they cannot, the law does more than simply keep children away from speech they have no right to obtain—it interferes with the rights of adults to obtain constitutionally protected speech and effectively "reduce[s] the adult population . . . to reading only what is fit for children." Butler v. Michigan, 352 U.S. 380, 383 (1957). The First Amendment does not tolerate such interference. See id., at 383 (striking down a Michigan criminal law banning sale of books—to minors or adults—that contained words or pictures that " 'tende[d] to . . . corrup[t] the morals of youth' "); Sable Communications, supra (invalidating federal law that made it a crime to transmit indecent, but nonobscene, commercial telephone messages to minors and adults); Bolger v. Youngs Drug Products Corp., 463 U.S. 60, 74 (1983) (striking down a federal law prohibiting the mailing of unsolicited advertisements for contraceptives). If the law does not unduly restrict adults' access to constitutionally protected speech, however, it may be valid. In Ginsberg v. New York, 390 U.S. 629, 634 (1968), for example, the Court sustained a New York law that barred store owners from selling pornographic magazines minors in part because adults could still buy those magazines.

The Court in Ginsberg concluded that the New York law created a constitutionally adequate adult zone simply because, on its face, it denied access only to minors. The Court did not question—and therefore necessarily assumed—that an adult zone, once created, would succeed in preserving adults' access while denying minors' access to the regulated speech. Before today, there was no reason to question this assumption, for the Court has previously only considered laws that operated in the physical world, a world that with two characteristics that make it possible to create "adult zones": geography and identity. See Lessig, Reading the Constitution in

Cyberspace, 45 Emory L. J. 869, 886 (1996). A minor can see an adult dance show only if he enters an establishment that provides such entertainment. And should he attempt to do so, the minor will not be able to conceal completely his identity (or, consequently, his age). Thus, the twin characteristics of geography and identity enable the establishment's proprietor to prevent children from entering the establishment, but to let adults inside.

The electronic world is fundamentally different. Because it is no more than the interconnection of electronic pathways, cyberspace allows speakers and listeners to mask their identities. Cyberspace undeniably reflects some form of geography; chat rooms and Web sites, for example, exist at fixed "locations" on the Internet. Since users can transmit and receive messages on the Internet without revealing anything about their identities or ages, see Lessig, supra, at 901, however, it is not currently possible to exclude persons from accessing certain messages on the basis of their identity.

Cyberspace differs from the physical world in another basic way: Cyberspace is malleable. Thus, it is possible to construct barriers in cyberspace and use them screen for identity, making cyberspace more like the physical world and, consequently, more amenable to zoning laws. This transformation of cyberspace is already underway. Lessig, supra, at 888-889. Id., at 887 (cyberspace "is moving . . . from a relatively unzoned place to a universe that is extraordinarily well zoned"). Internet speakers (users who post-material on the Internet) have begun to zone cyberspace itself through the use of "gateway" technology. Such technology requires Internet users to enter information about themselves—perhaps an adult identification number or a credit card number—before they can access certain areas of cyberspace, 929 F. Supp. 824, 845 (ED Pa. 1996), much like a bouncer checks a person's driver's license before admitting him to a nightclub. Internet users who access information have not attempted to zone cyberspace itself, but have tried to limit their own power to access information in cyberspace, much as a parent controls what her children watch on television by installing a lock box. This user based zoning is accomplished through the use of screening software (such as Cyber Patrol or SurfWatch) or browsers with screening capabilities, both of which search addresses and text for keywords that are associated with "adult" sites and, if the user wishes, blocks access to such sites. Id., at 839-842. The Platform for Internet Content Selection (PICS) project is designed to facilitate user based zoning by encouraging Internet speakers to rate the content of their speech using codes recognized by all screening programs. Id., at 838-839.

Despite this progress, the transformation of cyberspace is not complete. Although gateway technology has been available on the World Wide Web for some time now, id., at 845; Shea v. Reno, 930 F. Supp. 916, 933–934 (SDNY 1996), it is not available to all Web speakers, 929 F. Supp., at 845–846, and is just now becoming technologically feasible for chat rooms and USENET newsgroups, Brief for Federal Parties 37–38. Gateway technology is not ubiquitous in cyberspace, and because without it "there is no means of age verification," cyberspace still remains largely unzoned—and unzoneable. 929 F. Supp., at 846; Shea, supra, at 934. User based zoning is also in its infancy. For it to be effective, (i) an agreed upon code (or "tag") would have to exist; (ii) screening software or browsers with screening capabilities would have to be able to recognize the "tag"; and (iii) those programs would have to be widely available—and widely used—by Internet users. At present, none of these conditions is true. Screening software "is not in wide use today" and "only a handful of browsers have screening capabilities." Shea, supra, at 945–946. There is, moreover, no agreed upon "tag" for those programs to recognize. 929 F. Supp., at 848; Shea, supra, at 945.

Although the prospects for the eventual zoning of the Internet appear promising, I agree with the Court that we must evaluate the constitutionality of the CDA as it applies to the Internet as it exists today. Ante, at 36. Given the present state of cyberspace, I agree with the Court that the "display" provision cannot pass muster. Until gateway technology is available throughout cyberspace, and it is not in 1997, a speaker cannot be reasonably assured that the speech he displays will reach only adults because it is impossible to confine speech to an "adult zone." Thus, the only way for a speaker to avoid liability under the CDA is to refrain completely from using indecent speech. But this forced silence impinges on the First Amendment right of adults to make and obtain this speech and, for all intents and purposes, "reduce[s] the adult population [on the Internet] to reading only what is fit for children." Butler, 352 U.S., at 383. As a result, the "display" provision cannot withstand scrutiny. Accord, Sable Communications, 492 U.S., at 126–131; Bolger v. Youngs Drug Products Corp., 463 U.S., at 73–75.

The "indecency transmission" and "specific person" provisions present a closer issue, for they are not unconstitutional in all of their applications. As discussed above, the "indecency transmission" provision makes it a crime to transmit knowingly an indecent message to a person the sender knows is under 18 years of age. 47 U.S.C.A. §223(a)(1)(B) (May 1996 Supp.). The "specific person" provision proscribes the same conduct, although it does not as explicitly require the sender to know that the intended recipient of his indecent message is a minor. §223(d)(1)(A). Appellant urges the Court to construe the provision to impose such a knowledge requirement, see Brief for Federal Parties 25-27, and I would do so. See Edward J. DeBartolo Corp. v. Florida Gulf Coast Building & Constr. Trades Council, 485 U.S. 568, 575 (1988) ("[W]here an otherwise acceptable construction of a statute would raise serious constitutional problems, the Court will construe the statute to avoid such problems unless such construction is plainly contrary to the intent of Congress").

So construed, both provisions are constitutional as applied to a conversation involving only an adult and one or more minors—e.g., when an adult speaker sends an e mail knowing the addressee is a minor, or when an adult and minor converse by themselves or with other minors in a chat room. In this context, these provisions are no different from the law we sustained in Ginsberg. Restricting what the adult may say to the minors in no way restricts the adult's ability to communicate with other adults. He is not prevented from speaking indecently to other adults in a chat room (because there are no other adults participating in the conversation) and he remains free to send indecent e mails to other adults. The relevant universe contains only one adult, and the adult in that universe has the power to refrain from using indecent speech and consequently to keep all such speech within the room in an "adult" zone.

The analogy to Ginsberg breaks down, however, when more than one adult is a party to the conversation. If a minor enters a chat room otherwise occupied by adults, the CDA effectively requires the adults in the room to stop using indecent speech. If they did not, they could be prosecuted under the "indecency transmission" and "specific person" provisions for any indecent statements they make to the group, since they would be transmitting an indecent message to specific persons, one of whom is a minor. Accord, ante, at 30. The CDA is therefore akin to a law that makes it a crime for a bookstore owner to sell pornographic magazines to anyone once a minor enters his store. Even assuming such a law might be constitutional in the physical world as a reasonable alternative to excluding minors completely from the store, the absence of any means of excluding minors from chat rooms in cyberspace restricts the rights of adults to engage in indecent speech in those rooms. The "indecency transmission" and "specific person" provisions share this defect.

But these two provisions do not infringe on adults' speech in all situations. And as discussed below, I do not find that the provisions are overbroad in the sense that they restrict minors' access to a substantial amount of speech that minors have the right to read and view. Accordingly, the CDA can be applied constitutionally in some situations. Normally, this fact would require the Court to reject a direct facial challenge. United States v. Salerno, 481 U.S. 739, 745 (1987) ("A facial challenge to a legislative Act [succeeds only if] the challenger . . . establish[es] that no set of circumstances exists under which the Act would be valid"). Appellees' claim arises under the First Amendment, however, and they argue that the CDA is facially invalid because it is "substantially overbroad"—that is, it "sweeps too broadly . . . [and] penaliz[es] a substantial amount of speech that is constitutionally protected," Forsyth County v. Nationalist Movement, 505 U.S. 123, 130 (1992). See Brief for Appellees American Library Association et al. 48; Brief for Appellees American Civil Liberties Union et al. 39-41. I agree with the Court that the provisions are overbroad in that they cover any and all communications between adults and minors, regardless of how many adults might be part of the audience to the communication.

This conclusion does not end the matter, however. Where, as here, "the parties challenging the statute are those who desire to engage in protected speech that the overbroad statute purports to punish . . . [t]he statute may forthwith be declared invalid to the extent that it reaches too far, but otherwise left intact." Brockett v. Spokane Arcades, Inc., 472 U.S. 491, 504 (1985). There is no question that Congress intended to prohibit certain communications between one adult and one or more minors. See 47 U.S.C.A. §223(a)(1)(B) (May 1996 Supp.) (punishing "[w]hoever . . . initiates the transmission of [any indecent communication] knowingly that the recipient of the communication is under 18 years of age"); §223(d)(1)(A) (punishing "[w]hoever . . . send[s] to a specific person or persons under 18 years of age [a patently offensive message]"). There is also no question that Congress would have enacted a narrower version of these provisions had it known a broader version would be declared unconstitutional. 47 U.S.C. § 608 ("If . . . the application [of any provision of the CDA] to any person or circumstance is held invalid, . . . the application of such provision to other persons or circumstances shall not be affected thereby"). I would therefore sustain the "indecency transmission" and "specific person" provisions to the extent they apply to the transmission of Internet communications where the party initiating the communication knows that all of the recipients are minors.

Whether the CDA substantially interferes with the First Amendment rights of minors, and thereby runs afoul of the second characteristic of valid zoning laws, presents a closer question. In Ginsberg, the New York law we sustained prohibited the sale to minors of magazines that were "harmful to minors." Under that law, a magazine was "harmful to minors" only if it was obscene as to minors. 390 U.S., at 632-633. Noting that obscene speech is not protected by the First Amendment, Roth v. United States, 354 U.S. 476, 485 (1957), and that New York was constitutionally free to adjust the definition of obscenity for minors, 390 U.S., at 638, the Court concluded that the law did not "invad[e] the area of freedom of expression constitutionally secured to minors." Id., at 637. New York therefore did not infringe upon the First Amendment rights of minors. Cf. Erznoznik v. Jacksonville, 422 U.S. 205, 213 (1975) (striking down city ordinance that banned nudity that was not "obscene even as to minors").

The Court neither "accept[s] nor reject[s]" the argument that the CDA is facially overbroad because it substantially interferes with the First Amendment rights of minors. Ante, at 32. I would reject it. Ginsberg established that minors may constitutionally be denied access to material that is obscene as to minors. As Ginsberg explained, material is obscene as to minors if it (i) is "patently offensive to prevailing standards in the adult community as a whole with respect to what is suitable . . . for minors"; (ii) appeals to the prurient interest of minors; and (iii) is "utterly without redeeming social importance for minors." 390 U.S., at 633. Because the CDA denies minors the right to obtain material that is "patently offensive"—even if it has some redeeming value for minors and even if it does not appeal to their prurient interests—Congress' rejection of the Ginsberg "harmful to minors" standard means that the CDA could ban some speech that is "indecent" (i.e., "patently offensive") but that is not obscene as to minors.

I do not deny this possibility, but to prevail in a facial challenge, it is not enough for a plaintiff to show "some" overbreadth. Our cases require a proof of "real" and "substantial" overbreadth, Broadrick v. Oklahoma, 413 U.S. 601, 615 (1973), and appellees have not carried their burden in this case. In my view, the universe of speech constitutionally protected as to minors but banned by the CDA—i.e., the universe of material that is "patently offensive," but which nonetheless has some redeeming value for minors or does not appeal to their prurient interest—is a very small one. Appellees cite no examples of speech falling within this universe and do not attempt to explain why that universe is substantial "in relation to the statute's plainly legitimate sweep." Ibid. That the CDA might deny minors the right to obtain material that has some "value," see ante, at 32–33, is largely beside the point. While discussions about prison rape or nude art, see ibid., may have some redeeming education value for adults, they do not necessarily have any such value for minors, and under Ginsberg, minors only have a First Amendment right to obtain patently offensive material that has "redeeming social importance for minors," 390 U.S., at 633 (emphasis added). There is also no evidence in the record to support the contention that "many [e] mail transmissions from an adult to a minor are conversations between family members," ante, at 18, n. 32, and no support for the legal proposition that such speech is absolutely immune from regulation. Accordingly, in my view, the CDA does not burden a substantial amount of minors' constitutionally protected speech.

Thus, the constitutionality of the CDA as a zoning law hinges on the extent to which it substantially interferes with the First Amendment rights of adults. Because the rights of adults are infringed only by the "display" provision and by the "indecency transmission" and "specific person" provisions as applied to communications involving more than one adult, I would invalidate the CDA only to that extent. Insofar as the "indecency transmission" and "specific person" provisions prohibit the use of indecent speech in communications between an adult and one or more minors, however, they can and should be sustained. The Court reaches a contrary conclusion, and from that holding that I respectfully dissent.

FOOTNOTES

1. "Congress shall make no law . . . abridging the freedom of speech." U.S. Const., Amdt. 1.
2. The Court made 410 findings, including 356 paragraphs of the parties' stipulation and 54 findings based on evidence received in open court. See 929 F. Supp. at 830, n. 9, 842, n. 15.
3. An acronym for the network developed by the Advanced Research Project Agency.
4. Id., at 844 (finding 81).
5. Id., at 831 (finding 3).
6. Id., at 835 (finding 27).
7. Id., at 842 (finding 74).
8. Id., at 836 (finding 36).
9. "Web publishing is simple enough that thousands of individual users and small community organizations are using the Web to publish their own personal 'home pages,' the equivalent of individualized newsletters about the person or organization, which are available to everyone on the Web." Id., at 837 (finding 42).
10. Id., at 838 (finding 46).
11. Id., at 844 (finding 82).
12. Ibid. (finding 86).
13. Ibid. (finding 85).

14. Id., at 848 (finding 117).
15. Id., at 844–845 (finding 88).
16. Ibid.
17. Id., at 845 (finding 89).
18. Id., at 842 (finding 72).
19. Ibid. (finding 73).
20. Id., at 845 (finding 90): "An e mail address provides no authoritative information about the addressee, who may use an e mail 'alias' or an anonymous remailer. There is also no universal or reliable listing of e mail addresses and corresponding names or telephone numbers, and any such listing would be or rapidly become incomplete. For these reasons, there is no reliable way in many instances for a sender to know if the e mail recipient is an adult or a minor. The difficulty of e mail age verification is compounded for mail exploders such as listservs, which automatically send information to all e mail addresses on a sender's list. Government expert Dr. Olsen agreed that no current technology could give a speaker assurance that only adults were listed in a particular mail exploder's mailing list."
21. Ibid. (finding 93).
22. Id., at 846 (finding 102).
23. Id., at 847 (findings 104–106): "At least some, if not almost all, non commercial organizations, such as the ACLU, Stop Prisoner Rape or Critical Path AIDS Project, regard charging listeners to access their speech as contrary to their goals of making their materials available to a wide audience free of charge. . . . There is evidence suggesting that adult users, particularly casual Web browsers, would be discouraged from retrieving information that required use of a credit card or password. Andrew Anker testified that HotWired has received many complaints from its members about HotWired's registration system, which requires only that a member supply a name, e mail address and self created password. There is concern by commercial content providers that age verification requirements would decrease advertising and revenue because advertisers depend on a demonstration that the sites are widely available and frequently visited."
24. See Exon Amendment No. 1268, 141 Cong. Rec. S8120 (June 9, 1995). See also id., at S8087. This amendment, as revised, became §502 of the Communications Act of 1996, 110 Stat. 133, 47 U.S.C.A. §§223(a)%(e) (Supp. 1997). Some Members of the House of Representatives opposed the Exon Amendment because they thought it "possible for our parents now to child proof the family computer with these products available in the private sector." They also thought the Senate's approach would "involve the Federal Government spending vast sums of money trying to define elusive terms that are going to lead to a flood of legal challenges while our kids are unprotected." These Members offered an amendment intended as a substitute for the Exon Amendment, but instead enacted as an additional section of the Act entitled "Online Family Empowerment." See 110 Stat. 137, 47 U.S.C.A. §230 (Supp. 1997); 141 Cong. Rec. H8468–H8472. No hearings were held on the provisions that became law. See S. Rep. No. 104-23 (1995), p. 9. After the Senate adopted the Exon amendment, however, its Judiciary Committee did conduct a one day hearing on "Cyberporn and Children." In his opening statement at that hearing, Senator Leahy observed: "It really struck me in your opening statement when you mentioned, Mr. Chairman, that it is the first ever hearing, and you are absolutely right. And yet we had a major debate on the floor, passed legislation overwhelmingly on a subject involving the Internet, legislation that could dramatically change—some would say even wreak havoc—on the Internet. The Senate went in willy nilly, passed legislation, and never once had a hearing, never once had a discussion other than an hour or so on the floor."

Cyberporn and Children: The Scope of the Problem, The State of the Technology, and the Need for Congressional Action, Hearing on S. 892 before the Senate Committee on the Judiciary, 104th Cong., 1st Sess., 7–8 (1995).

25. Although the Government and the dissent break §223(d)(1) into two separate "patently offensive" and "display" provisions, we follow the convention of both parties below, as well the District Court's order and opinion, in describing §223(d)(1) as one provision.

26. In full, §223(e)(5) provides: "(5) It is a defense to a prosecution under subsection (a)(1)(B) or (d) of this section, or under subsection (a)(2) of this section with respect to the use of a facility for an activity under subsection (a)(1)(B) of this section that a person—"(A) has taken, in good faith, reasonable, effective, and appropriate actions under the circumstances to restrict or prevent access by minors to a communication specified in such subsections, which may involve any appropriate measures to restrict minors from such communications, including any method which is feasible under available technology; or "(B) has restricted access to such communication by requiring use of a verified credit card, debit account, adult access code, or adult personal identification number."

27. American Civil Liberties Union; Human Rights Watch; Electronic Privacy Information Center; Electronic Frontier Foundation; Journalism Education Association; Computer Professionals for Social Responsibility; National Writers Union; Clarinet Communications Corp.; Institute for Global Communications; Stop Prisoner Rape; AIDS Education Global Information System; Bibliobytes; Queer Resources Directory; Critical Path AIDS Project, Inc.; Wildcat Press, Inc.; Declan McCullagh dba Justice on Campus; Brock Meeks dba Cyberwire Dispatch; John Troyer dba The Safer Sex Page; Jonathan Wallace dba The Ethical Spectacle; and Planned Parenthood Federation of America, Inc.

28. American Library Association; America Online, Inc.; American Booksellers Association, Inc.; American Booksellers Foundation for Free Expression; American Society of Newspaper Editors; Apple Computer, Inc.; Association of American Publishers, Inc.; Association of Publishers, Editors and Writers; Citizens Internet Empowerment Coalition; Commercial Internet Exchange Association; CompuServe Incorporated; Families Against Internet Censorship; Freedom to Read Foundation, Inc.; Health Sciences Libraries Consortium; Hotwired Ventures LLC; Interactive Digital Software Association; Interactive Services Association; Magazine Publishers of America; Microsoft Corporation; The Microsoft Network, L.L.C.; National Press Photographers Association; Netcom On Line Communication Services, Inc.; Newspaper Association of America; Opnet, Inc.; Prodigy Services Company; Society of Professional Journalists; Wired Ventures, Ltd.

29. 110 Stat. 142–143, note following 47 U.S.C.A. §223 (Supp.1997).

30. See also 929 F. Supp., at 877: "Four related characteristics of Internet communication have a transcendent importance to our shared holding that the CDA is unconstitutional on its face. We explain these characteristics in our Findings of fact above, and I only rehearse them briefly here. First, the Internet presents very low barriers to entry. Second, these barriers to entry are identical for both speakers and listeners. Third, as a result of these low barriers, astoundingly diverse content is available on the Internet. Fourth, the Internet provides significant access to all who wish to speak in the medium, and even creates a relative parity among speakers." According to Judge Dalzell, these characteristics and the rest of the District Court's findings "lead to the conclusion that Congress may not regulate indecency on the Internet at all." Ibid. Because appellees do not press this argument before this Court, we do not consider it. Appellees also do not dispute that the Government generally has a compelling interest in protecting minors from "indecent" and "patently offensive" speech.

31. 390 U.S., at 639. We quoted from Prince v. Massachusetts, 321 U.S. 158, 166 (1944): "It

is cardinal with us that the custody, care and nurture of the child reside first in the parents, whose primary function and freedom include preparation for obligations the state can neither supply nor hinder."

32. Given the likelihood that many E mail transmissions from an adult to a minor are conversations between family members, it is therefore incorrect for the dissent to suggest that the provisions of the CDA, even in this narrow area, "are no different from the law we sustained in Ginsberg." Post, at 8.

33. Cf. Pacifica Foundation v. FCC, 556 F. 2d 9, 36 (CADC 1977) (Leventhal, J., dissenting), rev'd, FCC v. Pacifica Foundation, 438 U.S. 726 (1978). When Pacifica was decided, given that radio stations were allowed to operate only pursuant to federal license, and that Congress had enacted legislation prohibiting licensees from broadcasting indecent speech, there was a risk that members of the radio audience might infer some sort of official or societal approval of whatever was heard over the radio, see 556 F. 2d, at 37, n. 18. No such risk attends messages received through the Internet, which is not supervised by any federal agency.

34. Juris. Statement 3 (citing 929 F. Supp., at 831 (finding 3)).

35. "Indecent" does not benefit from any textual embellishment at all. "Patently offensive" is qualified only to the extent that it involves "sexual or excretory activities or organs" taken "in context" and "measured by contemporary community standards."

36. See Gozlon Peretz v. United States, 498 U.S. 395, 404 (1991) ("Where Congress includes particular language in one section of a statute but omits it in another section of the same Act, it is generally presumed that Congress acts intentionally and purposely in the disparate inclusion and exclusion") (internal quotation marks omitted).

37. The statute does not indicate whether the "patently offensive" and "indecent" determinations should be made with respect to minors or the population as a whole. The Government asserts that the appropriate standard is "what is suitable material for minors." Reply Brief for Appellants 18, n. 13 (citing Ginsberg v. New York, 390 U.S. 629, 633 (1968)). But the Conferees expressly rejected amendments that would have imposed such a "harmful to minors" standard. See S. Conf. Rep. No. 104-230, p. 189 (1996) (S. Conf. Rep.), 142 Cong. Rec. H1145, H1165–1166 (Feb. 1, 1996). The Conferees also rejected amendments that would have limited the proscribed materials to those lacking redeeming value. See S. Conf. Rep., at 189, 142 Cong. Rec. H1165–1166 (Feb. 1, 1996).

38. Even though the word "trunk," standing alone, might refer to luggage, a swimming suit, the base of a tree, or the long nose of an animal, its meaning is clear when it is one prong of a three part description of a species of gray animals.

39. 413 U.S., at 30 (Determinations of "what appeals to the 'prurient interest' or is 'patently offensive' . . . are essentially questions of fact, and our Nation is simply too big and too diverse for this Court to reasonably expect that such standards could be articulated for all 50 States in a single formulation, even assuming the prerequisite consensus exists"). The CDA, which implements the "contemporary community standards" language of Miller, thus conflicts with the Conferees' own assertion that the CDA was intended "to establish a uniform national standard of content regulation." S. Conf. Rep., at 191.

40. Accord, Butler v. Michigan, 352 U.S. 380, 383 (1957) (ban on sale to adults of books deemed harmful to children unconstitutional); Sable Communications of Cal., Inc. v. FCC, 492 U.S. 115, 128 (1989) (ban on "dial a porn" messages unconstitutional); Bolger v. Youngs Drug Products Corp., 463 U.S. 60, 73 (1983) (ban on mailing of unsolicited advertisement for contraceptives unconstitutional).

41. The lack of legislative attention to the statute at issue in Sable suggests another parallel with this case. Compare 492 U.S., at 129-130 ("[A]side from conclusory statements dur-

ing the debates by proponents of the bill, as well as similar assertions in hearings on a substantially identical bill the year before, . . . the congressional record presented to us contains no evidence as to how effective or ineffective the FCC's most recent regulations were or might prove to be. . . . No Congressman or Senator purported to present a considered judgment with respect to how often or to what extent minors could or would circumvent the rules and have access to dial a porn messages") with n. 24, supra.

42. The Government agrees that these provisions are applicable whenever "a sender transmits a message to more than one recipient, knowing that at least one of the specific persons receiving the message is a minor." Opposition to Motion to Affirm and Reply to Juris. Statement 4–5, n. 1.

43. The Government asserts that "[t]here is nothing constitutionally suspect about requiring commercial Web site operators . . . to shoulder the modest burdens associated with their use." Brief for Appellants 35. As a matter of fact, however, there is no evidence that a "modest burden" would be effective.

44. Transmitting obscenity and child pornography, whether via the Internet or other means, is already illegal under federal law for both adults and juveniles. See 18 U.S.C. §§ 1464–1465 (criminalizing obscenity); §2251 (criminalizing child pornography). In fact, when Congress was considering the CDA, the Government expressed its view that the law was unnecessary because existing laws already authorized its ongoing efforts to prosecute obscenity, child pornography, and child solicitation. See 141 Cong. Rec. S8342 (June 14, 1995) (letter from Kent Markus, Acting Assistant Attorney General, U.S. Department of Justice, to Sen. Leahy).

45. Citing Church of Lukumi Babalu Aye, Inc. v. Hialeah, 508 U.S. 520 (1993), among other cases, appellees offer an additional reason why, in their view, the CDA fails strict scrutiny. Because so much sexually explicit content originates overseas, they argue, the CDA cannot be "effective." Brief for Appellees American Library Association et al. 33-34. This argument raises difficult issues regarding the intended, as well as the permissible scope of, extraterritorial application of the CDA. We find it unnecessary to address those issues to dispose of this case.

46. For the full text of §223(e)(5), see n. 26, supra.

47. Thus, ironically, this defense may significantly protect commercial purveyors of obscene postings while providing little (or no) benefit for transmitters of indecent messages that have significant social or artistic value.

48. 929 F. Supp., at 855–856.

49. As this Court long ago explained, "It would certainly be dangerous if the Legislature could set a net large enough to catch all possible offenders and leave it to the courts to step inside and say who could be rightfully be detained and who should be set at large. This would, to some extent, substitute the judicial for the legislative department of the government." United States v. Reese, 92 U.S. 214, 221 (1876). In part because of these separation of powers concerns, we have held that a severability clause is "an aid merely; not an inexorable command." Dorchy v. Kansas, 264 U.S. 286, 290 (1924).

50. See also Osborne v. Ohio, 495 U.S. 103, 121 (1990) (judicial rewriting of statutes would derogate Congress's "incentive to draft a narrowly tailored law in the first place").

1. See, e.g., Alaska Stat. Ann. §11.66.300 (1996) (no minors in "adult entertainment" places); Ariz. Rev. Stat. Ann. §13-3556 (1989) (no minors in places where people expose themselves); Ark. Code Ann. §§5-27-223, 5-27-224 (1993) (no minors in poolrooms and bars); Colo. Rev. Stat. §18-7-502(2) (1986) (no minors in places displaying movies or shows that are "harmful to children"); Del. Code Ann., Tit. 11, §1365(i)(2) (1995)

(same); D. C. Code Ann. §22-2001(b)(1)(B) (1996) (same); Fla. Stat. §847.013(2) (1994) (same); Ga. Code Ann. §16-12-103(b) (1996) (same); Haw. Rev. Stat. §712-1215(1)(b) (1994) (no minors in movie houses or shows that are "pornographic for minors"); Idaho Code §18-1515(2) (1987) (no minors in places displaying movies or shows that are "harmful to minors"); La. Rev. Stat. Ann. §14:91.11(B) (West 1986) (no minors in places displaying movies that depict sex acts and appeal to minors' prurient interest); Md. Ann. Code, Art. 27, §416E (1996) (no minors in establishments where certain enumerated acts are performed or portrayed); Mich. Comp. Laws §750.141 (1991) (no minors without an adult in places where alcohol is sold); Minn. Stat. §617.294 (1987 and Supp. 1997) (no minors in places displaying movies or shows that are "harmful to minors"); Miss. Code Ann. §97-5-11 (1994) (no minors in poolrooms, billiard halls, or where alcohol is sold); Mo. Rev. Stat. §573.507 (1995) (no minors in adult cabarets); Neb. Rev. Stat. §28-809 (1995) (no minors in places displaying movies or shows that are "harmful to minors"); Nev. Rev. Stat. §201.265(3) (1997) (same); N. H. Rev. Stat. Ann. §571-B:2(II) (1986) (same); N. M. Stat. Ann. §30-37-3 (1989) (same); N. Y. Penal Law §235.21(2) (McKinney 1989) (same); N. D. Cent. Code §12.1-27.1-03 (1985 and Supp. 1995) (same); 18 Pa. Cons. Stat. §5903(a) (Supp. 1997) (same); S. D. Comp. Laws Ann. §22-24-30 (1988) (same); Tenn. Code Ann. §39-17-911(b) (1991) (same); Vt. Stat. Ann., Tit. 13, §2802(b) (1974) (same); Va. Code Ann. §18.2-391 (1996) (same).

2. See, e.g., Ala. Code §13A-12-200.5 (1994); Ariz. Rev. Stat. Ann. §13-3506 (1989); Ark. Code Ann. 5-68-502 (1993); Cal. Penal Code Ann. §313.1 (West Supp. 1997); Colo. Rev. Stat. §18-7-502(1) (1986); Conn. Gen. Stat. §53a-196 (1994); Del. Code Ann., Tit. 11, §1365(i)(1) (1995); D. C. Code Ann. §22-2001(b)(1)(A) (1996); Fla. Stat. §847.012 (1994); Ga. Code Ann. §16-12-103(a) (1996); Haw. Rev. Stat. §712-1215(1) (1994); Idaho Code §18-1515(1) (1987); Ill. Comp. Stat., ch. 720, §5/11-21 (1993); Ind. Code §35-49-3-3(1) (Supp. 1996); Iowa Code §728.2 (1993); Kan. Stat. Ann. §21-4301c(a)(2) (1988); La. Rev. Stat. Ann. §14:91.11(B) (West 1986); Md. Ann. Code, Art. 27, §416B (1996); Mass. Gen. Laws, ch. 272, §28 (1992); Minn. Stat. §617.293 (1987 and Supp. 1997); Miss. Code Ann. §97-5-11 (1994); Mo. Rev. Stat. §573.040 (1995); Mont. Code Ann. §45-8-206 (1995); Neb. Rev. Stat. §28-808 (1995); Nev. Rev. Stat. §§201.265(1), (2) (1997); N. H. Rev. Stat. Ann. §571-B:2(I) (1986); N. M. Stat. Ann. §30-37-2 (1989); N. Y. Penal Law §235.21(1) (McKinney 1989); N. C. Gen. Stat. §14-190.15(a) (1993); N. D. Cent. Code §12.1-27.1-03 (1985 and Supp. 1995); Ohio Rev. Code Ann. §2907.31(A)(1) (Supp. 1997); Okla. Stat., Tit. 21, §1040.76(2) (Supp. 1997); 18 Pa. Cons. Stat. §5903(c) (Supp. 1997); R. I. Gen. Laws §11-31-10(a) (1996); S. C. Code Ann. §16-15-385(A) (Supp. 1996); S. D. Comp. Laws Ann. §22-24-28 (1988); Tenn. Code Ann. §39-17-911(a) (1991); Tex Penal Code Ann. §43.24(b) (1994); Utah Code Ann. §76-10-1206(2) (1995); Vt. Stat. Ann., Tit. 13, §2802(a) (1974); Va. Code Ann. §18.2-391 (1996); Wash. Rev. Code §9.68.060 (1988 and Supp. 1997); Wis. Stat. §948.11(2) (Supp. 1995).

*Position Papers
on Regulation
and the Public Interest*

APPENDIX C

SERVING THE COMMUNITY
A Public-Interest Vision
of the National Information Infrastructure

Computer Professionals for Social Responsibility

EXECUTIVE SUMMARY

The National Information Infrastructure (NII) holds great promise for the future. The convergence of communications technologies and the expansion of network services will transform our society and create unparalleled opportunities. CPSR believes that the benefits of the NII, however, should not be framed solely in economic or functional terms. The nation's communications infrastructure should reflect the values of democracy. Ultimately, the success of the NII program will be measured by whether it empowers citizens, protects individual rights, and strengthens the democratic institutions on which this country was founded.

CPSR believes that the development of the NII must be guided by a set of principles that reflect public-interest values. CPSR endorses the principles proposed by the Telecommunications Policy Roundtable, which are discussed in detail in the body of this report. But principles alone are not enough. Despite the general agreement surrounding public aims, it remains unclear whether these goals will be realized. There are many aspects of the NII planning process that already raise concern, several of which are outlined in this report:

- The NII may fail to provide universal access.
- A small number of companies may dominate the network and exert undue influence on its design and operation.
- There is a danger that carriers will control content on the NII.
- NII services may emphasize commerce at the expense of communication.

- Public access to government information may be restricted.
- The NII may fail to provide a vital public space.
- The NII may be used to justify the elimination of other essential public services.
- The NII may fail to protect individual privacy.
- Global communication using the NII may be restricted.
- The hardware structure may be chosen without giving adequate consideration to the software implications.

To avoid these dangers, it is essential to adopt policy and design guidelines that will serve the public interest.

CPSR makes the following policy recommendations to the Information Infrastructure Task Force:

- Consider the social impact of NII development.
- Guarantee equitable and universal access to network services.
- Promote widespread economic benefits.
- Promote diversity in content markets.
- Provide access to government services over the NII.
- Protect the public spaces necessary to foster community development.
- Encourage democratic participation in the design and development of the NII.
- Think globally rather than nationally.
- Guarantee functional integrity throughout the network.

In addition, CPSR proposes the following guidelines for designers of NII services:

- Emphasize ease of use.
- Provide full service to homes, workplaces, and community centers.
- Enable all users to act as both producers and consumers.
- Address privacy and security issues from the beginning.
- Develop open and interoperable standards.
- Encourage experimentation and evolution.
- Require high reliability.

PART 1
SUMMARY OF PRINCIPLES, CONCERNS, AND RECOMMENDATIONS

One of the central goals of the Clinton administration has been to develop new policies that strengthen U.S. communications and information technology. The administration's vision of a new National Information Infrastructure was first presented in a

February 1993 white paper entitled "Technology for America's Economic Growth: A New Direction to Build Economic Strength." That vision was later refined in a report entitled "The National Information Infrastructure: Agenda for Action" issued in September 1993 by the National Telecommunications and Information Administration (NTIA).

The Clinton administration believes that the National Information Infrastructure, or NII, offers enormous potential for the nation. The Executive Summary of the NTIA report concludes that:

> The benefits of the NII for the nation are immense. An advanced information infrastructure will enable U.S. firms to compete and win in the global economy, generating good jobs for the American people and economic growth for the nation. As importantly, the NII can transform the lives of the American people—ameliorating the constraints of geography, disability, and economic status—giving all Americans a fair opportunity to go as far as their talents and ambitions will take them.

CPSR also sees great promise in the NII. At the same time, we believe that its potential benefits are not solely economic. The NII must promote the public interest along with private interests. The success of the NII program will depend on the extent to which it empowers all citizens, protects individual rights, and strengthens the democratic institutions on which this country was founded.

1.1 Fundamental Principles

We believe that the design of the NII must be guided by a set of principles that reflect the importance of the public interest in communications and information technology. CPSR strongly endorses the following principles set forth by the Telecommunications Policy Roundtable in Washington, D.C., of which CPSR is a member:

1. Universal access. All people should have affordable access to the information infrastructure.
2. Freedom to communicate. The information infrastructure should enable all people to effectively exercise their fundamental right to communicate.
3. Vital civic sector. The information infrastructure must have a vital civic sector at its core.
4. Diverse and competitive marketplace. The information infrastructure should ensure competition among ideas and information providers.
5. Equitable workplace. New technologies should be used to enhance the quality of work and to promote equity in the workplace.
6. Privacy. Privacy should be carefully protected and extended.
7. Democratic policy-making. The public should be fully involved in policy-making for the information infrastructure.

Our experiences as both designers and users of networking systems lead us to formulate an additional principle:

8. Functional integrity. The functions provided by the NII must be powerful, versatile, well-documented, stable, reliable, and extensible.

1.2 Areas of Concern

The principles outlined in Section 1.1 are widely accepted. In public discussions of the NII, most participants embrace a similar set of goals. For example, much the same principles are expressed in the "Agenda for Action" paper issued by the NTIA and in position papers issued by the telecommunications industry. At the level of general goals, there is broad consensus throughout the United States that the NII cannot be limited to the commercial sphere but must also serve the public interest.

As members of CPSR, we are encouraged by this consensus. We also recognize that stating a goal and achieving it are profoundly different things. Despite the general agreement regarding the public-interest principles, it is not yet clear how much those principles will influence the design of the NII. There are many other factors involved. When private interests conflict with the public interest, decisions must inevitably be made. In some cases, the decisions may make it difficult to satisfy public-interest principles, no matter how widely those principles are held.

After listening to much of the early debate concerning the NII, we have identified the following areas of concern:

• The NII may fail to provide universal access. The principle of universal access is much easier to articulate than to achieve. If network connections are not readily available, particularly in rural or economically disadvantaged areas, the NII will fail to serve those communities. If the pricing structure is not carefully designed, individuals and public institutions lacking the necessary resources may be frozen out. Even if the network itself is accessible at a reasonable price, the NII will remain outside the reach of most nontechnical users unless training programs and well-designed software tools are available. It is critical that the designers of the NII undertake the necessary measures to ensure full network access to people in all sectors of the United States.

• A small number of companies may dominate the network and exert undue influence on its design and operation. The NII is an extremely large and ambitious program that will require substantial investment on the part of private companies who undertake the task of providing the physical infrastructure. Because of the enormous scale of the project, barriers to entry into the carrier market will be high, creating a situation in which it is difficult to rely on market forces to ensure effective competition. If a small number of companies end up dominating the market, it will be harder to guard against monopolistic tendencies in that market and to ensure that the public-interest goals are met.

• There is a danger that carriers will control content on the NII. The enormous economic potential of the NII lies not in the network infrastructure itself but rather in the information and services that infrastructure carries. Even so, the carriers that own the network may seek to control the content that flows through it. Of serious concern, along with more traditional forms of censorship, is the danger that carriers may give preference to content that they control. The economic history of the United States provides convincing evidence that it is difficult to provide an equitable marketplace for content providers when single companies are allowed to control both carrier and content.

• NII services may emphasize commerce at the expense of communication. Judging from the way information networks are used today, people value being on-line primarily because it gives them new ways to communicate with other people. Much of the recent discussion of the NII focuses instead on using the network to market information services. Failure to understand what people want from the NII may adversely affect the design. Over the past two decades, for example, many companies have conducted trials of videotext systems focused on shopping and information retrieval. All have been dismal failures. Now, as we stand poised to develop the NII, telephone, cable TV, computer, and broadcast companies are again focusing on providing systems to promote electronic consumerism. Why? Part of the explanation is that, just as engineers tend to emphasize the engineering aspects of what they design, business people tend to emphasize the business aspects. Most Americans are neither engineers nor business people. The NII must be designed to meet the needs of all.

• Public access to government information may be restricted. In recent years, more and more public information has been turned over to private companies for distribution. In the absence of pricing regulations, much of this information has become unavailable except to the well-funded. If the trend toward privatization continues, the NII will be unable to satisfy its enormous potential as a source of public information.

• The NII may fail to provide a vital public space. In recent years, public participation in the political process and civic life has eroded considerably. By providing a framework for communication and community-building, the NII has the potential to reverse this trend. To achieve that potential, individuals and groups that represent the public interest must be an integral part of the NII design process. Otherwise, the NII is unlikely to meet the needs of that constituency.

• The NII may be used to justify the elimination of other essential public services. Although increased access to information can benefit and empower everyone in society, it is important to recognize that there are many other problems in society that the NII will not address. For example, making government documents available through the NII does not eliminate the need for reference librarians any more than providing on-line medical advice eliminates the need for local doctors.

• The NII may fail to protect individual privacy. As the NII develops and the amount of data accessible through the network grows, concerns about individual privacy become more pressing. Using the NII, government agencies and private companies would have unprecedented opportunities to gather and disseminate information about individuals. If no protections are built into the infrastructure to guard against abuse, such data collection threatens to erode the rights of citizens. Similarly, if the network itself does not protect the privacy of its users, they will be unable to communicate freely.

• Global communication using the NII may be restricted. Even more than the networks of today, the NII will be global in its scope. Moreover, by providing a common medium for international exchange of information, the NII will open up unparalleled opportunities for economic, scientific, and cultural exchange. To take full advantage of those opportunities, however, the NII must support and encourage international participation. Unfortunately, there is some danger policymakers will use economic competitiveness or national security to justify restrictions on international traffic. While imposing such restrictions may benefit a particular industry or special interest, it also runs the serious risk of isolating the United States from the international electronic marketplace, cutting us off from the enormous benefits that come from greater cooperation in this area.

• The hardware structure may be chosen without giving adequate consideration to the software implications. The NII requires considerable investment in physical connections, transmission lines, switching stations, and other forms of computing hardware. Even so, the most important challenges in the NII design lie elsewhere—in the software that makes it both powerful and easy to use. All too often, hardware considerations are allowed to dominate the initial design of such a project, to the point that the hardware choices end up placing severe constraints on what the software can achieve.

An imaginative view of the risks of an NII designed without sufficient attention to public-interest needs can be found in the modern genre of dystopian fiction known as "cyberpunk." Cyberpunk novelists depict a world in which a handful of multinational corporations have seized control, not only of the physical world, but of the virtual world of cyberspace. The middle-class in these stories is sedated by a constant stream of mass-market entertainment that distracts them from the drudgery and powerlessness of their lives. It doesn't take a novelist's imagination to recognize the rapid concentration of power and the potential danger in the merging of major corporations in the computer, cable, television, publishing, radio, consumer electronics, film, and other industries. We would be distressed to see an NII shaped solely by the commercial needs of the entertainment, finance, home shopping, and advertising industries.

CPSR believes that the principles outlined in Section 1.1 provide a standard by which to judge the success of the NII. If the design meets those principles, the NII will indeed serve the public interest, revitalizing our communities and the nation as a whole. On the other hand, if the potential dangers are ignored, the NII may fall short of its goals and thereby fail to bring the power of the information age into everyone's reach.

1.3 CPSR'S Recommendations

CPSR has developed a set of recommendations that we feel will help avoid many of the pitfalls outlined in the preceding section. Although there is some overlap, we have divided our recommendations into two groups. The first, directed primarily to the Information Infrastructure Task Force and other governmental agencies responsible for oversight and administration of the NII, consists of recommendations concerning policy. The second is directed toward designers and addresses more technical aspects of the NII.

Policy Recommendations

CPSR agrees with the conclusion expressed in the NTIA document that "the government has an essential role to play" in the development of the NII. We believe that the NII cannot meet its public-policy objectives without some combination of government initiative and regulation. In particular, we recommend that the Administration seek to establish the following general policies.

P1. Consider the social impact. Beginning with the initial design, the Administration must evaluate the impact of the NII on the society at large. It is essential to conduct periodic reviews as the NII is implemented and used to ensure that it continues to serve the public interest.

P2. Guarantee equitable and universal access. To the extent that free-market principles cannot guarantee affordable access to a full range of NII services, the Administration must be publicly accountable for the achievement of this goal through some appropriate mix of legislation, regulation, taxation, and direct subsidies.

P3. Promote widespread economic benefits. The Administration should evaluate the NII's economic success using measures that reflect its impact on the economy as a whole, not merely the profits of NII investors and service providers.

P4. Promote diversity in content markets. The Administration must recognize the distinction between the carrier of NII information services and the content that is carried over that infrastructure. In economic terms, the greatest potential of the NII lies in the marketplace it will create for content services, and the Administration must take whatever steps are necessary to ensure that the content market is both fair and open.

P5. Provide access to government services and information over the NII. The Clinton/Gore technology announcement of February 1993 explicitly recognizes that information technology can "dramatically improve the way the Federal Government serves the people," thereby making the government "more cost-effective, efficient, and 'user-friendly.'" The Administration must continue to make provision of government services a central aspect of the NII design.

P6. Protect public spaces. The Administration should promote the development of a vital civic sector by ensuring resources, training, and support for public spaces within the NII where citizens can pursue noncommercial activities.

P7. Encourage democratic participation. Government must prevent concentrations of economic power from controlling the design of the NII and the operational "rules of the game." Decisions that affect the public's use of the NII must be conducted openly and democratically. To this end, the Administration must ensure full public disclosure and actively promote democratic decision-making. In addition, the Administration should ensure that any committees, such as the soon-to-be-appointed Advisory Council on the National Information Infrastructure, include sufficient representation from the public-interest community to ensure effective participation and to reflect the diversity of that constituency.

P8. Think globally. The Administration should actively facilitate the seamless connection of America's NII with the information infrastructures of other nations by working to resolve such issues as security, censorship, tariffs, and privacy. Moreover, the NII should not be limited to the United States and the highly industrialized nations of Europe and the Pacific Rim. Because communication and information are vital resources for all nations, it is in the common interest to help the developing countries become part of the global information infrastructure.

P9. Guarantee functional integrity. To the extent that market forces alone cannot guarantee that the design recommendations discussed in the following section will be achieved, the Administration should take appropriate steps to ensure that the NII design satisfies these critical technical, functional, and safety requirements.

Design Recommendations

Our breadth of experience with existing networks and communications technology lead us to make the following recommendations about the technical aspects of NII design:

D1. Emphasize ease of use. Existing computer networks have fallen short of serving the public interest because they are difficult for nonexperts to use. The most significant challenge facing NII designers is to reduce the barriers to entry into the information network that the NII provides, so that using the NII for simple inquiries becomes as easy as using the telephone.

D2. Provide full service to homes, workplaces, and community centers. From the beginning, NII designers must strive to provide a high level of service to users where they live and work—to private homes, libraries, community centers, and businesses. If the public at large is offered only restricted, second-class service, the NII will be unable to serve as a medium for individual and community empowerment.

D3. Enable all users to act as both producers and consumers. Perhaps the greatest strength of existing networks is the opportunity for all participants to act as both producers and consumers of new products and information. By making it easy for individuals and small groups to develop new on-line services, today's networks display a vitality and openness that is difficult to find in other media. Individual initiative and entrepreneurship must continue to be supported in the NII design.

D4. Address privacy and security issues from the beginning. As is the case with reliability, it is difficult to implement privacy and security as an afterthought. In order to provide sufficient safeguards, it is essential that privacy and security be considered throughout the NII design.

D5. Develop open and interoperable standards. The NII will never be a single, static entity. It will instead continue to grow, driven in part by the general progress of technology and the extension of service to developing networks throughout the world. The NII community must develop standards that facilitate the growth of the network and allow for the broadest possible participation in the process.

D6. Encourage experimentation and evolution. On the basis of our experience with existing networks, it is clear that the most significant source of new network services and capabilities will consist of contributions by the NII users themselves. Many of the facilities that are now considered part of the core of the network were once experimental projects. Someone using the network recognized a need, developed a new service in response to that need, and then made that service available to others. As the community of users expanded, the service was then refined and standardized to the point that it became a widely accepted tool. The NII must allow for and encourage the same sort of experimentation and evolutionary development.

D7. Require high reliability. As use of the network expands into more and more sectors of the economy, the need for high reliability and fault-tolerance will become increasingly important. To meet the requirements of its users, reliability must be a central theme of the design at every stage of the process.

PART 2
TODAY'S INFORMATION INFRASTRUCTURE: LESSONS FOR THE NII

Although the National Information Infrastructure will be larger, more powerful, and more widely used than current computer networks, it is important to recognize that the underpinnings of such an infrastructure already exist in the United States today. In fact, it is difficult to go through a day without using some part of the existing information infrastructure. We use a computer network every time we make a phone call, watch TV, listen to the radio, get cash from an automated teller machine, reserve an airplane ticket, or pay with a credit card.

Despite the pervasiveness of computer networks, relatively few people understand them in any detail. As computer professionals, the members of CPSR have extensive experience working with networks as both users and designers. As citizens, we recognize that technical issues are only a part of the design considerations. Public policy issues must be considered as well. To enable everyone to participate effectively in the debate over public policy, it is important for us to share our technical expertise.

The NII of tomorrow will evolve from the networks of today. It will incorporate the services currently offered by cable companies, the telephone system, and broadcast media. Yet we expect that, in many technical ways, the NII will more closely resemble existing general-purpose networks that link computers throughout the world. Transmission using the NII will be digital, not analog as many of these media are today. Data will travel in individual packets and not through the dedicated circuits that have traditionally been used for telephone communication. Information will flow in both directions, in contrast to its behavior in the broadcast media. These are all characteristics of existing computing networks, which makes them a useful model for the NII.

The closest existing analogue to our vision of the NII is the Internet, a loose confederacy of computer networks that can exchange data freely. Understanding the Internet—what it is, how it works, where it has succeeded, and what its shortcomings have been—makes it easier to comprehend the challenges that face the designers of the NII. This part of the report provides an analysis of the Internet.

2.1 A Brief History of the Internet

Although the Internet incorporates many different networks with different histories, the current system can be traced directly to the ARPANET project, which provided the first large-scale demonstration of a new digital communications technology called packet-switching. Beginning in 1968, the Advanced Research Projects Agency (ARPA) of the Department of Defense provided grants to several universities and corporations to develop a nationwide digital communications medium separate from the existing telephone system. The purpose of the ARPANET was to link researchers at different sites and allow them to share hardware and software resources. Using the ARPANET, those researchers could send electronic mail to each other, transfer files of information from one site to another, and connect directly to a system that might be hundreds or thousands of miles away.

The early ARPANET experiment was quite successful and led to a dramatic growth in network technology. When the ARPANET first became operational in late 1969, the entire network consisted of four computers. After the first ten years of operation, the number of connected computers expanded to more than 100. At that point, however, the ARPANET began to exceed the capacity permitted by its initial design. As is usually the case with large, computer-based systems, the main problems were not in the physical hardware that comprised the network, but in the software-based procedures and conventions established to facilitate communication, which are known as "protocols." The original ARPANET protocols were not flexible enough to accommodate the ongoing expansion of the ARPANET itself or permit other networks to connect easily into the ARPANET framework.

In the late 1970s, a new family of message protocols was designed to address these problems. These new protocols were formalized in 1980, and their use became an ARPANET requirement in 1983. The most basic of the new protocols are the Transmission Control Protocol (TCP) and the Internet Protocol (IP), which together provide the facility by which computers can exchange messages. In addition to the TCP and IP protocols, the extended protocol family includes the Simple Mail Transfer Protocol (SMTP), the File Transfer Protocol (FTP), and a protocol to allow users to connect directly to and use a remote machine (TELNET).

Many computer operators quickly adopted TCP/IP as the message protocol for their systems. Those who could not convert—either because TCP/IP required faster hardware or because they did not have control over their system software—could still use TCP/IP by connecting to a "gateway" machine that converted the local protocol into the TCP/IP standard. Use of TCP/IP is now widespread in many different networks because it facilitates communication with an ever-growing community that shares this common protocol.

Meanwhile, other networks began to come into existence. Because ARPANET access was restricted to institutions with defense-related contracts, universities pushed for independent networks. To meet this need, CSNET and BITNET were created in the 1970s and 1980s to serve different segments of the academic community. As part of its own process to develop network standards, Europe began to deploy an information infrastructure of its own, based on another protocol called X.25. At the same time, several hardware vendors in the United States developed proprietary network technologies for their own internal use.

Because they used different protocols, many of these networks were initially isolated from each other. To communicate between different networks, it was necessary to have one computer linked to two or more networks so that it could serve as a gateway machine. Using these gateways to transfer data between independent networks was difficult, because doing so required a thorough understanding of all the different protocols involved. During this period in network history, gateways were developed as needed and operated with mixed results.

As the Department of Defense began to reduce ARPANET support in the mid-1980s, the National Science Foundation (NSF) stepped in and supported a new networking structure called NSFNET that was available to universities without restriction and to commercial concerns for a fee. The NSF also funded five supercomputer sites and a network of high-speed connections between them. That connection matrix, with its wide availability and its use of the TCP/IP protocols, allowed NSFNET to become the "backbone" of an entire collection of networks that is known collectively as the Internet.

By making it possible for many different networks to communicate with standard protocols over a common backbone, the deployment of NSFNET accelerated the pace of network expansion. As of 1993, the Internet has become an enormous global web linking over 1.5 million computers in more than 50 countries. Data traffic on the NSFNET backbone doubles every year.

2.2 Management and Pricing Structures on the Internet

Given the size and importance of the Internet, its management structure is surprisingly loose and decentralized. To a certain extent, the Internet runs itself. The community of users and institutions connected to the Internet has such a strong interest in keeping the network running that they perform much of the management themselves. Even so, a certain amount of additional coordination is required.

The diverse assemblage of over 2000 individual networks is held together by the Internet Activities Board (IAB). This group serves as the coordinating committee for Internet design, engineering, and management. The committee has several functions, including

- Defining Internet standards and organizing the process by which standards are set
- Acting as the Internet's international technical policy liaison
- Undertaking strategic planning for the network
- Taking advantage of long-range opportunities
- Solving problems as they arise

Much of the work of the IAB is done through two subcommittees: the Internet Engineering Task Force, which manages the evolution of Internet protocols, and the Internet Research Task Force, which fosters research into new network technologies.

The administration of the NSFNET backbone is managed by Merit Inc., which is the parent organization of the mid-level network connecting state-supported universities in Michigan. The physical network that forms the backbone—the wires and routing hardware—is administered by Advanced Network Services (ANS), which is a not-for-profit consortium funded jointly by Merit, IBM, and MCI. Commercial organizations use the Internet through a for-profit subsidiary of ANS called CO+RE Inc. Access to the NSFNET backbone is given to mid-level networks for a fee. Universities, corporations, and commercial service providers then buy access to the mid-level networks on an ability-to-pay basis.

Funding for the Internet is as piecemeal and diverse as the networks it comprises. Within the NSFNET itself and the regional subnetworks, institutions generally pay a flat monthly or annual fee based on the speed of the connection. For universities, some of these costs are met through federal subsidies that pay for connections to mid-level networks and by federal subsidy of the NSFNET itself. Commercial users must pay their own way. Because the fee structure is not based on the volume of traffic, however, institutions do not need to pass the marginal costs of additional use back to individuals. As a result, the costs of network services are completely hidden from individual users who use the Internet through their university or company.

The pricing strategy has a profound effect on the Internet. The fact that individual users are not normally charged for service encourages use of the network and promotes the development of a more inclusive Internet community. Moreover, the pricing structure encourages experimentation, which in turn leads to the development of new software tools that increase the value of the Internet itself.

In certain foreign countries, individual users are charged based on connect time and traffic volume. This policy has had a noticeably chilling effect on use abroad. Increasingly, Internet users who obtain access to the network through commercial services in the United States are charged for that service in a similar way. If "metered service" becomes the norm, individuals and public institutions may be disenfranchised. Moreover, the network may lose the sense of openness and free experimentation that have driven much of its development in the past.

2.3 Successes of the Internet

The Internet has had many profound successes, which must be kept in mind when designing future networks. The following are among its successes:

- The Internet has proven valuable to a large number of users. For any computer system, one of the best measures of success is the satisfaction of the user community. By this measure, the Internet has clearly been successful. Individual users have found the Internet an extraordinarily valuable tool for many different purposes: communicating with friends and colleagues, sharing data and software, obtaining access to information, and participating in the development of new on-line communities. The explosive growth of Internet use is a clear indication that people find it worthwhile. Since computers all over the world can instantly store and deliver information at minimal cost, the potential of the network can only increase.

- The structure of the Internet encourages participation and involvement. The value of the Internet comes primarily from the knowledge and creativity its users bring to it. Many services, such as bulletin boards and user-generated archives, are successful only when people contribute to them. By making individual contribution easy, the Internet has enabled those services to develop and grow.

- The pricing strategy of the encourages experimentation and growth. For users in universities or companies, access to the Internet usually seems free and unlimited. Costs of the network are paid by institutions for which individual researchers and developers work. Because the Internet pricing structure charges a fixed fee for the institutional connection, most users are not charged for individual use. This policy, which allows users to peruse the network casually, has generated forms of interaction that could not flourish in an environment of usage or connect-time charges.

- The Internet is run democratically. Even though the Internet requires some central coordination, its loose management structure has demonstrated the value of allowing widespread participation in the process of running the network. Because each site derives considerable benefit from being a part of the Internet, individual users and their institutions often feel a strong investment in its success. This sense of investment on the part of users encourages them to participate more actively in network maintenance and administration and thereby leads to more democratic involvement. Moreover, communication on the Internet is remarkably free from censorship, particularly on bulletin boards and other network services that provide space for public discussion.

• The Internet has demonstrated the value of open, interoperable standards. The protocols currently in use were designed to coexist with as-yet-unknown protocols and to permit evolution. The fact that the TCP/IP network protocol has enabled the Internet to sustain dramatic growth over the last few years illustrates the advantages of evolutionary standards.

2.4 Shortcomings of the Internet

Despite its considerable successes, the Internet also has certain inadequacies when viewed as a prototype for the NII. The Internet is dwarfed as a carrier of data when compared to the size and connectivity of the telephone system. A number of improvements must be made to transform the Internet into a system that can serve the whole country inexpensively at high speed. Most of the following trouble areas are already under investigation.

• The Internet is not connected with enough services of general interest. Although many people find the current Internet to be exciting and rewarding, it does not provide certain facilities that many people need. For many users, the facilities provided today seem esoteric and outside of the bounds of their daily lives. To make the network useful, those individuals need access to social services, to job-training programs, to better health care, and to communities of people who share their interests. Making sure that the services provided by the NII are the ones that people need is perhaps the greatest challenge in its design.

• Individual Internet connections are too expensive and difficult to obtain. The cost of providing an Internet connection directly to a home is too high—often as much as an automobile. Although service providers offer a compromise allowing individuals to dial in to a shared Internet connection, such connections usually offer only a minimum form of interaction. The price of home connection needs to compare move favorably with telephone or cable TV service.

• Human-computer interfaces for the Internet are not yet very sophisticated. A large development effort needs to take place if extremely sophisticated services are to be offered to unsophisticated users. The Internet does not yet allow widespread, easy-to-use multimedia interaction. It is generally aimed at people who are technically very experienced and knowledgeable. Adding new services often requires a high level of sophistication that many people do not have.

• Information overload is a significant problem. As a network grows, the volume of information and services available on it also expands. Making use of that information, however, requires that users be able to find what they need, without being overwhelmed by massive amounts of data. On the Internet today, the proliferation of new bulletin boards, discussion lists, information sources, and tools for retrieving information makes it harder for any user to locate a specific piece of information and represents a significant barrier to new users. It is crucial to provide better mechanisms for both finding and limiting information, especially for the NII, which will be much larger in scale than the Internet.

• The Internet offers no adequate mechanism for controlling antisocial behavior. Although free interchange is what makes the Internet valuable, it can sometimes be annoying. Individuals often abuse the privilege of global communication by posting silly, trivial, or redundant questions or comments. Commercial concerns are now contemplating the fact that, at no additional charge over basic Internet service, they can post electronic mail to absolutely everyone. The low fixed-price structure will not cope with an influx of advertising, or individuals capriciously broadcasting messages for their personal amusement to Internet mailboxes worldwide. Mechanisms need to be evolved to balance, and enforce, as-yet-unmade policies concerning both freedom of speech and the cost of speech.

• The Internet lacks sufficient mechanisms to guarantee privacy and security. The Internet does not provide adequate safeguards to ensure privacy and security. In today's Internet, it is impossible to ensure that individual communication is kept confidential. In addition, well-publicized attacks on the network by malicious individuals intent on gaining unauthorized access underscores the failure of current network security policies.

• The current Internet design suffers from several technical problems. Although the TCP/IP protocols have been extremely successful, there is concern that these protocols cannot easily be adapted for extremely high-speed machines. Moreover, the Internet protocols used for routing—the process of deciding how to send data from one network to another—are still experimental. Several competing routing protocols are in use, which can lead to complicated failures of network routing as a whole. In addition, several of the existing protocols, including those used for sending mail and identifying individual machines on the network, are likely to become unworkable as the network grows. Growth also presents a challenge to the protocol design, because the number of available IP addresses is too small for a large global system.

2.5 Further Lessons from the Internet Experience

Although the Internet has been an enormous success, the computer science community is still in the process of discovering how networking can best be done. Along the way, we have learned many useful lessons that will apply to the design of the NII as well. These lessons include the following:

• The technical development of a network is not an easy process. Particularly in the early days, researchers were surprised at how difficult network technology turned out to be, and all the problems are not yet resolved.

• Network design and development must be evolutionary. In the process of getting to the current design, many alternative strategies were attempted and then discarded. The right answers emerged slowly through experimentation. That experimentation continues today and must certainly continue into the future, if the NII is to respond to evolving needs.

• Substantial research and development funding is required to develop the technology. Over the years, the Internet and its predecessor networks have required significant investment of both public and private resources to overcome the difficult problems that arise in network design. New technologies and new uses for the network will require additional research and development on an ongoing basis.

• An open, cooperative environment is critical to network success. By combining the efforts of many researchers and building up a shared technological base, the network was able to grow and develop much more successfully than would have been possible using a less cooperative approach.

• Users tend to engage in communication rather than information retrieval. The most popular services on the Internet include electronic mail, bulletin boards, and programs to mediate on-line conversations. People enjoy the opportunity to communicate with other people and to build new communities that share interests or concerns. As an example of such community-building, the Internet is home to a discussion group for women who work with computers. The participants often find that they are the only women in their work group—sometimes, the only women in their company. The on-line group allows them to discuss problems they have encountered and to get advice on how to work through difficult situations. At the very least, they find sympathy and assurance that they are not alone. The NII ought to provide the mechanism for the formation of many such distributed communities.

The stakes are clear. The NII has the potential to introduce a uniform, centralized, oppressive viewpoint that further stratifies and polarizes society. With thoughtful design, however, the NII could provide universal access, support developing communities, and nurture true democracy.

APPENDIX D

SEVEN PUBLIC INTEREST PRINCIPLES

Telecommunications Policy Roundtable

1. UNIVERSAL ACCESS

All people should have affordable access to the information infrastructure.

Fundamental to life, liberty, and the pursuit of happiness in the Information Age is access to video, audio, and data networks that provide a broad range of news, public affairs, education, health, and government information and services. Such services should be provided in a user-friendly format, widely available to everyone, including persons with disabilities. Information that is essential in order to fully participate in a democratic society should be provided free.

2. FREEDOM TO COMMUNICATE

The information infrastructure should enable all people to effectively exercise their fundamental right to communicate.

Freedom of speech should be protected and fostered by the new information infrastructure, guaranteeing the right of every person to communicate easily, affordably, and effectively. The design of the infrastructure should facilitate two-way, audio and video communication from anyone to any individual, group, or network. The rights of creators must be protected, while accommodating the needs of users and libraries. Telecommunication carriers should not be permitted to constrain the free flow of information protected by the First Amendment.

3. VITAL CIVIC SECTOR

The information infrastructure must have a vital civic sector at its core.

For our democracy to flourish in the 21st Century, there must be a vital civic sector which enables the meaningful participation of all segments of our pluralistic society. Just as we have established public libraries and public highways, we must create public arenas or "electronic commons" in the media landscape. This will require the active involvement of a broad range of civic institutions—schools, universities, libraries, not-for-profit groups, and governmental organizations. It will also require vibrant public telecommunications networks at the national, regional, and state level.

4. DIVERSE AND COMPETITIVE MARKETPLACE

The information infrastructure should ensure competition among ideas and information providers.

The information infrastructure must be designed to foster a healthy marketplace of ideas, where a full range of viewpoints is expressed and robust debate is stimulated. Individuals, nonprofits, and for-profit information providers need ready access to this marketplace if it is to thrive. To ensure competition among information providers, policies should be developed to lower barriers to entry (particularly for small and independent services); telecommunications carriers should not be permitted to control programming; and antitrust policies should be vigorously enforced to prevent market dominance by vertically-integrated media monopolies.

5. EQUITABLE WORKPLACE

New technologies should be used to enhance the quality of work and to promote equity in the workplace.

Because the information infrastructure will transform the content and conduct of work, policies should be developed to ensure that electronic technologies are utilized to improve the work environment rather than dehumanize it. Workers should share the benefits of the increased productivity that these technologies make possible. The rights and protections that workers now enjoy should be preserved and enhanced. To encourage nondiscriminatory practices throughout the information marketplace, public policy should promote greater representation of women, people of color, and persons with disabilities at all levels of management.

6. PRIVACY

Privacy should be carefully protected and extended.

A comprehensive set of policies should be developed to ensure that the privacy of all people is adequately protected. The collection of personal data should be strictly limited to the minimum necessary to provide specific services. Sharing data collected from individuals should only be permitted with their informed consent, freely given without coercion. Individuals should have the right to inspect and correct data files about them. Innovative billing practices should be developed that increase individual privacy.

7. DEMOCRATIC POLICY MAKING

The public should be fully involved in policy making for the information infrastructure.

The public must be fully involved in all stages of the development and ongoing regulation of the information infrastructure. The issues are not narrow technical matters which will only affect us as consumers; they are fundamental questions that will have profound effects on us as citizens and could reshape our democracy. Extensive efforts should be made to fully inform the public about what is at stake, and to encourage broad discussion and debate. The policy process should be conducted in an open manner with full press scrutiny. Effective mechanisms should be established to ensure continued public participation in telecommunications policy making.

APPENDIX E

CYBERSPACE
AND THE AMERICAN DREAM
A Magna Carta for the Knowledge Age

Release 1.2, August 22, 1994

This statement represents the cumulative wisdom and innovation of many dozens of people. It is based primarily on the thoughts of four "co-authors": Ms. Esther Dyson; Mr. George Gilder; Dr. George Keyworth; and Dr. Alvin Toffler. This release 1.2 has the final "imprimatur" of no one. In the spirit of the age: It is copyrighted solely for the purpose of preventing someone else from doing so. If you have it, you can use it any way you want. However, major passages are from works copyrighted individually by the authors, used here by permission; these will be duly acknowledged in release 2.0. It is a living document. Release 2.0 will be released in October 1994. We hope you'll use it is to tell us how to make it better. Do so by:

- Sending E-Mail to MAIL@PFF.ORG
- Faxing 202/484-9326 or calling 202/484-2312
- Sending POM (plain old mail) to 1301 K Street Suite 650 West, Washington, DC 20005

(The Progress & Freedom Foundation is a not-for-profit research and educational organization dedicated to creating a positive vision of the future founded in the historic principles of the American idea.)

PREAMBLE

The central event of the 20th century is the overthrow of matter. In technology, economics, and the politics of nations, wealth—in the form of physical resources—has been losing value and significance. The powers of mind are everywhere ascendant over the brute force of things.

In a First Wave economy, land and farm labor are the main "factors of production." In a Second Wave economy, the land remains valuable while the "labor" becomes massified around machines and larger industries. In a Third Wave economy, the central resource—a single word broadly encompassing data, information, images, symbols, culture, ideology, and values—is *actionable* knowledge.

The industrial age is not fully over. In fact, classic Second Wave sectors (oil, steel, auto-production) have learned how to benefit from Third Wave technological breakthroughs—just as the First Wave's agricultural productivity benefited exponentially from the Second Wave's farm-mechanization.

But the Third Wave, and the *Knowledge Age* it has opened, will not deliver on its potential unless it adds social and political dominance to its accelerating technological and economic strength. This means repealing Second Wave laws and retiring Second Wave attitudes. It also gives to leaders of the advanced democracies a special responsibility—to facilitate, hasten, and explain the transition.

As humankind explores this new "electronic frontier" of knowledge, it must confront again the most profound questions of how to organize itself for the common good. The meaning of freedom, structures of self-government, definition of property, nature of competition, conditions for cooperation, sense of community and nature of progress will each be redefined for the Knowledge Age—just as they were redefined for a new age of industry some 250 years ago.

What our 20th-century countrymen came to think of as the "American dream," and what resonant thinkers referred to as "the promise of American life" or "the American Idea," emerged from the turmoil of 19th-century industrialization. Now it's our turn: The knowledge revolution, and the Third Wave of historical change it powers, summon us to renew the dream and enhance the promise.

THE NATURE OF CYBERSPACE

The Internet—the huge (2.2 million computers), global (135 countries), rapidly growing (10-15% a month) network that has captured the American imagination—is only a tiny part of cyberspace. So just what is cyberspace?

More ecosystem than machine, cyberspace is a bioelectronic environment that is literally universal: It exists everywhere there are telephone wires, coaxial cables, fiber-optic lines or electromagnetic waves.

This environment is "inhabited" by knowledge, including incorrect ideas, existing in electronic form. It is connected to the physical environment by portals which allow people to see what's inside, to put knowledge in, to alter it, and to take knowledge out. Some of these portals are one-way (e.g. television receivers and television transmitters); others are two-way (e.g. telephones, computer modems).

Most of the knowledge in cyberspace lives the most temporary (or so we think) existence: Your voice, on a telephone wire or microwave, travels through space at the speed of light, reaches the ear of your listener, and is gone forever.

But people are increasingly building cyberspatial "warehouses" of data, knowledge, information and *mis*information in digital form, the ones and zeros of binary computer code. The storehouses themselves display a physical form (discs, tapes, CD-ROMs)—but what they contain is accessible only to those with the right kind of portal and the right kind of key.

The key is software, a special form of electronic knowledge that allows people to navigate through the cyberspace environment and make its contents understandable to the human senses in the form of written language, pictures and sound.

People are adding to cyberspace—creating it, defining it, expanding it—at a rate that is already explosive and getting faster. Faster computers, cheaper means of electronic storage, improved software and more capable communications channels (satellites, fiber-optic lines)—each of these factors independently add to cyberspace. But the real explosion comes from the combination of all of them, working together in ways we still do not understand.

The bioelectronic *frontier* is an appropriate metaphor for what is happening in cyberspace, calling to mind as it does the spirit of invention and discovery that led ancient mariners to explore the world, generations of pioneers to tame the American continent and, more recently, to man's first exploration of outer space.

But the exploration of cyberspace brings both greater opportunity, and in some ways more difficult challenges, than any previous human adventure.

Cyberspace is the land of knowledge, and the exploration of that land can be a civilization's truest, highest calling. The opportunity is now before us to empower every person to pursue that calling in his or her own way.

The challenge is as daunting as the opportunity is great. The Third Wave has profound implications for the nature and meaning of property, of the marketplace, of community and of individual freedom. As it emerges, it shapes new codes of behavior that move each organism and institution—family, neighborhood, church group, company, government, nation—inexorably beyond standardization and centralization, as well as beyond the materialist's obsession with energy, money and control.

Turning the economics of mass-production inside out, new information technologies are driving the financial costs of diversity—both product and personal—down toward zero, "demassifying" our institutions and our culture. Accelerating demassification creates the potential for vastly increased human freedom.

It also spells the death of the central institutional paradigm of modern life, the bureaucratic organization. (Governments, including the American government, are the last great redoubt of bureaucratic power on the face of the planet, and for them the coming change will be profound and probably traumatic.)

In this context, the one metaphor that is perhaps least helpful in thinking about cyberspace is—unhappily—the one that has gained the most currency: The Information Superhighway. Can you imagine a phrase less descriptive of the nature of cyberspace, or more misleading in thinking about its implications? Consider thee following set of polarities

Information Superhighway	/	Cyberspace
Limited Matter	/	Unlimited Knowledge
Centralized	/	Decentralized
Moving on a grid	/	Moving in space
Government ownership	/	A vast array of ownerships
Bureaucracy	/	Empowerment
Efficient but not hospitable	/	Hospitable if you customize it
Withstand the elements	/	Flow, float and fine-tune
Unions and contractors	/	Associations and volunteers
Liberation from First Wave	/	Liberation from Second Wave
Culmination of Second Wave	/	Riding the Third Wave

"The highway analogy is all wrong," explained Peter Huber in *Forbes* this spring, "for reasons rooted in basic economics. Solid things obey immutable laws of conservation—what goes south on the highway must go back north, or you end up with a mountain of cars in Miami. By the same token, production and consumption must balance. The average Joe can consume only as much wheat as the average Jane can grow. Information is completely different. It can be replicated at almost no cost—so every individual can (in theory) consume society's entire output. Rich and poor alike, we all run information deficits. We all take in more than we put out."

THE NATURE AND OWNERSHIP OF PROPERTY

Clear and enforceable property rights are essential for markets to work. Defining them is a central function of government. Most of us have "known" that for a long time. But to create the new cyberspace environment is to create *new* property—that is, new means of creating goods (including ideas) that serve people.

The property that makes up cyberspace comes in several forms: Wires, coaxial cable, computers and other "hardware"; the electromagnetic spectrum; and "intellectual property"—the knowledge that dwells in and defines cyberspace.

In each of these areas, two questions that must be answered. First, what does "ownership" *mean*? What is the nature of the property itself, and what does it mean to own it? Second, once we understand what ownership means, *who* is the owner? At the level of first principles, should ownership be public (i.e. government) or private (i.e. individuals)?

The answers to these two questions will set the basic terms upon which America and the world will enter the Third Wave. For the most part, however, these questions are not yet even being asked. Instead, at least in America, governments are attempting to take Second Wave concepts of property and ownership and apply them to the Third Wave. Or they are ignoring the problem altogether.

For example, a great deal of attention has been focused recently on the nature of "intellectual property"—i.e. the fact that knowledge is what economists call a "public good," and thus requires special treatment in the form of copyright and patent protection.

Major changes in U.S. copyright and patent law during the past two decades have broadened these protections to incorporate "electronic property." In essence, these reforms have attempted to take a body of law that originated in the 15th century, with Gutenberg's invention of the printing press, and apply it to the electronically stored and transmitted knowledge of the Third Wave.

A more sophisticated approach starts with recognizing how the Third Wave has fundamentally altered the nature of knowledge as a "good," and that the operative effect is not technology per se (the shift from printed books to electronic storage and retrieval systems), but rather the shift from a mass-production, mass-media, mass-culture civilization to a demassified civilization.

The big change, in other words, is the demassification of actionable knowledge.

The dominant form of new knowledge in the Third Wave is perishable, transient, *customized* knowledge: The right information, combined with the right software and presentation, at precisely the right time. Unlike the mass knowledge of the Second Wave—"public good" knowledge that was useful to everyone because most people's information needs were standardized—Third Wave customized knowledge is by nature a private good.

If this analysis is correct, copyright and patent protection of knowledge (or at least many forms of it) may no longer be unnecessary. In fact, the marketplace may already be creating vehicles to compensate creators of customized knowledge outside the cumbersome copyright/patent process, as suggested last year by John Perry Barlow:

> "One existing model for the future conveyance of intellectual property is real-time performance, a medium currently used only in theater, music, lectures, stand-up comedy and pedagogy. I believe the concept of performance will expand to include most of the information economy, from multi-casted soap operas to stock analysis. In these instances, commercial exchange will be more like ticket sales to a continuous show than the purchase of discrete bundles of that which is being shown. The other model, of course, is service. The entire professional class—doctors, lawyers, consultants, architects, etc.—are already being paid directly for their intellectual property. Who needs copyright when you're on a retainer?"

Copyright, patent and intellectual property represent only a few of the "rights" issues now at hand. Here are some of the others:

• Ownership of the electromagnetic spectrum, traditionally considered to be "public property," is now being "auctioned" by the Federal Communications Commission to private companies. Or is it? Is the very limited "bundle of rights" sold in those auctions really property, or more in the nature of a use permit—the right to use a part of the spectrum for a limited time, for limited purposes? In either case, are the rights being auctioned defined in a way that makes technological sense?

• Ownership over the infrastructure of wires, coaxial cable and fiber-optic lines that are such prominent features in the geography of cyberspace is today much less clear than might be imagined. Regulation, especially price regulation, of this property can be tantamount to confiscation, as America's cable operators recently learned when the Federal government imposed price limits on them and effectively confiscated an estimated $_____ billion of their net worth. (Whatever one's stance on the FCC's decision and the law behind it, there is no disagreeing with the proposition that one's ownership of a good is less meaningful when the government can step in, at will, and dramatically reduce its value.)

• The nature of capital in the Third Wave—tangible capital as well as intangible—is to depreciate in real value much faster than industrial-age capital—driven, if nothing else, by Moore's Law, which states that the processing power of the microchip doubles at least every 18 *months.* Yet accounting and tax regulations still require property to be depreciated over periods as long as 30 *years.* The result is a heavy bias in favor of "heavy industry" and against nimble, fast-moving baby businesses.

Who will define the nature of cyberspace property rights, and how? How can we strike a balance between interoperable open systems and protection of property.

THE NATURE OF THE MARKETPLACE

Inexpensive knowledge destroys economies-of-scale. Customized knowledge permits "just in time" production for an ever rising number of goods. Technological progress creates new means of serving old markets, turning one-time monopolies into competitive battlegrounds.

These phenomena are altering the nature of the marketplace, not just for information technology but for all goods and materials, shipping and services. In cyberspace itself, market after market is being transformed by technological progress from a "natural monopoly" to one in which competition is the rule. Three recent examples:

• The market for "mail" has been made competitive by the development of fax machines and overnight delivery—even though the "private express statutes" that technically grant the U.S. Postal Service a monopoly over mail delivery remain in place.

• During the past 20 years, the market for television has been transformed from one in which there were at most a few broadcast TV stations to one in which consumers can choose among broadcast, cable and satellite services.

 • The market for local telephone services, until recently a monopoly based on twisted-pair copper cables, is rapidly being made competitive by the advent of wireless service and the entry of cable television into voice communication. In England, Mexico, New Zealand and a host of developing countries, government restrictions preventing such competition have already been removed and consumers actually have the freedom to choose.

The advent of new technology and new products creates the potential for *dynamic competition*—competition between and among technologies and industries, each seeking to find the best way of serving customers' needs. Dynamic competition is different from static competition, in which many providers compete to sell essentially similar products at the lowest price.

Static competition is good, because it forces costs and prices to the lowest levels possible for a given product. Dynamic competition is better, because it allows competing technologies and new products to challenge the old ones and, if they really are better, to replace them. Static competition might lead to faster and stronger horses. Dynamic competition gives us the automobile.

Such dynamic competition—the essence of what Austrian economist Joseph Schumpeter called "creative destruction"—creates winners and losers on a massive scale. New technologies can render instantly obsolete billions of dollars of embedded infrastructure, accumulated over decades. The transformation of the U.S. computer industry since 1980 is a case in point.

In 1980, everyone knew who led in computer technology. Apart from the minicomputer boom, mainframe computers *were* the market, and America's dominance was largely based upon the position of a dominant vendor—IBM, with over 50% world market-share.

Then the personal-computing industry exploded, leaving older-style big-business-focused computing with a stagnant, piece of a burgeoning total market. As IBM lost market-share, many people became convinced that America had lost the ability to compete. By the mid-1980s, such alarmism had reached from Washington all the way into the heart of Silicon Valley.

But the real story was the renaissance of American business and technological leadership. In the transition from mainframes to PCs, a vast new market was created. This market was characterized by dynamic competition consisting of easy access and low barriers to entry. Start-ups by the dozens took on the larger established companies—and won.

After a decade of angst, the surprising outcome is that America is not only competitive internationally, but, by any measurable standard, America dominates the growth sectors in world economics—telecommunications, microelectronics, computer networking (or "connected computing") and software systems and applications.

The reason for America's victory in the computer wars of the 1980s is that dynamic competition was allowed to occur, in an area so breakneck and pell-mell that government would've had a hard time controlling it *even had it been paying attention*. The challenge for policy in the 1990s is to permit, even encourage, dynamic competition in every aspect of the cyberspace marketplace.

THE NATURE OF FREEDOM

Overseas friends of America sometimes point out that the U.S. Constitution is unique—because it states explicitly that power resides with the people, who delegate it to the government, rather than the other way around.

This idea—central to our free society—was the result of more than 150 years of intellectual and political ferment, from the Mayflower Compact to the U.S. Constitution, as explorers struggled to establish the terms under which they would tame a new frontier.

And as America continued to explore new frontiers—from the Northwest Territory to the Oklahoma land-rush—it consistently returned to this fundamental principle of rights, reaffirming, time after time, that power resides with the people.

Cyberspace is the latest American frontier. As this and other societies make ever deeper forays into it, the proposition that ownership of this frontier resides first *with the people* is central to achieving its true potential.

To some people, that statement will seem melodramatic. America, after all, remains a land of individual freedom, and this freedom clearly extends to cyberspace. How else to explain the uniquely American phenomenon of the hacker, who ignored every social pressure and violated every rule to develop a set of skills through an early and intense exposure to low-cost, ubiquitous computing.

Those skills eventually made him or her highly marketable, whether in developing applications-software or implementing networks. The hacker became a technician, an inventor and, in case after case, a creator of new wealth in the form of the baby businesses that have given America the lead in cyberspatial exploration and settlement.

It is hard to imagine hackers surviving, let alone thriving, in the more formalized and regulated democracies of Europe and Japan. In America, they've become vital for economic growth and trade leadership. Why? Because Americans still celebrate individuality over conformity, reward achievement over consensus and militantly protect the right to be different.

But the need to affirm the basic principles of freedom is real. Such an affirmation is needed in part because we are entering new territory, where there are as yet no rules—just as there were no rules on the American continent in 1620, or in the Northwest Territory in 1787.

Centuries later, an affirmation of freedom—by this document and similar efforts—is needed for a second reason: We are at the end of a century dominated by the mass institutions of the industrial age. The industrial age encouraged *conformity* and relied on *standardization*. And the institutions of the day—corporate and government bureaucracies, huge civilian and military administrations, schools of all types—reflected these priorities. Individual liberty suffered—sometimes only a little, sometimes a lot:

• In a Second Wave world, it might make sense for government to insist on the right to peer into every computer by requiring that each contain a special "clipper chip."

• In a Second Wave world, it might make sense for government to assume ownership over the broadcast spectrum and demand massive payments from citizens for the right to use it.

• In a Second Wave world, it might make sense for government to prohibit entrepreneurs from entering new markets and providing new services.

• And, in a Second Wave world, dominated by a few old-fashioned, one-way media "networks," it might even make sense for government to influence which political viewpoints would be carried over the airwaves.

All of these interventions might have made sense in a Second Wave world, where standardization dominated and where it was assumed that the scarcity of knowledge (plus a scarcity of telecommunications capacity) made bureaucracies and other elites better able to make decisions than the average person.

But, whether they made sense before or not, these and literally thousands of other infringements on individual rights now taken for granted make no sense at all in the Third Wave.

For a century, those who lean ideologically in favor of freedom have found themselves at war not only with their ideological opponents, but with a time in history when the value of conformity was at its peak. However desirable as an ideal, individual freedom often seemed impractical. The mass institutions of the Second Wave required us to give up freedom in order for the system to "work."

The coming of the Third Wave turns that equation inside-out. The complexity of Third Wave society is too great for any centrally planned bureaucracy to manage. Demassification, customization, individuality, freedom—these are the keys to success for Third Wave civilization.

THE ESSENCE OF COMMUNITY

If the transition to the Third Wave is so positive, why are we experiencing so much anxiety? Why are the statistics of social decay at or near all-time highs? Why does cyberspatial "rapture" strike millions of prosperous Westerners as lifestyle *rupture*? Why do the principles that have held us together as a nation seem no longer sufficient—or even wrong?

The incoherence of political life is mirrored in disintegrating personalities. Whether 100% covered by health plans or not, psychotherapists and gurus do a land-office business, as people wander aimlessly amid competing therapies. People slip into cults and covens or, alternatively, into a pathological privatism, convinced that reality is absurd, insane or meaningless. "If things are so good," *Forbes* magazine asked recently, "why do we feel so bad?"

In part, this is why: Because we constitute the final generation of an old civilization and, at the very same time, the first generation of a new one. Much of our personal confusion and social disorientation is traceable to conflict *within us* and within our political institutions—between the dying Second Wave civilization and the emergent Third Wave civilization thundering in to take its place.

Second Wave ideologues routinely lament the breakup of mass society. Rather than seeing this enriched diversity as an opportunity for human development, they attach it as "fragmentation" and "balkanization." But to reconstitute democracy in Third Wave terms, we need to jettison the frightening but false assumption that more diversity automatically brings more tension and conflict in society.

Indeed, the exact reverse can be true: If 100 people all desperately want the same brass ring, they may be forced to fight for it. On the other hand, if each of the 100 has a different objective, it is far more rewarding for them to trade, cooperate, and form symbiotic relationships. Given appropriate social arrangements, diversity can make for a secure and stable civilization.

No one knows what the Third Wave communities of the future will look like, or where "demassification" will ultimately lead. It is clear, however, that cyberspace will play an important role knitting together in the diverse communities of tomorrow, facilitating the creation of "electronic neighborhoods" bound together not by geography but by shared interests.

Socially, putting advanced computing power in the hands of entire populations will alleviate pressure on highways, reduce air pollution, allow people to live further away from crowded or dangerous urban areas, and expand family time.

The late Phil Salin (in Release 1.0 11/25/91) offered this perspective: "[B]y 2000, multiple cyberspaces will have emerged, diverse and increasingly rich. Contrary to naive views, these cyberspaces will not all be the same, and they will not all be open to the general public. The global network is a connected 'platform' for a collection of diverse communities, but only a loose, heterogeneous community itself. Just as access to homes, offices, churches and department stores is controlled by their owners or managers, most virtual locations will exist as distinct places of private property."

"But unlike the private property of today," Salin continued, "the potential variations on design and prevailing customs will explode, because many variations can be implemented cheaply in software. And the 'externalities' associated with variations can drop; what happens in one cyberspace can be kept from affecting other cyberspaces."

"Cyberspaces" is a wonderful *pluralistic* word to open more minds to the Third

Wave's civilizing potential. Rather than being a centrifugal force helping to tear society apart, cyberspace can be one of the main forms of glue holding together an increasingly free and diverse society.

THE ROLE OF GOVERNMENT

The current Administration has identified the right goal: Reinventing government for the 21st Century. To accomplish that goal is another matter, and for reasons explained in the next and final section, it is not likely to be fully accomplished in the immediate future. This said, it is essential that we understand what it really means to create a Third Wave government and begin the process of transformation.

Eventually, the Third Wave will affect virtually everything government does. The most pressing need, however, is to revamp the policies and programs that are slowing the creation of cyberspace. Second Wave programs for Second Wave industries—the status quo for the status quo—will do little damage in the short run. It is the government's efforts to apply its Second Wave modus operandi to the fast-moving, decentralized creatures of the Third Wave that is the real threat to progress. Indeed, if there is to be an "industrial policy for the knowledge age," it should focus on removing barriers to competition and massively deregulating the fast-growing telecommunications and computing industries.

One further point should be made at the outset: Government should be as strong and as big as it needs to be to accomplish its central functions effectively and efficiently. The reality is that a Third Wave government will be vastly smaller (perhaps by 50 percent or more) than the current one—this is an inevitable implication of the transition from the centralized power structures of the industrial age to the dispersed, decentralized institutions of the Third. But smaller government does not imply weak government; nor does arguing for smaller government require being "against" government for narrowly ideological reasons.

Indeed, the transition from the Second Wave to the Third Wave will require a level of government *activity* not seen since the New Deal. Here are five proposals to back up the point.

1. The Path to Interactive Multimedia Access

The "Jeffersonian Vision" offered by Mitch Kapor and Jerry Berman has propelled the Electronic Frontier Foundation's campaign for an "open platform" telecom architecture:

> "The amount of electronic material the superhighway can carry is dizzying, compared to the relatively narrow range of broadcast TV and the limited number of cable channels. Properly constructed and regulated, it could be open to all who wish to speak, publish and communicate. None of the interactive services will be possible, however, if we have an eight-lane data superhighway rushing into every

home and only a narrow footpath coming back out. Instead of settling for a multi-media version of the same entertainment that is increasingly dissatisfying on today's TV, we need a superhighway that encourages the production and distribution of a broader, more diverse range of programming." (*New York Times*, 11/24/93, p. A25)

The question is: What role should government play in bringing this vision to reality? But also: Will incentives for the openly-accessible, "many to many," national multimedia network envisioned by EFF harm the rights of those now constructing thousands of non-open local area networks?

These days, interactive multimedia is the daily servant only of avant-garde firms and other elites. But the same thing could have been said about word-processors 12 years ago, or phone-line networks six years ago. Today we have, in effect, universal access to personal computing—which no political coalition ever subsidized or "planned." And America's *networking* menu is in a hyper-growth phase. Whereas the accessing software cost $50 two years ago, today the same companies hand it out free—to get more people on-line.

This egalitarian explosion has occurred in large measure because government has stayed out of these markets, letting personal computing take over while mainframes rot (almost literally) in warehouses, and allowing (no doubt more by omission than commission) computer networks to grow, free of the kinds of regulatory restraints that affect phones, broadcast and cable.

All of which leaves reducing barriers to entry and innovation as the only effective near-term path to Universal Access. In fact, it can be argued that a near-term national interactive multimedia network is impossible unless regulators permit much greater collaboration between the cable industry and phone companies. The latter's huge fiber resources (nine times as extensive as industry fiber and rising rapidly) could be joined with the huge asset of 57 million broadband links (i.e. into homes now receiving cable-TV service) to produce a new kind of national network—multimedia, interactive and (as costs fall) increasingly accessible to Americans of modest means.

That is why obstructing such collaboration—in the cause of forcing a competition between the cable and phone industries—is socially elitist. To the extent it prevents collaboration between the cable industry and the phone companies, present federal policy actually thwarts the Administration's own goals of access and empowerment.

The other major effect of prohibiting the "manifest destiny" of cable preserves the broadcast (or narrowband) television model. In fact, stopping an interactive multimedia network perpetuates John Malone's original formula—which everybody (especially Vice-President Gore and the FCC) claims to oppose because of the control it leaves with system owners and operators.

The key condition for replacing Malone's original narrowband model is true bandwidth abundance. When the federal government prohibits the interconnection of conduits, the model gains a new lease on life. In a world of bandwidth scarcity, the owner of the conduit not only can but must control access to it—thus the owner of the conduit also shapes the content. It really doesn't matter who the owner is. Bandwidth scarcity will require the managers of the network to determine the video programming on it.

Since cable is everywhere, particularly within cities, it would allow a closing of the gap between the knowledge-rich and knowledge-poor. Cable's broadband "pipes" *already* touch almost two-thirds of American households (and are easily accessible to another one-fourth). The phone companies have broadband fiber. A hybrid network—co-ax plus fiber—is the best means to the next generation of cyberspace expansion. What if this choice is blocked?

In that case, what might be called cyberspace democracy will be confined to the computer industry, where it will arise from the Internet over the years, led by corporate and suburban/exurban interests. While not a technological calamity, this might be a *social* perversion equivalent to what "Japan Inc." did to its middle and lower classes for decades: Make them pay 50% more for the same quality vehicles that were gobbling up export markets.

Here's the parallel: If Washington forces the phone companies and cable operators to develop supplementary and duplicative networks, most other advanced industrial countries will attain cyberspace democracy—via an interactive multimedia "open platform"—before America does, despite this nation's technological dominance.

Not only that, but the long-time alliance of East Coast broadcasters and Hollywood glitterati will have a new lease on life: If their one-way video empires win new protection, millions of Americans will be deprived of the tools to help build a new interactive multimedia culture.

A contrived competition between phone companies and cable operators will not deliver the two-way, multimedia and more civilized tele-society Kapor and Berman sketch. Nor is it enough to simply "get the government out of the way." Real issues of antitrust must be addressed, and no sensible framework exists today for addressing them. Creating the conditions for universal access to interactive multimedia will require a fundamental rethinking of government policy.

2. Promoting Dynamic Competition

Technological progress is turning the telecommunications marketplace from one characterized by "economies of scale" and "natural monopolies" into a prototypical competitive market. The challenge for government is to encourage this shift—to create the circumstances under which new competitors and new technologies will challenge the natural monopolies of the past.

Price-and-entry regulation makes sense for natural monopolies. The tradeoff is a straightforward one: The monopolist submits to price regulation by the state, in return for an exclusive franchise on the market.

But what happens when it becomes economically desirable to have more than one provider in a market? The continuation of regulation under these circumstances stops progress in its tracks. It prevents new entrants from introducing new technologies and new products, while depriving the regulated monopolist of any incentive to do so on its own.

Price-and-entry regulation, in short, is the antithesis of dynamic competition.

The alternative to regulation is antitrust. Antitrust law is designed to prevent the acts and practices that can lead to the creation of new monopolies, or harm consumers by forcing up prices, limiting access to competing products or reducing service quality. Antitrust law is the means by which America has, for over 120 years, fostered competition in markets where many providers can and should compete.

The market for telecommunications services—telephone, cable, satellite, wireless—is now such a market. The implication of this simple fact is also simple, and price/entry regulation of telecommunications services—by state and local governments as well as the Federal government—should therefore be replaced by antitrust law as rapidly as possible.

This transition will not be simple, and it should not be instantaneous. If antitrust is to be seriously applied to telecommunications, some government agencies (e.g. the Justice Department's Antitrust Division) will need new types of expertise. And investors in regulated monopolies should be permitted time to re-evaluate their investments given the changing nature of the legal conditions in which these firms will operate—a luxury not afforded the cable industry in recent years.

This said, two additional points are important. First, delaying implementation is different from delaying enactment. The latter should be immediate, even if the former is not. Secondly, there should be no half steps. Moving from a regulated environment to a competitive one is—to borrow a cliche—like changing from driving on the left side of the road to driving on the right: You can't do it gradually.

3. Defining and Assigning Property Rights

In 1964, libertarian icon Ayn Rand wrote:

> "It is the proper task of government to protect individual rights and, as part of it, formulate the laws by which these rights are to be implemented and adjudicated. It is the government's responsibility to define the application of individual rights to a given sphere of activity—to define (i.e. to identify), not create, invent, donate, or expropriate. The question of defining the application of property rights has arisen frequently, in the wake of oil rights, vertical space rights, etc. In most cases, the American government has been guided by the proper principle: It sought to protect all the individual rights involved, not to abrogate them." ("The Property Status of the Airwaves," *Objectivist Newsletter*, April 1964)

Defining property rights in cyberspace is perhaps the single most urgent and important task for government information policy. Doing so will be a complex task, and each key area—the electromagnetic spectrum, intellectual property, cyberspace itself (including the right to privacy)—involves unique challenges. The important points here are:

• First, this is a "central" task of government. A Third Wave government will understand the importance and urgency of this undertaking and begin seriously to address it; to fail to do so is to perpetuate the politics and policy of the Second Wave.

• Secondly, the key principle of ownership by the people—private ownership—should govern every deliberation. Government does not own cyberspace, the people do.

• Thirdly, clarity is essential. Ambiguous property rights are an invitation to litigation, channeling energy into courtrooms that serve no customers and create no wealth. From patent and copyright systems for software, to challenges over the ownership and use of spectrum, the present system is failing in this simple regard.

The difference between America's historic economic success can, in case after case, be traced to our wisdom in creating and allocating clear, enforceable property rights. The creation and exploration of cyberspace requires that wisdom to be recalled and reaffirmed.

4. Creating Pro-Third-Wave Tax and Accounting Rules

We need a whole set of new ways of accounting, both at the level of the enterprise, and of the economy.

"GDP" and other popular numbers do nothing to clarify the magic and muscle of information technology. The government has not been very good at measuring service-sector output, and almost all institutions are incredibly bad at measuring the productivity of *information*. Economists are stuck with a set of tools designed during, or as a result of, the 1930s. So they have been measuring less and less important variables with greater and greater precision.

At the level of the enterprise, obsolete accounting procedures cause us to systematically *overvalue* physical assets (i.e. property) and *undervalue* human-resource assets and intellectual assets. So, if you are an inspired young entrepreneur looking to start a software company, or a service company of some kind, and it is heavily information-intensive, you will have a harder time raising capital than the guy next door who wants to put in a set of beat-up old machines to participate in a topped-out industry.

On the tax side, the same thing is true. The tax code always reflects the varying lobbying pressures brought to bear on government. And the existing tax code was brought into being by traditional manufacturing enterprises and the allied forces that arose during the assembly line's heyday.

The computer industry correctly complains that half their product is depreciated in six months or less—yet they can't depreciate it for tax purposes. The U.S. semiconductor industry faces five-year depreciation timetables for products that have three-year lives (in contrast to Japan, where chipmakers can write off their fabrication plants in one year). Overall, the tax advantage remains with the long, rather than the short, product life-cycle, even though the latter is where all design and manufacturing are trending.

It is vital that accounting and tax policies—both those promulgated by private-sector regulators like the Financial Accounting Standards Board and those promulgated by the government at the IRS and elsewhere—start to reflect the shortened capital life-cycles of the Knowledge Age, and the increasing role of *intangible* capital as "wealth."

5. Creating a Third Wave Government

Going beyond cyberspace policy per se, government must remake itself and redefine its relationship to the society at large. No single set of policy changes that can create a future-friendly government. But there are some yardsticks we can apply to policy proposals. Among them:

• *Is it based on the factory model, i.e. on standardization, routine and mass-production?* If so, it is a Second Wave policy. Third Wave policies encourage uniqueness.

• *Does it centralize control?* Second Wave policies centralize power in bureaucratic institutions; Third Wave policies work to spread power—to empower those closest to the decision.

• *Does it encourage geographic concentration?* Second Wave policies encourage people to congregate physically; Third Wave policies permit people to work at home, and to live wherever they choose.

• *Is it based on the idea of mass culture—of everyone watching the same sit-coms on television—or does it permit, even encourage, diversity within a broad framework of shared values?* Third Wave policies will help transform diversity from a threat into an array of opportunities.

A serious effort to apply these tests to every area of government activity—from the defense and intelligence community to health care and education—would ultimately produce a complete transformation of government as we know it. Since that is what's needed, let's start applying.

GRASPING THE FUTURE

The conflict between Second Wave and Third Wave groupings is the central political tension cutting through our society today. The more basic political question is not who controls the last days of industrial society, but who shapes the new civilization rapidly rising to replace it. Who, in other words, will shape the nature of cyberspace and its impact on our lives and institutions?

Living on the edge of the Third Wave, we are witnessing a battle not so much over the nature of the future—for the Third Wave will arrive—but over the nature of the transition. On one side of this battle are the partisans of the industrial past. On the other are growing millions who recognize that the world's most urgent problems can no longer be resolved within the massified frameworks we have inherited.

The Third Wave sector includes not only high-flying computer and electronics firms and biotech start-ups. It embraces advanced, information-driven manufacturing in every industry. It includes the increasingly data-drenched services—finance, software, entertainment, the media, advanced communications, medical services, consulting, training and learning. The people in this sector will soon be the dominant constituency in American politics.

And all of those confront a set of constituencies made frightened and defensive by their mainly Second Wave habits and locales: Command-and-control regulators, elected officials, political opinion-molders, philosophers mired in materialism, traditional interest groups, some broadcasters and newspapers—and every major institution (including corporations) that believes its future is best served by preserving the past.

For the time being, the entrenched powers of the Second Wave dominate Washington and the statehouses—a fact nowhere more apparent than in the 1993 infrastructure bill: Over $100 billion for steel and cement, versus one lone billion for electronic infrastructure. Putting aside the question of whether the government should be building electronic infrastructure in the first place, the allocation of funding in that bill shows the Second Wave swamping the Third.

Only one political struggle so far contradicts the landscape offered in this document, but it is a big one: Passage of the North American Free Trade Agreement last November. This contest carried both sides beyond partisanship, beyond regionalism, and—after one climactic debate on CNN—beyond personality. The pro-NAFTA coalition opted to serve the opportunity instead of the problem, and the future as opposed to the past. That's why it constitutes a standout model for the likely development of a Third Wave political dialectic.

But a "mass movement" for cyberspace is still hard to see. Unlike the "masses" during the industrial age, this rising Third Wave constituency is highly diverse. Like the economic sectors it serves, it is demassified—composed of individuals who prize their differences. This very heterogeneity contributes to its lack of political awareness. It is far harder to unify than the masses of the past.

Yet there are key themes on which this constituency-to-come can agree. To start with, liberation—from Second Wave rules, regulations, taxes and laws laid in place to serve the smokestack barons and bureaucrats of the past. Next, of course, must come the creation—creation of a new civilization, founded in the eternal truths of the American Idea.

It is time to embrace these challenges, to grasp the future and pull ourselves forward. If we do so, we will indeed renew the American Dream and enhance the promise of American life.

APPENDIX F

TECHNOREALISM

Overview
[posted 12 March 1998]

In this heady age of rapid technological change, we all struggle to maintain our bearings. The developments that unfold each day in communications and computing can be thrilling and disorienting. One understandable reaction is to wonder: Are these changes good or bad? Should we welcome or fear them?

The answer is both. Technology is making life more convenient and enjoyable, and many of us healthier, wealthier, and wiser. But it is also affecting work, family, and the economy in unpredictable ways, introducing new forms of tension and distraction, and posing new threats to the cohesion of our physical communities.

Despite the complicated and often contradictory implications of technology, the conventional wisdom is woefully simplistic. Pundits, politicians, and self-appointed visionaries do us a disservice when they try to reduce these complexities to breathless tales of either high-tech doom or cyber-elation. Such polarized thinking leads to dashed hopes and unnecessary anxiety, and prevents us from understanding our own culture.

Over the past few years, even as the debate over technology has been dominated by the louder voices at the extremes, a new, more balanced consensus has quietly taken shape. This document seeks to articulate some of the shared beliefs behind that consensus, which we have come to call technorealism.

Technorealism demands that we think critically about the role that tools and interfaces play in human evolution and everyday life. Integral to this perspective is our understanding that the current tide of technological transformation, while important and powerful, is actually a continuation of waves of change that have taken place throughout history. Looking, for example, at the history of the automobile, television, or the telephone—not just the devices but the institutions they became—we see profound benefits as well as substantial costs. Similarly, we anticipate mixed blessings from today's emerging technologies, and expect to forever be on guard for

257

unexpected consequences—which must be addressed by thoughtful design and appropriate use.

As technorealists, we seek to expand the fertile middle ground between techno-utopianism and neo-Luddism. We are technology "critics" in the same way, and for the same reasons, that others are food critics, art critics, or literary critics. We can be passionately optimistic about some technologies, skeptical and disdainful of others. Still, our goal is neither to champion nor dismiss technology, but rather to understand it and apply it in a manner more consistent with basic human values.

Below are some evolving basic principles that help explain technorealism.

PRINCIPLES OF TECHNOREALISM

1. Technologies are not neutral.

A great misconception of our time is the idea that technologies are completely free of bias—that because they are inanimate artifacts, they don't promote certain kinds of behaviors over others. In truth, technologies come loaded with both intended and *unintended* social, political, and economic leanings. Every tool provides its users with a particular manner of seeing the world and specific ways of interacting with others. It is important for each of us to consider the biases of various technologies and to seek out those that reflect our values and aspirations.

2. The Internet is revolutionary, but not Utopian.

The Net is an extraordinary communications tool that provides a range of new opportunities for people, communities, businesses, and government. Yet as cyberspace becomes more populated, it increasingly resembles society at large, in all its complexity. For every empowering or enlightening aspect of the wired life, there will also be dimensions that are malicious, perverse, or rather ordinary.

3. Government has an important role to play on the electronic frontier.

Contrary to some claims, cyberspace is not formally a place or jurisdiction separate from Earth. While governments should respect the rules and customs that have arisen in cyberspace, and should not stifle this new world with inefficient regulation or censorship, it is foolish to say that the public has no sovereignty over what an errant citizen or fraudulent corporation does online. As the representative of the people and the guardian of democratic values, the state has the right and responsibility to help integrate cyberspace and conventional society.

Technology standards and privacy issues, for example, are too important to be entrusted to the marketplace alone. Competing software firms have little interest in preserving the open standards that are essential to a fully functioning interactive network. Markets encourage innovation, but they do not necessarily insure the public interest.

4. Information is not knowledge.

All around us, information is moving faster and becoming cheaper to acquire, and the benefits are manifest. That said, the proliferation of data is also a serious challenge, requiring new measures of human discipline and skepticism. We must not confuse the thrill of acquiring or distributing information quickly with the more daunting task of converting it into knowledge and wisdom. Regardless of how advanced our computers become, we should never use them as a substitute for our own basic cognitive skills of awareness, perception, reasoning, and judgment.

5. Wiring the schools will not save them.

The problems with America's public schools—disparate funding, social promotion, bloated class size, crumbling infrastructure, lack of standards—have almost nothing to do with technology. Consequently, no amount of technology will lead to the educational revolution prophesied by President Clinton and others. The art of teaching cannot be replicated by computers, the Net, or by "distance learning." These tools can, of course, augment an already high-quality educational experience. But to rely on them as any sort of panacea would be a costly mistake.

6. Information wants to be protected.

It's true that cyberspace and other recent developments are challenging our copyright laws and frameworks for protecting intellectual property. The answer, though, is not to scrap existing statutes and principles. Instead, we must update old laws and interpretations so that information receives roughly the same protection it did in the context of old media. The goal is the same: to give authors sufficient control over their work so that they have an incentive to create, while maintaining the right of the public to make fair use of that information. In neither context does information want "to be free." Rather, it needs to be protected.

7. The public owns the airwaves; the public should benefit from their use.

The recent digital spectrum giveaway to broadcasters underscores the corrupt and inefficient misuse of public resources in the arena of technology. The citizenry should benefit and profit from the use of public frequencies, and should retain a portion of the spectrum for educational, cultural, and public access uses. We should demand more for private use of public property.

8. Understanding technology should be an essential component of global citizenship.

In a world driven by the flow of information, the interfaces—and the underlying code—that make information visible are becoming enormously powerful social forces. Understanding their strengths and limitations, and even participating in the creation of better tools, should be an important part of being an involved citizen. These tools affect our lives as much as laws do, and we should subject them to a similar democratic scrutiny.

APPENDIX G

WHY GOVERNMENT IS THE SOLUTION, AND NOT THE PROBLEM

In the Pursuit of a Free Market
for Telecommunications Services

Gigi B. Sohn
Executive Director
Media Access Project

I am often asked by free market scholars to debate whether the government should have any role in ensuring that all Americans have affordable access to advanced telecommunications networks and services. They argue that government should have no such role, that it should stay out of the technology business, and that the market will determine who gets how much.

But this all-or-nothing approach not only ignores current realities, it is ultimately counterproductive. Libertarians must get past the notion that government is one day either going to disintegrate or legislate itself out of existence. And they must accept that subsidies benefitting the rich and the poor will not disappear overnight. Thus, the important questions become not whether government should be involved, but how it should be involved, and how can that involvement help libertarians reach the goals of smaller government and freer markets?

I would argue that government can play a constructive role in making markets work better, thereby lessening the need for government involvement in the future, and, in particular, obviating intrusive content-based regulation. It can do so by ensuring that all Americans have access to the tools that are becoming more and more central to education, the economy, social interaction, First Amendment values and democracy. And it can do so by making more competitive markets that are currently dominated by entrenched monopolies.

Affordable Access to New Technologies
Makes Markets Work Better

Nondiscriminatory and affordable access to telecommunications services is needed in the age of the Internet, more than ever. New technological advances—and those that are yet to come—will redefine telecommunications services and increase their importance well beyond ordinary telephone service. These technologies will bring new modes of exchanging opinions, information, news and viewpoints; new tools for education and skill development; new methods for conducting research and commercial activity; and new means of engaging in civic discourse. More than ever before, these technologies can promote important First Amendment and democratic values.

Ultimately, affordable access to new telecommunications services increases efficiencies that help markets work more efficiently and equitably. New technologies improve the distribution of information that is essential to participating in the market. Affordable access equalizes the receipt of this information, thereby erasing many of the inequities that exist today when some in the market are privy to greater intelligence than others. And when all speakers—commercial as well as those with political messages—can reach all individuals, the market will function even more efficiently.

When everyone has greater accessibility to connected individuals, reliance on government decreases and democracy flourishes. When people use advanced telecommunications services for education, research and job development skills, it benefits the economy and lessens the burden on government job training and welfare programs. When they use these services to receive news and information, they become more empowered to make informed choices at the polls, contribute to civic discourse and to the American system of governance. When they use these services to access public safety and health care information and assistance, they can fight crime and receive treatment for health problems.

What Kind of "Access"?

Access to the Internet and other advanced networks is essential to ensure full citizen participation in society. These networks are the backbone of the information age—and will soon become the principal means by which we communicate with each other. But unlike Newt Gingrich (who later apologized for his remarks), I am not advocating that government provide "a computer in every home." The fact of the matter is that equipment is inexpensive and often free—witness the greatly publicized donations of computer hardware and software to schools and libraries by Apple and Microsoft. Nor is the latest hardware necessary to access the Internet and other advanced networks. What costs money—big money—is access to the networks, whether by telephone wire, satellite, wireless, broadcast or other technologies. But there are no newspaper headlines about telephone companies or other telecommunications providers giving that kind of access away.

Ensuring free or low cost/affordable access to advanced networks is where government can play a constructive role. Such access should be provided broadly, not just to schools and libraries, which have long been the favored recipients of both corporate and government largesse. But by supporting "affordable" access, I am not advocating "equal" access, or even the best available access. Nor should the government mandate a particular technology or "pipe" through which access to advanced networks is provided. Instead, the government should ensure "adequate" access—in other words, that which is enough to enable an individual to participate in both the economic marketplace and the marketplace of ideas.

Affordable Access to Telecommunications Services Is Needed Because a "Free Market" Does Not Exist

The common belief of free market theorists is that, unburdened from government regulation, the market will determine the optimal level of technology necessary, and deliver it to those who need it. As to those with limited resources, the argument goes, K-Mart and McDonald's serve the poor, so why won't technology companies?

This analogy fails for two fundamental reasons. First, the telecommunications industry faces an entirely different cost structure and revenue expectations. Businesses serve customers where there is a profit to be made—that is, where revenues are greater than costs. McDonald's and K-Mart may make profits from the poor and rich, but telephone companies don't often do so in many rural and poor areas of the country. That is because it is enormously expensive to lay telephone wire in rural areas, a cost that is rarely offset by telephone usage. In poor urban areas, per capita costs may not be as high, but neither are revenues, particularly for advanced services. Thus, it is not difficult to find certain parts of the country where telecommunications companies have refused to deploy advanced services. For example, RBOC proposals to deploy "video dialtone" in the early 1990's did not include inner cities. And the cable industry's cable modem experiment in schools across America benefits mostly upper middle class suburbs.

Second, unlike the fast food and discount retail markets, the market for local telecommunications services is not now competitive. Nor will it be competitive just by simply announcing that "the local telecommunications market will now be competitive." The Telecommunications Act of 1996 has not begun to eliminate the discontinuities left after years of monopoly dominance by the Regional Bell Operating Companies (RBOCs), and it is unlikely ever to do so. Because the Act failed to provide a strong mechanism to require RBOCs to make their facilities available at reasonable prices, potential competitors are finding that the costs to enter the local telephone market are extremely high, and are therefore proceeding very slowly, if at all. Indeed, AT&T, with the deepest pockets, believed it could only compete if it merged with an RBOC; hence its failed attempt to combine with SBC Communications. And MCI's merger with British Telecommunications has met with great difficulty because of the escalating estimates of the costs to compete for local service.

Even if these companies and others do eventually provide some competition to the RBOCs, few believe that such competition will reach most residential users. In the meantime, according to a Bell Atlantic backed study, there are inner cities in the United States where home telephone penetration is about 50%. Thus, the most fundamental entry point to advanced networks is not available to many poor Americans. That some lack access to even a basic phone line renders irrelevant the argument that internet access is inexpensive (although mostly in cities).

What is the answer to the lack of competition in local telecommunications markets? Insistence on the old libertarian standard of "less regulation is better" simply will not lead to more competition and a freer market. Wishing the government away in this area will simply lock in the inefficiencies of an anticompetitive monopoly. The 1996 Act proved that. Instead, government can act to break down economic barriers and discontinuities in the local market by devising strict requirements that RBOCs open up their networks for facilities-based competition. And if, with government assistance, competition does ever develop for telecommunications services, a phase out of government subsidies could be appropriate.

The Benefits of Ensuring Non-Discriminatory Access Outweigh the Occasional Misplaced Government Subsidy

Even those who support government subsidies would not argue that they are perfect. They do occasionally benefit the undeserving along with the deserving. The current "universal service" scheme which subsidizes rural residents occasionally (and far more rarely) benefits the wealthy rancher or Aspen ski-buff. I would prefer targeted, needs-tested subsidies, such as that the FCC developed for school and library access to advanced services. Under that program, the neediest schools and libraries receive the greatest outlay of funds. And, while we may not agree on the benefits of subsidies, I agree strongly with libertarians that subsidies must not be hidden. If government is going to give out money, it should be subject to public disclosure, not buried.

But even in those cases where misplaced subsidies are unavoidable, I would argue that the benefits to society that redound from affordable access to telecommunications technologies outweigh the detriments of the occasional misplaced dollar.

The benefits to society of ensuring access to advanced telecommunications networks are many. As discussed above, access to technology actually decreases dependency on government by providing opportunities for education, jobs, civic participation and health care. And individuals, institutions and businesses all benefit from a telecommunications system where each is connected to all. What good would your telephone be if there were a significant segment of the population that you could not call? The need for similar externalities for new telecommunications networks increases daily as larger and large segments of the population rely on them to communicate.

To the extent that new technologies will reduce the public's reliance upon old forms of media for their news and information, that is also a net plus. Mass media consolidation continues unabated, and it is predicted that in the not too distant future, a handful of large companies will control most of the mass media in the United States. In addition, many of these large media companies are involved in joint ventures with each other, reducing any incentives they have to compete vigorously with one another. This concentration of ownership into fewer and fewer hands not only reduced competition, it also displaces independent voices, decreases diversity of viewpoints, and often leads to a type of corporate censorship in which information in which the large media company has an economic interest is kept from the public's eyes and ears. By contrast, those speaking in cyberspace can voice their opinion to many or few, with little fear of gate keepers. This is not to say that these networks will ever replace the mass media as the primary and most pervasive source of political speech, national and local information and news for Americans. But they will continue to have a bigger and bigger influence on public opinion and culture.

But perhaps the greatest benefit to society is what will be avoided if affordable access is ensured. Nearly 30 years ago, the Kerner Commission described the alienation, social unrest and other negative effects resulting from the lack of minority access to the mass media. The Commission found that the dearth of positive portrayals of, and news and information about, minorities contributed to their disenfranchisement—a situation that continues to impact society today. As the best education, well-paying jobs and the ability to communicate and participate in democracy become ever more dependent on access to new technologies, the gap between the information rich and poor will only be exacerbated if these critical tools are only available to those that can pay a premium for it. If that chasm is permitted to grow, the libertarian dream of free markets and smaller government will be subsumed by it, as political pressure to correct the resulting inequities will overwhelm market forces.

APPENDIX H

INTERVIEW WITH AN UMPIRE[1]

Michael L. Katz
Chief Economist
Federal Communications Commission

The following is the transcript of an interview conducted by Michael L. Katz of the Federal Communications Commission. His subject is Less-State, a noted hard-line economist, who believes that the role of government is to set up certain minimal rules for private behavior and then see that these rules are enforced. In light of the fact that Less-State does not exist in the corporeal world, one should not conclude that his views reflect the official position of either the Federal Communications Commission or its staff. Indeed, it is entirely possible that they do not represent his views either.

Katz: I would like to start by thanking you for taking the time to talk today.

Less-State: Think nothing of it. I have lots of time. Eternity, in fact.

Katz: That being the case, issues concerning how the [Federal Communications] Commission can increase the speed at which new communications services are brought to market probably mean a bit less to you than to the rest of us. In any event, perhaps you could begin by telling us what's so special about wireless communications services.

Less-State: Wireless communications services have two distinctive features. First, of course, they don't use wires. This fact gives rise to two potential advantages. One, wireless services can offer mobility, which is very valuable in many uses. Two, in certain situations, wireless technologies have significant cost advantages over wire-based communications technologies. Wireless technologies can be the cheapest way to create a network either where a lot of wire would be necessary per customer—a very sparse network, for example—or where installation of wire would be very expensive per foot installed, such as in a building lacking conduit or over some nasty mountains. Sometimes the distinction

266

between the two advantages blurs. The ease with which a wireless local area network (LAN) can be reconfigured within an office building can be thought of as either very low velocity mobility or a low cost of re-laying virtual wires.

A second distinction is that wireless technologies use spectrum. A lot of people believe that this is an extremely important distinction. The crowd I hang with, if you will pardon the pun, does not always agree. To my mind, the fundamental question is this: Is there any reason to treat spectrum differently than any of the thousands of other inputs used to produce communications services, or indeed other goods and services?

Katz: I'll ask the questions, thank you. Isn't spectrum different because it's scarce and thus needs to be allocated differently than other productive inputs?

Less-State: Absolutely not. Spectrum may be scarce, but with the possible exception of bad ideas, *all* inputs are scarce. Indeed, the whole point of having markets is to allocate scarce resources, and markets are generally recognized as doing a good job of it.

Katz: But what about *market failures?* Don't we need the government to correct them?

Less-State: You sound like a lawyer who has been hanging around economists too long. Sure, there can be market failures. That's not the question. The question is whether current U.S. spectrum policy is in any way based on correcting market failures and whether the government has the political will and analytic tools to identify and correct those market failures that may exist.

Katz: I said that I'll ask the questions around here. I think we need to go through these issues more systematically. Let's start by talking about why economists generally put so much faith in markets as a means of allocating scarce resources such as spectrum. Then let's talk about potential failures in the market for spectrum, from both equity and efficiency perspectives. Last, let's talk about what all of this means for current policy and its reform.

Less-State: I can't wait to get started.

THE VIRTUES OF THE MARKET SYSTEM

Katz: Economists generally favor using a market mechanism to allocate spectrum. We keep hearing that spectrum should be auctioned. Why?

Less-State: To most people, *the* reason to auction spectrum is to raise money for the government. But to an economist, the money raised is *not* the most important benefit of using an auction. Hey, don't laugh; I'm not kidding. This is a point that is very poorly understood by many of the people in government and industry who discuss these issues.

To an economist, the advantages of auctions over administrative process are threefold. First, the market process works faster than the administrative or political process. The Commission is famous for taking years to decide whether spectrum should be *allocated* to particular uses and then years more to decide to whom that spectrum should be *assigned*. Look at the allocation of spectrum for digital audio broadcasting by satellite. Satellite CD Radio filed a request to have spectrum allocated to satellite radio back in 1990, and we may still be years away from actually assigning licenses. Unfortunately, this situation is not unique. There are various estimates of the welfare loss due to the delay in the introduction of cellular services, ranging from $16.7 to $85 billion.[2] While one can criticize the methodologies used to derive these numbers, and there is quite a range, I think it is fair to conclude that the costs to society can be substantial. Now if these delays were simply the result of malevolence or incompetence, we could try to improve the Commission's personnel policies or the Senate's confirmation process. But that's not the central problem. The problem is the ridiculous administrative methodologies for spectrum allocation and assignment forced on the Commission by the U.S. Congress. If we had a market-based system, spectrum could change hands and uses in a matter of weeks or months.

A second advantage of a spectrum market over the administrative process is that the market mechanism creates less potential for privately valuable but socially wasteful actions aimed not at creating value, but rather at getting government-granted favors: so-called unproductive *rent-seeking activities*. Millions of dollars are spent on legal fees by parties filing comments in Commission allocation and assignment proceedings—it takes money to buy those years of delay. Frankly it is difficult for me to see much social value in the vast majority of these filings.

The third advantage of the market mechanism may be the most important one. Both the administrative process and the market process are supposed to put spectrum to its highest-valued uses. In my opinion, there is every reason to believe that the market process does a better job of this than does the administrative process.

Katz: What advantages could the market possibly have over well-intentioned civil servants? If nothing else, couldn't civil servants do what the market would do anyway, except where the public interest is served by doing something different?

Less-State: There are those who question the good intentions. I, of course, am not one of them. From my perspective, the problem is this: Absent conventional economic markets, policymakers will not have the information they need to allocate spectrum to its highest-valued uses. You can't simply go out and ask competing users how much they would be willing to pay for spectrum and then give it to the one who claims the highest value. Under such a system, there is no incentive to tell the truth, and every incentive to exaggerate your willingness to pay. Policymakers need what economists call an *incentive-compatible* mechanism, that is, a mechanism under which people have an incentive to tell the truth because doing so is compatible with their narrow self-interest.

The market provides such a mechanism. If you will pardon the cliché, the market makes a firm put its money where its corporate mouth is. I am much more likely to believe a company that says it's willing to pay $300 million for spectrum, knowing that it might actually have to pay that amount, than I am willing to believe a company that says the same thing but knows it will never actually have to pay any money. A properly designed auction reveals who truly places the highest value on use of the spectrum.

Katz: And you are saying that regulators can't tell who has the highest-valued use for spectrum? What about economic studies that com-panies commission to show all the social benefits that will flow if spectrum is given to them?

Less-State: These studies are a good thing; they keep my friends in silk capes. But they are no substitute for the market. Not surprisingly, each side in a dispute before the Commission typically has a study supporting its position. I don't believe that the Commission ever will have the resources to evaluate such studies in the detail that would be necessary to get to the bottom of the story, although I do want to commend the staff for doing the best that they can under the circumstances.

Moreover, the administrative approach to spectrum allocation tends to lock spectrum into a particular use, which necessitates making long-term predictions that no one is capable of doing with any confidence. A market process would allow reallocation to take place much faster if predictions turn out to be incorrect.

POTENTIAL SHORTCOMINGS
OF THE MARKET APPROACH

Katz: When you say that markets will allocate spectrum to its highest-valued uses, aren't you assuming that firms' willingness to pay for spectrum represents the social values of the different uses? It seems to me that this raises issues of fairness and also potential breakdowns in the workings of the market.

Less-State: Such as?

Katz: Let's start with fairness. It seems that proponents of auctions implicitly assume that, if each of us is willing to pay $1,000 for a license, the social value of putting the license in your hands is the same as the social value of putting it in my hands. But if you have a lot more money than I do, you may think nothing of paying $1,000 for something you don't really want much, while I would have to crave it to pay $1,000. It seems to me that a dollar is more "valuable" to a poor person than a rich one. Don't you agree?

Less-State: As you should have learned in your freshman economics course, "value" only makes sense as a relative term. If you mean that a poor person would be willing to give up more of her free time to get another dollar than would a rich person, then sure, I agree with you. But so what? It seems to me that your real concern is that certain low-income people don't have enough money. I share your concern, if not your pain. Be that as it may, having the government inefficiently allocate spectrum is as likely to make the problem worse as better. First, to have any idea of the effects of its policies on overall income distribution, the Commission would need to trace through the effects on the customers and owners of the firms acquiring spectrum and—where the customers are themselves other firms—the effects on the customers' customers and owners. I see no evidence that the Commission has done this, or could do it even if it wanted to. Inefficient spectrum policies will result in less income in the economy overall. I think almost all economists would agree that spectrum policy is an inappropriate means for effecting income redistribution.

Look, I can tell by your expression that this is just so much theorizing to you. In the end, I think the issue boils down to two points. First, you would be hard-pressed to convince me that the people benefiting from getting spectrum for free are not richer than the average American taxpayer. Second, if you are hell-bent on giving these people money, why not let them use the spectrum for anything they want, including selling it to others for different uses?

Katz: But doesn't free spectrum help viewers and consumers?

Less-State: Let's take free TV. What do you think would happen if broadcasters had to purchase spectrum? Do you really think that we would see the end of free, over-the-air broadcasting? And if you do think this, do you have any evidence to support your beliefs?

Katz: Okay. You are good at cursing the darkness. How about lighting a candle for us: How would you deal with income redistribution?

Less-State: Economists prefer explicit transfer payments, like the income tax system. First off, cash payments are more efficient because you are not distorting market allocations—the recipient is allowed to spend the income on whatever he, she, or it deems to be the most valuable. Suppose you were given the choice between \$140,000 and a Rolls Royce, with the understanding that you could not resell the car. Most people would prefer the cash, even when the Rolls has a sticker price higher than that. People should be allowed to make their own consumption choices, and cash transfers allow that flexibility. Second, economists tend to prefer that transfers be explicit so that the electorate can make informed choices. While many people dismiss economists as focused solely on efficiency, there is a strong ethical streak in economists' call for reliance on clear market mechanisms.

Katz: Enough about fairness. Let's talk about efficiency for a while. As I recall, there is a theorem stating conditions under which markets put resources to their highest-valued uses. What are the conditions?

Less-State: You are referring, no doubt, to the First Fundamental Theorem of Welfare Economics. Basically, the theorem says that the market outcome will be an efficient one if: (1) all markets are competitive; (2) there are no externalities; (3) firms and con-sumers have good information about the choices available to them; and (4) there are no indivisibilities. In a perfectly competitive economy meeting these conditions, each last bit of spectrum would be allocated to the uses in which it generates the highest net benefits to society.

Katz: That's a lot of assumptions. And some of them are unlikely to be satisfied in practice. So isn't it true that there is no guarantee that an auction allocates spectrum to its highest-valued uses?

Less-State: Yes, yes, it's true. Don't quote me on this [Our lawyers say we can.—Ed.], but there are at least three potential problems. One arises from the lumpiness of spectrum. While the spectrum is infinitely divisible in theory, in practice service providers need discrete blocks of spectrum. (I'll come back to spread spectrum technologies later.) This lumpiness—which economists call an indivisibility—gives allocation decisions something of an all-or-nothing character, which in turn can give rise to distortions.

Consider two firms, Firm A and Firm B—if I may be so colorful—bidding against one another for a block of spectrum. Firm A wants to go into business competing against cellular service providers and Firm B wants to offer a new service competing against those of television broadcasters. Does the fact that firm A is willing to pay more than Firm B mean that the spectrum will be put to the more valuable use by that firm? Not necessarily.

In deciding how much it values the spectrum, each firm considers the effect on its profits of obtaining the spectrum. If the firm could earn profits of a million dollars selling services using the spectrum, then the spectrum is worth a million dollars to it. But the firm's actions have effects on other parties as well. In particular, Firm A's decision to compete with cellular services will affect both incumbent cellular providers and cellular customers. These two sets of effects create wedges between the firm's private incentives and the overall effect of its decisions on the economy.

Katz: What sorts of wedges?

Less-State: Let's start with consumers of cellular services. They will benefit from Firm A's entry. Firm A will capture some of these benefits in its revenues. But some benefits will accrue to the consumers themselves. The difference between what consumers are in principle willing to pay for the service and what they actually pay—what economists call consumer surplus—will rise as result of the increased competition and new range of choices that Firm A's entry will induce. Since it does not capture these benefits for itself, Firm A ignores them in deciding how much to bid. Hence, Firm A will tend to bid too little from a social perspective.

At the same time, Firm A also ignores the negative effects that its entry will have on the profits of its competitors. Some of Firm A's profits will simply represent a transfer of income from the incumbents to Firm A; this is good for Firm A, but of no net gain to society. Thus, Firm A may tend to be willing to overbid for spectrum from a social perspective. In the end, we have one of those on-the-one-hand-and-on-the-other-hand situations for which my colleagues are so well known. And of course we have the added complication that the same considerations apply to Firm B's willingness to pay for spectrum.

Katz: So what do you think we should do?

Less-State: Throw our hands up in the air and ignore the problem. Seriously, we have no way of knowing in which direction the net biases run, but we do know from experience the markets tend to work well. So I favor accepting the market outcome. I suppose you could let a firm try to make the case that the market doesn't work for its service, but I would have an extremely strong presumption in favor of the market.

Katz: Haven't the radio and television broadcasters made the case for their service already?

Less-State: If so, it would be news to me.

Katz: But over-the-air radio and television are free. Doesn't that matter?

Less-State: Let's look at broadcasters' argument as I understand it. In essence, they say that because over-the-air broadcasting is free, it generates lots of consumer surplus. (They are also saying that broadcasting has a special role to play in society, and I'll come back to that later.) But the fact that broadcast services generate consumer surplus makes them no different than any other commodity. It's all a matter of degree.

Katz: Yes, but can't we say that broadcasting generates more consumer surplus than other services because it is free?

Less-State: No, we cannot. If all services had the same demand curve, we could. But they most certainly do not. If you want to take the consumer surplus argument seriously, then you should estimate the demand for television as well as the demand for other services that might use the spectrum. The resulting levels of consumer surplus could then be calculated and compared. Who knows, maybe broadcasting does generate more consumer surplus than other services. Whether it does or not, it is a sad state of affairs when policy is based on such an untested claim.

Katz: You said that there are other reasons why private and social values might diverge. What are they?

Less-State: Externalities are one. An *externality* exists when production or consumption decisions of one economic agent affect the welfare of another in ways that are not market-mediated. For example, interference could be an externality.

Katz: What do you mean, "could be"?

Less-State: Externalities arise where there are missing markets. If there were no spectrum property rights, then one party could begin transmissions that interfere with someone else's use of the spectrum and there might be no mechanism for making the interfering party take the costs of his actions into account.[3] But by defining spectrum property rights, the government can ensure that there is a market for interference. There is an important role for the government to play here, but it is in creating markets, not replacing them.

Katz: Could you say a little more about how a market for interference would work?

Less-State: It would be my pleasure. A license would grant the holder the right to transmit over a defined set of frequencies within a defined geographic area. She would be free to offer any service of her choosing. She would also have the right to prevent other people from interfering with her transmissions on the defined spectrum. Or, she could sell them the right to interfere, if she chose to do so.

Katz: Externalities are a problem because people don't take into account the effects of their decisions on others. Aren't there other problems along these lines? For example, what about potential coordination failures when a bunch of providers need to use adjacent blocks of spectrum to hold down the cost of receiving equipment? Isn't this an issue for mobile telephony—to facilitate roaming—and for radio and television broadcasting?

Less-State: Do you really think that broadcasters would suddenly locate all over the spectrum map? No one needs to tell retail stores to locate near to one another in a downtown shopping district; they figure it out on their own.

Katz: Let's go back to broadcasting for a moment. What do you make of the fact that broadcasting has characteristics of a *public good?* I am thinking in particular of the fact that consumption is nonrivalrous: Your decision to watch *The X-Files* has no effect on my ability to watch that show or any other. Consequently, the efficient price for the service is zero, which makes it difficult for the free market to provide the service.

Less-State: You are correct about the efficient price. But the problem you identified is far from unique to spectrum. It holds for almost any intellectual property, for instance. And to varying degrees, the same problem arises in markets subject to economies of scale, where marginal costs are much lower than average costs. The question is whether the problem is so severe, and its direction so clear, that we can be confident that the benefits of distorting the market in this instance outweigh the costs. We are really back to the "lots of consumer surplus" argument. I would also like to point out that, if you really believe this argument, then you should ask yourself: Why stop at free spectrum? Why not subsidize the transmission equipment and program development as well?

Katz: How about nonrivalry of a different sort? Some users can share spectrum, either because they have such low power levels or because they use spread-spectrum technologies.

Less-State: Actually, the nonrivalry is not that different from what we were just talking about. These parties do "consume" spectrum. For them to be able to use it, other uses have to be blocked. But once the spectrum has been set aside for these uses, they do not interfere with one another. Hence, the incremental cost is zero, *conditional on the initial allocation of spectrum.* This leaves us with the question of how to make the initial allocation to a shared-use block. Here, there does appear to be a role for the administrative process.

Katz: Anything else on your list of possible problems with a market for spectrum?

Less-State: Yes, *market power.* Market power can create a wedge between social and private values as firms try to use the acquisition of spectrum to block competition.

Katz: So you admit that there is another reason that we can't rely on free markets?

Less-State: You are jumping to incorrect conclusions here. We only need to place certain relatively minor restrictions on market participants, in the form of spectrum caps, to ensure that this is not a problem.

Katz: How would spectrum caps work?

Less-State: Any one firm would be limited in terms of the total amount of spectrum that it could control. For example, under the Commission's current rules, no one provider can control more than 45 MHz of spectrum in the personal communications service (PCS), cellular, and SMR bands.

Katz: Don't problems arise when setting a total megahertz cap for a company? Ten MHz for wireless cable might be nothing, while two MHz is a huge amount for paging.

Less-State: The issue isn't the service, it's the range of spectrum that can provide a service. Today, we have artificial zoning of spectrum, and thus caps need to be set zone by zone. If we moved to a market-based allocation policy, there would be less need to do this sort of fine tuning. Of course, there are differences in propagation characteristics across the spectrum and installed bases of receivers build up, so some market-driven zoning is inevitable. Hence, there likely will continue to be the need for some sort of band-specific caps. But with broad zones, relatively high caps still will constrain anti-competitive behavior.

Before we go any further, I can't resist saying that one of the biggest problems with market power is that the government may be tempted to exercise it by restricting the allocation of spectrum for particular uses in order to drive up auction values.

DO CURRENT POLICIES
CORRECT MARKET FAILURES?

Katz: In light of all the potential market failures, don't you think that government intervention of the sort we have today is needed?

Less-State: I agree that there are potential market failures. I just told you that we need to think through what to do about allocating shared-use bands and that certain limits on spectrum owner-ship make sense. But all of this is consistent with a policy that relies first and foremost on the market to allocate and assign spectrum licenses.

Let's remember that there are "government" failures too. I could argue for the presumption that the government could do no better than the market due to: (1) a lack of information; and (2) political pressures. The latter would not matter if political power were directly proportional to economic gains—it would be another form of the market at work. But this appears not to be the case. And, in any event, the rent-seeking activities often are unproductive. I think a good case can be made that current spectrum allocation and assignment policies are better seen as an example of government failure than as an example of solving market failures.

Katz: Those are strong words. Let's talk about some of the current exceptions to reliance on the market. Surely, you agree with people like Ken Robinson who believe that providers of health and safety deserve special treatment and shouldn't be fed to the jaws of supply and demand.

Less-State: Health and safety services providers may deserve special treatment, but that special treatment has little to do with spectrum policy. These organizations should buy spectrum like everyone else. For that matter, they should buy spectrum the way they buy all of the other inputs needed to produce health and safety services. If you think health and safety providers need more money, then give it to them.

Katz: But isn't that ultimately the same as giving them the spectrum?

Less-State: No, and that's the key point. First, a market makes the cost explicit rather than hidden, which should improve decision making, including policy making. (I know, I know, I'm back on that "good government" kick again.) Second, and more important, it gives health and safety providers incentives to economize on their use of spectrum.

Katz: But no one is going to give the health and safety providers the money they need.

Less-State: You are raising enough red herrings to feed the Russian army for a week. Seriously, I have two responses. First, it is easy for you and Ken Robinson to claim that, but what evidence do you have? If we were to sell the spectrum, how do you know what the sale proceeds would be spent on? Moreover, you have to explain to me why you want to subvert the political process in this case. My second response is this: If you don't want to make health and safety organizations pay for spectrum, at least let them voluntarily sell some of what they have.

Katz: But what good would that do? You are still giving them the spectrum.

Less-State: If we let these organizations sell some of "their" spectrum, then they will have incentives to economize on the use of spectrum and sell any that they consider to be excess. I simply can't think of any good reason not to let them do this immediately. In fact, I think the lack of political will to allow this in part illus-trates my earlier point that no one in Washington understands the real virtues of market allocations; instead they are entirely hung up on the money.

Katz: How about the need to maintain a "reserve," so that there will be spectrum for the innovative new uses that are certain to come down the pike in the future?

Less-State: The question is this—I know, I know, *you* ask the questions. In any event, the question is: Why is there any reason to expect the government to be better at this than the market? You can sit there and tell me that the government is better at taking the needs of future generations into account than the private market, but I see no evidence for this, and theory suggests the government may do worse. Politicians are concerned with the current generation because it is the one that votes. Profit maximizing firms, however, will reserve spectrum for future generations if there is reason to believe that they will pay for it. There are other problems as well.

Katz: Such as?

Less-State: The whole notion of a reserve is itself somewhat bizarre. Spectrum does not get used up the way oil does. The intensity of use today has no effect on the amount of spectrum available tomorrow. Hence, setting spectrum aside for future uses may be wasteful. It makes more sense to use the spectrum today but have a mechanism for transferring spectrum in the future to those who value it most highly at that time.

Katz: Public policy distinguishes between licensees who use spectrum to produce communications services that they sell to others and licensees who just use the spectrum for themselves, such as overnight delivery companies that use wireless systems to track their trucks. What do you think of this distinction between public and private networks?

Less-State: Try this experiment. Walk into an overnight delivery office and tell them you are a consultant shipping a valuable report to your client. Tell them you are going to charge the client $60,000 for the report itself, but you are not going to charge a cent for the shipping. Somehow I don't think the woman in purple and orange behind the counter is going to say, "Oh, in that case it's free." But let me know if she does.

Katz: I'm sensing here that you aren't a big fan of this distinction.

Less-State: Correct.

Katz: Okay. Let's move away from straight economic arguments. Let's talk for a few minutes about broadcasting and how—because of its pervasiveness—it plays a special role in our society as the principal medium of news dissemination and political discourse. Doesn't that make it imperative that we have lots of different broadcasters?

Less-State: Let me start by saying that this is an issue that is going to be of less and less importance as we see the continued growth of video delivery by wire and the rise of computer networks as sources of news. And, of course, there is always my old standby: If you want more stations than the market would otherwise support, subsidize them explicitly instead of through a hidden mechanism. Now, if you are talking about the pattern of ownership, rather than the total number of stations, I think there is merit to having ownership restrictions at the local level. This is just the spectrum cap issue again. It is somewhat harder for me to see the diversity benefits of national caps.

Katz: What about localism? Isn't there a danger that satellite technologies will wipe out local broadcasting unless satellite broadcasting is limited in some way?

Less-State: I tend to believe that if localism is so valuable, then local broadcasting will survive. And if you think it won't, then subsidize it, rather than trying to block innovation.

Katz: Doesn't the pervasiveness of broadcasting mean that we need to be concerned with the potentially negative effects of its content, particularly the effects on children?

Less-State: I thought that's what parents are for. Look, what does this have to do with spectrum policy? It doesn't matter to the kid whether the signal was broadcast, came over a cable, or is a videotape. And in any event, content prohibitions can easily be overlaid on an otherwise totally market-driven system.

Katz: What about the flip side of the coin, affirmative content re-quirements, such as children's educational programming?

Less-State: Here comes my good government and efficiency speech again: Why not pay for the content directly rather than subverting the market and having spectrum giveaways coupled with public-interest obligations that virtually everyone agrees are vague?

Katz: *Man*, explicit subsidies again. You sound like a broken record.

Less-State: There is a reason for that. Supporters of current spectrum policy keep making the same mistakes over and over, so I keep making the same corrections over and over.

POLICY REFORM

Katz: As you know, my colleagues at the Commission have been very busy conducting spectrum auctions. So why aren't you satisfied?

Less-State: When you have been around as long as I have, it takes a lot to satisfy you. I have been very pleased with the auctions, and they have done a lot to keep otherwise idle game theorists off the streets. But the auctions to date don't go far enough. They have been used in limited cases to pick the particular license holders for a given service, but they have not been used to decide the use to which a given block of spectrum is put. Congress will not allow the Commission to do this. We need to move to a system of flexible use. The only practical way to do that is to move to a market system.

Katz: You keep going on about the virtues of the market, but don't we essentially have a market-based system today since there are active secondary markets for many of the licenses? As I recall, many of the winners of the cellular lotteries simply turned around and sold the licenses to someone else.

Less-State: Secondary markets get us some, but by no means all, of the benefits of a full market-based system. They do nothing to overcome the delay in initial allocation and assignment, nor do secondary markets cure the problem of unproductive rent-seeking behavior I discussed earlier. Just think about the cost of the mountains of paper produced by firms and their lawyers hoping to get lucky in the cellular license lotteries. And secondary markets cannot by themselves overcome the overall restrictions on spectrum use that the administrative process imposes. Secondary market or not, a license cannot now be switched between television broadcasting and cellular services. Finally, the money from spectrum sales goes to the people lucky enough to get the initial licenses for free, rather than to taxpayers. This matters even to an economist who cares only about efficiency because an auction reduces the need to raise government funds through taxes, which almost always give rise to some efficiency losses.

Katz: So how do we move to a market-based system?

Less-State: The government defines property rights and lets the mar-ket work.

Katz: I think I understand how you would sell spectrum that the federal government newly turns over from its own uses. But what should be done about spectrum that has already been allocated and assigned by the Commission?

Less-State: In discussing this issue, it is helpful to separate equity from efficiency considerations. Purely from an efficiency point of view, there are several different approaches. One approach, which has been suggested by the Progress and Freedom Foundation, among others, would be to give title to the current licensees and let them use or sell the spectrum as they see fit. This approach would let secondary markets reallocate spectrum to its most valuable uses. Unlike the current system, the buyers would be free to choose what services they wanted to offer, rather than having each band tied to a particular class of service.

At the other extreme, we could auction everything off without restrictions. Now, before you get excited, recognize that there are tremendous advantages to incumbency, and in many cases spectrum would continue to be put to the same uses as today. But, and this is the whole point, there would be some significant changes.

The effects of the two approaches on spectrum efficiency would be the same. Remember that I told you at the start of our little chat that efficiency benefits of the market have little to do with raising money for the government, except that government auctions would improve efficiency by reducing the need to levy distortionary taxes to fund the government.

From an equity perspective, issues arise concerning who should get the proceeds of sales. One view holds that the licensees have no claim to the revenues since the spectrum is public property. At the other extreme, some licensees believe that the spectrum is theirs already, the language of the licenses notwithstanding. In the middle, you have many licensees pointing out that they have already paid in secondary markets for the spectrum they are using.

Katz: Let's talk about the argument that many license holders have already paid for their licenses in secondary markets. What do you think of this argument?

Less-State: My understanding is that many have paid for their licenses, which does raise fairness concerns about selling the licenses again. I think we shouldn't make people pay twice to buy the same thing. But we also need to look closely at what it is that they bought the first time around.

Katz: Are you referring to the fact that these licenses came with strings attached?

Less-State: Yes. There are two sorts of "strings," as you call them. One sort are the restrictions placed on how the spectrum can be used, such as the requirement that you use your license for UHF broadcasting. The other sort are affirmative requirements, such as children's educational programming or communications system build-out requirements. Although the analyses of the two sorts of strings are somewhat different, both have implications for the relationship between what licensees paid on secondary markets and what their licenses may be worth in the future.

Katz: Talk to me about restrictions on usage.

Less-State: As we have discussed, spectrum is currently zoned. Dropping these restrictions would raise the value of some licenses since they could be put to more valuable uses, while it might lower the value of others that would face increased competition. Some people have suggested that license holders must be protected from competition. As you know, I think this is a bad idea. Other people are concerned that holders of licenses that increase in value due to flexibility would receive an unfair windfall gain. In response, some people, notably Peter Huber, have suggested selling the flexibility. The danger of this approach, as he is aware, is that the flexibility has no social cost. Hence, charging for it is counterproductive and tends to lock spectrum into inefficient uses. So I think we need to be careful here not to stifle flexibility out of jealousy.

Katz: What about so-called public-interest obligations, like the build-out of networks to serve unprofitable areas or affirmative content requirements?

Less-State: The situation is a bit different with the public service obligations. In theory, at least, one could move to a system with no such obligations and levy a one-time charge on current licensees to capture the capitalized cost of the obligations. These funds could then go into the overall pool of government revenues or, if there is a consensus for continuing to promote the public service, the funds might be put into a public service trust fund.

Katz: Let's get to the bottom line here. Are so-called public interest obligations compatible with a market-based spectrum policy?

Less-State: Much as I hate to admit it, I think they are. But you have to be very careful not to distort the incentives to provide particular services. For example, if you have spectrum flexibility, but tell anyone who chooses to engage in television broadcasting that he or she has to provide children's educational programming, then you reduce the incentive to use the spectrum for broadcasting. To avoid this problem you need to decouple the obligation from the particular use of spectrum. For example, you could sell a license with the requirement that the licensee ensure that a certain amount of children's educational programming was aired. But you would not require the licensee to use his or her spectrum to broadcast it. Of course, the best way to do this would be to go to an explicit subsidy mechanism but I know you have already heard that from me.

CONCLUSION

Katz: Let me try out the following on you. The existing spectrum policy, for all of its problems, has brought us perhaps the most innovative and valuable set of wireless industries in the world. Why should we mess with a system that is working so well? Aren't you simply asking us to replace a misplaced faith in government with an equally misplaced faith in the market?

Less-State: I suspect that our success in broadcasting in comparison with other countries comes from the fact that we tend to interfere in broadcasting *[chuckles to himself]* less than do other countries. And there are those who might argue that the United States has not been the most innovative market, particularly in the area of mobile telephony.

In any event, the real issue is not whether markets have worked well to date, despite a misguided spectrum policy, but whether markets can work much better if given the chance. I believe that they can. Incumbents consistently use the administrative process to slow or block entry by new competitors. And in some cases, potential entrants slow themselves down by engaging in protracted legal battles to determine who will be given the license through the administrative process. Moreover, there are limited incentives to conserve spectrum. All of this tells me that the potential benefits of moving to a market system are huge.

Katz: I have just a couple of more questions.

Less-State: I'm sorry, but it's almost daylight. I really must be going.

Katz: I understand; there are many things in Washington that people hope will never see the light of day. Thank you for your time.

NOTES

1. I would like to thank the participants in the Aspen Institute for Information Studies' 1996 Annual Review conference, particularly Ed Lowry, for a variety of helpful comments and suggestions. I would also like to thank my colleagues Evan Kwerel, Greg Rosston, and John Williams for numerous stimulating discussions of these issues.

2. The lower figure is from J. Hausman and T. Tardiff, "Valuation and Regulation of New Services in Telecommunications," mimeo 1995. The higher figure is from C. Jackson, J. Rohlfs, and T. Kelley, "Estimate of the Loss to the U.S. Caused by FCC's Delay in Licensing Cellular Telecommunications," mimeo 1991, cited in Hausman and Tardiff.

3. While reviewing the transcript, Less-State asked to note that even in the absence of well-defined spectrum property rights, private parties might rely on contract law to reach some sort of accommodation. For example, the party being interfered with might pay the other one not to transmit.

FCC Speeches

APPENDIX I

EXCERPTS FROM

THE HARD ROAD AHEAD
An Agenda for the FCC in 1997

Reed E. Hundt, Chairman
Federal Communications Commission
December 26, 1996

The Chairman's speech provided a roadmap to problems of building new regulatory architecture and defining the public interest, 11 months into the post-1996 Act era. These excerpts feature the parts of his speech dealing directly with the implementation of the Act.

. . . Our principles are straightforward:

1. Make sure that the discovered truth about competition is nowhere frustrated by the chronic urge to monopolize. Like a Hindu tale of the struggle between good and evil, the battle between competition and monopoly will last as long as markets exist. And government should always be on theood side: the side of competition.

2. Guarantee that necessary public benefits from communications are distributed fairly and efficiently. The two means we should use are (a) competition and, where that doesn't work completely or equitably, (b) proactive social policies structured to be sustainable in a competitive environment.

3. Get rid of all the rules not necessary to reach these other two goals. We want to have a red-hot rule burning party every chance we get.

4. Make sure our operations are smart, simple, straightforward and slim. Our goal is to have the FCC be as fair, dedicated, responsive and effective as the best organization in the private or public sector in the world.

The Telecommunications Act of 1996 and the Communications Act of 1934 together state our charter. Congress said it sought to establish a "procompetitive, deregulatory" national policy framework for communications. "Procompetitive, deregulatory"—that is our mantra as we try to wake all markets from the slumber of monopoly and retail price regulation.

By the 1996 Act, Congress broke down the barriers that inhibited competition. The 1996 Act enabled local telephone companies to enter the video business, let cable, wireless, and long distance companies into local telephony, established conditions for the Bell telephone companies to enter long distance, and moved broadcasting from a business with a 1950's technology into the twenty-first century digital world.

There should be no mistake about any of these steps: Congress wants competition, not co-competition. We want a full competitive war, not a standoff in which incumbent companies warily eye each other, but never really enter each other's markets.

When I got to the Commission three years ago, everyone told me about inevitable and imminent "convergence" in which cable would provide telephony and the telephone companies would offer cable service. We still hope that eventually cable companies and telephone companies will compete with each other in all geographic markets, but as of now expectations for a full front two-wire war are not being met.

Financial markets have concluded that the telephone companies' threats to cable's video business have almost disappeared. According to Merrill Lynch, even if multi-channel video penetration increases to 85%–90% by 2005, the telco share is likely to stay about 1%. And just this month, there have been numerous announcements that phone companies are retreating from plans for offering wireless cable.

Meanwhile, Time Warner has said it won't be doing much telephony in the near future. TCI is shifting resources from battling telephone rivals to battling satellite video competition. There are some exceptions, such as Cox and to a degree Continental and Comcast. But, for the most part, Sanford Bernstein analyst Tom Wolzien got it right when he described the relationship of the cable and phone industries by saying "we may have the forming of a detente."

Detente is not what the Telecommunications Act of 1996 was supposed to be about.

So apparently it's no small job to create sufficient incentives for competition to dispense with the need for regulation of monopolies.

Nor should we expect the transition to competition to be fully and voluntarily undertaken by the incumbent companies who see their "home" market positions threatened. Those companies will seek to respond in the competitive arena. That's okay. But they will also respond by testing the government's resolve to stick to a pro-competition path. Think of this as a chance for Congress and state legislatures and federal and state agencies again to be able to do the right thing. When incumbent monopolies hire advertising agencies and political consultants and lawyers and lobbyists to push their agendas, think of it as a chance for the people's representatives to just say no, thank you—we insist on competition.

The importance of our country's future maintaining a clear and sustained commitment to competition cannot be overstated. When Keats wrote, "Hear ye not the hum of mighty workings of a distant mart," he might have been anticipating the sweet sound of robust competition, innovation, and economic welfare gains.

But the difficulty of maintaining the commitment to competition cannot be underestimated. After all it is, as Judge Bork said, the "paradox" of competition that although firms compete to win, the ultimate victory is monopoly. So the ever-present job of government is to write the rules that invent, revive and sustain competition, while inviting instead of deterring or inhibiting innovation, entrepreneurship and investment.

We know all this by our own American history. Let me illustrate with a story.

It is the middle of the last decade of the century. There are existing telephone monopolies. But the law changes, and within a few years the new entrants account for almost half the telephones. The incumbents respond with a three-part strategy of: (1) pricing below cost in response to entry; (2) denying the new entrants fair prices for interconnection; and (3) influencing local regulators to pass laws to institutionalize the prior monopoly. Within a few years the incumbents have reestablished and strengthened their prior monopoly. Then they hold it for 80 more years.

This story is what actually happened in this country between 1894 and 1912. This history, brilliantly set forth by President Richard C. Levin and Professor David F. Wyman of Yale in their 1994 article in *The Journal of Political Economy*, is a sobering reminder about the difficulties of competition. They describe the booming competition as the South got phones, from 1900 through 1910, after the Bell patents had expired. But Southern Bell then eradicated competition. The techniques they used were the construction of a long haul toll network to which new entrants were denied access, the denial of interconnection in local LEC markets, and the use of discounts to high volume customers. After finishing off its rivals, Southern Bell allied with big volume callers to form a regulatory compact that barred competition from coming back.

As Mark Twain said, history may not repeat itself but it does occasionally rhyme. It's a fin-de-siecle monopoly couplet that Congress absolutely does not want us to write in our rules.

For the most part, the 20th century history of telcom policy is a nightmare from which we're trying to awake. The Telecommunications Act of 1996 is a massive dose of caffeine. After all, as good as our telcom system is, imagine what wonders would already be achieved if we had woken earlier to the benefits of competition.

I. PROMOTING COMPETITION IN COMMUNICATIONS

. . . The most difficult issues that the Commission will continue to face in the coming year have the common theme of eliminating economic barriers to competition.

Congress addressed these economic barriers by giving new entrants in telecommunications three basic rights: (1) the right to pay a fair wholesale price so as to compete as resellers of an incumbent local exchange carrier's service; (2) the right to pay a fair price to lease and to combine elements of the incumbent carrier's network to create some of a new wire network (unbundled network elements); and (3) the right to pay and receive a fair price for interconnecting their own facilities to and terminating their traffic on the facilities of the incumbent.

Why is each of these three rights important? Because Congress rejected the approach that has been taken in other countries (such as the United Kingdom) of trying to enshrine into law and rules a "two-wire" industrial policy. Our various separate wire, cable, and wireless networks are too robust and too complete for us to be able to dictate that sort of policy. (By contrast, the United Kingdom could plan to have cable provide an extra phone line only because there was no cable industry in the U.K. when this plan was formed. Here our cable systems, comprising coaxial cables without a parallel phone line running down the conduit, already pass 95% of all homes. It's too late to order them to dig up all those systems just to fit policymakers' "two-wire" vision.)

Congress therefore rightly gave entrants in the local exchange markets a range of options for entry—from service resale, to purchase of unbundled elements, to partial facilities construction, to complete facilities construction. Then Congress trusted the marketplace to govern a new competitor's selection of the mode of entry for different demographic and geographic markets.

The second major principle Congress established to eliminate economic barriers to competition was that universal service must be implemented in a manner that is consistent and compatible with competition. Around the world, we have seen over and over that many believe competition is the enemy of universal service.

This pernicious myth leads countries to embrace monopoly, and to set up in local exchange marketplaces regulatory barriers against competition. Congress told the FCC to knock down these barriers in the United States. That's why the law prohibits hidden universal service subsidies in interconnection or unbundled network element prices. Congress recognized that competition lowers prices and increases deployment of telecommunications, making it the best friend of universal service, not its enemy.

The key proceedings in which the Commission must address these economic barriers to competition are interstate access reform and universal service. . . .

This proceeding will examine how, pursuant to the 1996 Act, we end the access charge system's role as a source of universal service subsidies; how we either move, or allow competition to move, to more efficient interstate access rate structures; and whether the marketplace or governmental direction should be the means of transition to economically efficient rate levels.

The universal service proceeding addresses the flip side of the golden coin of competition. How do we fund universal service when the law prohibits implicit subsidies and the evolving competitive marketplace undermines those implicit subsidies anyway? We must create an economically sustainable universal service system that explicitly compensates universal service providers for the true costs of providing universal service. We must create a universal service system that allows existing universal service providers—for now, primarily incumbent LECs—the capability to respond to competitors by reducing prices to high volume customers (the cream in the cream-skimming strategy of most new entrants), without requiring massive rate increases to other customers in order to pay for the total network. We must create a universal service system that allows companies to compete to provide universal service, so that universal service is provided with the highest quality and the lowest price possible. All this has been endorsed by unanimous vote of the Universal Service Joint Board. Now we have to write the rules that put these principles in operation. . . .

Of course the momentous and unprecedented Bell petitions for entry into long distance are another key component of the new law's pro-competitive framework. Congress envisioned a full competitive battle in all communications markets: both long distance and local. We will certainly be pressed to assure that the conditions are established that give all parties no more or less than a fair opportunity to compete in all the markets.

In the fullness of time we expect to receive 49 Bell petitions for entry. Each will bring us thousands of pages of filings. There will be nothing simple about those proceedings, precisely because Congress rejected the "date certain" approach to entry. No one can criticize us for calling on Congress to assure us the budgetary and other support necessary to discharge fairly our duties to rule on these petitions. The amazingly short 90-day deadlines mandated by Congress exacerbate the enormous pressure on us. But we will grant or deny, with or without conditions, each petition in the timeframe ordered by Congress. We are as impatient as Congress and the private sector in our zeal to do the right thing in telcom policy.

The FCC's commitment to competition has already led to radical deregulation and huge welfare gains in the long distance market. The average price per minute, adjusted for inflation, has decreased from about 34 cents in 1985 to about 12 cents in 1995—a drop of nearly 65%. There aren't too many things that have consistently fallen in price like that. Because of the many pro-competitive steps that have worked in the long distance market, the FCC has eliminated tariffing for all domestic interstate service.

Wireless services are another case in point. Here again the FCC has insisted on a policy of competition. As a result, the average cellular monthly bill has dropped by more than 27% in the past three years.

We have also had a pro-competition deregulating policy regarding DBS, and consumers have been well-rewarded. As Echostar has entered the DBS market, and as MCI prepares to enter, DBS installations that sold for about $1000 in 1994 retail for as low as $99 in some markets.

Still another area where the Commission has pursued a pro-competitive, deregulatory policy is payphones. In September, acting pursuant to the 1996 Act, the Commission eliminated regulatory barriers to entry and exit in the payphone industry. The Commission also eliminated certain subsidies that the Bells were receiving for payphone operations, and we deregulated payphone rates over the next two years. Again, our goal is to let competition, not government, be the regulator of the marketplace. (And again, there was substantial opposition from incumbents to these changes.)

In all of these cases, the Commission wrote rules to support competition and then when these efforts by the Commission put the markets on a path to competitively priced offerings, we stopped regulating retail prices. None of these steps is easy. For example, long distance companies vigorously opposed our refusal to let them file tariffs with us. They did not welcome our deregulatory efforts because the tariff filings were used to protect them from certain consumer complaints. But we wouldn't let government be the means of protecting companies from the just grievances of their own customers.

To facilitate competition and build the information highway, we also need to make sure we encourage, and do not inhibit, innovation. We will be doing so in a number of ways.

The FCC needs to analyze ways to continue to encourage investment and innovation in the networks protected by our dominant telephone companies. In February or March 1997, we will begin a proceeding to do just that. We will be working with manufacturers, incumbents, new entrants and market observers to determine how to promote innovation and investment, without abating the pro-competitive effects of the Act's unbundling and interconnection provisions.

We also are looking at what, if anything, needs to be done in response to increased demand for bandwidth for newly emerging services, including the Internet. . . .

The electromagnetic spectrum is a unique public resource. It should be used to maximize competition and public goods. . . .

Our spectrum policy rests on two key principles. First, we should make spectrum available to the private sector in an orderly but expeditious process, while relying on market forces to put spectrum to its highest valued use. Second, where appropriate, we should create public goods by establishing clear, specific, quantified public interest obligations that, like covenants or easements on real estate, remain with the spectrum licenses. . . .

Our pro-competition agenda is also at the heart of all our digital television proceedings. Some have viewed digital television as an opportunity to defend the status quo against new competitors. We view digital television as an opportunity for broadcasters to compete in new markets as well as competing more effectively in their core markets. . . .

As a result of radical changes in technology and markets, we have pressed significant changes to the FCC's approach to DTV. We should give broadcasters, and not the government, the right to decide whether multicasting or higher resolution is preferable. Broadcasters should make this decision on their own on a market-by-market, channel-by-channel, week-by-week, minute-by-minute basis. Some DTV broadcast should be free. But there's nothing wrong with letting broadcasters also offer subscription DTV. We don't ban subscription analog TV and we shouldn't prohibit or tax away the potential of subscription DTV. If our rules are procompetitive, broadcasters are more likely to have success with DTV and help preserve free TV in a digital age.

In addition to the DTV proceeding, the Commission should protect competition and diversity by means of our broadcast ownership rules. The 1996 Act substantially relaxed the radio ownership limits. There are now no FCC-set limits on the number of radio stations that can be owned nationally, and under the revised local limits a single entity can now own up to eight radio stations in the largest markets. We implemented this provision in new rules adopted last March. We are also reexamining our television ownership rules as called for by the Act.

We also are fostering innovation and competition in radio. The Commission is continuing to work with the radio industry to develop a viable terrestrial digital audio standard and a process for a transition to digital in-band. This whole process has taken far too long, although the rejection of the pioneer's preference approach was most welcome.

The Commission has ongoing proceedings examining its national and local broadcast ownership rules. The local rules currently prohibit television duopolies—the common ownership of two television stations in the same market. They also prohibit common ownership of a television station and a radio station in the same market. The Commission will waive this restriction if the transaction involves one of the top 25 television markets and if there would be 30 separately owned broadcast stations remaining in the market after the proposed transaction is approved.

The Commission's goal in this proceeding is to further competition, just as we seek to promote competition in other communications industries we regulate. But in our broadcast ownership rules we also seek to promote diversity in programming and diversity in the viewpoints expressed on this powerful medium that so shapes our culture.

What would happen to diversity if the Commission's rules allowed TV duopolies? That's a key question in the rulemaking proceeding. Plainly, allowing ownership of two stations would decrease diversity of ownership. But could it possibly increase diversity of viewpoint and diversity of programming, at least in some markets? . . .

The Commission also will reform the comparative hearing process for awarding new analog broadcast television and radio licenses. In 1993, the D.C. Circuit struck down the Commission's criteria for selecting among competing broadcast applicants. The D.C. Circuit said that the Commission's criteria were irrational, and few people disagree with that conclusion. The Court ordered the Commission to rethink the manner in which it awards broadcast licenses.

One way to decide among qualified competing applicants for new analog broadcast channels is by putting those channels on the auction block. As we've seen repeatedly since Congress granted us auction authority, competitive bidding is the fastest and fairest way of getting licenses into the hands of those who will put them to the best use.

Congress, however, has not given the Commission the authority to use monetary auctions in the broadcast context. Unless Congress acts, we have three options. One is to use the selection criteria that have not yet been invalidated. But few think that they make useful, meaningful and effective distinctions among applicants or that they are any more defensible than the one the D.C. Circuit invalidated.

Another option is to give new analog broadcast licenses to applicants whose programming will add the most to their communities. These are applicants who show by specific, quantifiable evidence that they are willing to provide free time for candidates, children's educational television, shows for minorities or other underserved segments of the community, and other valuable programming that the market demonstrably does not generate in sufficient amounts. (The assumption would be that the relevant market already provides sufficient entertainment programming). If spectrum is to be given away at no charge, this option at least provides the public with assurance that its property is going to those would return the most in terms of public interest programming otherwise not provided by the marketplace.

The last option is the worst: lotteries. The Commission could simply declare defeat and give analog TV licenses away randomly. The Commission has previously rejected the possibility of selecting new broadcast licensees by lottery. I hope the Commission doesn't now change its mind. . . .

The market has long discounted the effects of rate regulation. However, as the competition report will make clear, the cable industry still has significant market power in providing multi-channel video services. This is especially true for basic cable. Alternative multichannel providers such as DBS, MMDS and SMATV have increased their share of subscribers by approximately 2% a year since 1990, but cable continues to be the dominant provider of multichannel video programming— serving 89% of all multichannel video programming subscribers. Local markets for the delivery of video programming remain highly concentrated and structural conditions remain in place permitting the exercise of market power by incumbent cable operators. Nationally, concentration among the top cable MSOs has continued to increase. Although full competition has not yet bloomed, we see some hopeful signs.

The Commission has done much in the last year to promote competition in the multichannel video programming market. Within six months after the effective date of the 1996 Telecom Act, we adopted streamlined rules for Open Video Systems that will facilitate rapid entry by wireline competitors to cable. In addition, the availability of two-thirds of the OVS platform to unaffiliated video programmers will provide another potential source of multichannel video competition.

The competition policy put into place with the program access rules of the Cable Act of 1992 has had a significant benefit on competition by ensuring that new competitors such as DBS and MMDS have access to vertically integrated satellite delivered programming services. Our recent OVS decision extends this right to OVS operators. These rules have prevented strategic anticompetitive conduct with respect to distribution of satellite programming by vertically integrated firms to competitors. The program access rules prohibit unfair methods of competition and limit discriminatory conduct, including the use of exclusive contracts. By targeting and eliminating those vertical restraints that can impede entry into the video distribution market, the program access policy has fostered competition in both the video distribution market and in the programming market. . . .

We will shortly be finalizing our implementation of the cable provisions of the 1996 Act providing for the deregulation of cable rates when LEC or LEC-affiliated competition is present in a market. The challenge here will be to insure that the consumer is protected until actual competition exists. The recent announcement by Bell Atlantic/NYNEX that they are ceasing their investments in wireless cable shows that some caution is needed in this area. In that rulemaking, we will be taking a hard look at bulk discounts by cable for multiple dwelling units. And we will make sure that small cable operators will be receiving the relief that Congress intended. These issues should be resolved in early 1997.

One of the biggest surprises from this year's Competition Report will be the revelation that satellite providers DirecTV and Primestar now rank among the top 10 MVPD's in the nation when ranked by subscribership. In the past year, Echostar literally took off like a rocket. At this time last year, they did not have a bird in the sky, and now they have over 200,000 subscribers.

DBS is the most successful consumer electronics launch of all time. As we predicted when we auctioned the final national DBS slot, competition is causing price wars to break out. It remains to be seen, however, whether DBS will become a mainstream competitor to cable or will remain a niche market service. This depends to a degree on the long-run future of program access and the success of digital cable boxes. . . .

II. PUBLIC BENEFITS FROM COMMUNICATIONS

The second fundamental task of the Commission is to secure the public interest in communications.

Universal Service

This country has long recognized that there are benefits of the communications infrastructure that our society wishes to have but that even a vigorously competitive marketplace may not provide. That is why, for example, we have long had a policy of universal service in telephony.

The 1996 Act has forced us to transform these policies in light of the paradigm shift from regulated monopoly to deregulated competition. That is an immense task, and I appreciate all the hard and successful work that the Joint Board has done so far in this process. This re-write of universal service should revitalize the social compact between the communications industry and society. The ability of the communications industry to contribute to the public good is significant and it is vastly increasing in importance.

In Section 254 of the Telecommunications Act, Congress gave the FCC the authority to create a durable, efficient universal service system that will meet the three goals of keeping basic phone service low-priced, compensating fairly any company providing basic phone service, and making sure that new entrants and existing telephone companies each carry a fair share of the financial burden of keeping basic phone service affordable.

Moreover, in one of the most visionary provisions of the law, Congress mandated making modern communication services accessible to the 50 million students and teachers in the country.

Last month a bipartisan federal–state Joint Board made its recommendations to the Commission on universal service, providing for a number of measures to strengthen and renew the current system of universal service, such as strengthening the support mechanisms to get low-income, rural and insular consumers to get connected and stay connected.

The Joint Board also gave its unanimous support to a universal service plan that creates a federal–state, national–local partnership providing the funds to ensure that all schools, regardless of income or location, are able to share in the benefits of the Information Age. By providing up to $2.25 billion annually to help schools procure a wide range of communication services, internal network connections and Internet access, the Joint Board's recommendations articulate a visionary social contract between the communications industry and the public. This single issue alone will promote a revolution in the quality and equality of education. It shows America at its best.

It makes us the envy of the world.

Over the next five months, we will be working to write the specific rules to make this new vision of universal service an efficient, well-administered reality. As mandated by Congress, we will complete the universal rules by May 8. In fact, I've challenged our staff to get this done by the Commission's April meeting. Again, we need comments on the Joint Board recommendations, early guidance from Congress, and wisdom as we pursue the daunting task before us.

Because we are dedicated to making sure that universal service truly reaches every individual, we are working concertedly on improving access to communications technology and services for people with disabilities. I am asking the Disabilities Issues Task Force to publish an agenda for 1997 on the Internet by mid-January 1997.

This agenda will include a notice of proposed rulemaking seeking comment on proposed rules and an implementation schedule for closed-captioning of video programming. We also are working on issues of hearing-aid compatibility of new technologies and more generally on examining a broad range of ways to ensure equipment and services can be made accessible to individuals with disabilities.

Under Section 255 of the new Telecommunications Act, the Commission has enforcement authority to press for accessible equipment and technology. In particular, we will actively encourage makers of new equipment and services to incorporate the concept of universal design—designing products from the outset to be accessible for all needs—into the original conception of their products. Retrofitting equipment with accessibility options is often costly and unwieldy. Designing in such features from the beginning of the development process is far more economical and leads to elegant solutions that often benefit many people in the general population as well as members of the disabled community. . . .

Civic Debate

We also will provide Congress our views on ways to help improve political candidates' access to the public. Any successful campaign reform measure must take into account the fact that candidates need access to the most powerful medium of communication: television. Candidates and elected officials who must dedicate most of their energy to raising money to get onto TV necessarily will not have the time or the freedom to serve those whom they represent. . . .

The FCC could require that a reasonable percentage of digital television— 5%—be set aside for public-interest programming. We could ask that as part of that 5% broadcasters provide time during each election cycle to political candidates. Digital technology will vastly increase the potential of the spectrum, and existing broadcasters will get first crack at this new resource. Isn't it only right that the public should claim for itself a concrete benefit arising from the new, digital use of the spectrum?

That's not the only possibility offered by the transition to digital. Another mechanism to generate free political time is suggested by the 1996 Telecommunications Act's requirement that the Commission impose annual fees on broadcasters who offer digital subscription ancillary or supplementary services. What if broadcasters were permitted to pay these fees in kind, in the form of time, to a political-advertisement time bank? Candidates could then use that time for their political ads. . . .

CONCLUSION

An article in a computer magazine on the operations of the Commission ended this way, "Overall, there's something scary about the dynamism of the FCC. Perhaps the world isn't ready for a government agency that is efficient, creative and works hard to improve customer communication and service. What would comedians have left to joke about?"

We're not worried about the comedians. After all, they can always make jokes about lawyers. And we are proud of what we've already done. But we're very excited about the uncompleted agenda. If we can all just keep focused on the hard road ahead, this country will realize the full benefits of the communications revolution.

APPENDIX J

THE LIGHT AT THE END OF THE TUNNEL VS. THE FOG

Deregulation vs. the Legal Culture

Reed E. Hundt, Chairman
Federal Communications Commission
to the
American Enterprise Institute
Washington, D.C.
August 14, 1997
(As Prepared for Delivery)

A year-and-a-half after the President signed a law that replaced a hundred years of monopoly in communications with a commitment to competition, we should ask: is it working? Will Congress and the President see their intentions come true? Will we get competition and deregulation in local telephone markets—perhaps the largest remaining monopolized markets in our economy?

The answer is we have scarcely any competition in the local markets. The pace of investment and new entry is too slow; the success of our country's national deregulatory effort is jeopardized by the delays, missteps, and complexities of our legal culture.

Today I hope to describe some of the problems that our legal culture poses for rapid deregulation and some of the solutions that are possible.

As Jerry Mashaw of Yale Law School wrote in his brilliant book analyzing the failures of the 1966 Motor Vehicle Safety Act, "[L]egal culture . . . [is] expressed through the operation of judicial review, the separation of powers, 'federalism,' and associated 'checks and balances'."

And this legal culture, he wrote, determines the "ultimate success or failure" of any law that depends, as the Telcom Act must, on agency implementation.

As Mashaw explained, the Congressional intent behind the unanimously voted

Motor Vehicle Safety Act was hornswoggled by the legal culture. While the courts debated every nuance of every phrase of the law and every jot and tittle of the expert agency's implementation, for each of the first 15 years after the law was passed about as many Americans were killed on the highways as died in the entire Vietnam War.

When it comes to legislation, between the thought and the deed falls the shadow.

The shadow is cast by the million lawyers of America. I praise, respect, and try to convince other countries to adopt the American system by rule of law.

But respecting the rule of law is different from admiring the delays of the legal process.

The Telcom Act described a paradise of open markets, free competition, deregulation and growth in the information sector that is already one-sixth of our economy.

In my mind's eye, I see Congress and the FCC together in that paradise like Adam and Eve—we being the agency created by Congress like Eve from Adam's rib.

But now we two, like the First Family of Milton's *Paradise Lost*, are being exiled "hand in hand, with wand'ring steps and slow," from the Eden of promised deregulation into the harsh desert of the legal culture—with its thousand devices of tortuous delay and tortured questioning of every phrase, word, and punctuation mark of the Telcom Act.

Professor Mashaw wrote that an agency must "understand how hostile the legal culture can be toward certain forms of regulation. . . ."

And I might add, how hostile the legal culture can be even toward deregulation.

I admit that Congress asked us to undo the state-regulated local monopolies by forceful rulemaking action, not by passivity or mere jawboning.

Hostility is a fair way to characterize the reaction—from the telephone industry, from some states and even from the alleged new entrants, the long distance companies. An example: we dared order the long distance companies no longer to file tariffs with us. If they weren't regulated they'd actually be exposed to consumer lawsuits. So they got a court to enjoin us from deregulating!

I understand that for incumbent monopolists and other companies protected by regulation from market forces hostility may be a rational response to deregulation.

The problem is that the legal culture—just as Mashaw taught—validates that hostility, primarily by encouraging unceasing argument and ineffective delay-ridden decisionmaking.

Debates of interminable Jesuitical casuistry rage over the Congressional intent behind the word "cost" or—my personal favorite—the word "and", as in the phrase "business *and* residential."

I admire the lawyerly zeal that sees complexity behind these simple terms. Of course, that's because I am one of them—I myself am a lawyer. Worse, I'm a son of a lawyer. So I appreciate lawyerly cunning that can fog the plainest Congressional intent.

But how can we find our way to free markets through all this lawyerly fog?

Even now the telcos and the long distance companies and many other parties, including often the states, appeal virtually every paragraph of every one of our decisions to various courts of appeals. Moreover, the appellate courts don't consolidate the appeals; they scatter them across the country.

And as if there weren't enough litigation, Southwestern Bell has hired a brilliant lawyer named Tribe to argue in federal court in Wichita Falls that the Telcom Act the company itself lobbied about for years is unconstitutional.

I have two questions. First, SBC has just discovered the Telcom Act is unconstitutional? They lobbied this law for a decade. A year-and-a-half after it was signed, they just found out it violates the Constitution?

Second, the Bells asked Congress for a date certain by which they could get into long distance. They wanted three years after the law was signed: that would be February 1999. This lobbying effort they actually lost. And now they are irate to the point of starting Tribal warfare because only half-way through their own proposed waiting period they haven't yet made a record of opening local markets that passes the tests of the law. Is this reasonable?

The fog, the fog!

Meanwhile, after getting the Eighth Circuit to enjoin our clear national rule defining "cost" so that fair and final interconnection agreements could be quickly reached, GTE's taste for litigation is unslaked. So far, by our count, GTE has filed 23 federal court actions challenging the pricing decisions of 23 state commissions.

Of course, eventually the Supreme Court will resolve all disputes and the path to competition will be clear.

But the excruciating delays of the legal process recall the lawsuit known as *Jarndyce v. Jarndyce*, described in Dickens' *Bleak House*. Let me read a bit from that great book, and ask you to think of the interconnection lawsuit Dickens could so easily have been describing:

This scarecrow of a suit has, in course of time, become so complicated that no man alive knows what it means. The parties to it understand it least; but it has been observed that no two . . . lawyers can talk about it for five minutes without coming to a total disagreement as to all the premises. . . . The little plaintiff or defendant, who was promised a new rocking-horse when [the case] should be settled, has grown up, possessed himself of a real horse, and trotted away into the other world.

I myself perhaps can find that horse and ride away, the Senate so permitting when it returns in September.

And so will many, while the interconnection litigation drones on.

But there has to be a better fate for our country's competition policy than *Jarndyce v. Jarndyce*.

Dickens also wrote: "Facts alone are wanted in life. Plant nothing else, and root out everything else."

So let me plant a handful of facts.

Fact number one: after years of effort by many states, such as Ohio, Wisconsin, Illinois, Oregon and others—there is still scarcely any choice for telephone service in local markets. A year-and-a-half after the new telcom law, the new entrants to the local exchange markets of the U.S. have between one and two percent of total market share.

So far, scarcely any local competition has been delivered to residential or business consumers.

Fact number two: if our local telephone companies thought markets were truly open, at least one of them somewhere would be going into its neighbors' markets. For all intents and purposes, none of them is doing so.

And if local markets were truly open to competition, then all Bell companies in those markets would long ago have filed 271 applications for entry into long distance. Instead, only one Bell in one state, Ameritech in Michigan, has even tried to make a serious showing that one state is truly and fully open to competition—and there, neither Michigan nor the Department of Justice yet agreed!

By the absence of serious 271's and by the absence of telco-to-telco competition, the local telephone industry in effect admits that not one state market is truly open to competition at this time.

Fact number three: the congressional intent to open local markets on a national level has never, not for a day, been completely put into action. And that has mattered a great deal.

Since the day the law was signed, the incumbents have been arguing for prices so high that the new entrants would be, in effect, paying off the incumbents' past investments. If new entrants are forced to do that, they won't have enough money to pay for their own investments. Result: poof! no competition.

There has never been a day when any new entrant could be assured that interconnection pricing and network sharing pricing could be counted on to be, and to remain, fair in any state or region of the country. That means prices that are forward-looking or, in other words, set by the formula called TELRIC (total element long run incremental cost).

Yet, at last count, only 11 states have issued permanent interconnection and element pricing rules.

Meanwhile, does it matter that the Eighth Circuit last Fall enjoined the FCC's fair prices from going into effect?

GTE told the Eighth Circuit last fall that if the FCC's pricing rules went into effect, GTE would suffer "substantial and rapid losses of market share."

In other words, they said the FCC pricing rule would cause competition right away. They got an injunction from the Eighth Circuit: poof! the prospect for rapid competition went away.

The result: the telcos have lost hardly any market share since the law was passed.

So the judicial intervention in the interconnection case hurt competition badly.

Fact number four: the existing competitive efforts in local markets are tiny fish that will not survive in the presence of the incumbent, formerly government-protected monopolist, whale-sized telcos—unless state and national governments write and enforce pro-competitive rules.

All evidence suggests that as of now there is not effective enforcement of binding competition rules. And without that, competition will be undercut.

These are four key facts that tell us that we have a major challenge to introduce competition in the local telephone markets. And that challenge is not yet being met. Plainly investment in local competition is a necessity.

We need to promote investment by promoting rapid and wise decisions about how to open local telephone markets.

Justice delayed is investment denied.

Now I get to my most comforting *fact, number five:* legislation is not like the Ten Commandments.

The Commandments were brought down direct from the Supreme Being. They were not subject to judicial review. The tribes of Israel did not have divided jurisdiction over enforcing them.

Legislation is not so fine a thing. But legislation—this is its saving grace—is the work of mere humans and so mere humans can keep writing and rewriting it until courts finally submit to its direction.

So let us talk about how Congress could blow away the paralyzing fog the legal culture is spreading over the legislative and executive mandate to open the local markets.

Let us talk about how Congress, at least for this one fine law, might make sure its intent is truly realized.

I have four proposals for legislative action.

A. We need an immediate national definition of "cost" set forth by the FCC, so this key term won't vary confusingly and uncertainly from state to state.

Until the Eighth Circuit interconnection decision, no court in 60 years has issued a decision constraining this agency from defining terms in a congressional statute.

There is no doubt, however, that in a national law using the term 'cost' Congress intends a single national meaning for the term. The result of the Eighth Circuit decision is that up to 93 district courts will define the meaning of "cost" as they review hundreds of interconnection agreements. A dozen courts of appeal will then review these decisions. And if there is conflict among circuits ultimately—years from now—the United States Supreme Court will decide what "cost" means.

What fog this process will spew forth!

When Senators Lott, Hollings, Stevens and Inouye, and Congressmen Bliley and Markey told the Eighth Circuit that the FCC had the authority to define "cost," their words should have been treated by the courts as law. They were not. Now the law should be written to instruct the Court to follow the Senate Majority Leader by permitting the FCC to define the term now and have its definition respected by the courts, states, and parties.

B. The FCC should be given deference, as Supreme Court authority requires, for any reasonable interpretation of congressional intent and its application of policy.

In the 1984 case of *Chevron v. Natural Resources Defense Council*, the Supreme Court said that where "Congress has not directly addressed the precise question at issue, the [appellate] court does not simply impose its own construction on the statute." Instead, the Court said, an appellate court must affirm if "the agency's answer is based on a permissible construction of the statute."

But in the Eighth Circuit case, the court of appeals substituted its judgment for ours in striking down what it called the "pick and choose" rule, which we call the "nondiscrimination" rule.

The court of appeals "acknowledge[d] . . . that the FCC's approach [could reasonably be said to be] intended by Congress." [fn. 22]

If that's so, then under *Chevron* we should have been affirmed.

Instead, the Eighth Circuit inserted its opinion for ours regarding how interconnection negotiations were likely to proceed, and reversed the FCC.

This decision is a recipe for delay, doubt, and uncertainty.

If the FCC reasonably interprets the Telcom Act, the courts should rapidly affirm, not deliberately secondguess.

Congress should specifically instruct the 8th Circuit that our interpretation of the statute on this subject was correct, and that *Chevron* should be followed strictly by all courts reviewing our decisions.

If *Congress* does not like our interpretations, it can change them. But *courts* should give us *Chevron* deference.

C. Judicial review of FCC decisions interpreting and applying the telcom act should not be piecemeal or delayed.

I am confident that we ultimately will prevail in the Supreme Court on the Eighth Circuit's decision concerning our interconnection provisions. But, similar litigation over the 1992 Cable Act just ended last month, after *five years*, and it might have gone on for another year if the cable operators hadn't decided to give up.

We need a faster, cheaper, way to get the legal issues of competition policy resolved.

I will propose that Congress consider passing laws that would consolidate all appeals of section 252 agreements and all review of FCC decisions in a single court, bar stays of our orders for more than 30 days, and require for all such review expedited briefing and decisionmaking.

D. No state or federal competition rule will be of value unless it's enforceable.

I applaud the new Illinois statute that requires resolution of interconnection-related complaints within 60 days.

I will propose to Congress that it impose a similar rule on the FCC and on all states. Those states that won't follow such a rule, would have to relinquish enforcement to the FCC. In addition, I will ask Congress to increase the sanctions available to the FCC. We should have treble damage relief, in addition to equitable remedies, for all violations of our rules.

Congress, its agency the FCC, the Administration, and the country want a private, investment-built information economy in which the states and the federal government have no further need to regulate investment, wholesale prices or retail prices.

Lawyers—including both judges and recovering litigators, like me—need to learn from business people the real world consequences of delay and uncertainty.

While courts spar with Congress and its expert agency, while NARUC sues the FCC and never ever files a brief in support of us, the fog of uncertainty spreads like the famous fog of London described by Dickens as a metaphor for *Jarndyce v. Jarndyce*.

And in that fog an entrepreneur misses a window for launching a new satellite venture.

A would-be new entrant watches an incumbent obtain first mover advantage in offering a new product line. A banker agrees to finance an established business, while turning down the entrepreneur on the ground that the competition rules aren't clear yet.

The result—jobs are lost; money is wasted; choice does not come to the market; consumers are disappointed; productivity gains are not realized; other economies surge forward and we lose our edge.

These costs are real. They must always to be in our minds as we lawyers try to create a fair but efficient rule of law.

The competition policy of Congress should be realized by businesspersons solving economic and technological policies. It should not be tangled up by lawyers solving—or creating—word games about legislative intent.

Samuel Johnson said people disagree chiefly on means not ends. I'm sure we all agree on the ends of deregulation and competition. Let's work together in mutual respect to find more effective means.

APPENDIX K

EXCERPTS FROM

REMARKS BY WILLIAM KENNARD

Chairman
Federal Communications Commission
to the
National Association
of State Utility Consumer Advocates
February 9, 1998

. . . Oscar Wilde once wrote that "modern calendars mar our lives by pointing out that each day that passes is the anniversary of some perfectly uninteresting event."

Yesterday, we celebrated an anniversary that to most Americans must seem exactly that: the second anniversary of the Telecommunications Act of 1996.

But anniversaries are good opportunities to reflect on the passage of time—and what we've learned. . . .

The Act is all about competition. And with the advent of competition, consumer advocates will be more important than ever. You'll find yourselves drawn into new areas and facing new challenges. There's no question that as markets open to create new marketing opportunities and new products, consumers also face new risks.

So I want to talk today about how the growth of competition will change our role at the FCC, and the role of consumer advocates.

But first let's talk about what the Telecom Act has accomplished to bring competition about. And the work yet to be done.

There are those, of course, who have already declared the 1996 Telecom Act to be a failure. The King is dead.

Well, I say long live the King. Congress got it right: competition beats monopoly as the way to deliver the best telecom services to the American people. And the signs are that competition is indeed coming.

We recently held a hearing at the FCC on the status of local telephone competition. And it was clear to anybody paying attention that the Act has successfully moved us in the right direction—toward greater competition.

Have we moved far enough? Is competition as broad or as deep yet as we would like? No. But we're beginning to see the early, promising buds of competition.

We need to nurture those buds. Protect them from a premature frost. And make sure that the telecom garden is a hospitable environment for new growth.

I'm convinced that if cared for these buds will spread and bloom—like wildflowers—even for residential consumers. And like wildflowers, we won't see competition in just one color, but a multicolored array of choices.

Why am I so optimistic? First, its my nature. Second, and more importantly, there is good cause to be.

There are now over 100 competitive local exchange carriers [CLECs] around the country.

The top 10 CLECs have switches in 132 cities spanning 33 states and the District of Columbia.

Approximately 2,400 interconnection agreements have been created under the 1996 Act's framework.

Over the past two years, $14 billion has been invested in competitive local exchange carriers, and their combined market capitalization is over $20 billion. Clearly Wall Street sees opportunity here.

There are signs of the beginnings of facilities-based competition for residential consumers. At our recent hearing on local competition, we heard from an electric utility affiliated company focused on bundling voice, video and internet access. And some cable companies are doing the same.

What else has the 1996 Act accomplished?

Lower prices.

Wireless telephone prices are dropping rapidly. There was a big drop in the last nine months of '97—12% for low volume users of cellular and PCS services, and over 31% for high volume customers.

Long distance rates fell 5.3% between January 1996 and November 1997. Long distance prices are now the lowest they have ever been. And everyday, yet another long distance company interrupts your dinner to offer you an even better deal.

When we have full competition in all telecom markets, no one will ever have dinner in peace.

There have been setbacks, of course. We have seen Congress's careful design disrupted by judicial rulings that have added uncertainty, slowed investment and planning, and frustrated promising entry strategies.

Without these setbacks, we would be further along. And these decisions threaten to continue to hobble the development of competition and to deny our country the growth that broad telecom competition would create.

But still, to me, the results are clear. Two years after the enactment of the

Telecom Act, we are seeing the Act begin to deliver benefits to the American people.

What's ahead?

I believe that we must continue to work hard to promote competition. At the same time, we must continue to reform universal service, ensuring all the while that the essential universal service safety net remains in place. And we must be vigilant to ensure that consumers do not fall prey to unscrupulous practices as markets become more competitive.

At the top of my To Do list is delivering choice in telecommunications—especially local telecommunications. For the consumer, competition is all about choice. Residential subscribers want, need, and deserve more choice when it comes to local telephone providers and I'm determined that they will have that choice in the years ahead.

A second priority: affordable rates and comparable services for all Americans. We cannot allow our country to be plagued by an ever-widening gulf between information "haves" and "have-nots."

A third, but increasingly important, priority: consumer protection. In every market that becomes competitive, unscrupulous operators will find new ways to bilk consumers. "Slamming", "cramming" and outrageously high priced operator service calls are just a few examples. We have taken steps at the FCC to combat these problems, and will continue to do so. And we all must be ready to meet the challenges of consumer protection in competitive markets.

Let me first talk more specifically about competition and what we are doing at the FCC.

Competition is best viewed from the consumer's perspective, and I believe our job is to make sure that consumers have a basic set of rights. I call it a consumer Bill of Rights.

First and foremost, consumers must have the right to choose providers—from as wide a variety of providers as the market will bear.

The right to be able to move from one provider to the other.

The right to change carriers without changing telephone numbers.

The right to be able to have the same convenient dialing regardless of whether the consumer chooses a new entrant or the incumbent.

The right to change carriers without paying unnecessary fees.

One of the hardest tasks we continue to face is to create incentives to change telecommunications networks, which were built and engineered for a monopoly era, to accommodate these basic consumer rights.

Much of the Commission's efforts over the past year, and in the year to come, will continue to focus on creating this basic infrastructure—whether in numbering administration, number portability, or operational support systems for local competition.

And we must be able to be sure that the competitive infrastructure is working. We will shortly begin a proceeding to strengthen performance monitoring and reporting mechanisms that are critical to monitoring whether carriers are able to switch customers as easily as customers can sign up with an incumbent.

But unless we create this infrastructure and enforce the consumer Bill of Rights, consumers will not have real choice, and we cannot be said truly to have opened markets to competition.

The Act also provides us all with a mechanism to assist in creating this infrastructure, and to grade its adequacy: the Bell Company long distance entry process under Section 271.

The 1996 Act told the FCC that we are to permit the Bell operating companies into long distance when the Bell's have opened the door to competition in their local markets.

To help everyone get the job done, in December, I invited the Bell Companies, and all of the other interested parties, to join the FCC in collaborative discussions about how to meet the Act's preconditions for Bell long distance entry.

I am pleased to announce that all of the five Regional Bell Companies have taken us up on that offer. We've recently begun a series of what I hope will be constructive conversations with the BOCs, the states, the Department of Justice and others about the requirements of Section 271.

I look at these discussions as a collaborative process. We all are working to clarify the 271 process, to define the issues underlying the statute's requirements, and to help the companies and the Commission develop a better understanding of what is necessary really to create opportunity for choice to come to local markets.

These discussions will help Bell Companies file stronger applications, to be able better to demonstrate the effectiveness of the market opening steps they have taken, and to help the Commission to better understand the technical or business limitations that the Bell Companies and the entrants face.

I'm encouraged by the interest of the BOCs and others to engage in this collaborative effort. That will improve the process. I hope everyone involved participates in good faith and allows sufficient time for meaningful dialogue between the FCC and all interested persons.

That's what those discussions are about.

Here's what they're not about.

They are not intended to prejudge applications, but to build stronger applications and conserve everybody's resources.

Applications will be judged on the basis of what's contained in an application, and in comments filed by other parties. We will make decisions on the merits.

Universal service has been a hallmark of our telecommunications system since the invention of the telephone. The emergence and growth of competition requires that we re-double our efforts to preserve and enhance universal service. We cannot allow rural America to become a "have not" zone in the telecommunications age.

I have talked a lot about competition. But competition is not an end in itself. Competition is important only if it serves to build communities. Because our goal is not simply to bring lower rates and more choices to consumers. Our goal is to use those services and choices to foster the development of a telecommunication system that brings us together as a Nation.

The great federal interstate highway projects of the post World War II era were significant not just because they permitted the flow of commerce and allowed Americans to get more products faster and at cheaper price. The huge investment we made in those highway systems helped bring our Nation together. It connected communities and brought economic and social development.

Today it is the Information Superhighway that can bring us together as a nation. Or it can divide us. It can connect small and rural communities to the world of commerce and culture. Or it can leave them behind. It may be the most important factor in the economic development of our time.

This year, we must finish implementing a mechanism for sustainable universal service support to rural and high cost areas. There will be many difficult issues, such as how much does it really cost to build a network to serve rural America? What capabilities should that network be capable of delivering? And what is the appropriate allocation of responsibilities between the states—when is it fair to call upon lower cost states to shoulder more of the burden, and how much responsibility must high cost states bear for funding universal service within their own borders.

To help move the debate forward, I propose a set of principles. I assembled these principles as a balanced package to be taken as a whole—no picking and choosing.

There are eight principles. Here they are.

1. Universal service reform should not reduce the amount of explicit support that the state receives from the interstate jurisdiction. By this, I mean that costs that previously had been borne by the interstate jurisdiction because of the old high cost fund should continue to be borne by federal universal service mechanisms.

2. States have an obligation to take all reasonable steps as promptly as possible to reform existing intrastate universal service support mechanisms to make them compatible with competitive local markets by making the subsidies explicit and portable.

3. States should continue to collect as much of what is currently intrastate universal service support (whether implicit or explicit) from within their own state.

4. Where a state has fully reformed its own universal service mechanisms and would be collecting as much of what is currently intrastate universal service support as is possible, additional federal universal service support should be provided to any high cost areas where state mechanisms in combination with baseline federal support, are not sufficient to maintain rates at affordable levels.

5. Federal universal service support should be the minimum necessary to achieve statutory goals.

6. Federal and state universal support mechanisms should collect contributions in a competitively neutral manner.

7. Federal and state universal service support mechanisms should encourage efficient investment in new plants and technologies by all eligible telecommunications carriers.

8. Federal and state universal service support mechanisms should promote service to historically underserved areas—Native American nations, for example.

I believe that if guided by these principles, we can reform our existing universal service system for the competitive age.

Universal service has always been a shared responsibility of the state and federal governments. The 1996 Act told us to get rid of these implicit subsidies and to make the subsidies explicit. In doing so, there is no reason for the explicit federal contribution to universal service to shrink and I do not intend for it to shrink.

By the same token, each state has the obligation to get rid of its own intrastate implicit subsidies, to make those subsidies explicit, and to recover as much of what is currently intrastate universal service support (whether implicit or explicit) from within its own borders.

The goal is to move from implicit to explicit support without requiring subscribers to pay unaffordable rates. This is not a job that either the FCC or the states can do alone; we need to be—and are—working together. And we will need the help of all of you, both through Martha's work on the Universal Service Joint Board, through NASUCA, as an organization, and through the individual efforts of each and every one of you.

But simply creating choice and reforming universal service will not complete the work that all of us face. Consumer confusion and complaints are an inevitable byproduct of competition. The recent UCAN report on competition in San Diego demonstrated that consumers likely will have problems both with the incumbent as well as the new entrants.

How does a customer choose between all these new local service options? What role can NASUCA play along with state commissions in helping to educate consumers on their choices?

Consumer education is a must. For a competitive market to function flawlessly in providing value and choices to the public, consumers must be aware of what is being offered. Therefore, we must strive to provide consumers with the information they need to take advantage of the opportunities that competition provides.

Even today a large number of consumers subscribe to their long distance carriers' basic service plan and spend a lot more on long distance than they need to, because they are unaware that through a single phone call to their carrier they could sign up for another plan and start saving money right away.

NASUCA also could help play an important role by assisting consumers and state commissions in the filing, organizing, and prosecution of complaints. States have limited resources. And this is a problem that's going to get bigger as competition increases. They—and you—will have to do some creative thinking.

Perhaps NASUCA and state commissions should group similar complaints together in a single proceeding and have NASUCA assist in the prosecution of the complaint.

But we all also need to do more. We need to think about the basic consumer protections we will need for a competitive world. As tariffs become relics of the past and contracts become the norm, what consumer protections are necessary? How do we keep pace with and address problems not just of slamming, but billing problems such as "cramming"?

We will have to work together to find the most efficient means of addressing these problems and protecting the public.

We are all fortunate to be participants in this revolution in technology that is profoundly changing our Nation and the world. But that also gives us a special responsibility. We must seek to ensure that this booming revolution in communications markets is an inclusive one—one that creates opportunities for participation by all Americans. We must provide opportunities for employment, access and ownership, particularly for those who remain underrepresented in the ownership and employment ranks of these businesses—minorities, women, persons with disabilities.

The communications and information industries represent the fastest growing sectors of our economy—over $800 billion last year. We should create and expand opportunities in every sector of the communications marketplace. We shouldn't leave anybody behind.

Certainly not persons with disabilities. Last August, the Commission adopted rules to increase the amount of closed captioned video programming available to the 22 million Americans with hearing disabilities regardless of whether they receive their television signals from cable, DBS, wireless cable, or through over-the-air broadcast.

This is a vitally important step in making sure that Americans with disabilities get access. And in March, I plan to initiate another proceeding under Section 255 to propose ways to facilitate access to telecommunications equipment by persons with disabilities. I hope I can count on you to help us make sure that this proceeding is a success.

On this second anniversary of the Telecom Act, I'd like to leave you with one final thought. It's been only two years since President Clinton went to the Library of Congress and signed his name to the Act we've been analyzing today. It was such an appropriate place. Because here was a bill that would make everything in the Library of Congress available to every American with a few clicks of the mouse.

Not everyone was confident that he was doing the right thing.

Not everyone was confident that Congress had done the right thing.

Not everyone was confident that the FCC could handle the job of implementing that ambitious legislation.

Now, after twenty-four months, it's clear that they should have been confident on all counts.

After twenty-four months, the Act has produced important, tangible successes. There is much left to be done. But if we work together, we'll succeed. We will succeed in fulfilling the promise of the Telecommunications Act to bring competition and choice to consumers; to bring advanced services at affordable rates to all Americans; to bring new economic opportunity that can unite our Nation and narrow the gaps that divide us; and to fundamentally improve our country in ways unimagined just two years ago.

Index

About the Author

Patricia Aufderheide is a professor in the School of Communication at American University in Washington, DC. Aufderheide is a prolific cultural journalist, policy analyst, and editor on media and society, and has received numerous journalism and scholarly awards. She is the editor of *Beyond PC: Toward a Politics of Understanding* (Graywolf Press, 1992), and a collection of essays to be published by the University of Minnesota Press. She has been a Fulbright and John Simon Guggenheim fellow, and has advocated on telecommunications policy for the United Church of Christ. Aufderheide currently serves on the film advisory board of the National Gallery of Art, as a senior editor of *In These Times* newspaper, and on the editorial boards of a variety of publications, including *Communication Law and Policy*. She received her PhD in history from the University of Minnesota.